MR COLSTON'S HOSPITAL

MR COLSTON'S HOSPITAL

The History of Colston's School, Bristol, 1710-2002

JOHN WROUGHTON

THE SOCIETY OF MERCHANT VENTURERS

OF BRISTOL

First published in 2002 by
The Society of Merchant Venturers
The Promenade
Bristol BS8 3NH

ISBN 0 9504281 2 4

Typeset in 12 / 13 Times New Roman
Typesetting, design and origination by
The Lansdown Press, Bath

Printed in Great Britain by
The Cromwell Press, Trowbridge, Wiltshire

Contents

MR COLSTON'S HOSPITAL

Note on abbreviations:

When the full style is not used in the text, the Society of Merchant Venturers is referred to as either 'the Society' or 'the Merchants'. In picture credits, the abbreviation 'SMV Archive' is used.

Foreword

Brigadier Hugh Pye

Treasurer of the Society of Merchant Venturers and Chairman of Governors at Colston's Collegiate School

Ten years ago when I joined the governing board of Colston's School and anxious to learn more about it I asked for a copy of the school's history. I was amazed to discover that one had never been written. This seemed extraordinary for a school which had been founded in 1710 for 100 poor boys by the Bristol philanthropist, Edward Colston, and which has a rich and varied history, albeit a chequered one.

Edward Colston apppointed the Society of Merchant Venturers of Bristol to be Trustees of his generosity and since then the Society has carried out his wishes supporting the school in good times and in bad and often most generously. The Society, in the 21st Century, is very much involved in philanthropic work being trustee to many charitable endowments and trusts of which the school is a most important part and whose history they are delighted to have commissioned.

Shortly after I become a governor, the board was joined by Dr John Wroughton, a former Headmaster of King Edward's School, Bath. Dr Wroughton had already written a history of that school and I was delighted when he volunteered to write this spendid book. As a distinguished author of historical books he has brought to it his very special talents, making use of the excellent archives of the school held by the Society, personal reminiscences and many other sources.

At last we have a history portraying a fascinating story, beautifully presented and written, which I strongly recommend to anybody interested in the school and the development of education in Bristol.

HWKP
December 2001

Acknowledgements

The author wishes to thank the following people who have contributed in various ways to the publication of this book:

The Society of Merchant Venturers for giving him free access to their impressive archive and for trusting him with this publication; Brigadier Hugh Pye not only for his enthusiam, encouragement and support, but also for his constructive comments on the text; Mrs Pat Denney, his secretary, for her deep knowledge of the archives in Merchants' Hall and her practical assistance; and the staff of Merchants' Hall for their warm welcome and constant supply of coffee during his research.

Five Headmasters past and present (Nigel Gibbs, Graham Searle, Stephen Howarth, David Crawford and Graham Phillips); a former Headmaster's wife (Winifred Snaith); a former Chairman of Governors (Andrew Reid) and a former Governor (John Baker); plus a former Chairman of Governors and a former Governor of The Collegiate School (Mrs Gillian Woolley and Mrs Carole Jenkins) for their helpful submissions regarding their own involvement with Colston's.

Eight members of staff past and present (Gerard Boyce, Wally Feiner, Mike Graham, Ian Holmes, Alan Martinovic, Martin Tayler, Steve Waters and Keith Watts) for providing detail and colour out of their own experience; and three others (Graham Ricketts, Stephen Pritchard and Clive Warren) for their help with photographs.

Two Old Colstonians (Terry 'Fred' Forse, 1957-62, and George Moore, 1941-47) for their invaluable and unstinting help with archive material, including photographs - and twenty other OCs for contributing their personal reminiscences (Stanley Bowell, 1924-29; Jeffrey Cook, 1957-62; Norman Emmerson, 1916-20; David Faulkner, 1962-69; Richard Fullock, 1958-68); Alan Hale, 1958-64; John Harvey, 1940-47; Kenneth Hilborne, 1934-38; Nigel Hurley, 1959-65; Mike Jones, 1945-55; Doug Lodge, 1960-71; Pat Mahoney, 1940-46; Peter Mitchell, 1960-65; Mike Newman, 1947-55; Roger Newport, 1930-37; Dave Tooze, 1953-58; Bill Welland, 1959-66; Adrian Williams, 1956-64; Doug Winstone, 1942-50; and Michael Wood, 1950-56).

The staff of the Bristol Art Gallery, the Bristol Local Studies Library, the British Library and the Tate Gallery for their assistance in providing illustrations.

CHAPTER 1

Edward Colston and the Setting Up of the Hospital

'To provide...the Great House on St Augustine's Back to be forever hereafter used for a house, habitation and abiding place for fifty poor boys and one or more schoolmasters to inhabit in; and for a school to teach the said boys; and to find and provide for such boys meat, drink, washing, lodging and clothing of all sorts; and to place such boys apprentices, when and as they shall become capable'. (Settlement made by Edward Colston, 1708)

Edward Colston (1636-1721)

Edward Colston, the eldest of eleven children, was born in Bristol on 2nd November 1636 in a house in Temple Street, where his mother (Sarah) was visiting her parents. He was christened in Temple Church a few days later. His father, William Colston, was a wealthy merchant, a member of the Society of Merchant Venturers, an alderman of the city and, during the Civil War, an ardent supporter of the royalist cause. On the recapture of Bristol by the parliamentarians in 1645, therefore, he and his family were forced to flee from their house in Wine Street and leave their parish church (Christ Church), where William had served as a churchwarden.

For the next sixteen years, they made their home in London, where Edward undoubtedly received his schooling (possibly at Christ's Hospital). Then in 1654, at the age of eighteen, Edward was apprenticed to a prominent London merchant before eventually being enrolled as a member of the Mercers' Company in 1673. Although his parents returned to Bristol in 1661, Edward remained in London, where he chiefly lived for the rest of his life. He quickly became a highly successful and prosperous merchant, exporting cloth to Spain, the Canaries and the Mediterranean and importing wine and sherry. Later, in 1680, he became a member of the Royal Africa Company, which had the monopoly of shipping slaves from the west coast of Africa to the plantations in America and the Caribbean. He served on the company's numerous committees and was appointed its assistant governor in 1689.

From 1681, at the age of forty-five, Colston began to re-explore his

Edward Colston. Portrait by Sir G. Kneller. (By courtesy of the Society of Merchant Venturers)

roots, becoming more and more involved in the public life of Bristol - a decision prompted partly by the deaths of his father and younger brother (Thomas), both of whom bequeathed him city-centre property. During his extended visits to Bristol, he became a freeman of the city, a member of the Society of Merchant Venturers and an active merchant, trading in ships previously owned by his father and brother. Nevertheless, by 1689 he had returned to work full-time in London, living on the outskirts in a beautiful riverside house at Mortlake. He eventually retired from all activity as a merchant in 1708 at the age of seventy-two, thus freeing himself to devote more of his time to philanthropic activity.

Colston, a lifelong bachelor, used his considerable wealth to support charitable causes throughout the country. In London, for example, he became in 1681 a governor and benefactor of Christ's Hospital (a school for poor children), while at the same time making substantial donations to St Bartholomew's Hospital for the sick, numerous churches within the capital and the poor prisoners in Whitechapel. Increasingly, however, he focussed his attention on Bristol, the city of his birth. In 1695, he offered to provide maintenance for six poor sailors in the Merchant Venturers' almshouse in King Street on condition that additional rooms were built for their accommodation. A year later, he established the almshouse on St Michael's Hill, to be managed by the Society of Merchant Venturers, at the cost of £2,500.

The deep concern he showed towards the poor in general was reflected in his determination to provide a sound education for their children. Initially he concentrated his attention on supporting the work of Queen Elizabeth's Hospital for pauper children, funding the addition of six boys onto the school roll in 1695 and a further four in 1702. At the same time, he donated £500 towards rebuilding work there. However, his most generous offer of all was rejected by the Corporation in 1705, probably as a result of a deep clash of political and religious views (see below). By this, Colston would have agreed to support financially an increase of forty-six places at the Hospital, thus raising the total to ninety. It was therefore out of a feeling of utter frustration at his rejection that he contacted the Society of Merchant Venturers in 1706 with an alternative scheme for the education of poor children. These discussions regarding the setting up of a major new educational foundation were to result in the establishment of Colston's Hospital in 1710 (see below).

Not content with that achievement alone, he quickly proceeded to set up another school for forty poor boys in Temple parish, the parish of his birth. Established in 1710 in Tucker's Hall, the 'Temple Colston School' provided clothing for the boys and a sound education in reading, writing, cyphering and church catechism. Colston also contributed considerable sums to the refurbishment of city churches, including All Saints' in Corn Street (where his parents were buried), St Michael's, St Mary Redcliffe and Bristol Cathedral. In all, he contributed some £64,000 to charitable causes during his lifetime and a further £71,000 in his will (a total equivalent to over £10.5 million in today's currency).

Colston's philanthropic activity was greatly influenced by his deep religious beliefs. He was a High Church Anglican with a profound dislike of both Roman Catholics and protestant dissenters. He was also a Tory in politics with a great aversion to the Whigs, many of whom followed a policy of religious toleration, to which he was fiercely opposed. (He served briefly as Tory MP for Bristol between 1710 and 1713). These views, however, brought him into headlong conflict at times with Bristol Corporation, which was dominated by the Whigs between 1695 and 1710.

An obstinate, inflexible and intolerant man, he sought to ensure that all his charitable institutions - both almshouses and schools - strictly conformed to the rules he had imposed on them at the outset. In particular, those admitted were to have been baptised into the Church of England, attend prayer book services and live disciplined lives. In the case of children, they were also to be taught the church catechism and, on completing their education, to be apprenticed to masters who were members of the Anglican Church (and not, under any pretext, to dissenters). It is thought that his determination to impose similar conditions on the children admitted under his funding at Queen Elizabeth's Hospital was the principal reason for the rejection of his offer by a Whig-dominated Corporation in 1705.

His political views also brought him into conflict with an old friend, the Reverend Arthur Bedford, Vicar of Temple Church, whose parish school Colston had funded. Bedford had failed to vote for him in the Bristol election of 1710, preferring instead to to support a low-church Whig candidate in Gloucestershire (where he was also qualified to vote). As a result, Colston completely ended all further contact with the man - an action which was characteristic of his attitude to all those who opposed him.

Nevertheless, although he could be most difficult and awkward in his dealings with others, he was at the same time a most devout man with a great fund of compassion and kindliness. He supported the work of the Society for the Propagation of the Gospel, the Society for the Propagation of Christian Knowledge and the Society for the Reformation of Manners in Bristol. Furthermore, he sponsored an annual series of Lenten lectures in the city (fourteen a year), a monthly sermon to the inmates of Newgate prison and an annual sermon in Bristol Cathedral on his birthday to be attended by the boys from his Hospital. This day (Colston's Day) is still celebrated each year by the pupils of Colston's School, although the service is now held in the School Chapel instead of the Cathedral. [Although Colston was actually born on 2nd November, according to the Old Style or Julian Calendar then in use, the modern practice is to take the corresponding date (13th November) in the New Style or Gregorian Calendar, which came into force in 1752].

Colston's effigy on his tomb, designed by James Gibbs, in All Saints' Church, Corn Street, Bristol. (Author's collection)

Colston died on 11th October 1721 and was buried in All Saints' Church, Bristol. The funeral procession included the members of the Society of Merchant Venturers, the residents of his almshouses and the boys from his Temple and Hospital Schools (see *Personal Reminiscences 1*). In 1729, a tomb was erected to his memory inside the church, bearing an effigy of him designed by James Gibbs.

The Society of Merchant Venturers in 1710

The institution to which Edward Colston turned for help in establishing a new educational foundation was the Society of Merchant Venturers, formed by a group of merchants who traded overseas. Although a guild of merchants had existed in Bristol as early as 1217, it is generally believed that the Society itself originated in 1552, when Edward VI granted them a monopoly of all seaborne trade to and from Bristol - a charter later confirmed by Elizabeth I in 1566. Although this monopoly was rescinded by Act of Parliament in 1571, the Society was given a new charter with wide powers by Charles I in 1639, which was confirmed by Charles II in 1665.

By 1700 Bristol, with a population of around 25,000 people, had become the second largest city and the second most important port in England. Its prosperity was based partly on overseas trade (the volume of which was growing rapidly with the rise of the slave trade) and partly on trade carried along the rivers and coasts. Standing also at the hub of a network of major roads, it was without doubt the commercial capital of the West. Industries thrived within its bounds, especially those based on brewing, ship building, soap making, sugar refining, tobacco pipe making, glass making, metal crafts and leather working.

Membership of the Society, which reached a total of one hundred in 1707, could be achieved through birth within the city, through apprenticeship to a merchant who was already a member or through a 'fine' or entry fee (40 shillings in 1700). The Merchant Venturers exercised a dominant role in the affairs of the Bristol Corporation. During the seventeenth century, no fewer than 69 out of the 105 mayors elected were members of the Society, as were 65 of the 118 aldermen, 8 of the 11 city chamberlains and over half the sheriffs. They also accounted for 20 out of the 31 Members of Parliament elected to represent Bristol during the century. This overlapping membership helped to ensure that the Society and Corporation worked harmoniously together on most issues and that the interests of traders were largely protected.

At the beginning of the seventeenth century, the Corporation had given the Society a lease of the city's docks, which empowered it to charge anchorage, wharfage and cranage duties; control the haven-master, pilots and porters; regulate the use of the river and improve the port. This lease, which was not surrendered until 1859, enabled its finances to grow as receipts from port dues multiplied with the rapid growth of trade. At the same time, the Society made a number of shrewd property investments, which turned out to be most lucrative - including a large proportion of the manor of Clifton and various city-centre tenements in Bristol. By 1700, rents from these were producing between £150 and £200 per annum and its total annual income had increased to between £700 and £800. Much of this money was devoted to improving the port and funding its charitable work.

Merchants' Hall, near the Marsh Gate, in 1690. Drawing by A.C. Fare, 1926. (By courtesy of the Society of Merchant Venturers)

In the middle of the sixteenth century, the Society had taken over full responsibility for the Mariners' Almshouse (later called the Merchants' Almshouse), which accommodated a number of poor seamen, fluctuating between eight and nineteen. By 1696, the Society had built a new extension to house the additional six inmates funded by Edward Colston (see above). It also dispensed numerous gifts of pensions to distressed seamen or widows and single payments to free sailors imprisoned abroad. In 1690, it received almost one hundred applications for help from individuals connected with the sea.

By 1600, the Merchant Venturers had also shown their first interest in the field of education by taking responsibility for a school for mariners' children. Their involvement continued throughout the seventeenth century and, by 1700, the school (known as the Writing and Reading School) housed 62 boys in a basement room under the original Merchants' Hall in King Street (formerly the Chapel of St Clement, which had belonged to the Guild of Mariners). In 1737, the Society was to add another school to its list - the Navigation or Mathematical School, funded by two legacies, to instruct 20 boys in the art of navigation.

When, therefore, Edward Colston approached the Society in 1706, it was already receptive to the idea of giving support to the cause of education within the city.

The Establishment of the Hospital, 1706-1710

On 29th March 1706, the Society of Merchant Venturers received a letter from Edward Colston, which was read out at its meeting. It quickly became apparent that, although he was still seething at the rejection of his offer to Queen Elizabeth's Hospital (see above), he had not lost enthusiasm for his plan to support the education of 50 poor boys. He first explained that one option had been to take his money to London for the benefit of Christ's Hospital, where the reaction from the Corporation would have been far different from that received in Bristol. However, as he preferred to focus his efforts now on the city where he had drawn his 'first breath', he was approaching the Society with an offer to set up a school, on condition that they would undertake responsibility for managing it.

He expressed the hope that the Merchants did not share the opinion of some that schools for poor children were 'only a nursery for beggars and sloths'. He then went on to state that he had a site in mind - a field adjoining the almshouse he had established on St Michael's Hill, where a suitable house could be built. His initial thoughts on the funding of the enterprise suggested an annual sum of £600, which would include the maintenance of each boy (calculated at £10 per annum, as was the case at Queen Elizabeth's Hospital), the cost of teaching and an apprenticeship fee of £5 at the end of each boy's schooling.

The Society gratefully accepted the offer in a letter despatched next day and immediately established a committee to conduct detailed discussions. Although it agreed with Colston's general calculations on cost, it felt that a £5 apprenticeship fee was not realistic if the intention was to 'bind out' the boys to good masters. Negotiations continued until July 1707. Colston eventually agreed to increase his endowment to £627 per annum, whereas the Society now calculated that it would require

£640 to cover the basic costs (as outlined above) or £850 to include the payment of taxes, poor rates and house repairs. To provide income at this level, they suggested, would mean the possession of estates valued at £18,000 in total.

When the settlement agreement was finally signed on 25th November 1708 by the three parties involved (Edward Colston, the benefactor; twenty of the merchants, led by Sir John Duddleston, the trustees of the endowment; and the Society of Merchant Venturers, the managers of the Hospital), the finances had been amicably settled. An annual sum of £634 5s 0d was to be provided to cover the cost of maintaining and clothing 50 boys at £10 each (£500), binding them out apprentice after seven years at £10 each (£71 5s 0d yearly), paying a schoolmaster (£50) and routine repairs of the house (£13).

To cover this amount, Colston agreed to hand over to the trustees of his endowment two manors in Somerset (the manor of Beere, which produced £450 a year in rent, and the manor of Locking, valued at £250 a year), plus various lofts and cellars adjoining the school house (worth £20 a year). These properties therefore produced an annual figure of £720, leaving a surplus of £85 15s 0d to be applied to any unforeseen costs and legal fees associated with these properties. In addition, Colston agreed that he and his heirs would pay the estimated total of £62 14s 0d in taxes each year on the rents and holdings.

Meanwhile, a dramatic change of plan had already been announced. The lawyers had actually drawn up the agreement ready for signature as early as April 1708. It was at this point, however, that Colston suddenly decided that he would increase the number of boys to one hundred and would adjust the endowment accordingly. The Society readily agreed to this unexpected proposal, but pointed out that the enlarged school would require both an Usher and an assistant teacher in addition to the Master at an estimated extra cost of £40 per annum. Colston made allowance for this in his revised budget, which added a further £558 16s 0d to the annual income already pledged. This extra amount would be produced from ground rents of additional properties in Lincolnshire, Leicestershire, Dorset, Caermarthenshire and Essex, which now became part of his endowment.

Supplementary clauses were therefore hurriedly added to the original document. The Society agreed to maintain and teach the additional 50 boys at a total cost of £553 5s 0d a year (which was a lower figure than that accepted for the original group, because some of the overheads had already been covered in the first calculation). A sum of £10 out of the surplus from the combined income was now set aside for employing a clergyman to instruct the boys twice a week in the church catechism. Thus Colston had made provision for a total income of £1,278 16s 0d to support the school, plus the cost of taxes and other unforeseen expenses. In addition, in a surprise gesture, he generously provided in 1710 a complete suit of clothes for the first group of boys admitted, together with bedding, towels and cutlery - even though this had been agreed as the responsibility of the Society.

In the meantime, a site had been found for the school. After various options had been discussed, it was finally agreed in November 1706 that 'Mr Lane's house on Mr Colston's ground on St Michael's Hill' was the most suitable. Following a close inspection, the committee reported back that the house was 'firm and substantial and fit for Mr Colston's intended hospital' and that the asking price of £1,500 was 'not too dear'. In the event, Colston managed to purchase it for £1,300. The house in question was known as 'The Great House' in St Augustine's Back, in the parish of St Augustine - a most imposing building which had first been owned by Sir John Young, who had entertained Queen Elizabeth there in 1574. More recently used as a sugar refinery by Richard Lane, it consisted (in addition to the house itself) of a large number of outbuildings, warehouses, cellars, stables, gardens and orchards, some of which could be let out for profit. The Society realised that certain alterations would be necessary, including the stripping out of machinery used in the sugar refining process. The work was commenced under the supervision of a committee in October 1708 and was completed in time for the official opening of the Hospital in July 1710. The event was commemorated by a special service in Bristol Cathedral, after which the first scholars were led in procession by Edward Colston and his niece to the Great House. His family motto - *Go and do thou likewise* - was to become the motto of the school.

Sources used in Chapter 1

D.J. Eames, *The Contribution made by the Society of Merchant Venturers to the Development of Education in Bristol* (unpublished MA thesis for the University of Bristol, 1966), pp 1-37

Patrick McGrath, *The Merchant Venturers of Bristol* (Bristol, 1975), pp 209-10

Kenneth Morgan, *Edward Colston and Bristol* (Bristol, 1999), pp 1-12

Cecil Powell, *A Great West Countryman* (Somerset Year Book, vol. 35, 1936)

Society of Merchant Venturers' Archive:
   The Hall Book of Proceedings , vol. 3, 1694-1708
   Copies of Mr Colston's Settlements (printed volume containing his settlement of November 1708, his further directions of July

1715, his letter to the Society of April 1718 and clauses from his
will of May 1720)

Detail of a terracotta bust of Edward Colston by Michael Rysbrack, c.1726.
(By courtesy of Bristol Museums and Art Gallery)

A PIOUS & GRATEFUL PUPIL, 1719-25

Silas Told *(Old Colstonian 1719-25)*

[Silas Told was born near the Hotwells in 1711. His father, a physician, lost all his money in various business enterprises and died, leaving his wife almost penniless with five children to support. After his life at Colston's and then as an apprentice at sea, Silas became a school teacher in Essex before coming under the influence of John Wesley in London. He then ran a Methodist school in Finsbury Square before devoting much of the remainder of his life to the task of visiting prisoners in Newgate gaol. He died in 1779. This extract is taken from his autobiography, which was published ten years after his death with a foreword by Wesley. It shows just how strong the religious element was in the school at the time, a situation which was clearly appreciated by some of the boys.]

At the age of eight years [in 1719] my friends at Bristol made interest for me to be admitted into the Hospital of Edward Colston, Esq., based on St Augustine's Back. near the Quay of Bristol: a school, I dare venture to say, that cannot be surpassed by any throughout Great Britain for piety and Christian discipline, having a minister to attend twice a week regularly, for the instruction of one hundred boys in their duty towards God and man.

When I was first admitted into that school, the parting with my tender-hearted nurse brought me under much distress of mind; yet I constantly found the Spirit of God working powerfully upon me. My thoughts, when at prayers in the school three times every day, were carried up into heaven with the most solemn ardent desire; and when we assembled in the College Church, which we regularly did every sabbath day, the service there to me was a heaven upon earth. Here I drank deep into the bliss of the ever-blessed and adorable Jesus, till I arrived at the age of ten years; by which time I had made some proficiency in learning and was approved of by the Minister; so that, in a short time, I was entitled a monitor.

I then began to read pious books, especially the *Pilgrim's Progress*; and as there were a few lads in the same form as myself that were piously inclined, so we often read the *Pilgrim's Progress* together. One Lord's Day, many of our boys were deeply affected by the sermon, so that when we came home, several of us entered into an agreement to pinch the tongue of him that told a lie or mentioned the Lord's name in an irreverent way.

One day, the boys being permitted to go to visit their friends, I obtained permission likewise, although I had no relation or friend in the city. Several of the boys accompanied me that afternoon to a river called Broad Stony for the purpose of learning to swim; and, as I was strongly desirous of learning that art, several of the smaller boys with myself went into the pond adjoining to that river. I ventured beyond the others; but, in attempting to swim, struck out of my depth and was, for some time, struggling for my life. *[He was eventually saved by a Dutchman, who was making hay in a nearby field]* When I went back to school, Mr Samuel Gardiner, the principal Master of the Hospital, punished me severely, as a strict charge had been delivered by him that none of us should go near the water, one of his scholars having been drowned some time before.

Providentially I was in the school at the time of Mr Colston's death, when orders were given for all the children to learn by heart the 90th psalm, to sing before the corpse as it entered the city; which was at Lawford's Gate, where we joined the hearse and sang before it the space of five hours, amidst a most numerous and crowded audience. It is impossible to describe in what manner the houses and streets were lined with all ranks of people; and although the rain descended in torrents, none paid any regard thereto. We came at last to All Saints' Church, where he was interred under the communion table.

CHAPTER 2

The Management of the
Hospital, 1710-1861

'And that all the said boys should be ordered, governed, placed and, upon just cause,
displaced by the said Master, Wardens, Assistants and Commonalty of the Merchant
Adventurers within the City of Bristol'. (Settlement made by Edward Colston, 1708)

The Society's Role in Management

Under the terms of the settlement made with Colston, the Society of
Merchant Venturers agreed to become responsible for the management of
the Hospital and the collection of rents from the various properties
assigned to his endowment. It was to maintain The Great House as a
home and a school for the masters, servants and boys; to provide food,
clothing and laundry for the boys; to arrange apprenticeships when the
boys left the Hospital after seven years; and to appoint, pay and, if
necessary, dismiss the schoolmasters, who were themselves to teach the
boys to read and write and to learn both arithmetic and the church
catechism. The boys in fact were to be totally 'governed' by the Society,
who reserved the power to expel them when circumstances demanded
such action.

At the time of the settlement, Colston also drew up strict rules for
the conduct of both masters and boys (see chapters 4 and 5 for details of
these) and reserved the right to make additions during his own lifetime.
As part of his system of checks, devised to ensure that the rules were
being implemented, he required the Society to appoint 'a committee of
some of their members to visit the Hospital monthly, or least once every
quarter'. The purpose of these visitations was partly to investigate the
behaviour of the boys and decide whether any of them needed to be
reported to the Society for disciplinary action; and partly to enquire
how the boys 'are treated by their Master' and the quality of the food
he was providing. As a result of these instructions, the Society - after
further prompting in a letter from Colston - appointed a committee,
somewhat belatedly, to undertake these tasks on 27th November 1712.
This committee, which initially became known as the 'Colston

The Great House in 1574. Drawing by A.C. Fare, 1926. St Stephen's Church can be seen in the background together with ships on the River Frome, which ran close by until it was eventually culverted over. (By courtesy of the Society of Merchant Venturers)

Committee', met infrequently during the first ten years of the Hospital's existence and only visited the establishment in response to a particular crisis. For the rest of the eighteenth century, its work was taken over by the Society's Standing Committee, which rarely undertook visitations unless prompted by major complaints or problems.

It is abundantly clear that the Society was extremely negligent in the performance of its duties during the early years and quickly allowed the Hospital to plunge into a state of premature decline. An ineffective (and usually absent) Master, Mr Sylvester, had been appointed; the Colston Committee largely failed to visit; and the standard of teaching was dismal. In his will, dated May 1720, Colston castigated the Society for the lack of regular inspections. As a result, he stated, 'the boys have been so neglected by the schoolmaster, that when they were examined, it was found they had made so little improvement in their writing and cyphering, by the often absence of their Master from his school, that they were not fitly qualified to be put out apprentice; as likewise, that he had not given them sufficient allowance of provisions for their comfortable subsistence'.

This lack of control had also resulted in the Master taking his own decisions about the binding out of boys to apprenticeships, whereas it was clearly the responsibility of the Society to organise this according to Colston's strict instructions. Once alerted to the problem in August 1715, it resolved to take the matter into its own hands by advertising locally (February 1716) the fact that 20 boys in the Hospital 'are now of age fit to be bound and apprenticed' to 'good and proper masters'. Nevertheless, Colston himself was already uneasy about the manner in which boys were being apprenticed. He wrote to the Society in October 1716, urging it 'to take care in the putting out of apprentices'. This was a clear reference to additional rules he had drawn up for the Hospital in July 1715, which included the stipulation that the Society was to ensure that boys were apprenticed only 'to persons in all respects conformable to the doctrine and discipline of the Church of England'.

By this stage, he was desperately worried that the Society did not share his passionately held views on the chief purpose of education. He wrote a most sharply-worded letter to it in April 1718, stressing that he had not gone to the trouble of endowing his Hospital 'only for the bare feeding of one hundred boys', but chiefly that they should 'be bred up in the doctrine of our present established Church of England'. As governors of the school, they were therefore to ensure that 'the boys be so educated in future' and that, under no circumstances, should they be apprenticed to dissenters (i.e. protestant non-conformists). He concluded with the dire warning of God's own judgment on them. If they failed to comply, they would 'be answerable for a breach of their trust at the last and Great Tribunal, before which we must all appear'.

The Society had already been stung into taking action on other problems within the school by a previous letter from Colston in December 1716, urging it to enquire into various grievances which had come to his attention. The Colston Committee uncovered, on their resulting tour of inspection, a chaotic state of organisation within the Hospital. Mr Sylvester had not bothered to keep a record of the names and entry dates of the boys admitted or any detailed records of apprenticeships, expulsions and deaths within the community. He was therefore issued with a book for this purpose and instructed that all indentures (drawn up when apprenticeships were agreed) were to be housed safely in a chest at Merchants' Hall and not strewn around the Hospital.

Over the next year, the Society took its tasks more seriously and implemented a series of major decisions. First, it agreed to change the management system by abandoning the practice of buying in the provisions centrally (especially after the experience of Queen Elizabeth's Hospital, where serious losses had been incurred with a similar system). In future, therefore, the daily management of the school would be delegated to 'a chief master and two ushers'. The annual capitation allowance of £10 per boy, which had until now been controlled by the Society, would be given to the Master. Out of this sum, however, he was expected not only to pay the two ushers (£50 a year to be split between them), but also to feed and lodge them in the house; and to provide the boys 'with sufficient meat, drink, washing, clothing, writing books, pens and paper'. The Colston Committee would inspect 'from time to time' to ascertain that the system was working properly.

Secondly, the Society instituted, in February 1718, a new system for serving the boys at meal times and published a daily diet to ensure that they were properly fed (see Chapter 4). Thirdly, it dealt with the root cause of some of the Hospital's problems by sacking Mr Sylvester (December 1717) 'for not having performed his duty in relation to the boys in his care'. The Society then instructed the committee 'to look out for and treat with a master and two ushers, properly qualified, as desired by Mr Colston'.

Unbeknown to the committee, however, Colston had already decided 'to look out for' a replacement for Sylvester himself and was determined to find a man who would uphold his own principles. He acted quickly and, by February 1718, had written to the Society recommending a certain Mr Tooker as Master (a man no doubt of impeccable loyalty to the Church of England). The Merchants discussed the proposal a few days later and decided that he was 'not a fit person' to run the school, for they had discovered that he was an ardent Jacobite, who had refused to swear the oath of allegiance to King George I. One senses their relief on finding this undeniable excuse for ignoring Colston's suggestion, because they not only resented his interference in a decision that had clearly been delegated to them, but they had also by then earmarked their own candidate for the job.

They had decided in fact to look no further than Mr Samuel Gardner, their own Beadle, who was responsible for collecting the rents from their properties in Clifton and Bristol. He was therefore appointed initially for a probationary period of one year. Quite what his qualifications were for running a school is difficult to assess, just as it is impossible to ascertain how far the Society had looked in its search. This particular appointment clearly appealed to it for both its ease and its cheapness - for as Gardner was already paid £20 a year for his work as Beadle, it saw no reason to pay him an additional salary for his work as Master. The school was perhaps not yet sufficiently high on the Merchants' list of priorities, nor indeed could it be in the life of Mr Gardner, who had rents to collect as well as boys to teach.

Colston was furious when he heard the news and quickly wrote a letter to the Society expressing his great sense of hurt. He admitted that it had been empowered by him to make the appointment, but felt it discourteous in the extreme that it had rushed ahead with its own decision without first explaining to him why it had rejected his personal nominee. He confessed that he had had absolutely no hint of Tooker's political views or that the man had refused to swear the loyal oath - a confession that his own researches had not been quite as thorough as the situation required.

This uneasy relationship between Colston and the Society continued until his death in 1721. His will clearly reflected his concern that the Merchants were both inefficient and lax in their control of the school; and, at the same time, his deep sense of anxiety that they would not adhere to the religious principles on which his endowment had been based. Sadly, that ill-feeling spilled over beyond the grave. On 23rd December 1724, it was noted at a meeting of the Merchants that Colston's estate owed the Society a large sum of money, which they agreed to pursue. Then in October 1728, having failed in its earlier efforts, the Society sent its Standing Committee to 'wait on his kinsman' (Mr Francis Colston), who was then in Bristol. It demanded from him and the other executors of Colston's will 'the considerable balance' of money owed to the Society - and also the return of a portrait of Colston, which it had lent to Francis Colston some time earlier. Two years later, it again raised these matters in heated terms in a letter to Francis Colston and threatened to take legal action.

Nothing further on this matter was discussed for over thirty years, when it was was raised again with Lord Middleton, one of Colston's heirs. At stake were outstanding taxes on the income from the endowment, which the Society had paid, but which were in fact the responsibility of the heirs under the terms of Colston's settlement. Middleton argued that, in view of the fact that the Society had neglected to pursue its claim for nearly forty years, it had effectively lost its right to do so now. The Merchants agreed that they had not treated the matter with sufficient urgency or efficiency, but excused their neglect as stemming from simple human weakness. They pointed out that the large outstanding debt fell on the Society as a whole and did not hit 'the pocket of any particular man' or fall on any individual merchant to make good. 'If it had been in the hands of trustees who would have been obliged to pay the debt themselves', they confessed, 'certainly they would have taken more care'. Eventually, the dispute was settled in the Court of Chancery on 5th July 1768, when the heirs were ordered to pay the sum of £3,094 7s 3d - forty-four years after the matter had first been raised.

Colston's Nominees

It was just because of all these squabbles and the anxiety in Colston's mind about the future implementation of his wishes that he had put into place a number of checks to control the Society's management of the Hospital. In his original settlement of November 1708, he had set up a system for the recruitment of boys after his death (retaining, during his own life-time, the right to nominate all boys for entry). This stipulated that half the number should be placed by the Society and half by the executors of his will, who would be replaced on death by his 'Nominees' (the first twelve of whom were actually named, including his nephew, Francis). As individuals died, so the Nominees were - within three months - to elect replacements to join their body. The original function of the Nominees, therefore, was to share in the task of recruiting boys.

However, as Colston became more and more unhappy in his dealings with the Society in the ten years before his death, he dramatically extended the role of the Nominees by appointing them to be official 'Visitors' of the Hospital. Their function was therefore changed from that of a mere supporting body to that of a watchdog. These were, after all, handpicked men who shared his strict moral principles, his political views and his religious convictions. They were men to be trusted. When, therefore, he issued his further instructions for the management of his Hospital in July 1715, he made new stipulations which gave the Nominees, the right to dismiss the Master if he failed to comply with the rules which Colston had drawn up; if he failed to take the boys to church as prescribed; or if he failed to read Church of England prayers in the school twice a day.

They also gave the Nominees power to take action if the Society's committee neglected to visit the Hospital on a regular basis or if the Master of the school aided and abetted the education of boys in the religious ideas of dissenters. Any such faults were to be reported immediately to the Governors of Christ's Hospital in London, who were to seek immediate redress by visiting the school themselves or even by taking control the endowment income to ensure that it was spent in line with Colston's intentions. Colston made clear, in the same document, his utter disgust at the thought 'that any of the boys should be educated in fanaticism or any principles repugnant to those of our present established church'. His will also gave the Nominees the option of seeking legal advice, the cost of which would be borne by his estate.

Disputes between the Society and the Nominees, 1721-1836

Although it is possible to sympathise with Colston's growing concerns in old age, it is extremely sad that he should feel so much suspicion towards the managers of his school and that the realisation of his dream to educate poor boys should be tinged with so much anxiety at the time of his death. Much of the fault lies with Colston himself, a man whose obsessions and inflexibility made dealings with him difficult in the extreme. Nor is there any doubt that his division of power between the Society and the Nominees was a recipe for future disaster. The history of the Hospital, therefore, during the next century was, at least in part, the history of bitter feuds between these two bodies. There is little doubt that the school was badly administered, poorly disciplined, weakly led and shamefully equipped, at least until the 1830s. The Standing Committee reported only intermittently to the full meetings of the Society and visited the Hospital more in response to a crisis (of which there were many) than out of any sense of regular duty. Nevertheless, although it is easy to be critical, one needs to remember that the Merchants were inexperienced at running a school. Their main function, as illustrated by their minute books, was to undertake a vast amount of work involved with trade and the port.

The Nominees, on the other hand, were much more committed to the Hospital and much better organised throughout the century. Their minute books dealing the election of Nominees, which cover the period 1708-1874, clearly show the line of succession for each of the twelve places within the body, with replacements immediately installed on the death or resignation of any member. The Colston family continued to be well represented. Edward Francis Colston, for instance, was succeeded by his son in 1825 and by his grandson in 1847. The minute books of their actual meetings, which are intact for the period 1748-1875, give a good idea of their business-like approach to the responsibility with which they had been entrusted.

In June 1748, they agreed that in future they would meet four times a year (in March, June, September and December), gathering normally at The White Lion Inn at 11.00 am, before going on to the Hospital for a tour of inspection. They then returned to The White Lion for dinner, where they also wrote up and signed the minutes. Once the system was working, they even organised a kitty, requesting members to deposit 'a guinea to make a fund for defraying the expenses of such meetings'. Most of the meetings (with an average attendance rate of over fifty per cent) were devoted to the routine task of filling vacancies caused by boys who had left. They also checked up on the organisation of apprenticeships (ensuring that boys were bound out to masters who

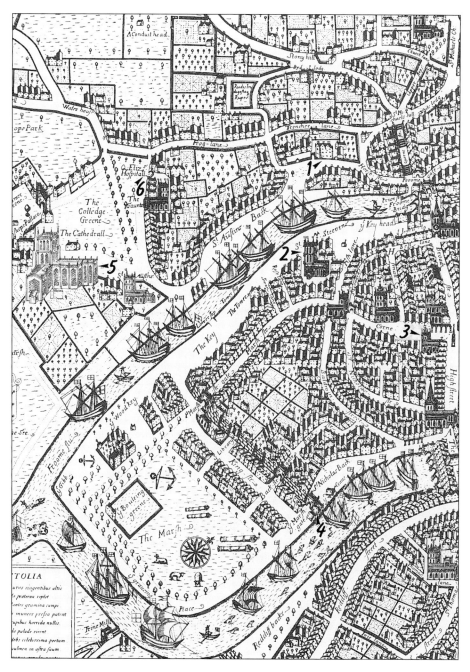

A section of James Millerd's Plan of Bristol, 1673, showing the location of (1) The Great House, (2) St Stephen's Church, (3) All Saints' Church (where Colston was buried), (4) Merchants' Hall, (5) The Cathedral and (6) Queen Elizabeth's Hospital. (By courtesy of the Society of Merchant Venturers)

attended the Church of England) and noted the names of boys who had been expelled. However, because they took their duties seriously, they also uncovered on occasions more deep-rooted problems. It was these that brought them into headlong conflict with the Society.

The Case of Mr Gardner and the 'Stinking Meat'

A major row broke out in 1757 and rumbled on over the next four years. It centred on Mr Samuel Gardner, junior, who had succeeded his father as Master in 1740. At their quarterly meeting in the March of that year, the routine work of the Nominees had suddenly been interrupted by 'some complaints'. As these turned out to be complaints against the Master for his non-attendance at school, the Nominees decided to seek legal advice. Nothing else was minuted about this problem until they visited the Hospital in November (a month ahead of their normal schedule). To their fury, they discovered that Mr Gardner was 'absent at the visitation, which was in school hours'. When the Usher informed them that the Master was at 'his country house at Westbury', the Nominees sent for him to return immediately. They severely cautioned him about 'his frequent absences from the school and several other personal neglects', which were contrary to Mr Colston's rules. Legal advice was again sought.

When the Nominees returned in December for their normal meeting, they were horrified that their warning to Mr Gardner had been totally ignored. Not only was he again 'not present at the school' during the whole visitation, he had (according to the Usher) been at his house for the last four days. The boys, when questioned (seizing no doubt the chance to stir up trouble), said that 'he had not been there for a fortnight'. It was not, however, until the October meeting of the following year (1758), that legal opinion was finally produced, recommending a stiff written warning. This was duly drawn up and signed by the Nominees at their meeting three months later. It reiterated the Master's duties, which 'you have by your late often absences from the school been very defective and, as the same is not to be done by a deputy, we admonish you to give a personal attendance on these duties for the future'. The Nominees agreed, when drawing up their dates for the next year's meetings, to vary the days and times on which they met and 'to keep the days a secret'.

This running battle with the Master subsided briefly over the following year, but broke out again with increased intensity during 1760. In June, the Nominees noted 'that several boys were badly apparelled without bands and badges, and Mr Gardner, the Master, was at home in the country'. For the first time in this saga, the Society of Merchant

Venturers was informed and it readily agreed to appoint a committee to visit the school to investigate the matter. Meanwhile, in September, the Nominees had received complaints from several of the boys concerning excessive punishments and poor food. They decided, therefore to interview as many of the boys as possible to see how serious the problems really were. They can scarcely have expected the grim picture that emerged in such graphic detail of brutality, terror and near-starvation. The witnesses, it has to be said, were perhaps not entirely unbiased in their evidence.

There were four main areas of complaint. First, the food was often bad with 'many instances of stinking meat' and cheese 'which for some time had been full of maggots'. Although the Master and Usher allegedly knew about this, the boys nevertheless had been obliged to eat it and had been offered nothing else in its place. Secondly, some of them had frequently been sent to carry heavy loads of material 'to and from Mr Gardner's country house at Westbury in school hours, as well as out of them'. Furthermore, they had often been whipped 'for wearing out their shoes going to Westbury'. On one occasion, a boy had picked an apple from a tree in Mr Gardner's garden and two more from the ground, but was caught in the act and beaten 'black and blue' with his large walking stick - and then whipped again next day.

Thirdly, the boys alleged that some of them were forced to perform domestic chores in the Master's school house during school time (such as gardening, cleaning and scrubbing floors), much to the detriment of their work - and that they were often beaten by his maids in the process. Fourthly, they claimed that Mr Worm, the chief Usher, had on several occasions 'corrected the boys unmercifully for small offences'. The Nominees were horrified by all this evidence and urgently summoned Mr Gardner to a meeting. He denied many of the allegations, but promised that he would endeavour 'to remove all occasions of complaint'. By the time of the Nominees' next meeting in December, however, he had clearly brooded over the matter and was now determined to confront them openly. There then followed a most unsavoury public row.

As the pupils were having dinner under the watchful eye of the visitors, Gardner suddenly addressed the Nominees in front of the boys and demanded to know which of his pupils had made the complaints. He angrily shouted that 'he was determined to correct very severely any boys who should in future make any such complaints'. When some of the Nominees objected to this behaviour, Gardner, 'amongst many other abusive sayings, declared that he did not give a farthing for them' (meaning the Nominees). They, with difficulty, shepherded him into another room, where Gardner declared that their cross-examination of the boys at their last visitation 'was very ungentlemanlike, clandestine and underhand, and made him as a scoundrel, which he would not take from any man'. He also said that he had reported the matter to the Society of Merchant Venturers, 'who had given him orders to correct any boys who should make future complaints'. In the face of this allegation, the Nominees then sought an urgent meeting with the Society's Standing Committee, at which the Merchants denied that Gardner had been given any such authority to beat complainants.

The Standing Committee then proceeded to conduct its own investigation by twice visiting the Hospital in the Spring of 1761 and eventually reporting back to the full meeting of the Society. The complaints were dismissed as being largely unfounded. Over the question of the bad food, the boys now admitted that the meat had only stunk on three occasions during the previous year and that, although 'five cheeses were decayed', they were not unfit to eat unless a boy 'had a dislike of strong cheese'. In any case, it was the fault of the boy who was the cheese monitor 'for not bringing down the cheese in proper time'. Secondly, the boys who had been beaten for stealing apples had only been given five or six lashes (the usual number for stealing or lying). Although the boys had given conflicting evidence over this (one saying that nine lashes had been given), the majority had agreed on five or six. Similarly, they found that the complaint against the Usher for unmerciful beatings was 'without foundation' - just as there were no grounds for censure over the matter of domestic chores.

The committee did, however, admonish the Master over his assertion that the Society had given him instructions to punish any boys who complained to the Nominees. No such order had been given. Gardner tried to claim that he had said no such thing to the Nominees, but the committee rejected this as being untrue. It also decreed that all future complaints should be made to the Society, 'who are the governors' of the Hospital, so that it could remedy the problems; and that it was the duty of the Nominees to alert the Society, if the difficulties had not been remedied.

The Nominees were most unhappy about these conclusions reached by the Society. They felt that the Merchants had ignored the central issue (namely, the incompetence of Mr Gardner) and had instead gone to 'great pains' exonerate the Master from a series of lesser complaints made by the boys. They put on record their right to interfere in school matters 'as superior visitors' and to insist that abuses were corrected. They condemned the Master's behaviour, which was intended 'to terrify the boys from making any complaints to the Nominees' - a suspicion confirmed by the sudden appearance of a notice in the school to that effect. This situation, they felt, would 'make any future visitation from them futile'. They therefore resolved 'that another paper be fixed up in some conspicuous place in the school, signifying that the boys *are* to complain to the Nominees on any occasion, as well as to the Merchants'.

Finally, after over four years of these unresolved problems with the Master, a joint meeting took place between the Nominees and the Standing Committee in July 1761 in an attempt to heal the breach. They resolved that Mr Gardner had had no authority for his declaration to the Nominees and that, in their joint opinion, 'he had behaved with ill manners to the Nominees and ought to ask their pardon and give assurance of his good behaviour to them for the future'. Mr Gardner complied with this instruction. Within a year, he had tendered his resignation.

This episode, however, highlighted a number of serious weaknesses in the management structure of the Hospital. The Society, which only discovered the problems after being alerted belatedly by the Nominees, had not been conducting its own quarterly visitations as stipulated. The Nominees, who had unearthed the problems, had dithered over a very long period at a time when dynamic action was urgently required. They had, after all, been given extensive powers by Mr Colston in 1715 for just such emergencies. Sadly, the respective rights of each body to take decisions independently or jointly had not been sufficiently well clarified in the settlement - nor had the matter of where the ultimate authority lay. These weaknesses undermined the confidence of both Merchants and Nominees and strengthened the position of the boys, who delighted in playing off the Nominees against the Master; and the Master, who relished the prospect of playing off the Nominees against the Merchants. The fact that the Master was not dismissed for his repeated absences from school, his neglect of teaching and his insubordination to the Nominees underlines a lack of strong leadership. This was to condemn the school to mediocrity for the remainder of the century.

Disputes between the two bodies continued to break out from time to time over the next seventy years. In September 1785, for instance, the Society suddenly admitted seven new boys into the Hospital, following a series of deaths which had reduced its own total of boys within the school to well below its allocation of fifty. In view of the fact that the number of those boys put in by the Nominees had remained constant, this move was designed to restore the balance. Its action, however, brought an immediate objection from the Nominees, who claimed that the election of so many boys at the same time was contrary to Colston's settlement. After a conference between the two bodies had failed to reach an amicable solution, the dispute continued to fester until they finally agreed to seek counsel's opinion. The verdict, given in February 1787, was that nominations by the two bodies for replacement pupils

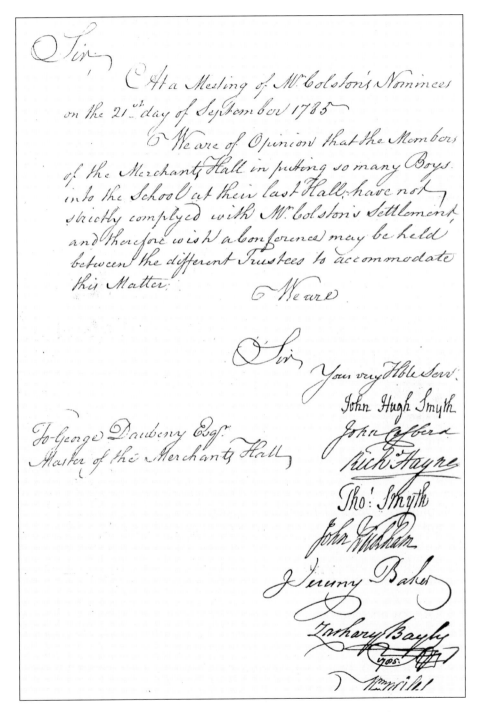

A letter from Colston's Nominees to the Society in 1785 protesting about its recent action in admitting boys to the school. (SMV Archive)

should alternate, irrespective of the total number of pupils the Society and the Nominees each had within the school. In view of the fact the all entries had been frozen during the fifteen months of the dispute, there were now 13 vacancies waiting to be filled. The interpretation of Colston's complicated settlement had again caused difficulties to the smooth running of the school.

A somewhat similar squabble had erupted earlier, in March 1745, over the right to nominate 'Boy Number 76' (see below). The two bodies also clashed in the summer of 1836 over the use of the Hospital's buildings. The Society had in fact granted the use of the school room and dining room to the British Association for the morning lectures at their annual conference during a week in August. As the school was still in session, however, it turned out to be 'a greater inconvenience than thought' and was therefore not to be regarded as a precedent. The Nominees, ever conscious of the duty to safeguard Colston's original settlement, stated at their meeting in September that it was the founder's intention that the Great House should be used exclusively as a school and a home for the masters and boys. The Society had breached the trusts by using it for other purposes, thus depriving the boys of its facilities for a considerable period. In response to their protest, the Society argued that it had granted permission 'for the honour of the city and the interests of science' and justified its action by the importance of the occasion.

This minor disagreement proved to be last serious division between the two bodies. Exactly one month after the Society had discussed the hiring out of the rooms, it took a most significant and far-reaching decision. On 8th November 1836, the Standing Committee was instructed to appoint a sub-committee with exclusive responsibility for the internal management of the Hospital. This was to result in the complete overhaul of the school and its workings (see below) and to herald a new era of enlightened leadership and tighter control. The Hospital was therefore to emerge from the first century and a quarter of its existence, which had been characterised by aimless ambition, apathetic management and repressive discipline, into a much more liberal era.

One by-product of this new regime was a far more harmonious relationship between the Society and the Nominees. The Society, for instance, in an attempt to promote 'good understanding' between the two bodies, kept the Nominees informed of all developments by giving them free access to its own minute books, class lists and reports from the catechist. It also made the Nominees feel involved and consulted on major matters, such as the date of a proposed public examination of the boys in 1845. The support and presence of the Nominees at the event, it stressed, would be essential in promoting 'the right feeling and impression on the minds of the boys'. When, three years later, the Society planned to increase the number of boys in the school, it conferred closely with the Nominees and worked out amicably the allocation of places. In return, the Nominees supported the decision wholeheartedly and thanked the Society most warmly for its consideration. The Society had at last managed to eliminate that source of friction and suspicion which Colston's settlement had generated for so long.

The New Visiting Committee, 1836

The new sub-committee held its first meeting on 12th December 1836. Consisting of six members (later seven), its sole task was to undertake the internal management of the school and to report back on its work to the Standing Committee. Its first members were Mr William Claxton (Chairman, who was also Master of the Society), Mr John Lunell, Mr Philip Protheroe, Mr Valentine Hellicar, Mr Robert Bruce, junior, and Mr Joseph Hellicar (Treasurer of the Society). The sub-committee kept its own minute book and presented an annual report on its progress to the Society each year in November from 1836 to 1857. It quickly became known as the Visiting Committee and, as such, continued to operate until 1875, when the new Governing Body was established. [It is also worth noting that, from the 1840s, its minute books refer increasingly to the Master as 'the Headmaster', the Society of Merchant Venturers as 'the Governors' and Colston's Hospital as 'Colston's School'].

The timing of this new major initiative, which was fundamentally to change the nature of the school, was influenced by a number of factors bringing pressure to bear on the Society. First, there was the arrival of an energetic new Master (Mr John Lewis), who had just been appointed on the retirement of Mr William Haynes, junior, through ill health. Mr Lewis was wholeheartedly in favour of reform. Secondly, the government had begun to take a rather inquisitive interest in the administration of charities and educational trusts and had established a committee of the House of Commons in 1815, under the chairmanship of Henry Brougham, to investigate the education of the poorer classes. He had duly requested detailed information about Colston's Hospital. Thirdly, the reforming Whig government had prompted the Charity Commissioners in November 1836 (the very month in which the Society had agreed to establish its new sub-committee) to demand the Society's minute books and all accounts relating the Colston's Hospital for inspection. For all these reasons, the Merchants felt that urgent action was now necessary to put the school into a fit state before outside bodies intervened.

From the outset, the new committee set about its work with enthusiasm, vigour and a real sense of purpose. Its status and power had been substantially increased by the permanent presence within its ranks of both the Master and the Treasurer of the Society. The intention of the Merchants was abundantly clear - namely, to transform Colston's Hospital into a totally different institution from what it had been throughout the previous century. For a hundred and twenty-five years the Society had run the school rigidly in accordance with the rules laid down by Edward Colston. It had therefore only provided the basic subjects of instruction, the minimal measure of food, facilities and comfort, and the strictest degree of discipline. Although it had successfully maintained the school's existence with the prescribed number of 100 boys throughout that period, it had largely been content to let the school run itself until an isolated crisis had demanded the Society's closer attention. The school therefore had drifted rather aimlessly during all these years with mediocre Masters at the helm. From 1836, however, this policy of *laissez-faire* was replaced by a policy of dynamic involvement.

At its first meeting, the committee set out its agenda for a major review of every aspect in the life of the school. Inspired by the energetic leadership of the Master of the Society (Mr William Claxton) and its Treasurer (Mr Joseph Hellicar), they worked at a furious pace, holding no fewer than thirty meetings during the first four months. Visits were made to other schools and local hospitals in a search for new ideas and methods. They examined the boys' diet, clothing and laundry; the daily routine; the system of rewards and punishments; the state of decoration; sleeping arrangements in the dormitories; kitchen equipment; the desks in the schoolroom; the boys' washroom; text books; the establishment of a library; a new curriculum with additional subjects; health and hygiene; leisure periods

Portrait of William Claxton, Master of the Society in 1836 and its Treasurer from 1841 to 1873. (By courtesy of the Society of Merchant Venturers)

and holidays; school excursions; furnishings for the Master's house; the introduction of gas lighting and heating; a covered play area; the Master's salary; the procedure for appointing Masters and Ushers; and the issuing of contracts to suppliers. (Details of the reforms emerging from these investigations will be discussed in Chapters 3 and 4). Even after this first flurry of activity, the committee continued to meet on a weekly basis until 1857, when it reduced to monthly gatherings.

As a result of the committee's work over the first ten years, the whole atmosphere of the school was changed with the comfort and welfare of the boys assuming far greater prominence. Nevertheless, throughout it all, the committee maintained with great enthusiasm and watchful diligence Colston's wishes over the Christian basis for education. Church attendance, religious instruction and daily school prayers continued to provide the cornerstone of life within the school.

Recruitment of Pupils

Throughout the entire period now under consideration (1710-1861), one aspect of the Hospital's affairs remained vital to the school's survival - namely, the recruitment of pupils. Although in theory the number of pupils specified under the terms laid down by the Founder in 1708 (i.e. one hundred) was maintained throughout this period, it was not always achieved in practice. According to the 1841 census, for instance, there were just 79 pupils resident in the school (together with three masters, a cook, a housemaid and a housekeeper).

In his original settlement, Colston had reserved to himself the right of nominating all boys for entry during his lifetime (though he did in fact sometimes ask the Society to make recommendations). After his death, nominations were to be shared equally between the Society and the Nominees, meaning in effect that each body eventually became responsible for having admitted 50 of the boys present in the school at any one time. The boys themselves were to be drawn from a genuinely poor background and, therefore, to be 'real objects' of the Hospital's charity. They were also to have been born within the city of Bristol or be the sons of freemen of the city - with the exception of twenty out of the allocation of the Nominees, who could be drawn from outside. In addition, Colston included instructions that, in filling all vacancies, priority should always be given to 'such poor boys who are or shall be of kin to the said Edward Colston, or of the name of Colston'. Other conditions for entry were stated clearly in his rules - namely, 'that no child be taken in, but whose parents will willingly submit to the rules and education of the House'; and 'that no boy afflicted with the evil, broken belly, idiot or other natural infirmity be admitted'.

He described his own method of recruitment in some supplementary instructions issued to the Society in 1714. His plan was to seek lists of suitable boys from the churchwardens of all the Bristol parishes - and he desired that this system should continue after his death, so that each parish could share in the benefits of the school in proportion to the number of poor boys within the parish. He did, however, put in a plea for special consideration to be given to the Temple parish, partly because it was the place of his birth and partly because 'the number of their poor is much increased'. He therefore stipulated that there should never be less than eight boys ('if not ten') from Temple within his Hospital.

Throughout the eighteenth century, therefore, the Hospital continued to recruit most of its boys from the parishes of Temple, St Mary Redcliffe, St Augustine's, St James's, St Stephen's, Christ Church, St Philip's, St Michael's, St Nicholas's, St John's, St Peter's and Clifton. On those occasions when the number of applications exceeded the number of places available, a vote was taken at the meeting to elect the most worthy. The Nominees regularly took up their option to recruit boys from outside Bristol - or 'foreigners', as they were called in the minutes. These were drawn not only from towns and villages in the neighbouring counties of Somerset, Gloucestershire and Wiltshire, but also from much further afield, including London, Yorkshire, Monmouthshire, Northumberland, Herefordshire, Devon, Oxfordshire, Worcestershire and Middlesex.

There was also a long succession of boys claiming to be of Colston's kin or to bear the name of Colston - boys who were drawn from a wide area stretching from Devon to St Andrew's in Scotland. Even in the nineteenth century, no fewer than 14 boys were recruited under this privilege between the years 1850-1873. All such claims were carefully considered by the Society and investigated locally for their authenticity. For instance, in March 1796, the Merchants read a genuine letter from a Mr Daniel Colston of London, who said that he had recently visited Bristol 'having heard it in my youth that we had once a great and good ancestor, that had left great charities at Bristol'. His fact-finding mission had proved fruitful, because he had bought a printed copy of Colston's settlement and had read of the preferential treatment given to the kin of the founder. He explained that his aged parents, who lived in Worcester, could no longer work and found it difficult therefore to support his brother (the youngest of twelve children), who was now seven - 'an active youth' with 'a great inclination for learning'.

Among all the genuine applications, however, there were always some from impostors, who tried to abuse the system. In 1791, for example, an application was received by the Nominees from a 'Mr George Colston' of Shepton Mallet, who wrote a heart-rending letter about his extreme poverty and the fact that he was the father of eleven children all still living. He had heard that 'persons of the name of Colston are entitled to a preference in being admitted' to the school and

A letter from Colston's Nominees in 1791 rejecting an application for a place, having discovered that the boy's name was not in fact Colston. If it had been, the boy would have warranted preferential treatment. (SMV Archive)

was therefore applying for a place for his son, Charles. The application, however, was rejected, because, in the words of the minute book, 'upon inspection of the registers of Shepton Mallet, the name of the family does not appear to be Colston'. Another application was refused in 1796 for a boy called 'James Colston' from Chacely in Worcestershire, after checks revealed that his name was actually 'Coston'.

As time progressed, the Society made a number of slight modifications to the entry system. From 1722, all boys admitted were required to bring a certificate of their baptism from their church minister and another from the churchwardens of the parish. This requirement was extended in 1796, when the Society ordered that no boy would be eligible for entry unless he had been baptised within one year of his birth (presumably to ensure that the parents were genuine members of the Church of England and not last-minute converts for convenience). By the early years of the nineteenth century, printed applications forms were being used to which the baptism certificates were to be attached. These were improved by the new Visiting Committee in 1837, when 'blank forms of petition' were printed for the use of applicants, together with information sheets (at a small charge!).

By the middle of the nineteenth century, there was also a strong move to vet candidates before their applications were considered. In 1841, for instance, the Nominees resolved that all boys who had been nominated should 'present themselves at the school at least a fortnight before the day of entry for examination by the surgeon'. This call for a preliminary medical examination resulted from the rejection of one of their candidates on the day of entry, because the school doctor had ruled him to be inadmissible 'on account of a bad head'. A year later, the Visiting Committee called for a preliminary enquiry into the life, means, habits and general character of the parents of each candidate - recognising for the first time the importance parental example and support. They also resolved that candidates should be cross-examined about their religious denomination before their cases were considered by the Society. The age of the entrance interview had arrived!

Nevertheless, when the Attorney-General suggested in 1856 that the school should consider changing its method of selection to include an 'examination in the rudiments of knowledge', the Nominees objected most strongly. The purpose of the Founder, they insisted, was to provide education for 'poor boys' and not necessarily for 'clever ones'. Another suggestion that they should consider taking in 'day scholars' was also dismissed in 1858 as 'undesirable' by the Society's Standing Committee. Progress continued to be made, however, with the actual system of entry and by 1859 a much slicker organisation was in place. Parents were first expected to pick up a printed 'form of petition' from Merchants' Hall, which was brought by the candidate to one of four 'vetting' sessions held each year by the Visiting Committee. The names of eligible candidates were then entered into the 'Candidates' Book'. After these initial interviews, Merchants were each entitled to nominate one candidate from that official list for each of the meetings held by the Society in April and October, when elections for entry took place. The Nominees operated their own system in relation to the fifty boys for whom they were responsible.

A form issued by Colston's Nominees to the Master of the School in 1819 to inform him of the admission of one of their nominations. (SMV Archive)

From 1716, the Master had been expected to maintain in a book a careful list of all the boys who had entered the school with dates of entry and leaving. These lists have survived in two volumes, covering the period 1718-1866. The boys were eventually given an admission number on entry, between 1 and 100, with each new boy receiving the number of the boy who had just left and whose place he was filling. However, thanks to the inefficiency of the Masters over the years, the numbering system became confused - hence the fact that, in 1843, the Society ruled that each boy on admission was to have his registration number clearly 'prefixed to his name'.

The importance of these numbers had been given a special significance in 1814, when Mr Philip Jones had invested £500 to establish a trust in favour of the school. Admitted to Colston's Hospital as 'Boy Number 76' in 1765, he now wished to express his gratitude for the start he had been given in life. His plan was that, out of the interest on the investment, £5 should be set aside each year to be paid as a lump sum to 'Boy Number 76' on leaving - and to each of his successors in that number thereafter. In addition, one shilling out of the interest was to be paid yearly to each of the other boys and the residue to the Master.

By 1842, the right to nominate 'Boy Number 76' (a number which was now highly prized) had become the source of some dispute between the Society and the Nominees. The Society claimed the right to do so, because Jones himself had originally been nominated by the Society and was a Bristol boy and that, although all the previous 'Number 76' boys since 1814 had been selected by the Nominees, this was due to poor administration of the numbering system by the Masters. The Nominees, on the other hand, pointed out that Jones had signified his his wish for the Nominees to control the nomination and to include 'foreign boys' from outside the city in their deliberations (which, of course, only they could do).

In the new spirit of goodwill, the dispute was settled amicably after a joint conference at which it was decided that the two bodies should alternate in making the nomination. By 1852, the Society had resolved to grant the privilege of nominating 'Boy Number 76' to the Master of the Society, whenever its turn came round. Later, in 1880, the newly-established Governing Board (see Chapter 7) decided to award this number (on the Headmaster's recommendation) to a boy who had been in the school for not less than one year or more than two years, as a reward for 'meritorious conduct' rather than for 'proficient study'.

Jones was by no means the only benefactor to use the school's numbering system in this way. William Vaughan of Monmouthshire left a sum of £125 to the Society in his will (dated 6th April 1798), the interest on which was to be awarded annually to the boys of the school on Colston's Day. He specified that, while each boy should receive one shilling, 'the doorkeeper for that week and boy Number 49' should each receive 2s 6d. If any money remained, then 'a great coat and gloves' should be bought for the use of the doorkeeper in bad weather. Boys had traditionally been employed to watch the gate, the Master appointing a new 'doorkeeper' each week. When this practice was later abandoned on the appointment of a full-time Porter in 1849, the 2s 6d allowed to the doorkeeper in Mr Vaughan's will was simply retained in the fund for general distribution. The first payments under this scheme were made in 1812.

Arranging Apprenticeships for the Boys

Edward Colston always considered that, whereas one essential ingredient
of a boy's education was a sound grounding in the doctrines of the
Church of England, the other was an apprenticeship on leaving with a
master, who was himself an active member of that church. Boys, who
were admitted into the school between the ages of seven and ten, were
expected to stay in the school for seven years, before going on to be
apprenticed. This meant that some of them were actually sixteen before
they eventually left school. Colston's endowment made provision for
the apprenticeship fee of £10 to be paid to the master, but with the
reservation that, if the master turned out to be a dissenter, then the fee
would be withheld and given instead to one of the charity schools set up
in four Bristol parishes. The placements were usually organised by the
Master of the school and then approved by the Society.

The record books, maintained by a succession of Masters from 1718,
show that the task of finding apprenticeships was efficiently organised
in the period to 1861. It is interesting to note that, during the 1740s and
1750s, boys went on to work in a great variety of occupations, many of
which were related to serving the needs of a fashionable, consumer
society. The masters listed included barbers, glovers, shoemakers,
perriwigmakers, staymakers, druggists, mercers, bakers, watchmakers,
tobacconists, papermakers, butchers and stationers. By the early
nineteenth century, the nature of their employment had noticeably
changed. In the eleven years from 1809, out of a total of 81 boys
apprenticed, 13 had gone 'to be educated as planters' overseas, 14 had
gone into service with merchants, 13 were ironmongers and 4 were
working for accountants. The remainder worked in various spheres,
some relating to crafts (cabinetmakers, saddlers, cordwainers and
carvers). One other feature was that some boys, who had been
apprenticed to one master, were subsequently 'turned over' to another.
Between 1789 and 1834, for instance, there were 84 such 'turn overs',
including 16 to plantation owners overseas.

On two occasions at least, in 1772 and 1785, the Merchants decided
to give a few of the senior boys work experience as clerks in their own
crane office at the port. This, they considered, would be 'of great service
to them in the future'. They also started the practice of encouraging
bright pupils to enter teaching. One boy (H.G. Brittan) was therefore
apprenticed to the Master at the Hospital in 1851, whereas four years
earlier a pupil had been placed with the Master of the Diocesan School.
So successful were these experiments that another school leaver
(Thomas Wedlock) was taken on as an apprentice at the Hospital for
five years from 1856. He was eventually followed in this capacity by

James Jones in 1864 (at a salary rising from £10 to £20), who was quickly judged to be so promising that he was given a permanent appointment as Fourth Master after only two-and-a-half years.

The Merchants became quite flexible in its approach to some situations. In 1782, they accepted an approach from Mr John Purrier to increase, during his lifetime, the apprenticeship fee to £15 for each boy - presumably to make it easier to secure better positions. In 1840, they waived their normal regulation requiring each boy to stay in the school for seven years, when Joseph Emmett's mother pleaded for his release after only five-and-a-half. She had found him a good placement with Mr Richard Illingworth, someone whom the Society applauded as 'a most respectable man and a churchman'. They were also very compassionate towards Walter Carr in 1838, who was due to leave but had no living relatives to help him. The Master, at the Society's prompting, worked hard on a solution and eventually found a good situation with a local baker at six shillings a week plus his board.

The Merchants, however, were equally hard on those who tried to abuse the system. They steadfastly refused to pay the £10 fee for Frederick Polson in 1841, whose mother had suddenly removed the boy without sanction and apprenticed him to Mr John Fisher of the schooner, *Eliza*; and they wrote a letter to Mrs West in 1846, warning her not to arrange an apprenticeship for her son William, until she had received their consent and had satisfied them 'that the intended master is a churchman'. A testimonial from her church rector would be required to that effect. They added a warm touch, however, expressing the view that that they were glad that William 'has now a prospect of a livelihood before him'. On the other hand, they firmly turned down an impudent application from Mr Charles Smith in 1830, informing them that Mr Mereweather would be taking his son as an apprentice and requesting that the £10 fee should be transferred to him (the father) in view of the fact that the boy would be living at home.

They were particularly strict in adhering to Colston's demand that the apprentice master should be a member of the Church of England. In 1840, for instance, the father of Edward Hobbs (a recent ex-pupil) wanted to apprentice the boy to B. Auckland & Son, ironmongers of Taunton. The Merchants refused, in spite of the threat of legal action, on the grounds that Mr Auckland was a dissenter. Earlier, in 1816, they had been worried by a letter from the Bishop of Bristol, stating that he had been informed from Newfoundland that a considerable number of young men, educated at Colston's School and apprenticed to Roman Catholics in violation of the founder's will, had themselves become bigoted Catholics. However, after a thorough investigation by Mr Haynes, the schoolmaster, this evidence turned out to be totally untrue. He had only sanctioned one apprentice to a non-catholic in Newfoundland and had turned down another request from a master, who was clearly a 'Romanist'.

The experience of boys from Colston's, who served apprenticeships, was not always a happy one. Silas Told later wrote of his own experiences, after enjoying six years in the sheltered environment of the Hospital (1719-25):

> In the year 1725, I was bound an apprentice to Captain Moses Lilly, in the ship *Prince of Wales*, and sailed from Bristol to Cork and Jamaica in the month of July. Here my sufferings began: being wrought on by the Spirit of God and totally ignorant of the maxims of the world, and having been six years in the Hospital, free from all intercourse with mankind, a sea life was very disagreeable to me.
>
> The first reception I met with on board, when the ship lay in Kings-Road, was this: the Chief Mate called the cabin boy, but he not being on board, he sent me to the cook to get him a plate of victuals, which I really imagined was meant for myself; and accordingly got a plate full, carried it down to the cabin and, having a keen appetite, made a very comfortable dinner. When the Chief Mate had done his business, he sent for me in order to bring his victuals. I told him understood it was for myself and that I had eaten it up; upon which, he knocked me down and began cursing and damning me at a horrible rate. This language I was never acquainted with; therefore I thought I should have broken my heart with grief; and, having no friend to whom I could apply for redress, I was forced to suffer repeated acts of barbarity, which continued for eleven years.

The Hospital's Finances

Colston had originally endowed the Hospital with estates at Beere and Locking, which were estimated to produce £700 a year, and ground rents in various places around the country, valued at £578 16s 0d - making a total income of £1278 16s 0d. During much of the eighteenth and early nineteenth centuries, their books failed to balance, partly because the level of income did not keep pace with the sharp increase in the cost of living (particularly severe during the period of the French Wars and the ensuing recession, 1790-1820). It was also partly due, however, to lax administration, which had permitted an outstanding debt from Colston's heirs of over £3,000 to remain uncollected for forty years (see above); and also, in 1748, arrears of £1,200, stretching back over twelve years, for ground rents from the Duke of Bolton's estate at Kidwelly.

The result was that the income from Colston's endowment was seldom adequate to maintain the Hospital throughout this period and that, for parts of the eighteenth century at least, the Hospital accounts were in debt to the Society - often by as much as £10,000. To their undying credit, through thick and thin, the Merchants continued to support 100 poor boys, even at a loss, in spite of the fact that Colston's settlement had given them powers to reduce numbers if the financial situation deteriorated. The situation certainly fluctuated. In 1788, William Haynes, junior, pointed out to the Society (as part of his campaign to increase funding for the Hospital) that the value of the endowment had risen by £692 a year to a new level of £1,970. However, when an investigation was conducted into the Hospital's finances in January 1807, the accounts showed clearly that spending had far exceeded income for several years. They also showed that, whereas the value of the estates in Somerset had risen from £700 to £2,300 a year in normal rents, the value of the ground rents in other counties had remained unchanged. It was therefore decided to seek permission to sell off the ground rents and invest the proceeds in land. Parliament eventually granted an Act in January 1808, enabling them to proceed with this. Over the next twenty-five years therefore, spasmodic attempts were made to sell off a number of these ground rents in Northumberland and Essex with the money so raised invested in additional property in Locking.

The Society also tried to control expenditure much more tightly after the establishment of its new sub-committee or Visiting Committee in 1836, (see above). Important savings were made by a decision to take over from the Master all responsibility for organising provisions, clothing and repairs and, instead, to control all supplies themselves through the award of contracts, after receiving competitive estimates from various local shopkeepers and manufacturers. A similar approach was adopted towards

An estimate from a contractor to The Visiting Committee in 1847, giving the cost of altering the iron bedsteads. (SMV Archive)

painters and craftsmen involved in the refurbishment of the fabric.

After the first year of operation, the committee was able to forecast an annual saving of £453 18s 0d, in spite of its large additional expenditure on salaries, books and refurbishment. Although this estimate was revised in 1843, the committee was still able to report the good news that expenditure, during the first six years of the new system, had resulted in a total saving over previous levels of £1,158 13s 7d (an average of about £193 a year). By December 1848, income had increased by approximately £600 a year (thanks partly to a new source of income from the Monkton estates - see below). By 1850, the total income had grown to about £3,590 a year, leaving a healthy balance in hand of around £1,273. Although this annual surplus tended to fluctuate, the Attorney-General estimated in 1856 that the potential surplus was still running at about £1,095 a year. In view of the fact that the finances were so buoyant, the Society began to give serious consideration to the possibility of expanding the size of the school to 120 and building extra accommodation (see Chapter 6 for the outcome of these proposals).

The fresh source of income (mentioned above) from the manor of Monkton in Stogursey, Somerset, had arisen after investigation by the Charity Commissioners into the records of the Society relating to Colston's Hospital (1836-39). In July 1839, the Attorney-General brought a suit against the Society, alleging that it had obtained the manor in its own right through a complicated transaction between 1709 and 1713. The crucial point was that, in order to achieve its objective, the Society had made use of some property in the transactions which it held in trust for the Hospital. At the end of a most complex and long drawn-out case, the Master of the Rolls (Lord Langdale) ruled in May 1842 that the Society had acted illegally and that the profit arising from the manor was therefore due to the Hospital. The Society had argued that Colston had, in his endowment, conveyed all the property absolutely to the Society for its own use, subject only to its undertaking to maintain 100 boys in the Hospital. As it had funded the school during years of loss, so it was entitled to benefit from the properties during years of gain. However, when the Society lost its appeal in January 1849, the income of the Hospital was immediately boosted by the rents of the manor of Monkton .

Sources used in Chapter 2

D.J. Eames, *The Contribution made by the Society of Merchant Venturers to the Development of Education in Bristol* (unpublished MA thesis for the University of Bristol, 1966), pp 37-99

John Latimer, *The History of the Society of Merchant Venturers of the*

City of Bristol (1903)

Patrick McGrath, *The Merchant Venturers of Bristol* (Bristol, 1975) pp
210-213, 360-70

Society of Merchant Venturers Archive (for exact location of source in
minute books use the dates supplied in the text):
Hall Book of Proceedings, vols. 4-22 (1708-1860)
Book of Orders and Minutes for Electing Nominees, 1708-1874
Minutes of the Meetings of Mr Colston's Nominees, 3 vols.,
(1748-70; 1780-1822; 1823-53)
Box of Appendices: Bundle 3 (petition of William Haynes)
Bundle 6 (apprenticeships, 1809-20)

*List of Boys taken in and bound out by Mr Samuel Gardner, Master,
1718-1762*

Copies of Mr Colston's Settlements (printed volume)

Book of Charity Proceedings, vol. 1, 1852-57

Annual Reports of the Colston's Hospital Visiting Committee, 1842-58

*A rare view of the inner courtyard of The Great House, c.1840s. A drawing by S.G.
Tovey. (By courtesy of Bristol Museums and Art Gallery)*

CHORES & PUNISHMENTS IN 1820

John Melhuish *(Old Colstonian)*

I was supplied with the number 78 and, on the Sunday after my admission, with a regular rig-out of the Colston regimentals, with the silver badge on the left breast of the coat, of which I felt not a little proud. I should say that each of our three coats bore a different badge - that on the everyday coat was of a heavy, rather coarse description, the holiday badge was of a finer sort, while the best was of silver and was only worn on Sundays.

On Sundays, we all marched to the Cathedral and occupied raised seats on each side of the altar. We attended morning and evening service (except in bad weather) throughout the summer and sometimes on a fine evening in winter. When we did not attend church, the time was devoted to reading the bible, one of the elder boys being called to the pulpit for that purpose. At intervals during the reading, a short cut of the usher's cane on the desk would be heard, with the demand, 'Number 60 - the last word?' If Number 60 failed to repeat the last word correctly, he was punished by having to stand up for the rest of the evening - and he was seldom alone.

On Monday mornings, after breakfast, some time was devoted to shoe-cleaning in the playground, when each had to polish up his three pairs of leathers - and this polishing was accomplished by the skimmings of the boiled beef (the grease). After this the whole of the shoes underwent examination and such as required mending were chalk-marked and handed over to the renovator of soles.

Thursday, once a month, was broken into by the washing of the dormitories. For this purpose some twenty-five or thirty of the boys were selected, to each of whom a particular duty would be appointed - and, on the previous day, their names would be shown on a slate, after the fashion of a programme, and each would know the lot assigned to him. There was the wet mop, the first brushes, the second mops, second brushes, mops again, and again dry mops, wringers, water carriers, splash boys etc. The cleansing of the two rooms occupied a good part of the day and the work was executed with the greatest deal of precision and regularity.

Punishment generally was of a mild character, a cut or two across the hand with a cane by the usher or, in bad cases, a sound thrashing on the back; but some of the monitors, who assumed a little brief authority in the absence of the usher, would amuse themselves with rapping the knuckles of the youngsters with a rather heavy ruler. Flogging was never resorted to but in extreme cases - and then the Headmaster, who was seldom seen in the school room except on such occasions, was always the executioner.

What was looked upon as the greatest punishment, however, was wearing the 'collar'. This article was a wooden instrument placed round the neck of the wearer; it was about an inch and a half in thickness and three inches in breadth, with a hinge at the back and locked in front. When the boys were at play or at exercise, the sufferer had to walk too and fro in a portion of the ground exposed to the view of the inhabitants of the houses nearby, and was supposed to be 'boycotted' by his fellows. The punishment was continued for a number of days according to the offence.

On 13th November, we attended service at the Cathedral and, on our return we were each entitled to receive two shillings, from which twopence was however deducted for broken windows; and an inspection of our belongings having been previously made, such of our books and slates as were found to be dilapidated were replenished and the cost deducted from the gratuity.

(From The Colstonian, *April 1895)*

CHAPTER 3

Masters and Ushers

'That the Master be a member of the Church of England, of sober life and conversation, and not under the age of five and twenty years; that hath good government of himself and his passions; one of a meek temper and humble behaviour and of a good genius for teaching'. (Colston's Rules for appointing the Master, 1708)

Qualifications and duties

Edward Colston made it clear from the outset what qualities he was looking for in the Master of his Hospital. The rules he drew up in 1710 were therefore strictly adhered to with all appointments throughout the period to 1861. By far the most important qualification was that he should be a member of the Church of England and a regular communicant. It was therefore essential that his application should be supported by some of the ministers in Bristol (although this stipulation was amended in 1715 to read the *majority* of the ministers in Bristol). In personal terms, he needed to be at least twenty-five years of age, a man of 'sober life and conversation', self-disciplined, 'of meek temper and humble behaviour' and fully in control of his own family. Although he was not necessarily expected to have gained formal qualifications, he was required to display 'a good genius for teaching', a firm understanding of the Christian religion and an ability both to write well and to calculate accurately in mathematics.

Colston also expected the selected Master to be totally reliable and obedient in implementing the rules drawn up for running the Hospital. It was therefore his duty to attend to school business between the hours of 7.00 am and 11.00 am and 1.00 pm and 5.00 pm in summer; and between 8.00 am and 11.00 am and 1.00 pm and 4.00 pm in winter. He stressed that it was the Master's 'chief business to instruct the children in the principles of the Christian religion' and to explain the meaning of the church catechism to them twice a week (with the help, if necessary of a local minister, who would eventually 'catechise' them in church). Furthermore, he was to read prayers, based on the Book of Common Prayer, twice a day in school. Great importance was also to be placed on encouraging good manners and good behaviour in the boys and discouraging 'the beginning of vice' - especially in relation to

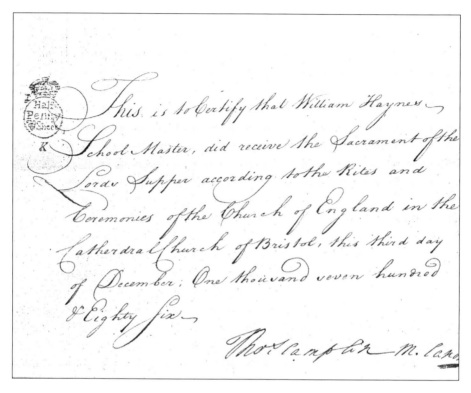

A certificate from Bristol Cathedral confirming that William Haynes, junior (who was shortly to apply for the Mastership of the School) had taken communion there in December 1786 (SMV Archive)

lying, cursing, swearing and blaspheming.

To strengthen all this training undertaken in school, the Master was to accompany the boys twice to church on Sundays and Holy Days, teaching them to 'behave themselves reverently while they are there' and to join in wholeheartedly with the service. Colston's chief concern, therefore, was with the spiritual and human development of the boys within his Hospital. In addition, of course, the Master was expected to teach them spelling, punctuation, reading, writing and arithmetic. He was not to teach any other children outside the school, nor was he to receive any money from the parents or friends of the boys 'upon any pretence whatsoever'. A copy of these rules was to be place prominently inside the school and the Master was to read them publicly at least four times a year in the presence of the Nominees. Edward Colston had therefore successfully stamped both his principles and his personality on the Hospital for the foreseeable future.

Salary

In establishing his settlement for the Hospital in 1708, Colston had built into the endowment sufficient resources to 'provide a convenient allowance' for the Master, as well as a capitation sum of £10 a year for the maintenance of each boy. The Master's salary was calculated at £50 with an additional £40 set aside for the appointment of two assistants. However, as early as 1717, the Society of Merchant Venturers had decided to abandon the original plan to control the operation centrally by buying in provisions and materials on behalf of the Hospital and, instead, to hand over that task to the Master along with the capitation fees.

When, therefore, Mr Samuel Gardner was appointed Master of the Hospital in 1717, he signed an agreement with the Society stipulating that, in return for £10 a year for each boy on the school roll, he would 'teach and instruct or cause to be taught' the boys 'to read, write and cast accounts'; and would provide them with 'meat and drink' (according to the specifications given), 'washing, pens, ink, paper or writing books, prayer books and reading books'. At Whitsuntide each year, he would buy for each boy a new suit of clothes and other items of uniform. Furthermore, he would be responsible for paying the salaries of the two Ushers (£50 a year to be divided between them) and providing them with board and lodging. If a boy left during the course of a year, then he would be expected to pay back to the Society a proportion of the £10 allowance already granted.

Therefore, although he was given food and rent-free accommodation for himself and his family in the Great House (repairs for which would be undertaken by the Society), the Master was not paid a salary. Nevertheless (as has already been discussed in Chapter 2), the Society compensated, in some measure, for the lack of salary by appointing each successive Master, until 1836, to the office of Beadle. This carried a salary of £20 per annum in return for the duty of collecting rents, on behalf of the Society, from their properties in Clifton and Bristol.

As the century progressed, this situation was to prove far from satisfactory. At a time of rising inflation, the Masters were increasingly tempted to cut costs by reducing the quality or quantity of the food and other supplies in order to maintain their own meagre standard of living. Periodic complaints about the inadequacies of the food were certainly made by both boys and parents. The problem had become acute by February 1774, when the Master, Mr William Haynes, senior, petitioned the Society over 'the price of provisions and clothing', which had 'greatly risen' since his appointment in 1762, leaving him much out of pocket. He pointed out that Bristol Corporation had granted special allowances under the circumstances to the Master of Queen Elizabeth's Hospital and the Mistress of Red Maids' School. The Society responded generously by granting Mr Haynes 100 guineas 'as a free gift'.

However, by the time that Mr Haynes's son had become Master in 1787, the situation had deteriorated even further - a process that was to continue throughout the period of the French Wars, which saw rampant inflation. He therefore petitioned the Society in the October of that year, making the extremely valid point that the £10 capitation allowance for the maintenance and clothing of each boy had been fixed some eighty years earlier and that no addition to it had been made, in spite of 'the great advance since that time in the price of provisions and every other necessity'. He also regretted that the recent dispute between the Nominees and the Society over the method of nomination (see Chapter 2) had left him with only 78 boys in the school, during those months when all the entries had been frozen. His revenue had therefore suffered greatly. Although the Society chose to ignore his request for increased capitation, it granted him 100 guineas on the basis of the points he had made.

Exactly a year later, Haynes again raised the question of the capitation allowance, but this time also mention the word 'salary' for the first time. He pointed out that Colston, in estimating costs in 1708, had made a provision of £50 a year in salary for the Master, but had left it to be fixed at the discretion of the Society'. He humbly submitted that 'since the original foundation of the school, no salary hath hitherto been paid to the Master'. On this occasion, the Society chose to ignore the point he was making about salary, but - in view of the increased value of the Clifton and Bristol estates - agreed to increase the capitation fees by £1 per boy, backdated to the previous December.

Then, with food prices almost out of control in the country at large, further increases followed rapidly - in November 1790, an additional allowance of £1 per boy; in April 1796, another increase of £1 per boy *and* an annual salary of £50 for the Master; in May 1800, a gift of 200 guineas to the Master 'as a temporary relief, owing to the very high price of provisions'; in November 1800, an increase in the capitation allowance to £15 per boy, 'considering the amount which the Master must be out of pocket'; in May 1801, a further gift of £200 in view of 'the enormous price of provisions'; in December 1810, an increase in capitation to £17 per boy (which was the sum that had been paid at Queen Elizabeth's Hospital for the past four years) and the Master paid a further £200 'for past expenses'; in November 1814, a further increase in capitation to £18 per boy, the Master's salary increased to £100 and a gratuity of 200 guineas granted 'for his past outlay'; and, in November

1818, a further increase in the Master's salary to £150. Although the capitation allowance was temporarily reduced to £15 per boy in November 1822 'in consequence of the reduced prices of provisions', it was again raised to £18 in June 1825 owing to further great rises in the price of food and clothing.

The Society must take great credit for keeping in touch with prevailing conditions (prompted no doubt by the Master's ready advice) and, at long last, for facing up to the need to provide a realistic salary for the Master together with index-linked capitation allowances. When eventually Mr Haynes, junior, retired in 1836, the Society decided, as part of its cost-cutting exercise (see Chapter 2), to take over control again of both the capitation allowance and the purchase of supplies for the Hospital. Although it was agreed to run this scheme as a one-year experiment, it became so successful that it became a permanent policy. The new Master, Mr John Lewis, was therefore paid a straight salary of £100 (increased to 200 guineas in August 1839), while still continuing to draw an additional £20 for his work as Beadle.

Appointments and Dismissals

Until 1836, the Society did not go to any great lengths in either selecting or appointing the Masters to the Hospital. As its ambitions for the school were strictly limited and its basic curriculum undemanding, the Society was far more interested in securing the services of reliable God-fearing men than searching for highly qualified Oxbridge graduates. It therefore tended to look locally for individuals who were already well known to both the Society itself and the parish clergy. By appointing them also to the salaried office of Beadle, it was able to regard them as very much one of the family. Indeed, family connections were so strong at times that the appointment almost became incestuous.

As we have already seen, the first Master, Mr Sylvester (July 1710 - December 1717), was not a great success. After a series of complaints, he was dismissed for 'not having performed his duties in relation to the boys in his care'. His successor, Mr Samuel Gardner, wrote in his record book that, when he became Master, he 'found most of the boys in a most deplorable condition in the school'. Little is really known about Mr Gardner (March 1718 - April 1740), except that he was actually styled 'a merchant' in his agreement and that he was already employed by the Society as it Beadle. He seems to have run the school in a steady manner, before dying in office after 22 years in charge.

He was succeeded by his son, Mr Samuel Gardner, junior, (April 1740 - September 1762) without any formality of application or interview. The Society merely recorded in its minutes that he would be 'admitted Beadle of the Society in the room of his father, deceased' and 'Chief Master of Mr Colston's Hospital in the place of his father and on the same terms and under the like rules and regulations'. This was certainly an economical method of operation, but it was also risky. In the event, Mr Gardner, junior, turned out to be a completely different character to his father and totally unsuited to the role of Master. The running battle between the Nominees and Mr Gardner over his frequent absences from school, his brutal treatment of the boys and his gross insubordination have already been described in Chapter 2. He resigned a year after his enforced apology to the Nominees, at the end of an unhappy era in the school's history.

For the next twenty-two years, the Master of the Hospital was Mr William Haynes (September 1762 - June 1784), who eventually died in office. It was a somewhat turbulent period in the life of the Hospital with regular indiscipline among the boys, merciless floggings and frequent attempts to run away (see Chapter 4). Haynes was succeeded by his brother-in-law, Mr John Watkins (June 1784 - February 1787), although it was evident from the outset that his role was merely that of a temporary caretaker. On the day of his appointment, Mr Haynes's son, William, was appointed 'Beadle and Collector of Rents in his father's place' - a significant hint that he was being groomed for the Mastership. Indeed, he had already been teaching in the school for several years, but, in 1784, was only 22 years of age - three years short of the lower age limit for the Mastership set by Colston. A keen member of the Church of England, who took communion at Bristol Cathedral, he had been baptised locally at St Augustine's church in January 1762. He was tailor-made for the post!

Mr Watkins duly tendered his resignation on 23rd February 1787 and thanked the Society for the Mastership 'and, more especially, for your permitting my nephew, William Haynes, to conduct the business for me'. By these words he revealed that, with the connivance of the Society, he had in fact been Master only in name and that young Haynes had been totally responsible for running the school. This was confirmed in a formal petition by Haynes to the Society requesting the Mastership on the same day that Watkins had resigned. He stated that 'for some years past' he had 'wholly managed' the Hospital and that therefore he flattered himself that he was 'capable of conducting the same' after the resignation of 'Uncle John Watkins'.

Mr William Haynes, junior (February 1787 - August 1836), who was a bachelor, retained the post most remarkably for over fifty years, either as Acting Master or Master. He saw the school though troublesome times with roaring inflation (see above) and frequent expulsions (see Chapter 4). In spite of his problems, however, he turned

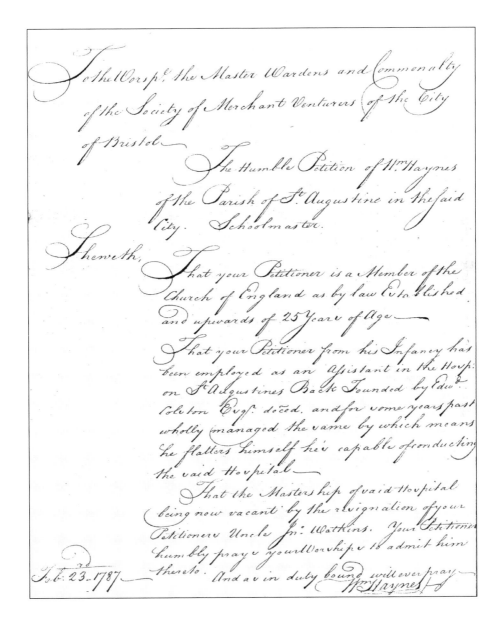

A certificate from Bristol Cathedral confirming that William Haynes, junior (who was shortly to apply for the Mastership of the School) had taken communion there in December 1786 (SMV Archive)

out to be a most reliable, energetic (at least in his earlier years), decisive and respected man. Indeed, the Visiting Committee later praised him for being 'in a great measure, the confidential agent of the Society of Merchants'. Sadly, he clung on to office for far too long and was obliged to leave the management of the school to others during his final years of failing health. On 1st August 1836, one member wrote to the Master of the Society of Merchant Venturers expressing his anxieties about the state of the school. 'Several circumstances lead me to fear that the establishment is not in all respects so well conducted as when under the immediate personal superintendence of our friend, Mr Haynes'. He went on to say that 'in the present state of his health,' he felt 'some difficulty in speaking to him on the subject', but believed that the nettle ought to be grasped and a sub-committee appointed to investigate.

Nine days later, Haynes resigned at the age of seventy-four. The Society recorded its immense gratitude for his Mastership, 'which he has so long discharged with so much credit to himself and so much satisfaction to the Society'. It was agreed - for the first time in the Hospital's history - that the post should be advertised in the press. A sub-committee was quickly formed and, out of twenty-one candidates, Mr John Lewis was appointed on 26th October. Travelling expenses were granted to those candidates who had attended the interviews 'from distant places'. The Society, however, explained to Mr Lewis that he could not yet take up residency in the Great House, because Mr Haynes's poor health prevented him from being moved. He died in the following March, when the new Master was finally able to take possession of the school and to move into fully furnished accommodation. Although Mr Haynes had purchased all his own furniture, the Visiting Committee believed that a capital outlay now would eliminate 'injury to the house by the removal of furniture' on the change of Mastership - and thus save the cost of redecoration.

Mr John Lewis (October 1836 - August 1848), a married man, took on his responsibility with great energy, flare, enthusiasm and drive. He supported the Visiting Committee wholeheartedly in its desire to transform the school and displayed considerable initiative in the introduction of new ideas. The members of the committee, in return, were warm in the appreciation of his efforts - particularly in their annual reports to the Society. In 1839, they commented: 'There is much reason to be pleased with the general improvement of the boys both as to general good conduct and attainments in learning during the past year.' In 1841, they praised 'the zeal and ability' with which Lewis carried out the new system, 'the advanced moral tone of the school' and 'the confidant and orderly behaviour of the boys'. Such was their satisfaction with his work that they had by then already recommended the doubling of his salary to 200 guineas. The sweetness of all this acclaim, however, was soon to turn sour.

For all his good qualities, Lewis could be both self-willed and obstinate - and also perhaps, after his initial success, a trifle over-confident. He therefore ran headlong into a Visiting Committee, the members of which were equally stubborn in their determination to uphold the regulations imposed by the founder. The first signs of trouble ahead occurred in August 1842, when the Society expressed its displeasure at the fact that the Master had purchased some books quite contrary to the instructions of the Visiting Committee. This was apparently not the first time that he had shown 'disregard' to its directions. Then, four months later, one of the Nominees (Canon Lord William Somerset) complained that the Master and boys had failed to attend the Cathedral service on 5th November and that the Master did not always accompany the boys to church on Saints' Days. The Society ruled that this behaviour was quite contrary to the express directions of the founder, that Lewis had been 'highly culpable' and would be dismissed if again found guilty of this offence. Almost exactly one year later, the Visiting Committee received complaints that Lewis was 'in the habit of attending places of worship other than the established church', which was totally contrary to the spirit of Colston's stipulation 'that anything approaching dissent' was to have have no place in his Hospital. After his admission that the allegation was true, he was firmly warned that, if this practice continued, he would be dismissed.

Foolishly, he continued to brood over the question of church attendance and again raised the matter in a sharply-worded memorandum to the Visiting Committee in 1846. In particular, he disputed the need to take boys to church twice on Saints' Days and Holy Days (as specified in Colston's instructions). The practice of attending only once was 'of long continuance', he argued, and even the boys at the Cathedral Middle School never attended in the afternoons, which were vital for recreation. After all, some other sections of Mr Colston's rules had been modified 'to meet the altered requirements of the age'. He particularly pleaded with the committee not to enforce the 'twice-a-day' rule at Christmas, Easter and Whitsuntide and on Saturday afternoons 'as being universally devoted to the purposes of relaxation in all schools'. Otherwise, he would be forced to request the employment of a 'charwoman' to free the boys from washing and scrubbing the dormitories - thus releasing time for their recreation to compensate for that lost by going to church. He then added a most impertinent final remark (for he was clearly seething with anger as he drew to the end of his memo). He suggested that a further saving of time might be effected if the committee 'were pleased to meet fortnightly or perhaps monthly, as prescribed by Mr Colston in

Rule 18' (implying, of course, that their normal weekly meetings were a waste of his time).

Although the members of the Visiting Committee chose to ignore these comments, they were merely biding their time for the final confrontation. Matters came to a head in January 1848, when the committee reported its discovery that, fifteen months earlier, Lewis had 'surreptitiously changed the relative positions' and responsibilities of the Senior and Junior Ushers, without informing the Society. After a brief investigation, Lewis admitted the charge, but said that he had made the switch for 'the benefit of the Hospital' and had not informed the committee through a desire 'to spare the feelings' of the man demoted. The Society rejected his arguments and stated that the offence was of the gravest nature, especially in one 'entrusted with the education of youth'. Bearing in mind that it had twice before given him a most severe warning, it now concluded that he was 'not a fit and proper person to be continued in the management of the Hospital'. He was therefore dismissed with effect from 1st August 1848. The Society stuck firmly to its decision, refusing his plea in May to be reinstated or at least granted a 'retiring pension'; and refusing a request in September for extracts from the annual reports praising his work and for an extension of his salary to the end of September. It is, however, interesting to note that in 1937 the Society did give a pension to a Miss L. C. Lewis, an aged lady, who was described as being the daughter of a former Headmaster of Colston's Hospital. She was granted a sum of between £1 and £1 10s a week at the discretion of the Master of the Society.

The Society, with its new and ambitious policy for the development of the school, was determined to cast its net over a wide area in a search for a first-rate replacement and to include the university cities of Oxford and Cambridge. The Visiting Committee was therefore given the task of advertising for a 'Head Master' in *The Times*, *The Chronicle*, *The Herald* and *John Bull* in London; *The Oxford Journal*, *The Cambridge Chronicle*, *The Midland Counties' Herald*, *The Edinburgh Evening Post* and *The Dublin Evening Mail*. Candidates were sent details of the salary (£200), the boys' diet, the Master's House and Colston's Rules. Eventually six candidates, who were selected for the short list out of 34 applicants, attended interviews before a full meeting of the Society. Mr Richard Rowlatt (August 1848 - December 1870), who worked at a school at Bloomsbury in London, was finally offered the post on 23rd June.

The Ushers

From the foundation of the Hospital in 1710, two Ushers or assistants were always appointed to help the Master with both teaching and controlling the boys. In 1717, the Society ruled that they should be paid £50 (to be divided between them) and be provided with board and lodging in the school. Their duties, in return, included the supervision of the dining room 'at eating times to see that each boy has his due proportion of meat and drink'. There is no doubt that they were very much on the front line, in daily contact with the boys, as they supervised their out-of-school activities from dawn to dusk. They often needed to be tough disciplinarians, for many of the pupils were drawn from rough backgrounds where polite behaviour and honesty were not the norm. From time to time, ugly confrontations erupted, which normally resulted in expulsions or brutal floggings - or both (see Chapter 4).

Little detail emerges about the life and work of the Ushers until the early nineteenth century, after the appointment of the Visiting Committee to overhaul the workings of the school (see Chapter 2). Although the Society had strangely ruled on the retirement of Mr Haynes in 1836, 'that it would not appoint an Under Master', it quickly relented after the arrival of the new Master, Mr John Lewis, in 1836 and appointed Mr William Stephens at an annual salary of £50. Even so, it deliberately stopped short of appointing a second Usher, which had been the normal convention. Mr Stephens, aged 32 years, had successfully superintended Kingswood Hill School in Bristol as an assistant. Within a year, however, he had been reprimanded for using 'too much authority' and had resigned in January 1838 after a period of illness. He was replaced by Mr Henry Long, who had taught very successfully at the Diocesan School for many years. He was allocated a sitting room and a bedroom. The latter had been specially created for him and was strategically placed between the two boys' dormitories. Thus, by means of two partially glazed doors in this cleverly-arranged observation post, he was able to keep an eye on the behaviour of the boys in both dormitories at the same time.

Sadly, things did not work out well for Mr Long. In October 1841, Mr Lewis was forced to complain to the Visiting Committee about the conduct of his Usher. Long was duly interviewed and told of 'a serious charge against him for frequently remaining out at night after 10 o'clock, contrary to the rules of the Hospital'. When reminded of the impropriety of such conduct, Long did not deny it, but stated the he did not intend to change his ways. In view of his attitude, the committee gravely warned him that dismissal by the Society was highly likely but, as this would 'materially injure his future prospects in life', recommended that he should offer his resignation at the next meeting - which he did. It has to be stated, however, that Long had been suffering from poor health during the previous year and had been given a week's leave of absence on one occasion to assist his recovery. The case highlights most clearly the lack of time available to an Usher for his own social activities - a point emphasised in the rules drawn up for his successor (see below).

Mr Lewis was now determined to gain more assistance for the arduous task of running the school. He therefore wrote to the committee recommending the appointment of two Ushers 'in accordance with Mr Colston's settlement, page 44'. [As we have already seen, Mr Lewis was very keen on quoting chapter and verse for his evidence!] It would, he argued, be especially valuable for the 'moral good', which would 'be greatly promoted among the boys by a general system of supervision during the hours of recreation'. This was particularly so when the boys were 'walking out of doors', washing themselves or undertaking domestic chores - and during 'the first hour at night in the dormitories', when the boys were settling down.

Furthermore, the additional Usher would greatly relieve the growing pressure on Lewis himself, who was 'overburdened' by mounting administration - including 'keeping of the account books, writing out the various orders for provisions and clothing, superintending the wear and tear of shoes, examining boys clothes and presses [i.e. the shelved cupboards used for clothes and books], filling up petitions for the school and almshouses, correspondence on school matters, interviews with boys' friends, preparing lists of candidates for Merchants' Hall and papers for Nominees' meetings, copying reports and letters into committee minute books and indexing the same' - all of which 'interfere much with the school arrangements and leave me little time for relaxation'. Furthermore, in order to relieve the pressure on his one Usher, Lewis had 'taken charge of the boys, after school hours, for four evenings every week'. Lewis was, in effect, not only Head Master of the school (with a full complement of teaching duties), but also its Bursar, Secretary and Clerk to the Governors.

This invaluable insight into the work of an early nineteenth-century Headmaster undoubtedly impressed the committee at the time. Having recommended the appointment of two new Ushers, it then proceeded to advertise the posts in the local press and draw up job specifications. The Ushers were to have the same food as the boys, except for those occasions on which the boys were given 'pudding and broth', when a dinner would be provided for them by Mrs Lewis. The latter would also supply them with groceries and butter for their breakfast and tea, sending accounts quarterly to the committee for the money spent. They would be given a guinea a quarter in cash for the purchase of their beer - and Mr Lewis would be permitted to employ an extra servant to cover the additional work involved (with £6 a year set aside for wages).

The Ushers' duties were now clearly defined. They were to provide 'a constant supervision of the boys at rising in the morning, prayers, meal times, washing, church, bed-time and recreation, dividing their duties between them to ensure that one Usher was always on duty. In addition, they were to supervise classes, as directed, and to organise the domestic duties of the boys (including making beds; cleaning shoes, washing hands, face and feet; combing hair; scrubbing the dormitories and sweeping the yards). Absences outside the school would only be sanctioned with the Master's permission and they were not to take on other engagements, but exclusively 'to seek the improvement and comfort of the children' under their charge. They would be appointed initially on three months' probation at salaries of £50 for the Senior Usher and £40 for the Junior Usher. These positions respectively were accepted in December 1841 by Mr William Cox and Mr Richard Harding, who had been selected out of only four candidates to apply.

Within a few years, however, Mr Lewis was having serious doubts about the competency of his Senior Usher. Without informing the committee, he proceeded to switch the roles and responsibilities of Mr Cox and Mr Harding - a move which was eventually to bring about his dismissal (see above). Although Mr Richard Rowlatt, who succeeded Lewis as Master in August 1848, inherited both Cox and Harding, he quickly made it clear to the committee that it was impossible for him to carry out his own methods of education or conduct the business of the school 'with the present Ushers'. Under subsequent pressure from the committee, Mr Cox quickly sent in his letter of resignation, whereas Mr Harding refused to co-operate and was therefore dismissed with three months' notice. The Society eventually appointed Mr William Friel as 'Second Master' (the first time that this expression had been used) on 9th March 1849, at an increased salary of £80 per annum, and Mr Alexander Griffin as 'Third Master' at £50 per annum.

To complete the hierarchy, the Society had also agreed in 1849 to the appointment of a 'Porter' to supervise the playground (thus relieving the Ushers of this extra burden) and the gate (which had previously been watched over by boys on a weekly rota system). A section of the old cellars was duly converted into a Porter's lodge. The Visiting Committee expressed satisfaction in its 1850 report, that the Porter had 'a good control over the boys in play hours' and had 'put an effectual stop to idling at the door'. By the middle of the century, therefore, Headmasters at Colston's increasingly favoured the idea of running the school with the help of their own hand-picked team, especially in view of the high expectations placed on them by the Society in general and the Visiting Committee in particular.

Sources used in Chapter 3

D.J. Eames, *The Contribution made by the Society of Merchant Venturers to the Development of Education in Bristol* (unpublished MA thesis for the University of Bristol, 1966), pp 31-4, 42-4, 57-65

Patrick McGrath, *The Merchant Venturers of Bristol* (Bristol, 1975), p 360

Society of Merchant Venturers Archive:

Copies of Mr Colston's Settlements (printed copy)

Box of Appendices: Bundle 3 - Mr Haynes's petition, 1788
                         Bundle 11 - papers of Mr Haynes, 1786
                         Bundle 13 - letter from Mr Lewell, 1836
                                     - memo from Mr Lewis, 1846
                         (Unnumbered) - payment Mr Gardner
                                     - agreement with Mr Gardner

Hall Book of Proceedings: vol. 4 (1708-23);   vols. 10-21 (1772-1855)

Minutes of the Meetings of Mr Colston's Nominees, 3 vols., (1748-70; 1780-1822; 1823-53)

Proceedings of the Colston's Hospital Visiting Committee, vol. 1, 1836-41

Annual Reports of the Colston's Hospital Visiting Committee, 1842-58

Book of Charity Proceedings, vol. 1, 1852-67

MEALTIMES IN THE 1820s

John Melhuish *(Old Colstonian)*

In the early part of the year 1824, I was admitted into Colston's School and remained there for nearly five years. I was left one evening at the School in charge of the usher and was introduced by him to the school room. I was rather astonished when I entered the room as I had never been in so large a place before.

Bedtime arrived soon after my advent, and I was placed in a sleeping berth in the front dormitory with two other youngsters for my bedfellows, from whom I learnt a good deal about the routine of the school. There were two dormitories, I should mention, the beds in the first being occupied by three of the smaller boys, while two only of the elder boys slept together in the back room.

At about half-past six o'clock the next morning, at the call of 'rise' by the Usher, all jumped out of bed and, after dressing ourselves, bedmaking was proceeded with, which completed, all marched down to the school room and, prayers having been read by one of the senior boys, breakfast was served.

This consisted of a quarter of a cake of brown bread with a small quantity of butter served out to each boy. No plates nor knives nor table cloths, and those who did not possess such a thing as a pocket knife tore the cake open and spread the butter with the thumb. The portions were served out from a large basket, which was carried around by two of the elder boys, while another followed with the butter on a large trencher. Then came two large copper cans of milk and water, cold in the summer, considerably warmed in the winter, but minus sugar or other sweetening. This was served out, a hornful to each, passing from the first to the last.

The bread supplied to the school was in cakes of two weights - one pound cakes and twelve ounce cakes (brown). The pound cakes made a breakfast for four scholars, while those of less weight sufficed for the supper of two; and the boy of seven, who came into the house only last night, fared the same as the growing lad of fourteen, who would leave on the morrow. The supper allowance had the addition of a small piece of cheese - such a piece as would, at the present day, pass through the post for a penny; and we could have a 'horn of beer' only, or as much water as we liked. All liquids were served in horns, no glass or china was seen in the school.

Dinner was served at twelve o'clock and consisted, on Sunday, of boiled mutton and potatoes (neither warm nor cold); on Monday and Saturday, of what was called milk broth - this was milk with rice boiled in it, but without any sweetening, and was rather insipid; on Tuesday and Thursday, boiled beef and potatoes; and on Wednesday and Friday, pea soup with neck of beef in it. The latter was the fare most generally liked, being most filling each boy had the allowance of a quarter of a pound of bread cake; but at times the peas or the rice did not boil well and proved too hard to be pleasant.

The potatoes, after being well washed, were boiled in their skins in large coarse bags and, when drawn from the boiler by pulleys, were beaten in the bags into a pulp and served out skin and all. The meat and potatoes were served upon wooden trenchers and the soup in large wooden bowl - and four boys ate from a bowl. All entered the dining hall two-and-two, according to their size, and took their places on each side of the long tables. The quantity of meat allowed to each boy was supposed to be half a pound, inclusive of bone, but the bones must have been large or the meat must have lost in the cooking, for the residue was really quite small.

(From The Colstonian, *April 1895)*

CHAPTER 4

Life and Work in the Hospital, 1710-1861

'The desks in the school room were very improper, especially for the eldest boys, who were obliged to write in a crooked, standing position; they were inconveniently small and in a very ruinous state'. (Visiting Committee Report, 1837)

It appeareth to the committee that the crime of running away is becoming very prevalent'. (Standing Committee Minutes, 1783)

The Daily Routine

Life was undoubtedly spartan for the boys in Colston's Hospital throughout the eighteenth century and routine seldom varied. Even after the introduction of the major reforms in 1837, the actual pattern of each day remained much the same as it had been when first established by the founder in 1710. The boys rose just before six in the morning, when they were expected to wash, comb their hair, brush their shoes and make their beds. They then went into the school room for prayers, the reading of scripture and the singing of psalms. This was followed by work on their spelling, before breakfast was taken in the dining room. Between eight and nine o 'clock, they went for exercise out in the courtyard (which had been paved for this purpose in 1715). Traditionally, this meant 'stamping in pairs around the court', although the introduction of a more understanding approach saw the erection of a seat in 1837 and a covered shed in 1841 to provide shade from the sun.

Morning lessons took place between nine and twelve, after which they reported for dinner and then enjoyed more free time in the yard until two o'clock. Afternoon lessons continued until five, when a further hour was spent in the yard (always, of course, under the tight supervision of the Ushers). At six o'clock, supper was served, followed by a final half-hour in the yard and a period for washing. Half an hour was devoted at seven to 'preparing lessons', before the boys took part in evening prayers, scripture reading and psalms. They were all in bed, whatever their age, by eight o'clock.

In between all these fixed activities, the boys were also required to

The Great House, which became the home of Colston's School between 1710 and 1861. A drawing by S.H. Grimm in 1789 showing a boy in traditional dress in the street. (By permission of the British Library - reference Add.Ms. 15,540)

undertake various chores on a rota basis under the control of the Ushers. These included scrubbing the floors of the dormitories and sweeping the yard outside. There were, of course, modifications to the programme at weekends. On Saturdays, lessons only continued until eleven o'clock in the morning, when the boys were given time to mend their stockings and repair their uniforms. But whereas Colston had decreed that Saturday afternoon was to be devoted to learning the church catechism, from 1837 the boys were given a half-day holiday for visiting their own homes. On Sundays, instead of ordinary lessons, they spent the morning 'reading church lessons' before going to church; and the afternoon in religious instruction and further church attendance. From 1837, it became no longer obligatory to spend recreation time out in the yard. The purchase of 'Sunday' books in that year (all of a religious nature) and the establishment of a school library in 1839 (see below) meant that boys were now able to put their leisure to more constructive use. The Visiting Committee was quick to applaud 'the increasing disposition of the boys during their leisure hours to read instructive books' for pleasure.

The Boys' Clothing and Uniform

In 1710, Edward Colston himself presented the Hospital with its initial set of clothing for the first 100 boys enrolled, insisting that it should be worn every day. It consisted of one suit of clothes (a long dark blue tunic and breeches), blue cap, shirt, shoes, scarlet stockings, bands, buckles and girdle for each boy, together with a spoon and a trencher. The Society matched this gift by providing each boy with a spare set for special occasions. By 1761, each boy was in possession of three complete sets of clothes - the best being worn on Sundays, the next best on school holidays and the worst inside school.

The two best sets also carried a badge bearing Colston's own crest, which featured a dolphin. This had apparently been chosen by him (and used on his coat of arms) after one of his ships, returning from the West Indies with a valuable cargo, had been seriously holed. The water was already rising rapidly, when, by chance, a dolphin accidentally became stuck in the damaged hull, thus stemming the flow and saving both crew and cargo. The badges, initially made in silver, were replaced in 1776 by Mr John Purrier (a former pupil) 'out of most grateful remembrance for the place where he was brought up'. Twenty-four years later, another former pupil (Mr Collier of London) presented the Society with 100 brass badges and a die for casting them - a gift that was replenished again by Mr Purrier in 1828. It is probable that these brass badges were not worn by the boys on their best clothes, because a new set was cast from Mr Purrier's die in 1843 specifically for their 'everyday clothes', whereas at the celebrations for the Queen's coronation in 1838, the boys wore their silver badges.

The dolphin badge worn by boys on their uniform. (Author's collection)

From the outset, Colston had made it clear that, if a boy had been expelled for bad behaviour, then the Society was to take back the clothes that had been issued and recycle them with the pupil admitted as a replacement. This rule was also extended in 1838 to any boy who had been suddenly taken away by his parents without prior sanction from the Society. On the other hand, the Merchants could be equally sympathetic to a genuinely poor boy who left school at the end of his statutory seven years, but whose parents were so destitute that they were unable to provide any clothes at all. In 1838, the Society authorised the Master to spend up to £2 on such cases. Andrew Fisher was therefore presented with a jacket, trousers, waistcoat, shoes, cap, stockings, shirt and handkerchief, causing a minor flood of similar applications in consequence!

In 1837, the Visiting Committee was alarmed to discover that previous Masters had requested parents to supply their boys on admission with various items of linen and other articles of clothing, often costing these impoverished people up to fifty shillings in total. This practice, which was clearly contrary to the spirit of Colston's settlement, was quickly halted, as was the more recent habit with some parents of providing their boys with winter waistcoats. The committee firmly ruled that no article of clothing whatsoever was to be furnished by relatives or friends 'to the inmates of the Hospital' - although waistcoats were provided by the Society to all boys soon afterwards (in 1848) on medical advice. In addition, with a growing emphasis on health and hygiene (see below), the committee agreed to the Master's request in 1837 that boys should be issued with two shirts a week for everyday wear instead of just one, which became far too dirty 'by being worn day and night for a whole week'. Pyjamas were not yet part of the allocation!

The basic 'Hospital' uniform of long tunic and breeches continued to be worn throughout much of the nineteenth century, although it was called into question in December 1856 when the Attorney-General suggested that the school might consider 'abolishing the present dress of the boys' as part of an entirely new scheme of management. The Nominees, however, stoutly defended the existing uniform by stating that 'such a dress has been found to prevent an abuse of the charity'. They argued that wealthy parents (i.e. those 'of a class not contemplated by the Founder'), who could well afford to pay for their sons' education, had been discouraged from applying to Colston's by the prospect of seeing their children in 'the dress of a charity school'.

The Daily Menu

In February 1718, the Society approved a weekly menu for the boys, which continued largely unaltered until 1837. To enable the system to work as intended, the boys were divided into 'messes' or groups of eight, which were then be issued with a bulk allocation of the food listed on the menu, together with a gallon of beer for each meal. [The beer was a weak, 'small beer', which was brewed on the premises]. A half-pint 'horn cup' was provided for each mess and was passed round the table for the consumption of the beer. Although each boy had been issued on entry with his own knife and 'trencher' (or wooden plate), the lack of forks and spoons ensured that fingers were largely used for the consumption of food. Mealtimes were therefore noisy, quarrelsome and ungracious occasions with Ushers much in attendance 'to prevent', in Colston's own words, 'disorder'. The Nominees and Visiting Committees also made it part of their regular duty to 'watch' the boys having dinner - and to comment accordingly.

The fixed allocation for each mess was as follows:

Sunday: Breakfast — Two 12 oz. loaves

Dinner — Four 12 oz. loaves and a piece of beef weighing 4 lbs before being boiled

Supper — Four 12 oz loaves and 40 lbs of mutton, roasted for the 100 boys and divided between the messes

Monday: Breakfast — Two 12 oz loaves and either broth or water gruel

Dinner — Four hot 12 oz loaves and 12 oz butter

Supper — Four 12 oz loaves and 1 lb cheese

Tuesday: Breakfast — Two 12 oz loaves and 8 oz butter

Dinner — Four 12 oz loaves and 12 lb beef (before being boiled)

Supper — As Monday

Wednesday: Breakfast — Two 12 oz loaves and 8 oz butter

Dinner — Four 12 oz loaves, 8 oz butter and a quart of raw pease boiled [mashed to form pease pudding]

Supper — As Monday

Thursday: Breakfast — Two 12 oz loaves and 8 oz butter

Dinner — 45 lbs mutton boiled and divided equally between the 100 boys

Supper — As Monday

Friday: Breakfast — Two 12 oz loaves and mutton broth

Dinner — Four 12 oz loaves, 8 oz butter and a quart of raw pease boiled

Supper — As Monday

Saturday: Breakfast   Two 12 oz loaves and 8 oz butter
                   Dinner   Four 12 oz loaves and milk pottage [a
                                          soup or stew]
                   Supper   As Monday

Although it was a monotonous and meagre diet, which was doubtless deficient in both protein and vegetables, it probably represented a far better deal than most of the boys would have had at home. This did not, however, prevent a group of 'women, mothers and grandmothers' of several boys in the school complaining in 1736 at the lack of food provided - a complaint rejected by the Society as being 'frivolous and trifling and without foundation'.

Complaints clearly continued into the first quarter of the nineteenth century, judging by a letter published in the *Bristol Times and Farley's Bristol Journal* in November 1856. A former Colston boy, who was at school between 1812 and 1819, stated that in his day the boys were 'half-starved', being 'fed on less than a penny cake a day'. Nevertheless, he said, in spite of many hardships, the experience proved invaluable for later life. 'Compelled as we were to do all sorts of drudgery in all weather, against which it was utterly useless to complain...with a prison crop and worse than prison fare; going without stockings or shoes when scrubbing the courts, schoolrooms and dormitories; fed twice a week on just water and gruel and at other times with scarce enough to sustain nature - yet we furnished the West Indies with a constant supply of hearty and healthy lads, and were much more hardy and fit for the Crimea than those at the school today. And this, too, at a time when our tidal river was almost at a standstill, and dead dogs, cats and pigs covered its surface as often as did ships'. His conclusion was that the school 'was the means of giving him 'a hardiness and strength of constitution', which enabled him 'to endure anything'.

It was not until 1837 that the Visiting Committee took major steps to improve both the diet and the arrangements for eating. Its members made a particular point, in their report on the new system, in stressing that 'each boy is now allowed a knife, fork, spoon, earthenware cup and basin - the former system of serving the meals being considered highly objectionable.' The 'mess' system was therefore abandoned and each boy was issued with his own ration of food.

Under the new system, breakfast each day consisted of 6 oz of bread and 0.5 oz of butter for each boy, together with half a pint of milk and water mixed together - although, as a treat on Sundays, the drink consisted of half a pint of tea. Supper was always the same - 6 oz of bread and 1.5 oz of cheese with water (although toast was substituted for the plain bread in winter). The real difference came with dinner, the main meal of the day, which was served at 12.30 pm. The weekly menu for this was as follows:

Sunday: 8 oz of cold roasted beef and 6 oz of bread

Monday: 8 oz of boiled mutton with an unrestricted amount of potatoes (about 1 lb to each boy)

Tuesday: Broth from mutton liquor with oatmeal, herbs and vegetables (unrestricted in quantity)

Wednesday: 1 lb plum pudding, made with flour bread, suet, allspice and raisins

Thursday: 8 oz of mutton with unrestricted potatoes

Friday: 8 oz of boiled beef with unrestricted potatoes

Saturday: Broth from the boiled beef with oatmeal, herbs and vegetables (unrestricted)

This was a much more substantial diet (particularly appreciated, no doubt, by the older boys) and far better balanced with the introduction of vegetables and a greater range of meats. A slight modification was made to this menu in 1840, when bread and cheese were substituted for broth at dinner on Saturdays; and, a few years later, when it was agreed to provided salt fish for dinner on Ash Wednesdays and Good Fridays. The Visiting Committee also stipulated in 1837 that water jugs were to be placed on the tables for each meal and replenished as often as required. This highlighted the fact that beer had now been taken off the menu as a result of the increasing availability of clean fresh water.

Although the boys' feelings on this are not recorded, it is interesting to note that the Master was reprimanded in 1843 for allowing the boys to go to a public house to fetch beer. The committee rejected Mr Lewis's justification for this, adding that its opinion of the Master 'tended to weaken' as a result of this lapse. Meanwhile it did its level best, through its newly-established system of contracting for supplies, to ensure the quality of food provided. Although it bartered furiously with the suppliers on prices and discounts, the tenders it issued called for guarantees of the highest standards. This meant that committee members, sitting earnestly in their committee room in the Hospital, were frequently spotted examining individual cakes, loaves or potatoes to test their worth.

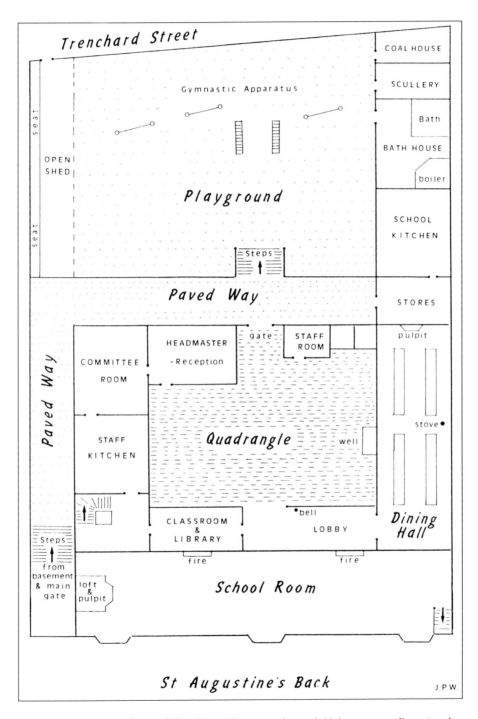

Plan of the ground floor of The Great House in the mid-19th century. (Drawing by John Wroughton)

Recreation and Holidays

Quite apart from a much more varied diet, life became far better for the boys of the school with the introduction, from 1837 onwards, of much more varied activities. Particularly enjoyable were the excursions which the Master arranged to coincide with special events - a microscope exhibition in 1840, an art exhibition 'at the top of Park Street' in 1842, a day trip to Tintern Abbey in 1849 (as a reward for good behaviour during a cholera epidemic in the city) and an 'excursions treat' to Dawlish in 1857 'through the liberality of the directors of the Bristol and Exeter Railway'. The excursions were regarded as privileges which could be lost for misconduct. When, for instance, the Master reported to the Visiting Committee that the boys had not conducted themselves properly on one occasion, Mr Claxton (the Society's Treasurer) withdrew his intention of asking for a holiday to enable the boys to see the *Great Western* steamship, which had just been launched. Nevertheless, the highlight of the year from 1855 was undoubtedly the annual excursion to Badminton (owned by the Duke of Beaufort, a member of the Nominees), which gave the boys a wonderful opportunity to play games in the park and to enjoy the Duke's generous hospitality.

In addition to a growing number of such outings, the boys were normally invited to play a prominent part in any major events within the city. Probably the most exciting occasion during this period was the Coronation of Queen Victoria on 28th June 1838. The Master outlined to the committee his plans for the Bristol celebrations. The boys would walk in the special procession through the streets of the city in their best clothes with the silver badges and would wear white satin rosettes. Two specially-made banners would be carried by their contingent, one bearing the initials 'VR' and the other showing 'Colston's Hospital' in gold letters. The Master requested that each boy should also carry a bunch of flowers and be awarded a small medal as a memento. On their return to the school, the celebrations would continue with a plum cake and a glass of wine for each boy, together with a gift of a shilling. Afterwards permission was granted for the boys 'to view the illuminations' under the direction of the Master. When, in February 1840, the Queen's wedding took place, the boys were granted a holiday and again enjoyed the cake, the wine and a shilling as a further treat. They were also involved in another great procession with the Mayor and Corporation in October 1856 to celebrate the proclamation of the peace with Russia - just as each year they processed to St Stephen's Church for the Society's Charter Day on 10th November.

As part of the general review of school life, in 1837 the Visiting

Committee fixed the annual allocation of holidays. There would in future be three whole-day holidays to mark special events - the Monarch's Birthday, the Charter Day of the Society of Merchant Venturers (10th November) and Colston's Day (13th November); and holidays to commemorate the three great Christian festivals - three weekdays after Christmas Day; Easter Monday and Tuesday; and the Monday and Tuesday after Whitsuntide. There was no thought of an annual summer holiday until the first one was granted in 1865. However, in addition to the fixed holidays as described, the Nominees could call for four extra individual days throughout the year - and the Society for one extra day - to reward good conduct or to celebrate special events.

For instance, Mr Maze (the newly-elected Master of the Society) requested a day's holiday in November 1837 on the day of his accession to office. In 1840, the Visiting Committee recommended that the boys should be granted a whole week's holiday at Christmas, instead of the normal three days. This, however, was not to be regarded as a precedent, as it was only awarded on the basis of good behaviour. The allocation of the actual days at Christmas was always dependent on the positioning of the Holy Days. For instance, in 1842, it just happened that Monday 26th, Tuesday 27th and Wednesday 28th were all Holy Days. As the boys, in accordance with Colston's rules, were compelled to attend morning service in the Cathedral on each Holy Day (even though by then the afternoons were granted as free half days), their Christmas holidays could not be taken until the Thursday, Friday and Saturday of that week.

Half-day holidays on Saturday afternoons also commenced in 1837, although the newly-favoured doctrine of 'rewards and punishments' meant that these could always be cancelled if necessary. In the September of that year, for instance, the Master reported that a number of the boys had used the previous Saturday afternoon to visit the fair, knowing full well that it was contrary to his wishes. The Visiting Committee ordered that, as punishment, the boys would not be allowed to leave school on the next Saturday until 4.00 pm. This 'detention' would therefore prevent them from attending Ryan's Circus, to which all the charity children had been granted free admission. Boys were required to return to school by seven o'clock from all holidays (including half days). The one exception to all these arrangements was that boys living in the country were granted a fortnight's holiday at Whitsuntide.

Sickness and Health

Colston's rules, issued in 1708, made it abundantly clear from the outset that any boys with any kind of permanent physical or mental sickness would not be admitted into the hospital. Over the following years, the Society dutifully adhered to that stipulation, even to the point of harshness. In 1732, for instance, it 'turned out' a boy, who had already been in school for three years, 'for being blind'; in 1736, it removed Richard Cox, who had remarkably been on the roll for nine years, but who was now 'deprived of his senses and lunatic' (although, to be fair, it provided him with clothes and sent him into the parish's care); in 1757, it sent away Thomas Harding who for some time had had 'a leprosy on him, for which he can find no relief'; in 1786, it removed Samuel Viney, who was so 'defective in body and mind as to be incompetent'; in 1788, it expelled Joseph Parker, 'who squinted very much'; and in 1782, it discharged 'with all convenient speed' a boy named William Reece, who had been found by the surgeon to have 'the Evil' (a disease which caused painful swelling of the joints). The surgeon reported that he had discovered the bones of his right hand and wrist were 'foul from the Evil, attended with spreading ulcers'. In spite of treatment and seven weeks in hospital, 'the disease had ruined the joint', which called for amputation of the right hand to prevent any further spread. The Society quickly resolved that the boy's presence in the Hospital was 'contrary to Mr Colston's regulations'.

Even in the more tolerant and enlightened times of 1838, the Visiting Committee reacted to a report by the school surgeons (Messrs Maurice & James) that a boy named Merrick was afflicted with scrofula (which was very similar in symptoms to 'the Evil') and a serious infection of the bowels, by removing him with a considerable sense of urgency. During the eighteenth century, medical help had been called in as and when required. Under the old capitation system (see Chapter 3), the Master was expected to pay for all medical expenses, although the Society occasionally came to his rescue during an epidemic. In 1766, for example, the Master paid £28 7s 0d on medicine and the fees of a surgeon and nurse, during 'the violent fever that lately raged in the Hospital, in which 45 boys were afflicted and two died'. Similarly, in 1779, the Master's bill for medical attendance and medicine during outbreaks of smallpox and fever over the previous seventeen years (together with the cost of funerals) was calculated at £124 8s 8d. On both these occasions, the Society agreed to foot the bill.

There was always the constant fear that an epidemic would spread through the school like wildfire, bearing in mind the cramped conditions in which the boys lived in their dormitories. In 1825, the Master reported that several boys had become ill with typhus and that some of these had been removed to their parents at home. Sadly one boy died, although the Master assured the committee that every precaution was being taken to stop the spread of the disease. In 1853, the Nominees

Gentlemen;

I have drest for some time past Wm Reece a Boy belonging to Mr. Colston's Hospital, & find the Bones of his right Hand & armwrist are foul from the Evil, attended with spreading Ulcers, & that notwithstanding all means that have been us'd by his friends at home & at the Infirmary, where he was 7 weeks an In-patient, & was discharg'd. The disease has now ruin'd the Joynt; & it has been necessary for some time past & more so now, that his right Hand should be amputated to prevent the farther progress of the Disease.

I am, Gentlemen,

Yr most obedt. Servant

Wm Barrett —

Colston's Hospital
6 May 1782 —

Report in 1782 from the school's surgeon, William Barrett, concerning the need to amputate William Reece's hand. (SMV Archive) were informed that one of the boys had fallen sick of 'brain fever'. The medical officer feared in fact that scarlet fever had been introduced into the school 'through the imprudence of the parents of one of the boys' and that it might spread. Although this proved to be a false alarm, the Society had already considered the desirability of closing the school 'for a few weeks'. Deaths of Colston's boys were, however, by no means infrequent in the eighteenth century. Between 1721 and 1755, for example, twenty boys died (including five who were at home at the time). Nevertheless, by 1843, the Society was able to report that, although one boy had died 'through a presence on the brain', that death was the first in seven years within the school - a tribute in part to the provision of both better medical care and a healthier diet.

By the early nineteenth century, the Society's minutes increasingly referred to 'the school surgeon', a local doctor who was called in for emergencies. In 1838, it decided to offer a contract to the school surgeons, Messrs Maurice & James, in line with the contracts now offered to suppliers of food and clothing. The surgeons readily agreed, offering to treat and provide medicines for the masters, servants and boys for the inclusive charge of £35 per annum. The Visiting Committee, now well practised in the techniques of barter, managed to negotiate a reduction to £25. These school doctors played an increasingly important part in the life of the school and gradually introduced a more tolerant attitude towards sickness. They frequently recommended that a sick boy should 'have a change of air' by going home for a spell. When this happened, the Society usually granted the parents five shillings a week to support the boy while under their care. In 1839, it continued to help William Mead in this way for almost a year, until it was finally decided that he should leave, as there was now 'no hope of recovery'. In 1848, it even paid for the school doctor to attend a boy at his home on account of his mother's 'great poverty'. The boy eventually recovered and returned to school.

As part of the major reforms, which were introduced from 1836, the Society had also appointed a 'medical attendant' to be responsible for all matters of health within the school on a daily basis. From 1843, he was required 'to keep a book in which to register his proceedings' and to report regularly to the Visiting Committee. There was an increasing awareness of the need to prevent sickness by taking sensible precautions. The medical attendant, for instance, drew the Society's attention to the lack of proper ventilation in the boys' dormitories in 1854 and to the need for a proper sick room, where he could isolate boys 'visited with fever, cholera or any other dangerous epidemic'. Although reference had been made in the minutes of 1840 to six boys who had been 'in the sick ward with measles', this presumably had only been a temporary arrangement to deal with a particular crisis. Indeed, six years later, the medical attendant successfully requested the appointment of a 'nurse to superintend the sick rooms' and to ensure that his orders were properly carried out. She was also detailed 'to look after the linen and keep it mended' and later, in 1849, to supervise the twenty youngest boys in a newly-created attic dormitory. In 1847, the medical attendant was provided with his own room for examining patients - a further indication that the system was becoming more professional.

By 1850, the Society had already taken a number of preventative measures, including its insistence that, prior to entry, all boys should be both vaccinated against smallpox (agreed in 1820) and medically examined (ordered in 1838). Its members also realised that additional facilities, too, could improve the health and welfare of the boys - a lamp near the two flights of steps, where a boy had fallen in the dark in 1775 and broken his arm; the introduction of gas heating into the schoolroom in 1837; and the piping of water up to the level of the dormitories in 1848. Water had previously been carried up the stairs in buckets from the yard outside and the slops carried down in similar fashion. The whole question of sanitation was now given much more urgent attention. In 1850, the Visiting Committee strongly recommended the replacement of the existing lavatory, privy and urinals - 'the latter are not only insufficient, but offensive and, in the opinion of the medical officer of the establishment, prejudicial to the health of the school'. Two years later, they condemned 'the inconvenience, inadequacy and unreliability of the system for procuring water from the pump in the yard and advocated instead an agreement with the newly-formed Bristol Water Company to supply piped water. This was quickly undertaken at a cost of £35 for installation and £16 10s 0d a year for supply.

Perhaps the most needed new facility, however, had arrived in 1843 with the installation of 'a plunging bath' (fed by a large reservoir of water), which was large enough to take between twelve and fifteen boys at a time. The boys were thereafter required to take a bath 'every Friday, unless from any illness of the boys it should be considered improper'. The Master was always be the judge of such instances, usually after taking advice from the medical attendant. A suggestion by the Visiting Committee in 1852 that a swimming bath should also be installed was delayed partly on grounds of cost and partly to await a decision on major structural changes to accommodate a possible increase in numbers.

The Society at least saw the 'plunging bath' as a major step towards 'the healthful improvement of the boys' - an attitude which was reiterated in 1846 by the Visiting Committee, when it issued a set of instructions to promote health within the school. Believing that 'cleanliness was of so much importance to health and even in some

measure to the good training of youth', it requested weekly reports of
the times when the bath was used, insisted that every boy in future
should sleep 'in a night shirt provided for him and kept for this purpose
alone' and issued each boy with 'a separate hair brush and comb to be
kept in a bag marked with his number in a place specially arranged to
receive them'. Although the cost of these reforms had been considerable,
the committee had already noticed one major benefit - the recent
outbreak of ring worm, which had affected sixteen boys, had now been
contained and would soon be eradicated.

By 1852, the Visiting Committee was expressing delight that
structural alterations and changes to procedure had all helped to make
the Hospital a most healthy place. Praise was also lavished on 'the
judicious watchfulness and care' of the medical attendant. Underlying it
all, however, was a fundamental change in attitude to the sick, who were
no longer expelled or despatched home at the first opportunity. In 1853,
the parents of James Bridges, who had died from 'water on the brain'
while still resident at school, offered 'their fervent gratitude to Mr and
Mrs Rowlatt for their unbounded attention and kindness to their child
during his painful and protracted illness'.

By far the best example of this new approach came with the case of
Washington Tremblett in May 1857. The boy, who had been out with
friends on Ashley Hill during the afternoon, was later found on Horsfield
Common in a collapsed state 'with a wound in his side, his clothes cut to
pieces, his buckles being cut from his shoes and his stockings and cap
thrown away'. The school's medical attendant (Mr Bartley) was alerted
by the Vicar of Horfield, who was looking after the boy in his house. Mr
Bartley and Mr Rowlatt (the Master) rushed to see Tremblett, who on
examination was found to have a small self-inflicted wound near the
heart, caused by the use of pen-knife. It transpired that he was a
naturally 'sullen' boy when under the 'normal restraint of the school',
who (according to the medical attendant) seemed to be 'the subject of
impulsive acts amounting almost to those of an insane person'. He added
that 'his mother and sister are at present in a lunatic asylum'.

Tremblett stayed with the Vicar of Horfield for the next two days,
but was constantly visited by both Bartley and Rowlatt and was kept
company by a friend from the school. The Visiting Committee went to
enormous lengths to discuss the best possible solution for the boy with
both medical advisers and Mr William Spark, a friend of the family.
Eventually it was agreed that, as the boy's return to school would be
unwise for his own safety, Mr Spark would undertake to look after him.
There had been no thought this time of beating the boy for damaging his
school clothes or running away! Bartley was voted a gratuity of five
guineas for 'his extraordinary civility' and compassion.

Meanwhile, the Society had continued the theme of the improvement of boys' health in 1843 by appointing a 'Drill Sergeant', at one guinea a month, to give the boys regular exercise. Four years later, however, it voiced its disappointment that the drilling did not produce 'such good effects as were anticipated'. Although the experiment was therefore discontinued, the Visiting Committee felt that 'a system of gymnastics' might be more 'productive of health and happiness'. This plan was duly put into operation carried out and, by 1849, had been voted a success - although, seven years later, 'a drilling master' was again appointed to visit the school on a monthly basis.

Comfort and Ambience

Quite apart from the 'plunging bath', the installation of heating into the school room and the provision of a covered area in the playground, the Society spent a large amount of money from 1837 on a major programme of refurbishment and improvement. It has to be said, however, that the fabric of the Hospital had been shamefully neglected during the period 1710 to 1836. In 1767, a committee which inspected the buildings noted that the dormitories had not been painted for nearly forty years and the school room for at least sixteen. The floor of the Ushers' sitting room was in a state of disintegration and the outer gates were totally beyond repair.

The situation, which faced the Visiting Committee on its appointment in 1837, was little better. Its members noted in their first annual report that 'the premises had not been painted for many years past' and that the school room floor was in a terrible condition. There were two basic problems - the floor itself was badly worn as a result of 'the nails in the boys' shoes' and the room was bitterly cold, thanks to the lack of a ceiling in the warehouse below to provide some level of insulation. Undaunted by the size of the task, the committee first conducted a most thorough survey, drawing up a detailed action list to cover every area within the school, and then unleashed a team of masons, carpenters, plumbers, tilers, plasterers, painters, glaziers and smiths on priority tasks.

A major redecoration programme was set in train between 1837 and 1843 to include the dormitories, the school room, the entrance hall and the exterior of the building. It was later agreed that all rooms were to be 'well washed' during the Whitsuntide holidays (supervised, of course, by the Master) in order to maintain their newly-painted appearance. The dormitories were also refurbished with some of the walls 'cased with wood to prevent the great dampness hitherto experienced on the outward walls'. The school room floor was repaired, a washstand built

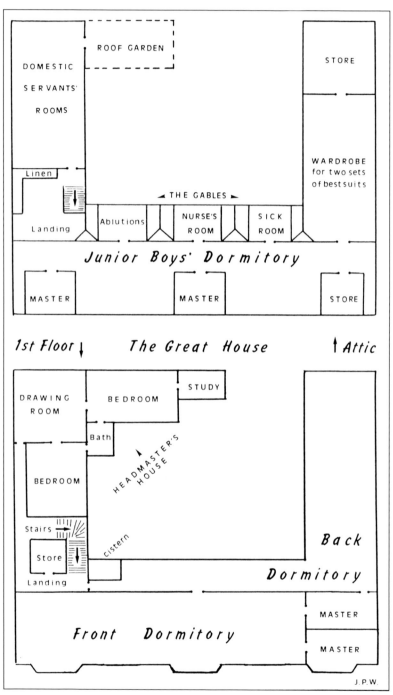

Plan of the first floor of The Great House in the mid-19th century. (Drawing by John Wroughton)

in the dining room 'for the boys to wash their hands' and a new 'roaster' purchased for the kitchen.

The old desks in the school room were replaced with new desks and forms 'applicable to the sizes of the several boys'. The committee noted that the previous the desks had been 'very improper, especially for the eldest boys, who were obliged to write in a crooked, standing position; they were inconveniently small and in a very ruinous state'. Nor was the Master himself forgotten during this large-scale refurbishment of the school, for his house was freshly papered and carpeted. As a result of their programme, the committee reported at the end of their first year that £384 had already been spent on repairs and alterations and £385 on new furniture.

Some of this expenditure had been allocated to a most important area in the life of the boys - namely, their sleeping arrangements. The committee had discovered that there was an acute shortage of beds, which meant that 'in some cases, the boys were sleeping three in a bed'. It had also found that the bedding itself was old and in poor condition. Its immediate task, therefore, was to buy more beds and then to squeeze them into the two dormitories as best they could. Fourteen iron bedsteads with new bedding were quickly purchased in 1837 to provide single beds for the older boys. Then, after a prolonged debate in 1837 over the various options open to them, the Society purchased thirty more bedsteads with bedding for the front dormitory, selecting beds that were two feet and six inches wide. By placing the beds just twelve inches apart and adapting the room so that extra beds could be fitted in under the windows, the committee achieved its objectives. These cramped conditions were greatly eased in 1849 when a new dormitory was created in the attic for twenty of the youngest boys. The rear dormitory was fitted out in the following year. By 1843, the committee was also able to claim, in its annual report, that it had managed to achieve not only better bedding, but clean linen and sheeting as a result of improved laundry facilities.

Crime and Punishment

It has already been seen that life in Colston's Hospital during the eighteenth century was most uninviting. The boys were cooped up like prisoners in a confined space with just an exercise yard for leisure and a church parade on Sunday for variety. They were forced to endure a meagre diet, a cold school room, a damp dormitory, unsympathetic teachers and a brutally harsh regime. It is therefore not surprising that some of the boys were truculent and others openly rebellious.

Colston had briefly outlined in the rules he had issued in 1708 the system of discipline which was to operate within his Hospital. The Master would be responsible for reporting to the Society's Standing Committee any serious examples of bad behaviour. The Society then had the power either to expel any boy, if he 'remained incorrigible' after warnings had been issued or if the crimes were 'heinous and often repeated'; or to order his flogging, which was inflicted by the Master in the presence of the committee. There were two weaknesses to the system - the Master had little independent authority over serious cases and he was often forced to delay punishment until the next meeting of the committee (perhaps months ahead). On the other hand, both he and the Ushers had the power or flog boys for lesser offences without reference to the committee - and they often did!

At first few details of punishments were recorded in the minute books. In 1737, however, the mother of John Gingell demonstrated her disgust with the school by publicly cutting off 'the badge from the said boy's coat in the cathedral' and then keeping him away for three months. The boy was duly expelled. Attacks like this on school uniform became a regular feature of defiance towards the school. Clothing, after all, (unlike Ushers) presented a much easier target for a release of anger or hatred. After this isolated example, there was a spate of eleven expulsions during the last seven years of the Mastership of Mr Gardner, senior (which ended in 1740). But worse was to follow.

The Hospital went through a most turbulent period between 1775 and 1796, when first Mr Haynes, senior, and then his son were at the helm. The frustration of some boys erupted into spasmodic violence, vandalism and gross insubordination. Other boys simply seized the first opportunity to escape from the horrors of daily life by running away. James Collier, who had been guilty of several thefts, did so in 1775 and was flogged for his pains. John Thomas and John Strange ran away in 1779, because 'they were cruelly used by the Usher'. They, too, were flogged in the presence of the Standing Committee.

In 1778, four other boys (Birch, Luckett, Anderson and Jones) did what many other boys attempted to when making their escape - namely, to cut up their uniform to look more like an ordinary jacket and trousers, hoping thereby to become less conspicuous as they made their get-away through the streets of Bristol. When eventually they were caught, Birch was named as the ringleader: 'a very bad boy, having come home drunk and having been often admonished, but remains incorrigible'. The Society instructed the Master not only to flog all four 'with a degree of severity', but to keep them in their damaged uniform and to 'to put the wooden collar on Birch and Anderson'. [For a description of this collar and how it was used, see *Personal Reminiscences 2* on page 40] Apart from those mentioned here, many other boys ran away during this period and were flogged without mercy on their return.

After two more boys had run away in 1783, the Standing Committee solemnly noted in its minutes: 'It appeareth to the committee that the crime of running away from the school is become more prevalent'. It therefore introduced a standing rule that any boy who ran away in future would not be readmitted - which was apparently the rule adopted by Christ's Hospital in London. Although this measure did not in itself reduce the flow of escapees, it did greatly increase the number of boys expelled (or, rather, 'not readmitted'). In seven years (1789-1796), during the Mastership of Mr Haynes, junior, no fewer than 28 boys were removed (or 'taken away by friends to prevent being expelled'), mostly for what was now referred to as 'elopement'.

In 1786, the committee even put an advertisement in the local press, offering a reward for the apprehension of John Pearce and Walter Nicholas (who had run away with their school clothes) - just so that they could be formally expelled! Petty theft, involving other boys' property, was also prevalent in the school. William Webb, for instance, who was found guilty of various thefts and branded 'a very great liar' and a troublemaker, had also run away one at least one occasion. The Master was ordered to flog the boy and to inform his parents that, if they did not remove him, he would be expelled forthwith.

Theft was also at the root of one of the most serious cases of indiscipline reported during this period. In 1780, Daniel Morgan was caught red-handed stealing a plate. When the Usher, after cross-examining the boy, was about to punish him, Morgan took out two knives and 'stabbed him in two places'. It turned out later that this was all premeditated and that two other boys (Strange, an accomplice, and Westcoat, who had provided a penknife) had conspired with Morgan to corner the Usher, presumably to settle an old score. The Standing Committee immediately laid this case of assault before the local magistrates, who ordered Morgan to be whipped by the City Beadle and then (with his parents' consent) sent to sea with the Royal Navy. The other two boys were flogged by the Master and expelled.

The punishment meted out to Morgan was now seen by the committee as a new weapon for their armoury in their battle against crime. Their next chance to use it came in 1781. George Wilway, a notorious tearaway who 'had shown an exceeding bad example to the school', had had the effrontery to steal not only a penknife from one of the other boys, but also an old coat and waistcoat belonging to Mr Haynes. The boy's plan was to make good his escape from the school by changing out of his own clothes into those of the Master. The committee ordered Mr Haynes to 'have him taken up' from Bath (to where he had fled) and put into the Bridewell at Bristol (i.e. the workhouse or 'house of correction'). He should then arrange for a flogging by the City Beadle before delivering him up for service in His Majesty's fleet.

Probably the worst case of all was that reported to the Standing Committee in 1785, when the Master levelled charges of gross misconduct against 14 of the boys. These were all boys with bad disciplinary records, including previous punishments for running away, lying and theft. On this particular occasion, prior to what can only be described as a mass break-out, five of the boys 'had made an attempt to cut off the Usher's hair in the night'. Several of the gang had also cut up their school coats and 'made them into trousers'. James Case, who had been involved in the hair incident but who had not tried to escape, nevertheless aided and abetted the others. He persuaded several of the boys to run away, 'offering Stephen Lewis three pence to do so and assisting the boys in getting over the roof of the house'. He also shook hands with them and wished them well.

The ringleader, however, was undoubtedly Joseph Millard, who called himself 'Young Turpin' and was notorious for cursing and swearing - not to mention his appalling behaviour in church on Sundays. He was extremely rude to the Usher, who caught him climbing over the roof, calling him 'a long-shanked fool' and warning him that, if he hit him, he would be stabbed. He also used more threatening language to the effect that, if he were expelled, 'there should not be a window in the house left unbroken'. The committee took decisive action against these rebels by ordering that eleven of them, including Millard, should be whipped in their presence, kept separate from the other boys and fed chiefly on bread and water until the Society's next meeting. Eight of the worst offenders were then expelled and the six others flogged - a task which was carried out, according to the minute book, 'with much seriousness'.

There is no doubt that, during the eighteenth century, Colston's Hospital was institutionally brutal and that its Masters and Ushers (particularly Mr Haynes and his son) were compulsive floggers. They had little else to offer. Furthermore, the members of the Society's Standing Committee watched the endless beatings with the sort of morbid satisfaction with which Londoners of the same period watched public executions. All this was to change in a most dramatic way with the appointment of the new Visiting Committee in 1836, which heralded the arrival of a much more enlightened and humane era .

In its first annual report, given to the Society in 1837, it stated: 'It is hoped that, owing to the improved system of education which is adopted, and the inculcation of higher principles, corporal punishment may hereafter be wholly abolished'. The report went on to highlight its new policy of 'rewards and punishments', which would bring a much more constructive approach to the area of school discipline. The process would take time but, 'as the boys who have been under the old system leave the school', the opportunity to establish 'a more perfect one' would be presented. The key objective henceforth was to be 'the moral improvement of the boys' - in other words, to tackle crime at its source!

This 'whole school' approach consisted a number of elements, including the importance of making the school a more congenial place in which to live (see above) and the vital role of encouragement rather than repression - hence the 'rewards' offered as holidays for good behaviour and as prizes for good performance in academic work (see below). Underpinning it all was a continual emphasis on church attendance and a more active programme of religious instruction by the catechist. There was also a desire by the Visiting Committee to be much more personally involved in the task of inculcating higher moral standards into the boys.

Its first opportunity for action came in July 1840. Richard Astat, Charles Jones and Joseph Dear had escaped from the school via the dormitory fire escape ladder and over the walls, before the rest of the boys were up, taking with them 13s 9d belonging to Thomas Walker and stolen from under his bed. The committee did three things in consequence. First, it took decisive action by immediately expelling the three boys and, when Astat's father failed to collect his son from school, sent the boy home by coach, instructing the driver to deliver him safely to his father in Bath.

Secondly, its members addressed the whole school at some length on the seriousness of both theft and running away, pointing out the long-term injury that such conduct would have on themselves and the distress it would cause to their parents. Thirdly, they sent out a letter to all parents, not only stressing that running away would always incur expulsion, but also emphasising the importance of parental co-operation in underlining to their sons the necessity of strict obedience. Shortly afterwards, Mr Claxton (the Society's first full-time salaried Treasurer) went with the boys to the cathedral and then, having returned with them to the school, 'addressed them upon their religious duties' and the advantages they gained by attending Colston's Hospital. By doing all this, the Society displayed a most enlightened approach, which was well in advance of its times.

The phasing out of flogging was also central to the committee's plans. In 1837, following a complaint that the Usher (Mr Stephens) had 'used too much authority against certain boys', the Visiting Committee warned him that he was not to exercise 'any severe punishment' in future, except by the direction of the Master. They went even further in 1842, when they banned the Ushers altogether from administering corporal punishment, which henceforth was to be solely reserved for use by the Master. Needless to say, the older boys who had been brought up on a more ruthless approach to discipline, quickly detected and exploited this softening of attitude. The committee expressed its sadness and frustration at this turn of events in a minute dated October 1846:

> The committee regrets to state that the happiness and discipline of the Hospital has been interrupted by the influence and bad example of some few of the boys, whose conduct has been insubordinate, having not infrequently treated the Under Masters with insolence, amounting in some cases to defiance and threats; who being restricted from inflicting punishment without reference to the Master of the Hospital, have repeatedly been under the necessity of reporting their conduct.

The minute went on to stress the measures they had undertaken to reform one boy in particular - 'punishments and restrictions have been resorted to, but with little effect' and 'repeated intimations of his misconduct have been conveyed to his parents', but all to no avail. The committee therefore 'had the painful duty of communicating with his widowed mother this distressing and deplorable intelligence' with the result that she decided to remove the boy (much to everyone's relief). The other offenders were given 'a solemn warning in the presence of the whole school' and the Master asked to keep a watchful eye on them, imposing 'a strict, but kind discipline'. The words used in this report were far removed from the words used by their eighteenth-century predecessors in similar cases. The emphasis of the Society was now increasingly that of gaining co-operation from the boys, based on a realisation that expulsion would have serious consequences for their future success. Flogging was no longer considered an option.

Occasional lapses were inevitable - as in 1840, when the committee 'were extremely grieved to hear of the misconduct of the boys during divine service in the cathedral'. The boys were not only severely reprimanded and lectured on good manners by the committee, but were also subjected to a special admonition by the catechist, who was increasingly enrolled to set the moral tone for the school. Although three boys 'eloped' in 1838 (with the connivance of two boys who were on duty as 'door keepers') and were expelled for their pains, the committee was able to report in 1841 that 'only one case of running away' had occurred since that incident, 'forming a great contrast with former experience'. Two years later, it was delighted to announce that 'order and discipline is in a sound and good state'. Indeed, the attitude of the pupils had gradually changed under the new regime. Although boys were still boys and still capable of extreme naughtiness, they had learnt to recognise right from wrong and the need for remorse. In 1854, the annual Prize Giving was saved from cancellation because 'the boys have voluntarily and publicly expressed their sorrow for their misconduct in August last'

Work in the Classroom

Colston's rules in 1708 for the running of the school established a programme of work that was to remain almost intact until 1836. The boys were simply taught the basics of reading, punctuation, spelling, writing, arithmetic and church catechism. The first change of any significance took place in 1830, when, at the prompting of the Master of the Society, the Standing Committee undertook an investigation into 'the expediency of extending the system of instruction'. When its suspicion was confirmed that the old programme was no longer adequate, it agreed to add two new subjects - history and geography - to the curriculum. Orders were therefore placed for class sets of Goldsmith's *History of England*, Goldsmith's *Histories of Greece and Rome* and Guy's *Geography for Schools.*

This, however, was only a start. After the appointment of a new Master (Mr Lewis) and the establishment of the Visiting Committee in 1836, a major review was launched. Members of the committee underlined just how outdated the programme was in their first annual report, published in 1837: 'No alteration in the course of instruction having been made since the foundation of the Hospital, it is almost unnecessary to state that the course adopted was unsuited to the present time. The Hospital education was inferior to that of parochial schools under the improved system of tuition'. They went on to record that they had therefore introduced 'a more general system of education' with the adoption of 'useful and amusing books', instead of the restricted and formal range previously used. Furthermore, they had successfully introduced 'the class system of learning' (based on age) - and also gas lighting into the schoolroom, which meant that the full teaching programme could be maintained throughout the winter and that the boys could use the room for 'amusing reading' during their leisure time on dark evenings.

They quickly drew up a new weekly programme of lessons, which provided 32 hours for classroom teaching. Within this programme, the following allocations were made: arithmetic 9 hours, writing 5 hours, bible reading 4.5 hours, catechism 4 hours, grammar 3 hours, geography 2.5 hours, history 2 hours and history reading 2 hours. In addition, the boys had half an hour each day before breakfast of 'spelling lessons', amounting to 3 hours a week. In order to make this programme work properly, the committee ordered a new stock of slates, pencils, paper, ink and writing books, together with a large supply of new class books in sets of 18 or 24. These included Johnson's *Dictionary*, Crosby's *Calculations*, Lennie's *Grammar*, arithmetic tables, class reading books, bible spelling books, church catechisms, *Outlines of Geography* and Pinnock's *England*. A large map of the world was also purchased in 1840.

Further developments quickly followed with the introduction of a more formal approach to the teaching of singing. As early as 1775, the Standing Committee had complained that the boys did not sing the psalms, during morning and evening prayers, in a proper manner, having picked up bad habits over the course of time. The committee had therefore decided at that time to employ a man to teach them to sing properly and to buy copies of the new version of the psalms. Mr Bourne was duly appointed at the rate of £2 per annum.

These singing lessons continued through to 1842, when the Visiting Committee recommended that the sum paid for singing instruction should be increased to £15 a year to enable the boys 'to be taught on Mr Hullah's system'. This method, devised by John Hullah, was a system of sight-singing used before the later tonic sol-fa method was more widely adopted. The Hullah approach was therefore taught at the school until 1847, when the Society dismissed the teacher (Mr Dobson) for his 'considerable negligence' in attending classes and decided to pay the Junior Usher an extra £10 for taking over singing duties (carried out, presumably, as an extra outside the normal timetable). The cause of music within school life was advanced in 1855 by the purchase of a harmonium (costing £25) 'for the improvement of the boys in singing' and a variety of other instruments for five guineas - followed four years later by a decision to pay for the instruction of boys in brass band music.

All this effort clearly paid dividends. The improvement in the quality and variety of school music was particularly evident on the Society's Charter Day, held in St Stephen's Church each year in November. Whereas (according to the Treasurer, William Claxton), the boys' chanting of the canticles and the psalm 'was not so satisfactory as usual' in 1847, two years later it had improved out of all recognition. By 1852, they not only 'performed the chanting most admirably' in church, but also entertained the guests in Merchants' Hall over lunch with 'several nice glees and choruses'. They had extended their repertoire to include 'several airs on their drums and fifes' in 1855 and various tunes 'on their brass instruments' in 1857. By 1863, the school's brass band was leading the procession to the church. The boys reward for all this entertainment remained the same throughout - a piece of plum cake and a glass of wine.

A start was also made to the introduction of drawing as a subject. In 1853, the Visiting Committee recommended that the Hospital should co-operate with other schools in the city in establishing an elementary Drawing School. The Society agreed in view of the fact that it would only require an initial expenditure of £7, plus an annual payment of £5 to cover the cost of one lesson a week for the whole school. The scheme clearly proved viable, because six years later the Society sanctioned an increase in its annual payment to the drawing master at the School of Practical Art. In 1857, an examiner from the London branch of that institution examined the boys' drawings and designs, before awarding eleven prizes (including one 'first class'). Two years later, twenty-nine boys entered the examination held at the Gallery of Arts, twenty-one of whom came away with prizes.

The introduction of drill under a drill sergeant has already been mentioned (followed by some gymnastics in 1847). It was, however, the establishment of 'navigation' as a subject within the curriculum in 1845 that caused most controversy. A report into the reorganisation of the Merchants' Hall School had recommended that a class of up to twenty boys at the Hospital should be taught 'navigation and mathematics'. When the Society decided to proceed with this idea, the Master (Mr Lewis) objected. He argued that, as this would mean the appointment of a new mathematics teacher (a subject which he himself taught), he would be somewhat overshadowed and 'would therefore be looked upon as a nonentity'. Furthermore, he continued, very few of the Colston's boys went to sea, but rather sought a living 'with the pen' as clerks. In spite of the Master's objection, navigation was introduced and was taught by Mr Babb (the Master of Merchants' Hall School). The Society allocated £15 for books, instruments and two globes. Quite how the subject fitted into the timetable is unclear.

Although 'church catechism' had been taught throughout the school's history, the subject took on an even greater prominence with the introduction of the new curriculum in 1837. The task of appointing a catechist (traditionally a minister from one of the local churches) had always fallen to the Nominees, who had conscientiously filled the post whenever a vacancy had occurred. A new level of enthusiasm and organisation, however, was set with the appointment of the Reverend G.N. Barrow (the minister of St Paul's, Bedminster and himself one of Colston's Nominees) in March 1838. In giving his annual report on his work (another new initiative), he stated that, during his first seventeen months, he had made 58 visits to the school and had pursued a systematic plan of religious instruction, based on the bible and the prayer book. In his weekly sessions with the older boys and monthly meetings with the younger ones, he had covered aspects of the Christian faith as well as the procedure of the Church of England. During Lent, according to normal custom, the whole school had attended a service in St Augustine's Church, where they had also been 'publicly examined by the minister' on the faith. Boys were regularly sent forward for confirmation - thirteen over that particular year.

The whole school, of course, continued to attend the Cathedral on Sundays, Holy Days and special occasions - such as the day of Solemn Fast and Humiliation, ordered by the Queen in 1847, in consequence of the Irish potato famine. The boys contributed £1 1s 2d out of their own pockets to the collection in aid of relief. One significant change to the normal routine of cathedral attendance was agreed in 1856, when boys were permitted to attend the afternoon service at Clifton Church on the first Sunday of each month 'to hear sermons addressed to young persons by the Reverend W.W. Gibbons' - or at least 'whenever the state of the weather may not render this undesirable'.

The Reverend G.N. Barrow also played a significant role in the establishment of a school library in 1839. The Visiting Committee reported that, as a result of 'the increasing disposition of the boys, during their leisure hours, to read instructive books, the Reverend Barrow was requested to submit for consideration a list of books which might form the commencement of a good school library'. His list, which was quickly approved at a cost of £20, included 26 books on religion, 24 on history and biography, 19 on voyages and travels and 31 on fiction, science, natural history, poetry and arts. Book cases were duly purchased and the first school library had been established.

Two years later, the Society expressed its delight that the library had been 'greatly used' and voted a further £10 for the Master to spend on books. With this sum, he was able to purchase over 100 new volumes, including an increased range of history and fiction. Thereafter, the Society gave regular amounts annually to the library, normally of £10, while individual members frequently donated books of their own. In 1847, the list of books acquired included a large number of 'replacements' of earlier purchases because, as the Master explained, those particular books 'are popular in the school and many are now in an imperfect state'. The boys' particular favourites included *The Life of Marlborough*, *Tales and Stories from History*, *History of the Plague*, *Travels in Africa*, *Travels in South-East Asia*, *Anson's Voyage*, Hall's *Voyage to Java*, *Church Scholars' Reading Book* and various books on animals and wildlife. By 1861, Colston's Hospital was in possession of a library, which far bettered anything on offer in the local parochial schools.

Examinations and Prizes

Fundamental to the Society's transformation of the atmosphere within the school was its system of 'rewards and punishments', which was gradually developed between 1831 and 1850. Part of the scheme was based on providing opportunities for the public acclaim of the boys' efforts in order to develop their sense of self-respect. In January 1845, therefore, the Visiting Committee put forward the proposal that there should be 'a public examination of the boys in Merchants' Hall by a clergyman of the established church and any other members of the Church of England to be selected by the Visiting Committee'.

Alongside this was the suggestion that 'rewards' should be presented on the basis of the boys' achievement throughout the previous year. These were to be in the form of books (not exceeding the value in total of £20 for any one year), which would be distributed by the Master of the Society at the annual 'examination'. To enable the committee to draw up the list of 'rewards', the Headmaster was to 'keep a register of each boy's conduct and attainment', which would be shown to the committee each week, with a much more detailed analysis every six months. In order to encourage and motivate the boys, marks were to be entered in the register each day so that 'each boy shall be aware of his position' - and the registers 'kept in the school library', where they would be available for easy consultation. Furthermore, every three months, the Master was to read out to the whole school the latest situation in the mark order.

Merchants' Hall in King Street (destroyed by bombs in the Second World War). A drawing by E. Willis Paige, 1933. (By courtesy of the Society of Merchant Venturers)

The 'rewards' ceremony was, of course, the origin of the modern Prize Giving. The Visiting Committee decided to place the prizes in two categories - the first for 'general proficiency' in work, accompanied by 'good conduct' throughout the year; the second, for 'marked good conduct, where proficiency may not be so great, but is equal to the boy's ability'. It is interesting to note that prizes could never be won without good conduct (however excellent the academic achievement) and that some prizes were reserved for boys who were not naturally clever, but who had performed to the very best of their ability. In this way, the Society hoped to motivate every boy within the school.

The first 'Public Examination' was therefore held in Merchants' Hall on 12th June 1845 in the presence of the Mayor of Bristol, the High Sheriff, the Duke of Beaufort, Mr E.F. Colston, several other distinguished guests and many Merchants and Nominees. The Society's aim in providing such a fine setting and impressive atmosphere was to give the boys a real sense of the importance of the occasion and therefore the importance of their achievement. It also believed that the boys would benefit in two other ways from the experience - it would help them to develop 'their religious and moral improvement' and it would produce a spirit of 'emulation', as they were inspired to equal the performance of the twenty-two prizewinners.

The 'examination', which was conducted by the Reverend Canon Barrow (the Secretary to the Nominees and the school's previous catechist), was not intended to be an examination of each individual boy in the normal sense. It was rather an opportunity for a group of boys (in this case, the 1st Class, averaging 14.75 years) to demonstrate some of what they had learnt during the year. The programme was as follows:

> **The Venite** to be chanted
> **Examination** of the boys by the Reverend Canon Barrow
> **Address** by the Master of the Society of Merchant Venturers to
>   such boys as shall receive from him the prizes to be
>   awarded
> **Address** from the Reverend John Hensman, Chaplain of the
>   Society of Merchant Venturers, to the whole school
> **National Anthem**

The occasion was voted such a success that it was decided to make it an annual event with a more sophisticated classification of prizes. In 1846, therefore, the Visiting Committee drew up a more detailed list of the 'rewards' on offer. Each of the five classes in the school would have five subject prizes available for the most proficient in arithmetic; penmanship; recitation and grammar; church catechism; and geography and history (all again dependent on good behaviour as well as good work). In addition, there would be either one or two good conduct prizes for each class, plus one prize to be awarded to the navigation class. The Public Examinations held in 1847 and 1848 were less formal affairs, being held in the Hospital in the presence of the Standing Committee rather than in Merchants' Hall.

By 1850, the idea of a really large ceremony had somewhat lapsed. When, in that year, Mr John Saunders provided £6 to be shared by the three boys considered 'to have attained the highest characters for moral conduct', the Visiting Committee suggested that the annual visitation of the Hospital by the Standing Committee might provide an appropriate occasion for the awards to be presented. It went on to suggest that 'it might have a further good effect to distribute a few prizes in books to some of the boys for other attainment' (not exceeding £5 in value). Thus the idea of a Prize Giving was revived in some measure and, by 1858, a sum of 15 guineas had been set aside for the books each year. The ceremonies continued to be held in the Hospital with the examination normally conducted by either the Master of the Society or a local clergyman. Quite apart from this annual examination organised by the Standing Committee, the Nominees also seized the opportunity to examine the boys each year during one of their own quarterly visitations. In 1853, for instance, they questioned the boys on scripture, ancient history, the history of England, geography, arithmetic, algebra and geometry.

Meanwhile, the Society itself continued to extend the principle of rewards, as well as punishments. In 1842, therefore, it had started the tradition of presenting each leaver with a copy of both the Bible and the Book of Common Prayer subject, as always, to his good conduct throughout the school - a stipulation which was rigidly adhered to. Whereas, for instance, in 1851 all eighteen leavers received the awards, in 1853 only six out of sixteen did so. The books, which were stamped on the outside with 'The Gift of the Society of Merchant Venturers', contained an engraved plate on the inside bearing the Society's arms and signed by both the Master of the Society and the Master of the School. The aim was two-fold: first, to provide a source of reference for their future lives; and secondly, 'to cherish in them and their families a remembrance of the great advantages derived from the sound religious education received under the fostering care of the Society of Merchant Venturers'. In the following year, each leaver was also required to take with him a copy, in his own handwriting, of a passage praising the life and work of the founder.

The idea of examinations continued to develop, even if the school's own 'Public Examinations' were being held in a slightly lower key. The first five boys ever to be entered for an external examination took 'the Cambridge University Examinations of students not members of the University' in December 1858. With three of them passing on that occasion, the idea was considered to be so worthwhile that the Society set aside a sum of money in each following year to cover the fees of boys from impoverished homes, together with any special books required in their preparation.

Sources used in Chapter 4

D.J. Eames, *The Contribution made by the Society of Merchant Venturers to the Development of Education in Bristol* (unpublished MA thesis for the University of Bristol, 1966), pp 45-94

Patrick McGrath, *The Merchant Venturers of Bristol* (Bristol, 1975), p 214

Society of Merchant Venturers' Archive:
> *The Hall Book of Proceedings*, vols. 4-22 (1708-1860)
> *Minutes of the Meetings of Mr Colston's Nominees*, 3 vols., (1748-70; 1780-1822; 1823-53)
> *Proceedings of Colston's Hospital Visiting Committee*, vol. 1 (1826-41)
> *Annual Reports of Colston's Hospital Visiting Committee* (1842-58)
> *Copies of Mr Colston's Settlements* (printed volume), pp 17-20 ('Rules, Orders and Directions')
> *Box of Appendices:*   Bundle 3: letter from Wm Barrett, surgeon
>   Bundle 13: examination programme, 1845
> *Lists of boys taken in by Samuel Gardner,* 1718-62
> *The Diary of William Claxton,* vol. 1(1841-63); vol. 2 (1863-73)
> *The Society's Book of Charity Proceedings,* vol. 1 (1852-67)

The Bristol Times & Farley's Bristol Journal, 15th November 1856

MONEY LENDING IN THE 1840s

Edward Colston *(Old Colstonian, 1841-48)*

On 26th April 1841, I was admitted to Colston's School on St Augustine's Back (where the Colston Hall now stands). I remember well ringing the gates for admission, having longed for the happy day to be made a Colston boy. I became on very friendly terms with the Masters, although I deserved no doubt a little punishment at times - the punishment inflicted usually being kept in for an hour or two on holiday or sometimes for the whole day. Birching was at times inflicted for any serious misconduct, but such was not very frequent as our Headmaster [Mr Lewis] was very forgiving.

There was an old market women allowed into the playground every Tuesday from twelve to two o'clock, selling sweets, cake and fruit. It was a custom for the boys to congregate near her basket and for the boys that had any spare cash to lend boys a halfpenny for a penny on the next holiday [i.e. the return of capital plus interest] - or, if cash was plentiful, you could borrow a penny for three halfpence, thus gaining a halfpenny on other boys' cash. The money lenders did remarkably well.

In illustration of this, a close companion of mine named Jarrett (Number 30), having heard that I purchased a galvanic ring on our last holiday - and coming across a boy having a headache - persuaded this boy to purchase the ring, stating that it would cure him. So having effected a sale, we started a partnership. Having sold it for a penny, the day following we got the Door Keeper to purchase a penny worth of lozenges at Mrs Stokes's shop, consisting of nine lozenges. Disposing of them at three for a halfpenny, we profited a halfpenny on the investment. We repeated the same as soon as our stock became exhausted so that, by the time the market woman commenced disposing of her stock the following day, we were able to start money-lending. In a few weeks our cash increased considerably.

We were frequently taken on a walk on Durdham Down to play cricket, having a club of our own - payments into which enabled us to procure bats and balls. We prided ourselves as very successful players.

Sometimes whilst on the Downs, by paying a penny, we could ramble through the wood in which stands the far-famed Cook's Folly - swings etc being provided.

About the year 1843, Prince Albert visited Bristol to launch the Great Britain Steamship, which was a very remarkable day. All Bristol was on holiday. The Colston schoolboys had a platform erected for them by the generosity of the Society of Merchants, near Hotwell House. The Prince, on arriving at the Hotwell House, took a glass of the spa water; and, whilst staying there to partake of this, a passenger was sent in a basket across the bar that spanned the Avon (where is now constructed our most wonderful Suspension Bridge). The Prince then proceeded to the dock facing the gasworks to launch quite the largest steamship in the world. The Colston boys then proceeded to Brandon Hill, from whence a splendid view of the launch was obtained.

Whilst the boys were stationed on the platform, an uncle of mine (my foster father) invited me, when we dispersed (as it was a holiday), to join them for a drive around the city. But, as I knew that uncle would therefore be away from home, it was a very good opportunity to invite a few of my school mates to visit his garden; and, as the gooseberries were in their prime, we stripped all the trees and took them in our handkerchiefs to school. On the next holiday, he gave a stern reproof.

In the year 1844, Thomas Warren (number 75) left the school. As he had said Grace for the boys before and after meals, I was selected to that duty for the remainder of my time. I spent a very happy time whilst at school - I may say the happiest of my life. Several members of our family were educated in the school - my two grandfathers, my father, myself, two of my sons and a grandson. We could claim admission on the grounds of our name being the same as the Founder.

(Written in 1910, a copy of this was sent to the school in 1946, when the writer's grandson was was considering Colston's for his own son. It reflects the more enlightened atmosphere)

CHAPTER 5

The Hospital in Perspective, 1710 - 1861

'We trust that God will bless the means used in bringing up the young and that many valuable members of society may have reason to feel eternal gratitude to Him for the blessings here bestowed upon them'. (Colston's Hospital Visiting Committee's Annual Report, October 1846)

Background to the School's changing fortunes

By 1861, the Society of Merchant Venturers had, with much credit. successfully steered Colston's Hospital through the first 151 years of its history. Although some changes had been made, particularly during the last sixteen years of this period, Colston's fundamental principles had remained intact - the school still provided a free boarding education for one hundred poor boys, who were given instruction in the three 'Rs' and then found apprenticeships; and it was still firmly based on the doctrines of the Church of England.

It is easy to criticise the harsh conditions in which the boys lived and the brutal floggings they endured until a more enlightened regime took control in 1836. However, it must be borne in mind that the majority of boarding schools in England, including the most famous, were equally uncivilised places during the eighteenth century. At Eton, for instance, boys were obliged to wash outside at the pump and the Headmaster was reputed to have flogged eighty boys on one day in 1832. Similarly the stabbing of the Usher at Colston's in 1780 and the mass break-out in 1785, however serious, were nothing in comparison with what was happening in other schools, where boys organised violent protests. Partly inspired by the French Revolution, boys at Winchester staged a number of rebellions. One, in 1793, saw a two-day seizure of school buildings under the red flag of liberty. Another, in 1818, ultimately required intervention by soldiers with fixed bayonets. Meanwhile, boys at Rugby School used gunpowder in 1797 to blow open the door of the Headmaster's study. Life at Colston's, by contrast, was distinctly tame.

When eventually the Visiting Committee (under the watchful eye of the Society's Standing Committee) began to transform life and conditions at the Hospital in 1836, its members were motivated by a number of factors. In particular, they found themselves in the middle of what nationally became known as 'The Age of Reform'. Mounting pressure in the country at large brought about not only a measure of parliamentary reform in the Great Reform Bill of 1832, but also a succession of reforms over the next fifty years in the spheres of local government, factories, law and education. The spirit of reform, therefore, was very much in the air. Three great Headmasters, Samuel Butler of Shrewsbury, Thomas Arnold of Rugby and (later) Edward Thring of Uppingham began to revise teaching methods, examinations and curricula in the public schools to meet changing needs. There was, too, a great improvement in the tone of these schools as life there became less spartan - although the roasting of small boys before an open fire was not completely unknown at Rugby even in the days of Mr Arnold. Nevertheless, it is fair to say that Colston's Visiting Committee was very much ahead of its times when it stated its intention, as early as 1837, to phase out corporal punishment. At King Edward's School, Bath, the Headmaster was still defending his right in 1856 to birch boys 'on the bare skin' in front of the whole school.

The Visiting Committee was also inspired by the national upsurge in religion, as reflected in the rise of Methodist, Evangelical and Oxford Movements - movements which all stressed the need to tackle poverty, slavery and social conditions. These developments served to reinforce Colston's own principle that education at the Hospital should be firmly based on the teachings of the Church of England. The committee's annual report of 1841 was unrestrained in its fervour: 'Train up a child in the way he shall go and, when he is old, he will not depart from it', became their unofficial motto. The members earnestly believed that 'some benefit must accrue to those who are brought up in the fear of God', especially if they were boys who were previously 'neglected and despised' - a benefit far greater than could have been achieved if the same boys had attended ordinary schools. The new compassionate approach was therefore based to a large extent on religious zeal.

Nevertheless, it is also true to say that the minds of the members of the committee were more sharply concentrated on the need for reform by the appointment of the Charity Commissioners in 1838 with powers to investigate all endowment trusts. The commissioners, with instructions to ensure that resources were being properly applied, finally descended upon Colston's Hospital in 1836, when the Society was ordered to produce all its minute books and ledgers relating to the school. During this investigation, which lasted until 1842 (for details see Chapter 2), the Society was most anxious to demonstrate that the Hospital was being well run and the endowment funds wisely spent. The Merchants were also distinctly edgy following the passing of the Municipal Corporations Act in 1835, which had transferred control of all charitable institutions previously under the control of Bristol Corporation (including Queen Elizabeth's Hospital) to a new body of Bristol Charity Trustees. William Claxton, the Society's Treasurer, firmly believed that this Whig-dominated body, which was strongly sympathetic to dissenters from the Church of England, was 'determined to set their rapacious claws on Colston's Hospital' for they 'could not abide' the thought that the school was strictly based on the Anglican faith. Indeed, he was convinced that they had mischievously sparked off the enquiry by the Charity Commissioners. In the end, although the Society was found guilty in 1842 on a technical offence relating to its use of its trust funds, the Attorney-General complimented the Society's control of the Hospital by stating his belief that it was 'very well managed'.

But whatever the real motivation behind the Society's wholesale reforms after 1836, the fact remains that the members of the Visiting Committee threw themselves wholeheartedly into the task. Meeting at least once a week (and more during the early stages), they personally presided over a whirlwind of change - inspecting the refurbishments, dealing with estimates, awarding contracts, visiting other establishments to pick up ideas, keeping accounts and badgering the Master. Furthermore, they became involved in the daily life of the school as never before - seeing 'the boys have their dinner', hearing 'the boys go through their arithmetic', observing lessons, reprimanding or advising individuals, lecturing or encouraging the whole school and accompanying the boys to church.

The fruits of this labour were evident to visitors. When, in 1856, the Reverend Alexander Wilson (Principle of the National Society's Training Institution at Westminster) visited the school, he commented that 'he had never visited an institution where the relations of masters and pupils were more beneficially and beautifully carried out'. The Society deserves much credit for this. In some ways at least, Colston's Hospital was ahead of the field.

Education in Bristol

At the beginning of the eighteenth century, the provision made in Bristol for the education of most of its children can best be described as dismal. Apart from Colston's Hospital (founded in 1710), there was Queen Elizabeth's Hospital (founded in 1590 as a boarding school by John Carr, merchant, to provide the barest elements of schooling for 36 poor boys and based in former monastic buildings near College Green); Red Maids' School (founded in 1634 by John Whitson, alderman of the city, to teach 42 poor girls to read); Redcliffe Grammar School (established in Elizabeth I's reign in an ancient chapel within the cemetery of St Mary Redcliffe for about 12 children); the King's School or Royal Grammar School (later Bristol Cathedral School, founded by King Henry VIII in 1542); and, for the sons of tradesmen, the Free School or Bristol Grammar School (founded in 1532 by Robert Thorne, merchant, as a day school situated in the old buildings of St Bartholomew's Hospital, near Christmas Steps, and run by the Corporation).

In addition, there were three or four private 'writing schools' and one or two Poor Law schools, where a few pauper children were taught to read. However, because each of the schools listed above catered for just a handful of children, the total number educated within the city (with a population of 25,000 people) was exceptionally low. Thousands of children from the homes of labourers and artisans found themselves completely without provision, while many wealthy businessmen were still unable to write their names.

In order to combat this situation, a movement gradually gained momentum within Bristol to establish charity schools within each parish, based on the example of similar institutions in London. This first indication of this came in 1699, when Miss Mary Gray left £50 in her will (less 6s 8d for an annual sermon in the parish church) to fund the teaching of seven poor fatherless children in Temple parish. Ten years later, the Reverend Arthur Bedford, vicar of that parish, drew attention to the fact that out of 232 poor children resident there only three were being taught by the poor Law guardians. In the light of this, he successfully called for subscriptions from within the parish (including £10 a year from Edward Colston) and then proceeded to open a school for 30 boys in August 1709. Colston himself became so enthusiastic about the project that he not only gave a further £80 a year to clothe and educate an increased total of 40 boys in that school, but also provided a site for the erection of a suitable building, which finally opened in December 1711.

Other such charity schools quickly followed - a school for 20 girls in Temple parish (1713), a school for boys in the combined parishes of St Michael's and St Augustine's (1714) and a joint school for 40 boys from the parishes of St Mary Redcliffe and St Thomas's (which moved into a new school house in Pyle Street in 1739). Much later, in 1858, the parishes of St Nicholas's and St Leonard's joined forces to set up a school with a newly-built room and playground in Back Street. Parochial charity schools such as these all aimed at the education of poor children in reading, writing, arithmetic and the beliefs of the Church of England. The Diocesan School, which was established in 1812 with similar intentions in Nelson Street, was eventually converted into a Trade

School in 1856 and later became the Merchant Venturers' School.

Two other schools are also worthy of mention - the presbyterian school for poor children, established in 1722 by Abraham Hooke, merchant, in Stoke's Croft; and a school to teach ten boys the art of navigation, established in 1712 on the Quay by Lady Susanna Holworthy. Ten years later, this was moved to a new location - an old kitchen inside Merchants' Hall. By 1738, the Society of Merchant Venturers had taken over responsibility for its endowment and management.

Little further progress was made during the eighteenth century to the general spread of education in Bristol. It is true that a number of small boarding schools were established in the city for the sons and daughters of more wealthy citizens - such as the one for young ladies by Mrs Becher in College Green in 1743 and the one for boys by Mr Steward in Christmas Street in 1747. Nevertheless, the fact remained that seventy-five per cent of the city's work force were totally illiterate - a situation not helped by the attitude of the local Sunday Schools' Commission. In its report of 1786, it stated that 'the instruction to be obtained at a Sunday School is fully adequate to all the purposes of the lower classes of people'. Nor had the situation greatly changed by 1836, according to evidence presented at the annual congress of the British Association in Bristol. Out of a population of 112,000, there were 20,000 children of school age - yet only 5,200 were actually being taught in schools.

The boys who attended Colston's School during this period, therefore, were part of a highly privileged minority.

Thomas Chatterton

Given the nature of the school, the limited ambition of the curriculum and the recruitment of boys from impoverished backgrounds, it is hardly surprising that Colston's Hospital failed to produce, during these early years, a long line of distinguished statesmen, generals, surgeons, judges and academics. Nevertheless, it is true that many boys went on to do well for themselves in various spheres, as testified by those who presented gifts or prizes in appreciation of the start they had been given in life.

One young man, however, defied all the odds stacked against him by becoming one of the most famous and admired poets that this country has produced. Thomas Chatterton was born on 20th November 1752 in a small tenement behind the Pyle Street Charity School, where his father had been Master until his untimely death earlier that year. His mother was soon forced by poverty to move into a much smaller house in a courtyard near St Mary Redcliffe Church and to set up a sewing school from which to earn a living. At five years of age, the young Thomas showed little spark and was regarded by his mother as 'little better than an absolute fool'. Indeed, he was rejected by Pyle Street School, after a short stay, as being too dull and incapable of learning his alphabet.

Then, quite suddenly, a remarkable transformation took place. One day, as he approached his seventh birthday, he happened to notice the illuminated capitals on his father's old music book. His total fascination with these sparked off an insatiable curiosity to learn more. His mother seized the opportunity to teach him the alphabet through these letters and eventually to teach him to read from an old bible. Within a year, he had become such an avid reader that he was successfully nominated for a place at Colston's Hospital by the vicar of Henbury. He was almost eight, therefore, when he started his school career on 3rd August 1760. From this moment on, his potential was released in a most dramatic manner.

It is true that Chatterton, anxious to extend the range of his learning, was soon frustrated that the school only offered basic teaching in reading, writing and arithmetic. Indeed, Mrs Edkins (a family friend) later recalled that, although he had at first been very proud of his election to the Hospital (thinking that he would gain all the learning he wanted), he soon seemed 'much hurt' and said 'he could not learn so much at school as he could at home, for they had not enough books'. Nevertheless, the Hospital provided him with a structured and disciplined environment for these formative years. Furthermore, he found a great ally in the junior Usher, Thomas Phillips, who gave him support and encouragement. The Master, Mr William Haynes, said later that Chatterton 'was a lad of quick conception, but that he had several contemporaries whose parts were at least equal to his - and three or four of them having a poetical turn, he had been informed they used frequently to send little detached pieces of poetry to each other'.

Chatterton completed the normal period of seven years at the school and was confirmed by the bishop in 1762 - after which occasion, according to his sister, he made 'sensible and serious remarks about the awfulness of the ceremony'. He also took his turn alongside the other boys with routine chores in the dormitory and around the playground. His sister (Mrs Mary Newton) later wrote that, during his week on duty as doorkeeper at the school gate, Thomas eased his boredom by writing eighteen lines of poetry on 'The Last Day' and paraphrasing the 9th chapter of the Book of Job, together with part of the Book of Isaiah. He was not a rebel, although he was severely punished on one occasion, after being caught red-handed writing some satirical verses on the senior Usher.

Most of his satisfaction and development, however, came through the opportunities provided by his leisure hours. He spent a lot of time inside St Mary Redcliffe, where his uncle was sexton, studying the ancient writing and heraldic designs on tombs. He spent even more time in his attic room, drawing knights in armour and satisfying his thirst for reading. He spent his pocket money on borrowing books from circulating libraries or buying them from second-hand bookshops. By the age of eleven, he had drawn up a list of over seventy books, which he had already read, chiefly on history and religion. His sister later wrote that 'his school mates informed us that he retired to read at the hours allotted to play'. Within one year, he had completely filled a pocket book, given to him by his sister, with his own writings - and his first poem had been published in the *Bristol Journal* (1764). Articles and other poems quickly followed.

On one visit home from school, Chatterton made what turned out to be a most significant discovery - a piece of old parchment, which was being used by his mother as a silk winder. The parchment had come from the old muniment room in St Mary Redcliffe, where the chests housing ancient manuscripts had been broken open some years earlier. His father had apparently taken a few bundles of these, which were generally considered worthless, and had used them to cover books at the school. Two full boxes, however, still remained in the house. The boy, who was thrilled with this discovery, collected together the various pieces and carried them off to his room. From this began his study of ancient spelling and old English words, which he compiled into his own glossary. He also built up his knowledge of mediaeval history from reading Camden's *Britannia*.

Armed with this material and a boyish sense of humour, he now commenced work on a different type of writing. In 1764, he spread the word around amongst his school friends that he had numerous old documents at home, which had come from St Mary Redcliffe. He then showed a piece of stained parchment to Thomas Phillips, on which was written a poem, *Elinowe and Juga*, convincing the unsuspecting Usher that it was genuine. Chatterton, of course, had composed it himself, using antiquated spelling and words drawn from old English dictionaries. [It was published five years later in *Town and Country* magazine].

Although he left school on 1st July 1767 (when he was approaching his fifteenth birthday), he was determined to pursue his new interest even more vigorously. He was apprenticed as a scrivener to John Lambert, an attorney on St John's Steps (the Society of Merchant Venturers paying the normal £10 indenture fee). In spite of the fact that his working hours were long (7.00 am to 8.00 pm daily), the tasks set were not arduous and there were long periods of inactivity. This enabled him to set his lively mind and imagination to work on both his poetry and the continuing process of self-education. Shortly after leaving school, for instance, he corresponded with a boy (Thomas Cary) who had been his bedfellow at Colston's and who was now bound apprentice to a New York merchant. The letter consisted of a collection of all the hard words he could find in the English language - with a request to his friend that he should reply in the same style!

Within a year, he had written *A description of the mayor's passing over the Old Bridge, taken from an old manuscript*, a description of events in Bristol five hundred years earlier, couched in ancient language and spelling. This was published by the *Bristol Journal* on 1st October 1768 - the first time one of his spurious ancient documents had been seen in print. His claim that the manuscript had been found at St Mary Redcliffe was accepted. Encouraged by this success, Chatterton soon found a number of patrons in Bristol who were only too pleased to receive his 'discoveries'. Henry Burgum, a pewterer, was thrilled when the boy announced that he had found among the Redcliffe parchments the heraldic devices of the De Berghams with descent established to the time of William the Conqueror. Burgum paid well for a painted drawing of the arms, a handwritten book on his family history complete with elaborate references and a poem allegedly written in 1320 by one John de Bergham. Sadly, the Heralds' College in London, when approached, could find no trace of the De Berghams!

Mr George Catcott, a pewterer friend of Burgum and amateur archaeologist, rewarded Chatterton for a document called *Bristowe Tragedie* and other 'compositions' by Thomas Rowley, a fifteenth-century monk. Mr William Barrett, an eminent surgeon and local historian, was delighted when Chatterton was regularly able to provide missing evidence for his planned history of Bristol in the form of writings by a monk named Turgot (translated, of course, by Rowley). In this simple boyish way commenced the 'Rowley Romance', which over the next few years occupied the young Chatterton in fabricating the poetry not only of Rowley, but of eleven other imagined medieval poets. It was during this period that he wrote some of his best poetry, including *The Tournament*, *The Battle of Hastings and Aella* (which many judge to be his masterpiece). He shared his secret with no one.

Meanwhile, Chatterton had set his sights on bigger game. Noticing that Horace Walpole had recently published his *Anecdotes of Painting*, he sent him a manuscript entitled *The Ryse of Peynctene in England* by Rowley and later *Historie of Peyncters yn England*. Walpole and his poet friends were not deceived, however, leaving Chatterton embittered at the harsh manner in which he had been rejected. In the meantime, in an attempt to supplement his meagre salary, he had contributed in 1769 alone no fewer than sixteen poems and essays to *Town and Country*

Extract from Chatterton's handwritten book on the history of the De Bergham family - produced for Henry Burgum. (By courtesy of Bristol Central Library)

Magazine, including a touching *Elegy on Thomas Phillips*, the recently-deceased Usher of Colston's Hospital. By now, he was becoming increasingly depressed by the meanness of his Bristol patrons, the miserliness of literary editors and the drudgery of life in the attorney's office. Mr Lambert was quick to burn any of Chatterton's writing which was not related to the business, deriding it merely as 'stuff'. Such was his state that, in April 1770, he decided that suicide would be the only solution to the misery he was suffering. He drew up his 'Last Will and Testament', written 'in the utmost distress of mind', and placed it in a conspicuous position on his desk in the office for Mr Lambert to find. He was instantly dismissed.

He then went to live in London, almost penniless, lodging at first with an aunt in Holborn, where for the first time in his life he had a room to himself. Later he moved to a garret apartment at 13 Brock Street in Gray's Inn. Whenever possible, he wrote to his mother and sent presents to the family. He worked furiously in the hope of earning a living, producing an endless flow of prose and verse but receiving a mere

Signed extract from Chatterton's 'Last Will and Testament'- the last item reading: 'I leave my Mother and Sister to the protection of my Friends, if I have any'. (By courtesy of Bristol Central Library)

pittance in return from the eleven leading magazines which published his efforts. Sadly, his hopes of gaining the patronage of Lord Mayor Beckford were shattered by the man's sudden death. He told his cousin, who saw that 'he was perfectly frantic', that he was ruined. Nevertheless, he managed to produce, in July 1770, *An Excelente Balade of Charitie*, one of his most delightful Rowley poems. It was rejected. Such was his desperate plight that he gradually starved to death, often surviving on a diet of water and cake and rejecting offers of food from his landlady, Mrs Angell. During his last three days, with no food to revive him, he completely lost his sanity. He died from the effects of arsenic poisoning (the near-empty phial still in his hand) on 25th August 1770 at the age of seventeen. When, a few days later, he was buried in a pauper's grave in Shoe Lane, his publishers still owed him almost £12.

This remarkable story of a child prodigy, who spent almost half of his short life under the care of Colston's Hospital, presents a fine example of the hidden potential of youth. His genius was widely celebrated after his death, the first edition of his collected works being published in 1777. His poetry was greatly admired by Shelley, Coleridge, Keats, Johnson, Walpole, Malone ('the greatest genius that England has produced since the days of Shakespeare'), Rossetti ('as great as any English poet whatever') and Wordsworth ('the marvellous boy').

Painting by Henry Wallis, 1856, which depicts the death of Chatterton in 1770 in his London garret. (© Tate, London 2001)

A Visit to Colston's Hospital, 1844

A local newspaper correspondent was invited to cover the visit of the Mayoress to the school's annual examination in November 1844. His delightful description gives a fascinating insight into life inside the Hospital and the great strides that had been made in improving its atmosphere during the previous twelve years.

'The house is a quadrangle, surrounding a spacious courtyard, into which you enter by a stately gateway, ornamented with escutcheons. The schoolroom extends the whole length of one side and the dining room of another; over each are the dormitories with beds for more than one hundred boys. The third side is occupied by the committee rooms and master and matron's apartments. In front of the building, and pleasantly situated on a slope, is a dry flagged playground, a portion of which is covered in as a provision for outdoor exercise on wet days; there is also a large plunge bath, supplied with good water, for the boys; and everything presented the appearance of the utmost cleanliness and cheerful comfort.

'...Appealing to the large bell at the outward gate, we were admitted by one of the little boys (the porter for the day), who made his obeisance and, taking his leave, directed us to the schoolroom, where the lads were being examined by the Reverend G.N. Barrow in the presence of the Mayoress...After singing the National Anthem, the boys at command formed two lines and then, filing off in military order, proceeded to the dining room. [There an interesting sight awaited the visitors]...At two lines of tables, each the entire length of the room, were seated these little bluecoats to the number of one hundred; before each were a pile of potatoes and a plate of beef, and in a moment, after the conclusion of the blessing, one hundred pairs of arms and jaws were energetically at work...The ladies looked smilingly on, hardly knowing whether more to admire the capacity of their minds or the acuteness of their appetites. They had not, however, proceeded far with their pleasant occupation, when the command of the schoolmaster ordered them to 'hold' and arrested the progress of many a piece of beef and potato midway between plate and mouth. [The Headmaster announced a half day holiday, requested by the Mayoress]...From full mouths and empty, a cheer burst forth at this announcement...

'Passing to the two sick wards, we were pleased to find both tenantless; and, if further proof were required of the health of the whole establishment, it was furnished in the spectacle which awaited the visitors on returning to the playground, where the lads, with two standard bearers, were being put through all the evolutions of the drill by an 'old soldier'. At the close of this martial display each boy, as he passed by a large box filled with twopenny cakes by the kindness of the Mayoress, was handed one; and this ceremony closed the day's proceedings with which all parties were exceedingly gratified'.

Sources used in Chapter 5:

H.C. Barnard, *The History of English Education, 1760-1944* (1947)
Dictionary of National Biography (1900) - article on Thomas Chatterton
John Dix, *The Life of Thomas Chatterton* (1838), pp 306-8
D.J. Eames, *The Contribution of the Society of Merchant Venturers to the*

Development of Education in Bristol (unpublished MA thesis for the University of Bristol, 1966)

G. Gregory, *The Life of Thomas Chatterton* (1789), pp 17-24, 100

John Latimer, *The Annals of Bristol in the Eighteenth Century* (1893), pp 12, 16, 80, 99-100, 198, 241-2, 358, 374-5, 385-9

John Latimer, *The Annals of Bristol in the Nineteenth Century* (1887), pp 4-5, 46, 202, 230, 336-7, 365-6

E.H.W. Meyerstein, *A Life of Thomas Chatterton* (1930), pp 25-36

Society of Merchant Venturers' Archive:
    Annual Reports of the Colston's Hospital Visiting Committee, 1852-8

Newspaper cuttings in William Claxton's working copy of *Colston's Settlements*

A rare view of the fine gateway into the inner courtyard of The Great House c.1840s, showing two boys on duty as 'door keepers'. A drawing by S.G. Tovey. (By courtesy of Bristol Museums and Art Gallery)

THE GREAT HOUSE IN THE 1850s

An Old Colstonian

The main entrance was external to the building at its south corner, where the columns of stonework, surmounted by dolphins, supported heavy wooden doors. The schoolroom extended along the entire front of the ground floor to a depth of 20 feet and had a painted wainscot of wood 6 feet high. A heavy baize curtain was drawn across it in winter so as to enclose the end near the Master's residence for lectures and recitations.

The kitchen for the staff lay beyond the staircase. In it the fireplace had an iron spit above the fender, probably part of the original structure. It was turned by a smoke-jack in the chimney and required a powerful upward draught to work it. Though the cook was addressed by the boys as 'Mother', none was allowed to enter her realm.

At the west angle of the mansion was the committee room. Here Mr Colston's Nominees held quarterly meetings and the committee of the Colston Fraternal Association their monthly consultations. In this room was laid dinner at noon for the assistant staff to avoid transit across the quadrangle to their small sitting room. The Headmasters' residence adjoined. From an antiquarian point of view, his reception room well repaid a visit, as it was lined from floor to ceiling with a wainscot, on which prominently carved were bunches of fruit and the mouldings - an ideal interior, save for the mice which found a harbour there.

Against the dining room stood a force pump with a heavy wheel, which was turned by the bigger boys under the supervision of the Porter, who was responsible for the supply to the main cistern, which stood on the first floor level. A flight of steps led up to the playground. It was also paved. At one extremity was an open shed and at the other the kitchen, where the boys' meals were prepared, and the bath house. Tradition was current that the bath house was built for brewing beer, also that small beer was served to the boys at certain meals once on a time.

The gymnastic apparatus stood in the playground. It was of simple form - viz., horizontal bars and ladders, two giant strides and a lofty swing, by which at high elevation a passing view of St Stephen's tower could be snatched. The atmosphere of the playground would often be depressing on account of the smoke issuing from the shaft to the sugar factory at the foot of Host Street, the high wall to Trenchard Street tending to render a breeze inoperative. This drawback was removed when the factory got burnt down, as it was not rebuilt. It happened on a Saturday morning and put a stop to school work - it was a spectacle and so near. Further it curtailed the half-holiday, as the boys were not allowed to leave the premises until the fire was reported under control.

The first floor contained the front and back dormitories with rooms for the staff at the east corner. From the landing on the staircase, the Master had direct access to his residence. The drawing room at the west corner encouraged hospitality. In it were assembled once a year the thirty winners to select their prize, when accommodation was found for all. The attic floor comprised a dormitory for the juniors with rooms for the nurse and staff in the gables. In winter at eventide, the very youngest dormitories supplied many visitors to Nurse's sanctum; the attraction was a cough mixture, applicants for which had to enter their number on a slate beforehand. In the north wing was the wardrobe. Suits of clothes not in wear were suspended by the girdle from numbered pegs - on either side a hundred.

There was no musical instrument possessed by the school when I entered. The singing master brought in his pocket a wooden pipe from which the keynote was got. In those days, it was mostly scale practice, to which the singing of *Three Blind Mice* in three relays was always a welcome change. The Trenchard Street door was seldom used by the school. On Sundays, the boys proceeded by twos through it, each bearing a bible and a prayer book, to attend services at the Cathedral.

(From The Colstonian, *Spring 1921)*

CHAPTER 6

The Move to Stapleton: Years of Dramatic Change, 1861-1873

'What a change the new school was from the old. How delightful to be transplanted from the dingy neighbourhood of Host Street to the open country, from a paved playground enclosed with high walls to a real field surrounded by beautiful trees and shrubs'. (James Jones, Head Monitor in 1861, writing later in 1894)

Agreement to Expand the School

When the Society lost the case brought against it in 1839 by the Attorney-General, the finances of Colston's Hospital received a valuable new source of rent income from the manor of Monkton in Stogursley (see page 38). Taken in conjunction with the increase in rents from other property and savings made through tighter budget control, this boost soon resulted in an annual surplus of over one thousand pounds.

By 1848, therefore, the Society had begun to think in terms of using these additional funds to bring about an expansion of the school. In its annual report of November that year, the Visiting Committee, after drawing attention to requests made by Mr Rowlatt (the new Headmaster) for increased classroom space and other structural changes, recommended that these should be considered alongside a broader plan to enlarge the intake of pupils. At its meeting in February 1849, the Society accepted the committee's report and estimated that funds would permit an increase of 20 boys, bringing the total school roll to 120. It believed that the extra pupils could be accommodated by converting a number of adjacent stables, cellars and sheds, which were then being rented out. The Nominees, who were closely consulted throughout and shown a drawing of the proposed alterations (which preserved 'the style' of the Hospital), gave their unanimous backing to the plan. A draft scheme was duly prepared for submission to the Court of Chancery for approval.

It would seem, however, that the court delayed its deliberations, because nothing relating to the matter appears in any of the minute books until November 1856, when the Nominees discussed a letter they had received from the Attorney-General. He stated that he was in the process of preparing a new scheme for the administration of the school in the light of the plans he had received from the Society for accommodating increased numbers 'in new buildings' and now sought the views of the Nominees. Would they, instead, prefer 'the removal of the school to the neighbourhood of Bristol?' In their reply, they stressed that they 'would prefer the enlargement of the present building to the removal of the school from the present site, because by adopting the former course a large expenditure would be avoided; and the present site, affording ample space for enlargement, had always been found extremely healthy and in every respect convenient for the charity'. They also took the opportunity of urging the Attorney-General to ensure that, in any increase in numbers, 'the Founder's will' would be respected in maintaining the proportion of 'country boys' born outside the city of Bristol (for whom they were responsible).

By 3rd August 1857, after further discussion between the Society and the Attorney-General, a new scheme of administration had been approved by the Master of the Rolls, giving the Society authority 'to enlarge and alter the present school buildings of the Hospital by adding classrooms and dormitories with such other accommodation as may be required by reason of the increased number of boys' (and to borrow up to £4,000, if necessary). Exact details of the alterations, however, would first need to be sanctioned by the Charity Commissioners. Confirmation was also given, to the delight of the Nominees, that the proportion of 'town' and 'country' boys would continue as before in the ratio of 4:1. However, in view of the rapid expansion of Bristol and the fact that recruitment of 'town' boys had been limited by Colston's settlement to those born within 'the ancient limits' of the city, the new scheme ruled that in future the limits should be extended to those of 'the present borough'.

In spite of gaining this approval, however, the Society began to show a marked hesitation in putting the scheme into operation. Nine months later (May 1858), it was even wondering whether the school needed new buildings at all. The Visiting Committee was therefore instructed 'to ascertain if an additional number of boys could be received into the present building' - or whether it would be better 'to postpone the same' until a larger outlay became available. After inspecting the buildings, the committee stated firmly that, in view of the sanitary condition of the school, 'it would be extremely inadvisable, if impracticable, to add to their number in the present building'. Furthermore, it advised the Society to seek the opinion of the Charity Commissioners before employing an architect to design any additional accommodation. Serious doubts were clearly now evident about pursuing that course of action, which had been so confidently and enthusiastically promoted just one year earlier. By the autumn the plan had been abandoned in a dramatic turn of events.

Decision to move to Stapleton

On 9th September 1858, the Society reported to the Nominees that it had been 'found difficult and very costly, if not impossible, to enlarge the present school buildings' to accommodate the additional boys. It therefore asked the Nominees to comment on the possible 'removal of the school into some healthy situation in the neighbourhood', adding that the former Bishop's Palace at Stapleton was now on the market - a fine building, which had been the episcopal residence of the Lord Bishop of Gloucester and Bristol (James Henry Monk) from 1840 until his death in 1856. The seven Nominees present gave their unanimous backing to the proposal. Next day, the Society's Charity Committee (formed in 1852 to deal with the affairs of all its charitable operations), having resolved 'that the present buildings and accommodation are insufficient', considered the 'eligibility and expediency of purchasing Stapleton Palace and estates for the purposes of the Hospital'. Events now moved with such speed that, on 22nd October 1858, the Society signed a contract to buy the house itself and 9.5 acres on behalf of the Hospital for £6,000 (to be raised by loans at 4% interest and paid off as income permitted) and the remainder of the estate for the Society's own use for a further £6,000 out of its own funds.

Having obtained the support of the Charity Commissioners, the Society quickly put forward its plans to the Master of the Rolls for approval. Meanwhile, the Society's decision had aroused a storm of protest. Thirteen members of the Society (led by Mr John Salmon), one of Colston's Nominees and the widow and family of Mr E.F. Colston (as kin of the founder) filed objections to the Attorney-General, while other opponents included many members of Bristol Corporation, several Bristol clergy (led by the Reverend John Hensman) and some 400 leading inhabitants of the city. In all, six past Masters of the Society voiced their opposition in various ways. Their arguments against the removal of the school, put forward in the Court of Chancery and summarised in the local press, were based on a mixture of fact, emotion and sentiment.

The present site, they argued, 'was, in point of health, quite on a par with the other parts of the city - as substantiated by a study of the register of deaths at times of epidemic; the present buildings could in fact be adapted for extra pupils at a cost of no more than £2,000; it was 'undesirable to violate the will of the founder by removing the boys from the city with which their friends are connected and in which, in all probability, they are destined to live'; the boys 'would have luxuries, which they ought not to receive'; and the the city itself would lose an institution which was 'calculated to operate with force as a moral example'. Furthermore, the Hospital was 'an object of affection and regard to them, as one of the ornaments of the place'; its removal would be injurious 'to the general lustre and importance of the city itself', as witnessed each year by the procession of the boys at the Colston's Day celebrations.

This more emotional response was underlined by one local citizen in the correspondence column of the *Bristol Mirror*: 'I lived in College Green and the neighbourhood for many years and it was to me and many others a most pleasing sight to see Colston's boys go regularly to the

A drawing of The Great House and the boys in Hospital dress. (From J.W. Arrowsmith's Dictionary of Bristol)

cathedral. It was a living monument to a great man...It was an excellent example to others to do likewise. Now, alas, the boys are gone from the old city to a palace at Stapleton - an unhealthy, damp place with low rooms and want of ventilation'.

The Society's case, on the other hand, was summarised in the press as follows: 'It was contended that the confined nature of the present building was inimical to the health of the pupils, to keep whom in health the Master was compelled to give them frequent walks to the downs, two miles off; that its dimensions are inadequate to the accommodation of a large number of boys; and that it could only be enlarged at an expenditure of £4,000 and with the purchase of adjacent property costing an additional £3,000. That the present schoolroom looks out on St Augustine's Place, in which, on Sundays and at other times, large numbers of idle boys and girls are in the habit of congregating; that the neighbouring buildings are occupied by persons in a low class of life ; and that the boys, in passing through those areas, are exposed to the influence of bad example; and that it was desirable to remove the school to a locality where there would be, physically and morally, a more healthy atmosphere'.

In summing up, the Master of the Rolls said that the main issue was 'what was for the benefit of the charity'. He had therefore discounted much of the evidence concerning loss of lustre to life in Bristol. These sentimental arguments were 'of too thin and slender a description'. In concentrating therefore on what was for the greatest benefit of the boys, he had concluded that the present premises were 'extremely cramped for room' and that the boys would undoubtedly benefit from being in a more airy situation 'measured in acres...instead of being cooped up in a place measured by scores of yards'. In giving judgment for the Society, he added that he had been influenced by the fact that the vast majority of the Trustees and eleven out of twelve of the Nominees, all of whom cared deeply about the school, were in favour of the plan. Nevertheless, he urged the Society to ensure that that the school continued to be involved in the life of the city, including the annual Colston's Day procession - even if this meant providing transport for the boys.

Opening of the New School

Once the plans for transferring the Hospital to Stapleton had been approved by the Court of Chancery on 2nd May 1859, the sub-committee charged with overseeing the operation wasted no time in organising necessary alterations and additions to the former Bishop's Palace. After an inspection of the site by the Treasurer and Headmaster at the end of August 1861, it was agreed that, 'if all the painting were postponed until the next summer holidays,...the boys might be located there by 30th September'. Indeed, the situation was already urgent. The Great House had been sold by auction on 29th August with handover guaranteed by 20th December. The Visiting Committee therefore instructed the Headmaster to make all preparations for effecting the removal of equipment and furniture 'by degrees and in the quietest possible manner' by Tuesday 1st October. In view of an all-day excursion planned for the boys on Wednesday 9th, it was agreed that the boys should afterwards return to their own homes for a long weekend before assembling 'at the new Hospital at Stapleton' the following Monday. The new premises at Stapleton, therefore, were first occupied on 14th October 1861.

The official opening, which took place on 25th January 1862, was attended by the Lord Bishop (Dr Thompson), the Mayor of Bristol, the Master and Members of the Society, the Nominees and several local clergy. These all processed with the boys to Stapleton Parish Church, where a sermon was preached by Canon Barrow, who was himself a member of the Nominees. He stressed that, in spite of its new home, the school would remain 'essentially a Bristol school...Still, as heretofore, when the boys shall be permitted to visit their friends, the streets of the old city will be gladdened by the going to and fro of numbers clothed in the well-known dress and bearing Mr Colston's honoured badge'. After the service, they processed to 'the private chapel of the school', where the bishop conducted the consecration and the boys sang the 100th psalm. All those present were encouraged by a letter of good wishes from Mr Edward Colston, who had originally opposed the move.

The school chapel, which stood just inside the main entrance to the school building, had in fact been the private chapel of the former bishop when he was living in the Bishop's Palace. It had also been used by the parish of Stapleton during the building of their new church, which was consecrated in April 1857. In point of fact, the chapel was not used at first for the school's twice-daily prayers (held instead in the Dining Hall). According to E. Matthews, who had joined the school in 1861, 'the only use of the chapel after the formal opening was as a store room, where the band practised on Saturday mornings. The pulpit was there all my time, and the band members used in turn to go into it and deliver a mock sermon - I think I was one of them'. The chapel was not properly refurbished for school services until 1873 (see page 152).

Financial Implications of the Move

The transfer of the Hospital to Stapleton proved costly and placed the school's finances under considerable strain during the next ten years. The

Society had in fact spent a sum of £14,332 on the new buildings (including £6,000 for the original purchase and £8,332 for alterations and additional furniture). Part of this money (£9,081 in total) was raised from an existing surplus of funds (£3,161), a tax rebate (£920), the sale of the Great House (£3,000) and the sale of some stock held by the charity (£2,000). The remainder (£5,200) was borrowed from the

Statement of accounts relating to the purchase of the Bishop's Palace at Stapleton.
(SMV Archive)

Society of Merchants at 4 per cent interest. They calculated that the annual cost to the charity of all this, to be provided out of income, would amount to £575, including interest on the loan (£208), contributions into a sinking fund to pay off the debt in 14 years (£260), loss of income on the stock sold (£66) and the wages of an extra man (£41). This analysis did not take into account, of course, the cost of boarding, maintaining and teaching the 20 additional boys (who finally entered the school on 20th January 1862) or the need to provide them with books, clothing, bedsteads and bedding.

It quickly became apparent that other charges were also necessary. An additional Undermaster (who became the 'Fourth Master') was hurriedly recruited in December 1861 to teach the extra pupils. By September 1862, the Visiting Committee was considering requests for an increase in salary, to compensate for the increased numbers, from the Medical Officer (raised from £25 to £50 per annum), the Catechist (£10 to £25) and the Singing Master (£15 to £25). By 1868, the situation was becoming so critical that the Visiting Committee confessed in its annual report that it was deeply worried about 'the present state of income'. Indeed, the Society had appointed a sub-committee to examine the state of the Colston Hospital Trust's finances. Its report of 12th June 1868 indicated that, although the Trust still owed the Society £5,200 on its mortgage account, the debt would be paid off from the sinking fund within six years. However, the Trust was also £3,543 in debt to the Society on its current account (including £1,184 in interests payments on the loan) - a sum which was likely to increase by a further £1,000 until the loan was finally cleared. In view of all this, the Visiting Committee was asked to look for ways of saving money through a policy of prudent cuts.

Although this request immediately resulted in delays in the programme for redecoration, an even better opportunity for economy presented itself in the May of that year. When the Second, Third and Fourth Masters resigned in quick succession, Mr Rowlatt (the Headmaster) suggested a restructuring of the staff. The present Porter (who, after nineteen years of service controlling the gate and supervising the playground, was incapacitated 'from advanced age') would be pensioned off and replaced by a 'Commissionaire', who would combine the job of Porter with that of the Drill Sergeant and band instructor. At the same time, the Fourth Master would not be replaced and Mr James Jones, a former pupil and now the Headmaster's apprentice teacher, would be raised to Third Master at a substantially lower salary. The attraction of this plan to the Visiting Committee was considerable. Whereas previously £157 12s 0d had been expended in total on the Third Master (£54 4s 0d), the Fourth Master (£50), the Drill Sergeant

(£12) and the Porter (£41 12s 0d), now only £110 12s 0d would be spent on Mr Jones (£30), the Commissionaire (£54 12s 0d) and the former Porter's pension (£26). The annual saving on staff (£47 4s 0d) was therefore impressive - but the inevitable cost to the quality of teaching was incalculable.

A Healthy Situation

One of the most convincing arguments used in favour of moving the school to Stapleton had been that the situation there would be much healthier than that of central Bristol. James Jones, who was Head Monitor at the time of the move, later wrote: 'What change the new

James Jones, who was a pupil (1858-65) and Head Monitor when the School moved to Stapleton, shown here wearing the traditional Hospital uniform. (SMV Archive)

school was from the old. How delightful to be transplanted from the dingy neighbourhood of Host Street to the open country, from a paved playground enclosed with high walls to a real field surrounded by beautiful trees and shrubs; and from the old, heavy schoolroom with its high windows to the bright reception rooms of the Palace with their French windows, marble fireplaces and ornamental ceilings'. This rosy picture of the new school, however, is somewhat contradicted by E. Matthew, who saw things through the eyes of a younger boy:

> I entered the school 11th November 1861, and I was the first new boy to enter. There was no gas laid on and we had to grope our way about the place; only two candles in the long dorm and one or two on the dining tables. It was dismal and I felt fairly miserable; the other boys seemed to enjoy the darkness, and many a joke was played and traps laid in the passages. The playground was just a rough field and had to be levelled; that fact gave us plenty of fun in wheeling the barrows of turf and gravel.

In most respects, forecasts of good health proved to be accurate. There were, however, a number of teething problems, which seemed to threaten the welfare of the community. It was belatedly discovered (September 1861) that no gas supply was available in Stapleton. Hurried negotiations with the Bristol Gas Company, however, brought an agreement whereby they would supply gas to the school for £50 per annum for a contracted period of five years. The cost would then be reviewed, if the village of Stapleton had meanwhile taken supplies. The heating system, however, proved sadly unreliable, breaking down in both 1866 and 1867.

Far more serious, however, was the problem of sanitation. As early as June 1862, the Visiting Committee 'inspected the boys' privies and urinals and found them very offensive'. The Society's surveyor was asked to produce an urgent report, especially in view of fears that the water supply might have been contaminated through seepage and 'eruptions having broken out on many of the boys'. Fortunately, samples of water taken from the three sources of supply were analysed by a chemist and declared unharmful. Nevertheless, bearing in mind the proximity of the toilets to the kitchen, serious anxiety continued to be expressed by the Nominees, who reacted strongly to the Medical Officer's report on the state of the drains (December 1863). A heated and extensive correspondence ensued between them and the Visiting Committee on this subject. The problem centred partly on the difficulty of gaining proper drainage from the toilets as a result of the geology of the site and partly on the lack of adequate water pressure for the purpose of flushing. It was finally decided (February 1866) that the solution was to empty the tank every three years and to bury its contents in an adjacent field. All parties were happily reassured that, in spite of the appalling smell, there had been no hint of any typhoid outbreak during the first five years of the school's occupation of the site.

The health of the boys, in fact, remained good throughout the decade. There was some sickness, including an outbreak of measles in 1870, which caused the postponement of Prize Giving; and a mild outbreak of scarletina two years earlier, which caused a certain degree of panic. The six infected boys were hurriedly placed in isolation at a house in Montpelier (much to the consternation of local residents); the next half-holiday was cancelled as a precaution; and the changing hut by the swimming pool was hastily dismantled and rebuilt as a sanatorium for future use near the kitchen. The boys soon recovered. Although occasional deaths were reported, arousing a great deal of compassion, the mortality rate remained extremely low, when compared with that experienced in the late eighteenth century. Nevertheless, in 1867, 'a little country boy', named Murray, 'died at the Hospital from rheumatic affection of the heart and, having no parents, was buried at the Bristol cemetery at the expense of the Colston Fraternal Association'.

The sound health of the pupils was undoubtedly due in part to the greater opportunities afforded by the new site for exercise and fresh air. As early as October 1861, the Visiting Committee had given priority to the creation of a substantial playground with a large covered section for shade and shelter. Several trees were ceremonially planted around this area by the Master and Treasurer of the Society during the course of the first year. One of the most important advances, however, came in 1862 with the construction of an enclosed swimming area at the local 'bathing place' by the river. The Visiting Committee decided that it should be one hundred feet in length, surrounded by a wall and served by a 'bathing house' for changing. The pool was officially opened in March 1863 during a visit by the Master of the Society. The committee noted in its minutes: 'The day being very warm and the sun resplendently brilliant, the first class boys were permitted to open the new bathing place'. The members present were gratified not only 'at the thorough enjoyment of the lads', but also at the thought that this new facility would create 'health, happiness and comfort to the poor boys who will there be brought up'.

Other recreational activities also became possible. At the Headmaster's request, a large area of ground was converted into a kitchen garden in 1864 'to give some employment for the idle hours of the elder boys' (under supervision, of course). Croquet, too, was introduced and quickly developed into a popular pastime, although the evidence suggests that it was played in a somewhat boisterous manner.

The 'bathing place' by the river Frome, opened in 1863. By 1906 there were no changing facilities - note the clothes strewn on the bank behind. (SMV Archive)

The list of equipment, maintained by Mrs Rowlatt (who really acted as Matron on the boarding side), reveals that in June 1862 there were 20 hoops, 16 hammers, 6 stumps and 16 balls. By August, 7 hammers, 5 stumps and 3 hoops had been broken - and three items of equipment were missing. On dark winter's evenings indoor entertainment was occasionally provided by magic lantern shows with sets of slides labelled 'astronomy', 'antediluvian' and 'comic'. Boys were sometimes given passes after school hours to visit their friends in Bristol, particularly on the occasion of their birthdays.

Membership of the school's brass band or drum and fife band undoubtedly provided the boys with one of the most popular forms of leisure activity. Although band music had previously been taught by either one of the Ushers or a visiting instructor, from 1868 this duty became the responsibility of the new Commissionaire, who was also the Drill Sergeant. The first man appointed to the post, Daniel Shannon, had been drum major in the 47th Regiment and was allegedly 'a fine player of the cornet'. In view of the fact that the boys were trained by him to give martial displays on major school occasions and to march in a military manner, it can be argued that Colston's Hospital was already developing a type of cadet force. The bands were highly successful and much admired, although the Visiting Committee repeatedly turned down invitations for them to play at charity bazaars. They regularly led processions to the Cathedral on Colston's Day or to the railway station when the boys went out on whole-day excursions; they gave concerts at Prize Giving (in conjunction with the choir) and played interlude music during the annual public examinations.

Judging from a list of available scores for sopranos, altos, tenors and bases, drawn up in 1862, the repertoire of the choir was quite extensive. It consisted of two psalters, six services of canticles, ten anthems (including *The King shall Rejoice* and *Lord of all Power and Might*) and various hymns (mostly contained in the *Congregational Hymn Book*). Their range also extended to a collection of twenty glees (including *Bold, Bad Robin* and *The Village Chorister*) and sixteen songs and choruses (including *Hearts of Oak* and *Cheer Boys, Cheer*).

Every Wednesday evening, the boys assembled in the dining hall for a series of recitations and playlets performed in front of the Headmaster and his guests. According to Charles Rosling, writing thirty-five years later, 'the boys whose names were down had to give a display, either good, bad or indifferent; or else a play or portion of one would be performed, often with no mean skill. Scenery, properties and a drop curtain were all constructed by the boys, and were long in use'. At the time of the 1868 election, The Bell Inn in Stapleton became a committee room for the West Gloucestershire Tory candidate. 'This seemed to fire our political souls' recalled Gosling, 'and we determined to have an election of our own. Candidates immediately sprang up, addresses were issued, and harangues innumerable were uttered, many collisions

The School Band in 1867, the year before the first-ever Drill Sergeant was appointed to train the boys in marching and martial displays. (SMV Archive)

occurred between the contending parties until, upon the same day as the election in the City of Bristol, our polling took place at duly appointed booths within the Playground Shed, and, as returning officer, I had the keen satisfaction of announcing the triumphant return of the Church and State candidate by a whacking majority'.

Excursions and Holidays

The Visiting Committee encouraged with great enthusiasm the new policy of major excursions to broaden the boys' horizons and to make their experience of school enjoyable. The highlights of each year were undoubtedly the invitations they received to visit the estates of the Duke of Beaufort at Badminton, Mr Tufton Knyfton at Uphill Castle (near Weston-super-Mare) and Colonel Master at Knowle Park (near Almonsbury). All three men were members of Colston's Nominees and were visibly delighted to lavish the most generous hospitality on the boys. The sense of adventure, fun and mischief experienced on a visit to Knowle Park in June 1868 was well captured by the local press correspondent. After catching a train provided by the Bristol and South Wales Union Railway from Stapleton Road station to Patchway, the boys marched to the park in military formation with their two bands at the head. After lunch on the lawn, they went into the park for various amusements - some playing cricket, football or leapfrog, while others wandered around the grounds 'in search of subjects of interest'. Their hosts should really have known better! The boys were not disappointed in their search, for 'a hedgehog and several birds were caught'. At 2.00 pm, 'the school marched to the lawn to the appropriate melody of *The Roast Beef of Old England*. Sitting at large tables the boys ensured that the various joints and pies provided 'were dispatched with great gusto'. Sports were then resumed, including a cricket match organised by Mr Tagg, the butler, between his scratch eleven and fourteen of the boys. Young Brooks, who carried his bat for 49, was presented with a new cricket ball as 'man of the match'.

The visit to Uphill Castle in 1867 was just as enjoyable. The boys marched from the station in Weston-super-Mare via the 'new pier', seizing their opportunity to sample donkey rides on the beach. Dinner, which was served in a large tent, was even more impressive with 'rounds of beef of 70 lb weight, veal, lamb, ham, tongue and chicken, with drinkables of a like quantity, and then plum puddings'. After various games, the boys were then 'drawn up in martial order by their drill instructor' and entertained their hosts to a concert of singing, playing and recitation. Then there were races with cash prizes; then 'tea cakes in abundance'; then a shilling for each boy; and, finally, a bun each. It has

to said that Mrs Knyfton, the lady of the house, was a blood relation of
the founder's family.

Some excursions of a more educational nature were organised by the
Headmaster and funded by the Society - including trips to London by
the Great Western Railway for the Great Exhibition in 1862; the
agricultural show of the Bath and West Agricultural Association on
Durnham Down and the Wombwells Menagerie at the Zoological
Gardens on the same day in 1864; and a meeting of the Church
Missionary Society in Bristol in 1870. Other outings, of a more social
nature, were arranged by the Colston Fraternal Association and again
funded by the Society - to Weymouth (1867 and 1870), Teignmouth
(1868) and the Crystal Palace (1869), the latter of which required two
trains to convey the 1,800 members, wives and boys who made the trip.

The Colston Fraternal Association, which held its inaugural meeting
at the school in November 1854, had been largely prompted by the
Headmaster (Mr Rowlatt) and inspired by a similar one at Christ's
Hospital in London. However, the actual spark, which set in motion the
train of events, was a written appeal signed by six boys at the school on
14th November 1853 to their 'friends and patrons'. It read:

> We, the undersigned boys of Colston's Hospital, in the name of the whole
> school, taking into consideration the great difficulty often experienced by our
> schoolfellows on leaving the Hospital, to provide themselves with clothes
> suitable to their several occupations, have resolved, with God's blessing, to
> raise a fund among ourselves to assist each other under these trying
> circumstances.
>
> We confidently appeal to our patrons and friends, and more especially to those
> gentlemen who have been educated in this noble institution, not only to give a
> smiling approval to our plans, but their active co-operation. We purpose that
> every boy in the school on this ever-to-be-remembered day shall give one
> shilling, and henceforward subscribe one penny per week. The money collected
> to be placed in the hands of a treasurer, as soon as we can find a gentleman
> who will kindly undertake the office.

The appeal did not go unheeded. Although it was made, in the first
instance, to the Society of Merchant Venturers and the members of
Colston's Nominees, it was also directed to former pupils of the school.

In fact the sixty or so men, who attended the inaugural meeting in
1854, had all been educated at Colston's and had been convened by
circular letter. According to the *Bristol Mercury*, the aims of the
proposed society were 'to assist boys with outfits on leaving the school;
to advance them sums upon loan, repayable by instalments, as aids to
their starting in business; to relieve them by donations in time of

sickness and misfortune; to help them with pensions in old age, and also to give temporary relief to the widows and orphans of deceased members'. This speaks volumes about the loyalty felt by the 'Old Boys' towards the school, their admiration for its founder and their appreciation for the start they had been given in life. One of their first decisions was to accompany the boys' procession to the Cathedral each year on Colston's Day. Meanwhile, a temporary committee of five, including the Headmaster, was elected to draw up rules for the proper establishment of the association. By the 1860s, the Association had started holding a dinner in November to coincide with the annual meeting and also a summer festival in July (attended by the boys), which included a service in Stapleton Church, dinner and tea in the school dining room and recreational activities outside.

The boys of the school were soon to benefit from the generosity of this group - not only through their annual excursions, but also by means of generous cash donations. At their annual meeting in December 1869 (which preceded the annual dinner, attended by 100 guests), the chairman was able to announce that the association had raised a sum of over £2274 in subscriptions since its inauguration sixteen years earlier. During that period, it had given financial assistance totalling £512 to 171 boys on leaving the school and a further £170 in 'special aid'. During the previous year alone, they had given £3 to each of the 28 school leavers, plus other 'special aid' of £24. It is interesting to note that the association's income included money raised from 'the boys' weekly pence', which had been mentioned in the original appeal. The fund had also benefited in 1865 from its first-ever legacy of £400 from an Old Boy, Charles William Hicks, followed by a further £1,000 ten years later on the death of his sister.

The close relationship between the Association and the school was underlined in 1856, when boys were also present at the annual meeting. According to the *Bristol Times*, 'a beautiful banner' was brought into the gathering, bearing Colston's arms and surmounted with the inscription: 'The Colston Fraternal Association'. A pupil, John Edgell, then stepped forward and said: 'Mr Chairman, Ladies and Gentlemen - the Master and boys of Colston's School, having subscribed for this banner, and I, having had the honour of painting it, hereby present it to the Colston Fraternal Association'.

The move to Stapleton enabled the Society to revise and extend its programme of main school holidays. Although the boys still attended Stapleton Parish Church each Sunday, they were no longer bound by the founder's stipulation enforcing their attendance on Saints' Days and Holy Days at Bristol Cathedral - a policy which had, for instance, resulted in Christmas Day always being spent in school. The new situation, therefore, meant that the Christmas holidays could be extended to four weeks (instead of the previous three days) from December 1861; and that midsummer holidays of four weeks from mid-July could be introduced for the first time in 1862. The Easter and Whitsuntide holidays remained unchanged with just two days (Monday and Tuesday) allocated, although two more days (including Good Friday) were added to those at Easter from 1868.

Sadly some boys, who had no close relatives or who lived a long way from Bristol, were unable to go away for the holidays. In 1862, for example, 5 boys remained at school for the midsummer holidays, 17 at Easter, 24 at Whitsuntide and 9 at Christmas. Additional days and half days continued to be awarded to celebrate special events - a day in February 1863 to celebrate the wedding of the Prince of Wales; half a day in March of that year to mark the planting of an oak tree in the front of the school by the Master of the Society; and the traditional whole day, requested by the Master each year at the end of Prize Giving.

Events of civic importance also took the boys out of school on several occasions throughout the year. The Society was only too well aware of the criticism it had received for removing the school to Stapleton and it was determined to heed the words of the Master of the Rolls concerning the Colston's School's continued involvement in the life of the city. When, therefore, the school was invited to attend the Mayor and Corporation in their perambulation of the city bounds in August 1863, the Visiting Committee readily agreed, 'considering it an excellent opportunity for showing the public that the school was still connected with the city of Bristol'. Similarly, in the following year, it agreed that the boys should take part in the procession for the opening of Clifton Suspension Bridge. A month earlier, they had marched with their brass band and banners to the stone-laying ceremony for the new buildings at Temple Colston School, where they sang several psalms and hymns for the audience. Fourteen months later, they were back for the official opening of the new buildings, having been transported in omnibuses provided at the Society's expense. The school continued, of course, to process each year to the Cathedral for the Colston Day service and to St Stephen's Church for the Society's Charter Day celebrations. Colston's School, therefore, remained very much in the public eye - just as Colston himself remained in the memory of the school. In August 1863, a memorial tablet with a bust of the founder was erected in the entrance hall of the school, while in October 1864, a copy of the portrait of Colston was presented by Mr R.S. Parkman in gratitude for his son's education there. This portrait was subsequently 'trimmed with laurels' each year at Prize Giving.

Control and Discipline

The arrangement of the new buildings at Stapleton enabled the Headmaster and his wife to exercise general supervision over the key areas of school life. The Headmaster's house, part of the additions made to the old Palace, consisted of three rooms on two floors. A door opened from his ground floor rooms into the boys' dining room and another gave access from his upstairs rooms into their dormitories. The Ushers (or Undermasters, as they were now called) had separate bedrooms nearby. Mrs Rowlatt was closely involved in the boarding side of the operation, looking after the boys' clothes and controlling their games equipment. Discipline within the buildings was undoubtedly helped by the more spacious accommodation provided. The Upper Dormitory housed 31 beds with 8 more provided in each of two smaller rooms nearby. There were a further 33 beds in the Middle Dormitory and 40 in the New Dormitory - giving a total of 120 in all. The days of overcrowding, with two or three boys sleeping in a bed, had long since disappeared.

Richard Rowlatt, Headmaster, 1848-1870.
(SMV Archive)

By this stage in the school's history, senior boys were being actively used in the control of younger pupils in all areas within the life and work of the community. In the year 1861, for instance, there were fifty-two monitors who had been chosen with specific tasks to perform under the leadership of a Head Monitor. The list included eight for duty in the dining room (with two monitors on each table), seven for the dormitories, six to assist with clothes, three for supervision of the library and three to help with classes. Others were in charge of ink, bibles, drawing materials, caps, lavatories, bathrooms, combs and brushes, while four individuals assisted the drill sergeant and music instructor with the two bands and the drill. One monitor was responsible for gas, but quite what that entailed is not revealed! Mrs Rowlatt, however, was alone responsible for checking the condition of boys' clothes when they reported back from holiday, listing all those items which were returned 'not properly repaired', 'torn' or 'dirty'.

Although the atmosphere within the school was now much more happy and relaxed, boys unsurprisingly continued to get into trouble. The Pupils' Record Book, 1861-62, contains not only their weekly assessments for performance in the classroom, but also a grade for their contribution to chores assigned to them in the dormitory, the dining room and the playground. The final column with comments on their general behaviour and appearance is most revealing. Boys were frequently described as being 'slovenly', 'ragged', 'dirty', 'untidy' or 'skulking'; presenting themselves with 'dirty hands' or 'dirty badge'; and 'losing books', 'lying', 'being on the [covered] shed', 'copying' or 'telling stories'. Punishments for these offences were recorded by the class teacher. It is therefore interesting to note that, although the public and merciless flogging of boys was now a thing of the past, the cane was used quite regularly for such offences as disobedience, idleness, losing books and being very dirty or troublesome. Other punishments included those of being sent to bed and being kept in detention after school or on Saturday afternoon.

There is little hint in the minute books of boys running away, tearing up their clothes or of being expelled during the school's first ten years at Stapleton. The standards of honesty, set so rigorously by the Society and reinforced by the Catechist, seem largely to have prevailed. Nevertheless, a serious crisis arose in December 1868 when Edward Daniell, a bright boy who had been entered for the Cambridge University Local Examinations in Bristol, was caught red-handed at the end of an examination with a packet of pens belonging to the Fine Arts Academy. Although he had acted 'impulsively' and was extremely remorseful, the Visiting Committee suspended him immediately and recommended his expulsion to the Society. Furthermore, the committee summoned the whole school into the schoolroom, where the Warden spoke to them about the case. 'The boys all appeared deeply to feel the disgrace brought to the school', noted the minute describing the episode. 'They listened with the utmost attention'. He then went on to urge them 'to let those facts sink deeply into their hearts with the earnest prayer to Almighty God that they may be kept by His gracious help and guidance from the most trivial offences'. The committee's personal involvement undoubtedly made a deep impact on the school. Nevertheless, when the matter was brought to the next general meeting of the Society, it was decided not to accept their recommendation for expulsion, but rather to impose a milder punishment instead.

Examinations and Prizes

From 1858, the school regularly entered the eight or so most able boys for the external examinations of the Cambridge University Local Examination Board in Bristol - usually with commendable success. In 1867, the Society responded favourably to a request from the Board to contribute annually to a prize fund so that awards could be made to the most gifted candidates. It therefore agreed to offer 10 guineas each year to the fund, stipulating its wish to endow the following three prizes - Religious Knowledge (4 guineas), English (3 guineas) and Pure Mathematics (3 guineas). Needless to say, the Merchants were delighted when J.M. Hatherley of Colston's was announced as the first winner of the Religious Knowledge Prize against national competition.

Even more popular were the annual drawing examinations set by the Science and Art Department in South Kensington and held at the Academy of Arts in Bristol. From 1853, the school had drawn on the services of the School of Practical Art in Bristol for weekly instruction of all the pupils. Although this arrangement had been temporarily suspended in 1861, when the school moved to Stapleton, it was revived three years later at a cost of £5 per annum. The subject quickly blossomed. Whereas a total of 43 boys had taken the examination in 1864, the number grew to 62 in 1865, 88 in 1867 and 109 (almost the entire school) in 1868. The results were extremely good. Indeed, in 1868, only 8 failed, whereas 18 were graded 'excellent' and 58 'proficient'. Two years earlier, the organisers had considerably tightened up the regulations for controlling the examination by insisting on strict and adequate supervision. So seriously was this taken by the Society that they agreed to supply the Master, the Warden and one other Merchant as invigilators, who would then dispatch the sealed entries to South Kensington 'by the first post'. This was yet another example of the Society's active involvement in the life of the school and its desire to set the highest moral standards as an example to the young.

The school itself continued to hold its own internal examinations. From 1845, the teachers had maintained a daily register of each boy's performance in each lesson, grading his achievement from A to D. Examinations were then held in each subject at Christmas and midsummer with marks duly totalled and positions allocated. All this evidence was then taken into account when prizes were awarded. In addition to these tests, there was the annual 'Public Examination' and Prize Giving, which had also commenced in 1845 (see page 83) and was traditionally held to coincide with the Standing Committee's annual visitation of the school in November. In 1863, it was decided to switch this event to either June or July in the hope of better weather for outdoor activities. Parents were now encouraged to attend.

By 1869, the occasion had taken on a distinct format. The guests arrived at noon for a buffet lunch in one of the classrooms with the ceremony itself commencing at 2.00 pm. The schoolroom was decorated with the school's banners and with what the *Bristol Times and Mirror* called 'creditable specimens of the boys' mapping, writing and drawing'. The proceedings opened with a short concert of sacred and secular music by the boys conducted by Mr Greenwood, the singing master, at the harmonium. The examiner, Canon Barrow, then conducted an oral examination of the boys in scripture, catechism, history, grammar and geography. Musical interludes were sung by the boys in between each subject examination to relieve any boredom felt by the guests. He explained that, for the first time ever, he had already examined the boys in mathematics by means of a written examination. This clearly set a precedent for, in the following year, the examiner (the Reverend E.J. Gregory, who was a former secretary of the Cambridge Local Examination Board) conducted the entire examination 'by paperwork extending over three whole days'. This proved to be the start of school examinations in their present form.

After the public examination had been completed, prizes were presented (over forty in number) to boys who had excelled in both work and behaviour throughout the year. The books, which had been selected individually by the boys, were beautifully bound in leather. After the speeches, each boy was presented with a new shilling by the Master of the Society, who then awarded the school a whole day's holiday in celebration. Finally, there were the customary three cheers for the Queen, the Mayor, the Society, the Nominees and the Ladies, before the school marched out into the playground to music provided by their bands. There, under the direction of their drill sergeant, they put on a display of drill manoeuvres for the entertainment of the guests.

Storm Clouds: the Schools' Inquiry Commission

In many ways, the move to Stapleton made little impact on either the daily life of the school or the system of management. The boys continued to wear their traditional uniform, to attend church on a regular basis, to be catechised each year as a group, to be confirmed when they were older and to be apprenticed when they left. It is true that the number of apprenticeships slowly declined. Whereas earlier in the century, most boys would have expected to have gained training in this way, only 5 out of 16 leavers secured apprenticeships in 1866 and 5 out of 19 in 1868. The Society's Visiting Committee still met at the school at least once each month, organising contracts with suppliers, dealing with requests from possible leavers, discussing invitations, sorting out problems and organising new appointments. The Standing Committee still made its annual visitation to the school each autumn, visiting classes and listening to the formal reading through of Colston's rules in front of the whole school; and the Nominees still met to organise their half of the yearly intake.

Boys with the name Colston were still given priority on entry - so much so in fact that, in December 1868, the Nominees expressed their alarm that this provision in the original settlement was in danger of subverting the founder's actual intentions. They recorded this unease and their fear of abuse in their minutes: 'The number of boys claiming admission to the school under the name Colston is yearly increasing. Large families of the name are known to the Nominees in London, Worcestershire, Gloucestershire, Monmouthshire and Somerset. Five families of the name are now settled in Bristol. During the present year applications for four country boys and two Bristol boys of the name Colston have been received, that is for nearly one-third of the average number of vacancies'. They went on to warn that, unless a check on this development was made, 'the Hospital will become, and that at no very distant time, a school of Colstons instead of Colston's School'.

The academic side of school life, too, had changed little since the reforms inaugurated between 1836 and 1845. The class system of teaching, which had been introduced then, was still operational in 1862 with just three classes (the 1st, 2nd and 3rd in descending order of age) covering the whole school. By 1869, this had been modified to provide a Monitor Division of 26 boys at the top, an Upper Division of 47 boys in the middle (subdivided into the 1st and 2nd classes) and a Lower Division of 45 boys (subdivided into the 1st, 2nd and 3rd classes). The curriculum, however, had changed little, except that boys in the Monitor Division, in addition to being taught all the regular subjects, were given lessons in book-keeping, algebra, geometry and trigonometry - together with 'voluntary studies' in French and Latin.

This continuity, however, was soon to be shaken by powerful forces from outside the school. On 18th December 1865, The Visiting Committee heard that Mr Charles Stanton, assistant commissioner of the Schools' Inquiry Commission had visited both the school and Merchants' Hall. He had 'made many enquiries' in both places, but had expressed himself 'well pleased' with what he had seen. Established in 1864, the commission (which was also known as the Taunton Commission) had been detailed by the House of Lords to inquire into the management of educational endowments. Stanton's report, which was eventually published in 1868, dealt with the three endowed boys' schools in Bristol - the Free School (Bristol Grammar School), Queen

Elizabeth's Hospital and Colston's. He was quick to praise the Society's decision to move the school to Stapleton; noted that the selection of boys at Colston's was fairly made and without any political bias; and admitted that much within the school was 'excellent'.

Nevertheless, he observed that the standard of education was not as high as that at Queen Elizabeth's Hospital, even though the boys stayed for much longer. This he attributed to the reluctance of the Society to introduce more challenging or academic subjects, fearing that by doing so they would raise the education to a level, which was above the social class for whom the school was intended. He noted that even the brightest boys were forced to study 'out of school hours' for the Cambridge Board's Local Examinations. Mr Stanton had observed 'several big boys about sixteen years old, whom the Master was obliged to keep in the upper class on account of their size, but who by no means deserved that place from their attainments'. He went on to wonder if the school was doing enough 'to promote the cause of education' or whether education was taking second place to the Society's desire to give 'charitable support and entertainment' to poor boys. He concluded by expressing his belief that the school had greater potential than was then being realised and that, 'with some little alteration, greater and more worthy results might follow'.

The report, which stung the Society into immediate action, was referred to the Visiting Committee on 5th February 1869 with instructions to consider the age of a pupil's entry and the length of his stay; the desirability of introducing ' a preliminary examination' on which to base selection; and the feasibility of 'extending the education at the school to include natural sciences'. A week later, the committee reconvened to hear the advice of Canon Henry Moseley of Bristol Cathedral, the former Professor of Natural and Experimental Philosophy and Astronomy at King's College, London. They explained to him that the Society's desire was to introduce natural sciences, so that boys on leaving would be 'better fitted than at present for employment in the manufactures and trades of the city'.

Canon Moseley spoke in forthright terms about the deficiencies of their present system, emphasising that the boys remained at school for far too long. The books read by the boys in the Monitor Division, for instance, were no more advanced than those used in the city's elementary schools, while the boys in the Duke of York's School in Chelsea covered all that was taught at Colston's, but left school two years earlier at the age of 14. He strongly urged the adoption of science, although such a system would require a Master and Undermasters who were specially trained and responsible for it, together with 'a laboratory and necessary apparatus'. Practical science should be confined to boys in the Upper Division, entry to which would be determined by examination. He went on to recommend an entrance examination for the school itself, which would remove from masters the burden of having to teach many boys to read; a qualifying age for admission of 9 or 10; and a leaving age of 14 or 15.

Canon Moseley's views, however, did not find favour with Canon Barrow and the Nominees, who felt that the proposals threatened to undermine the basic character of the school. Edward Colston had intended the school to provide a religious and elementary education that would prepare poor boys for 'the humbler employments and duties in life' (for example, jobs as clerks in banks and offices). To introduce an entrance examination and to bring about fundamental changes to the curriculum would constitute a serious breach of trust and a misuse of the charity's funds. The Visiting Committee, on the other hand, was totally supportive of Canon Moseley's plan, believing that the school should now become much more progressive by providing education of a more practical and technical kind. After lengthy discussion and a little compromise, the Nominees gave way and the committee presented its report to the Society on 17th March 1869.

First of all, the report recommended an entrance examination, which would consist of reading aloud a short passage, writing a slowly dictated sentence, calculating a sum of money and - at the insistence of the Nominees - showing knowledge of 'the principles of the Christian religion as laid down in the church catechism'. It then went on to propose a leaving age of 14, except for those going on to take practical science, who would be permitted to remain until the age of 15 or possibly 16 in exceptional circumstances; half-yearly examinations by an external examiner for boys studying practical science; and half-yearly examinations by the Headmaster for the rest of the boys in reading, spelling, writing, geography, history, English grammar, arithmetic and algebra as a test of their suitability to progress into the practical science section.

The Teaching of Science and the Resignation of Mr Rowlatt

The Visiting Committee duly set about the task of implementing the plan. On 26th October 1869, therefore, the first-ever entrance examination was held, conducted by the Visiting Committee and the Catechist on behalf of the Society and Canon Barrow on behalf of the Nominees. The introduction of science, on the other hand, required far more detailed discussion and planning. The Visiting Committee therefore sought advice in December from Mr Coomber, Headmaster of the Bristol Trade and Mining School in Nelson Street. He recommended that mathematics, mechanical physics, experimental physics, chemistry, geography, machine drawing, magnetism and electricity, heat and light and building construction should be taught in the Upper Division of the School. Based on their discussions with Mr Coomber, the Visiting Committee finally presented its report to the Society on 7th January 1870. It recommended that a craftsman or 'sapper' should be appointed to provide instruction in the use of tools; and that, in order to receive grants from the Science Department of the Council on Education, the Headmaster should be qualified in science, either as a graduate or as someone who had passed the advanced grade of the government's science examination at first or second class.

The committee had, in fact, already conveyed the gist of the report to Mr Rowlatt three weeks earlier (18th December 1869) and had firmly stated: 'You as Headmaster will be required to instruct the subject classed under experimental physics and chemistry, while probably your Second Master would take the mathematical subjects and descriptive geography'. He was therefore requested to take the government's science examination forthwith. Rowlatt was furious and wrote back immediately stating 'that he would not think of submitting to the examination of the Science Department, unless he could be sure of passing in the honours list; and, as it was quite beyond his powers to do so, he should not attempt to pass the examination'. Although he felt perfectly competent to teach the subjects, he thought that the Headmaster should be responsible only for 'the moral training and the discipline of the school, as well as the house management'.

The committee remained adamant that the school needed a scientist as Headmaster. Therefore, in spite of his loyal service to the school spanning twenty-one years, Mr Rowlatt was forced to resign on 4th March 1870. He was later asked to stay on until at least the following Christmas, in view of sudden complications which had arisen (see below). Although he agreed to do so, relationships became increasingly bitter, culminating in a most unseemly public row with the Master of the Society in October. This was set against a background of a public examination of the boys, conducted by the Reverend E.J. Gregory, which had for the first time consisted entirely of written papers (see above). It proved to be a much more searching test than those in previous years - so much so, in fact, that the boys had performed badly. At the subsequent Prize Giving, the Master of the Society - in a masterpiece of understatement - expressed in his speech his regret that the standard was 'not quite so high as they had hoped for'; and, at the same time, rather glossed over the Headmaster's resignation. Mr Rowlatt, incensed at the comments made, loudly interrupted the Master - his resignation 'had been forced upon him'; the examination 'was

'The tall, upright figure of the Headmaster with his kindly face and penetrating eye, white neckerchief and long frock coat'- the description of James Jones, who worked under him as a teacher. (SMV Archive)

hurried'; and the boys had not received 'fair play at all'. He even turned to the boys to confirm the inaccuracy of the Master's facts over the number of them who had sat the papers.

As a result of this deterioration in standards and relationships, the Society had no choice but to terminate his employment on 21st December 1870. He was given six months salary in lieu of notice and a pension of 100 guineas a year. Thus the Society had effectively dismissed two successive (and successful) Headmasters, who had steered them through a series of momentous changes in a most creditable manner. Although Mr Rowlatt's departure was undertaken amid considerable bitterness, time proved to be a great healer. After his death in May 1885, the Governors eventually agreed (1896) to erect a brass plate, provided by the Old Colstonians, to his memory in the chapel. His former pupils were always full of praise for his qualities. James Jones, who served under him as boy and teacher, later wrote: 'The tall, upright figure of the Headmaster, with his kindly face and penetrating eye, white neckerchief and long frock coat, seemed not only to make one at once feel his authority, but his stately presence thoroughly harmonised with the old-fashioned Elizabethan school premises...Mr Rowlatt, as a schoolmaster, was a very strict disciplinarian of the old-fashioned kind. A boy took his well-deserved flogging without fuss - yet our Headmaster always strove to be just. He was, indeed, a terror to evil doers, but he had also kindly praise and encouragement for those who did well'.

Charles Gosling, another former pupil, later stressed this human side of Mr Rowlatt's character: 'I have many happy memories of summer evenings, during the year 1870, spent in company with some of the older boys and our dear old Head upon his lawn, where we literally sat at his feet and imbibed knowledge from the large store of learning poured forth from his well-furnished mind. The lessons generally ended with the twilight, and usually an adjournment was made to his strawberry beds or other homes of fruit within his garden, where nourishment for our bodies was as readily supplied to us as nourishment for our minds had been a short while before. Mr Rowlatt was extremely fond of a game of chess, and would often bring his board and men up to one of the classrooms during the winter evenings. Great would be the honour and glory of the lucky lad selected by the Head as his antagonist.'

A New Threat: The Endowed Schools' Act, 1869

Change of a dramatic and far-reaching nature nature was already in the air by the time that Mr Rowlatt had left Stapleton, for great strides were being made by the government in the country at large to establish a national system of education. The Education Act of 1870, therefore, established School Boards in each district to plug gaps in provision by building elementary schools in areas where church schools did not exist. The Endowed Schools' Act of 1869 sought to ensure that long-established schools with charitable endowments (like Colston's) played a part in the new system by using their resources to the best effect. Consequently the Act, which was based on detailed research by the School's Inquiry Commission between 1864 and 1869, aimed at modernising those institutions by drawing up a new scheme of management for each of them after a thorough inspection. Schools would then be classified into three grades, depending on the leaving age which had been assigned to them: i.e. 18 or 19 years of age for first grade schools (designed for professional classes aiming at university); 16 years for second grade schools (targeted at middle class children wishing to enter business or the army etc); and 14 years for third grade schools (catering for children of more humble background, destined for jobs as clerks and artisans).

At the very moment when the Society was drawing up its own plans to introduce science and more practical subjects into Colston's School, the Endowed Schools' Commission sent Mr I.G. Fitch, their assistant commissioner, to Bristol to report on all its endowed schools. After conducting a detailed investigation in 1869, he revealed that, although the three Hospital schools in the city (Queen Elizabeth's, Red Maids and Colston's) had a joint income of £14,000 a year, they only educated some 436 children in all out of a total population of 160,000. He consequently condemned the schools for not using their endowments wisely for the public good - endowments which, if properly employed, could result in a vast increase in the number of boy and girls being educated, especially in day schools. Furthermore, it was wasteful to devote their resources exclusively to the provision of free basic education for poorer children, when many of their parents could afford to pay the two or three pence a week charged by local elementary schools.

Mr Fitch therefore went on to propose, in September 1869, that the trustees of Colston's endowment should in future be responsible for a day school of 300 boys, a day school of 200 girls, a trade school teaching technical subjects to day pupils and a boarding school of 100 boys. All four would be third grade schools with a leaving age of about 14 and would be required to charge modest fees for the majority of pupils. The Society was profoundly shocked by these radical proposals, which would fundamentally change the nature of Colston's School. Therefore, after a meeting with Mr Fitch to discuss his plan in March 1870, the Master and Wardens drafted their initial response. They hoped to find an alternative based on their scheme to introduce practical science, but were quickly advised by their own Charity Committee to abandon all such plans for the time being.

Warned by the commission in August 1870 that it would be two years before their final proposals were published, the Society used the intervening time wisely and spared no effort in a campaign 'to preserve the main design of the founder' by influencing the commission's thinking *before* the scheme was actually finalised. Legal advice was obtained (July 1870), which cast doubt on the Act's authority to overturn Colston's specific wishes on free boarding education for poor boys; detailed counter-proposals were drawn up (March 1871), which sought compromise while maintaining essential principles; a visit was made to the commission in London to discuss these proposals (July 1871); and a petition to both Houses of Parliament was carried by the Duke of Beaufort and Mr Samuel Morley, MP for Bristol, on behalf of the Society (June 1871).

Although the commission's Draft Scheme was at last received in November 1871, the Society remained deeply concerned about the threat posed to the charitable nature of the school by the commission's insistence that all boys should be fee-paying. After heated correspondence between the two bodies, the Society appointed a sub-committee to draw up an Alternative Scheme, which was finalised in February 1872 and forwarded to the commission. It sought to retain the Society's control over the school as governors and preserve its charitable nature for the benefit of 100 poor boys drawn from elementary schools. It agreed that entrance should be by examination and proposed that the Society should take over the Bristol Trade and Mining School by incorporating it with the Hospital. Finally, in a masterly move, it offered to endow the Hospital with a total of £10,000 (including a sum of £5,000 to write off the debt owed to it by the Colston Trustees) - on condition that an amicable agreement was reached by 31st December 1873. This generous gesture was to bring weighty pressure to bear on the eventual outcome of the dispute.

Meanwhile, the Society continued to apply pressure behind the scenes by joining in London the powerful lobby of Church of England Schools, which were similarly threatened by the Act, and sending a representative to sit in on meetings of the Select Committee, appointed by the Commons to monitor the implementation of the Act. For their part, the commissioners eventually produced an Amended Scheme in the light of the Society's alternative proposals. Finally, after further consultations in London, an agreement was reached in July 1873.

The main points of the New Scheme, which was to have a major impact on the life and management of the school, were as follows. The objective of Colston's Hospital Trust (whose responsibilities were now extended beyond the scope of the original school) would in future be 'to supply sound practical and liberal education, not being merely elementary education, in accordance with the principles of the Church of England, for boys and girls by means of schools in or near Bristol'. Colston's Boarding School (which was classed as a third grade school) would be managed by a Governing Body of 23 members, consisting of the Bishop, the Rector of Stapleton, 13 members of the Society of Merchant Venturers, 3 representatives of the Bristol School Board, one representative each from the Justices of Gloucestershire and Somerset and 3 co-opted Governors. Much to their surprise and delight, therefore, the Society was to be given majority control.

As an interim measure, the Nominees were initially asked to fill the five places allocated for Justices and co-optative Governors. Much to the relief of the Society, too, the school was essentially to remain a boarding school for 100 boys, admitted on exhibitions providing free education, food and accommodation (plus clothing 'in special cases of poverty'). The exhibitions were for 'poor boys', now defined as those who had attended an elementary school for at least one year, where fees did not exceed six pence a week. Eighty of these boys were still to be drawn from inside the limits of the borough of Bristol, with the remaining twenty taken, as before, from Gloucestershire, Somerset and Wiltshire. On a further charitable note, the scheme stipulated that preference could be given to fatherless boys or boys whose fathers were 'permanently incapacitated'.

Prospective pupils would be required to take an entrance examination, which would consist of reading 'an easy narrative', writing in 'text hand' and calculating 'easy sums'. If the school found itself oversubscribed with successful candidates, selection was to be made 'in order of merit'. The boys, who needed to be 'of good character' and 'sufficient bodily health', would not be admitted until the age of 10 and would be expected to leave at the end of the term in which they reached 15. The Society and the Nominees, therefore, lost their power to nominate pupils, as they had done under Colston's original scheme. Similarly, the Nominees surrendered their right as official Visitors of the school to the Crown (to be exercise through the Charity Commissioners).

In addition to the 100 exhibitioners, who were to be distinguished by wearing Colston's badge, the Governors were also empowered to admit additional pupils, as space permitted, on payment of an entry fee (not to exceed ten shillings), a tuition fee (between £2 and £6 a year) and boarding fees ('as low as the Governors can fix them'). All pupils would be taught reading and spelling; writing; arithmetic and elementary mathematics; English grammar, composition and literature; French or Latin or both; history; geography; natural sciences; drawing and vocal music. The Society's ambitious plans to introduce more practical scientific and technical subjects were therefore abandoned, although some science and language teaching now appeared in the curriculum.

The Governors were instructed to set aside £100 a year for maintaining a number of leaving exhibitions, which would be open to competition and tenable at any grammar school or approved place of 'liberal or professional education'. This made it possible in future for bright boys at Colston's to progress to Bristol Grammar School, for instance, and eventually on to university. In addition to this new element of competition, accountability also became a fundamental principle of the new scheme. The pupils would be subjected to a yearly examination by a paid external examiner, who would report in writing to the Governors; and the Headmaster would submit his own report to them on the year's achievement.

The Society's concern to maintain the religious nature of the school was largely satisfied - the Headmaster was still required to be 'a communicant member of the Church of England and religious education was to be 'in accordance with the doctrines of the Church of England' - although a conscience clause was inserted at the last minute, giving parents the right to apply in writing to the Headmaster for a pupil to opt out of prayers, worship or religious instruction. This, of course, seriously breached Colston's instructions on the question of dissent (see Chapter 1).

Quite apart from its responsibility for the boys' boarding school, the Colston Hospital Trust was also charged with the task of establishing Colston's Girls' School, a third grade school for 200 day pupils; and taking over and expanding the Bristol Trade and Mining School (which had been established in 1656 in Nelson Street), as and when funds would permit. All these plans were delayed, however, by the depression which hit agriculture during the 1870s, thus seriously reducing the income of the Colston Trust from its Somerset estates. In 1885, however, the Society agreed to help the Trust by taking over responsibility itself for the Trade and Mining School 'for the promotion of scientific and technological teaching'. The school, which became known as the Merchant Venturers' School (and later as the Merchant Venturers' Technical College), moved into new premises in Unity Street which had been purpose-built by the Society. This generous action freed the Trust to devote all its resources to supporting Colston's Boys' School and establishing Colston's Girls' School for 300 pupils (a hundred more than stipulated) on a site in Cheltenham Road. This eventually opened in January 1891, offering 10 free places for girls from elementary schools (the remainder paying £5 a year).

Meanwhile, the Amended Scheme for Colston's Boys' School had been finally ratified in April 1874, coming into operation in March 1875. Although from that point on, the Society of Merchant Venturers was no longer legally responsible for the school, it continued to act as trustee of Colston's endowment and manager of all trust property (except for that occupied the school). Furthermore, as the Merchants continued to dominate the Governing Body, their actual influence was as strong as ever.

Sources used in Chapter 6

D.J. Eames, *The Contribution of the Society of Merchant Venturers to the Development of Education in Bristol* (unpublished MA thesis for the University of Bristol, 1966), pp 97-142

Patrick McGrath, *The Merchant Venturers of Bristol* (Bristol, 1975), pp 370-375

Endowed Schools' Commission, *Scheme for the Management of Colston's Hospital in Bristol 1873* (printed in Eames, Appendix 1)

Society of Merchant Venturers' Archive:

The Hall Book of Proceedings, vols. 22-25 (1855-75)

Visiting Committee's Minute Books, vol. 2, 1848-70; vol. 3, 1870-75

Visiting Committee's Annual Reports, 1842-58

Minutes of the Meetings of Mr Colston's Nominees, vol. 4, 1854-75

Book of the Society's Charity Proceedings, vol.1, 1852-67; vol. 2, 1867-81

Pupils' Records, 1861-62

Files labelled *Colston's Hospital* and *Move to Stapleton* (typed and printed extracts from minutes, letters, news cuttings etc)

The Colstonian, June 1894, February 1895, Autumn 1934

Bristol Times & Farley's Bristol Journal, 27th December 1856

Cribsheet (The Old Colstonians' Newsletter), February 1987 & February 1989

LIFE AT STAPLETON IN THE 1860s

Charles Rosling *(Old Colstonian)*

A day at school in those old times commenced with the clanging of the bell, lustily wielded by the old porter, Lake, somewhere about six in the morning; beds were made, boots cleaned and washing done by seven. That hour saw us ready for the first morning school, which, consisting mainly of preparation of the day's lessons, lasted until eight. Morning Prayers followed in the Dining Hall, preceded by a report by the Head of the School, and succeeded by a presentation of delinquents by the various Form Masters; punishment sharp and decisive usually followed, and those unlucky mortals then ate their breakfast with what relish they could and forgot their sorrows in a quick burst of healthy play, until that merciless bell brought us in again for morning school at 8.45. Work ran on till noon. Dinner was served at 12.30. Afternoon school lasted from two till five, when a welcome breathing time awaited us ere supper was served at six. Preparation, in a strict sense did not exist, the various assistant masters giving us *en masse* a lesson on some general topic of interest until 7.30, after which quiet relaxation was permitted till Evening Prayers were read at eight, when all of us went off to bed.

Our masters entered largely into our out-of-door life, and one could generally see the tall form of the Head looking on at our games, usually carrying a particularly long and flexible cane beneath his arm, and often have I felt its sting in the playground, most commonly for being ragged and untidy. In that time, we all wore the old style dress - and most inconvenient we found our long tails when at play, the consequences often being that we pursued our games in a condition rather worse than that of Falstaff's ragged regiment. After a sound thrashing for such carelessness of appearance, we generally found ourselves sent off to bed, there to stay until we had played the tailor sufficiently well and long enough to render ourselves presentable again.

A periodical function was a Court Day of members of the Governing Body, when a visit was paid by them to the Hospital, and a quaint and curious custom took place. The whole school awaited their arrival in the Dining Hall, the boys being grouped around an old wooden pulpit which then stood beneath the portrait of Colston at the end nearest the Headmaster's house. The Governors were received upon their arrival with a lusty rendering of the National Anthem, sung with vigour by us all, for Colston boys in my day were nothing if not loyal; to this succeeded the reading *in extenso* of the original set of rules drawn up by the Founder for the better government of his Hospital. Then a glee or so would be sung and the inspection of writing and drawing, of which each boy held a specimen, would take place. A tip would generally be bestowed on the lucky fellow nominated by any Governor then present *[i.e. one of the Nominees, who had put forward a boy's name for entry]*; and, if fine, a short parade would be held, and the rest of the day kept as a holiday.

The Bath was an institution greatly valued by us all during the summer, and the Bath House of those days was a building I have seldom seen excelled, so well suited was it for its purpose. It was afterwards removed and the materials used to build a Sanatorium below Parker's Nursery. I very well remember the fun some of us had in hauling up the beams from the Bath to the site on which the new building was to stand. Boys then bathed in the middle of the day, and left school to do so at 11.45. I have often taken a shivering plunge myself in late September or even October, just to escape the few extra moments of school. For during those months, out-door bathing was optional on our part.

(From The Colstonian, *June 1894)*

CHAPTER 7

Years of Stagnation, 1873 - 1901

'Almost daily we have to contend against falsehood, fraud, selfishness and dirtiness in some form or other. These seem to be characteristic propensities of the majority of the boys who come into the school'. (The Headmaster's Annual Report to the Governors, 1889)

The New Scheme in Operation

By fighting an effective rearguard action, the Society of Merchant Venturers had managed to salvage important elements of Edward Colston's original plan for the running of the Hospital. The New Scheme for the school retained its basic provision for one hundred 'poor boys' to be educated free of charge in accordance with the doctrines of the Church of England; and the Society itself effectively retained control of its management. Nevertheless, important changes had been made, which (at least in theory) opened up new and exciting challenges for the future. In particular, the school had ceased to be a purely elementary school; the entrance examination offered the hope of improving the quality of the yearly intake; and the leaving exhibitions provided the brightest boys with the prospect of a ladder of advancement through grammar school to university.

At the annual dinner of the Colston Fraternal Association in December 1869, Mr Proctor Baker (the Master of the Society) was visibly excited about the introduction of the entrance examination. The aim, he said, was 'to raise the whole standard of education...Hitherto boys were admitted who had not even the rudiments of learning: there were boys in the school at present, who were unable to read and who had a natural inability for learning'. The time, talents and patience of the masters, he concluded, were consequently being wasted 'by boys to whom it was impossible to teach anything'.

When, therefore, the new Governing Body met for the first time on 25th March 1875, hopes were high that the school would quickly rise from its recent depths, as typified by the disastrous examinations experienced just five years earlier (see above). The Governors, under the

The Staff of Colston's School in 1874 shown in front of the door into the
Headmaster's house. From left to right - back row: *Louis Antony (French); John*
Hancock (Headmaster); James Greenwood (Music); middle row - *Richard Chester (3rd*
Master); James Jones (2nd Master); Patrick Bourke (4th Master); front - *C.D.*
Rosling. (SMV Archive)

chairmanship of Mr Proctor Baker, decided to meet normally on a termly basis in Merchants' Hall, although much of the detailed work was delegated to their Management Committee (fully responsible, like the previous Visiting Committee, for routine control and planning).

It was perhaps fortunate that a new Headmaster had already been appointed in January 1871 and was therefore able to bring fresh ideas and considerable experience to the new situation. Mr John Hancock, who was 38 years old and married, had been selected for the post from 250 applicants at a salary of £210 per annum (later increased by a capitation fee of £1 for each paying pupil under the new arrangements). An Associate of King's College, London with a first class certificate from both the Council of Education and the Science Department, he had previously been Headmaster of Marylebone Eastern District School for 400 boys, before teaching at Cheltenham Proprietary School. By 1875 (when the New Scheme commenced), his staff consisted of Mr James Jones (Second Master with a salary of £100 per annum), Mr Richard Chester (Third Master, £80), Mr Patrick Bourke (Fourth Master, £50), M Louis Anthony (French teacher, £35) and the Reverend I.F. Marillier (Catechist, £25). There were eight female servants (together costing £100 per annum), a Porter (who also taught drill, 21 shillings a week) and a gardener (who was also in charge of the sanatorium, 15 shillings a week).

Early Disillusionment

In March 1875, the school roll totalled just 88 boys (including no fewer than 39 orphans), the slump in numbers being attributed to the fact that admissions had been largely frozen while the future of the school had remained uncertain. The Governors, therefore, wasted no time in attracting new recruits, placing advertisements in local and county papers to advertise the availability of places for both 'exhibitioners' or 'foundationers' (i.e. boys on free places from elementary schools) and fee payers. A prospectus was also circulated to attract the latter, stressing that the school had been 'adapted to the wants of the sons of farmers, tradesmen, clerks and others'; listing the subjects taught and the facilities on offer; and itemising the fees of £31 per annum (including £5 for tuition, £20 for board and lodging, £5 for uniform and £1 for books and stationery). By 1876, the numbers had risen to 108 (including 17 fee payers) and, by 1878, to 145 (including 49 fee payers). Over the next four years, the total numbers fluctuated between 122 and 137, including an average of 46 fee payers.

Although these numbers were encouraging at first sight, the Headmaster (Mr Hancock) quickly became disillusioned about the general situation within the school. In a series of forthright annual reports to the Governing Body, he launched scathing attacks on both the attitude of the pupils and the terms of the New Scheme. The standard of exhibitioners coming into the school was abysmal - they were, in the main, 'hardly mediocre' with several 'particularly dull and backward'. To compound the situation, they were 'incorrigibly idle'. The number of applications for entry was often so disappointing that the school was obliged to lower the standards it had set. Indeed, in 1879, with only 22 eligible candidates to consider as exhibitioners, the Governors were forced 'to depart from their usual practice of electing no boy who obtained less than half marks in the examination'. The Headmaster particularly bemoaned the fact that, with the younger leaving age imposed by the New Scheme, these weak pupils now had just four years at most to improve and reach the expected level. This was impossible.

Furthermore, the behaviour of the exhibitioners was often deplorable. Shortly after his appointment, Mr Hancock had been forced to discipline three boys who had sneaked out of school one Saturday evening in 1872 to drink at The Bell public house opposite. 'If we are to have tippling, in addition to lying, cheating and dishonesty,which already are rife', he complained, 'heaven only knows where we shall drift next'. The situation had not improved by 1878, when he confessed to the Governors that he had dealt with 'a greater amount of fraud, falsehood and theft, obscene language and actions, low swearing and wilful blasphemy' than ever before.

Such had been the impact of this on the school that he had received letters of complaint from parents of the better boys (especially the fee payers), who were unwilling to subject their sons to 'influences so strongly adverse to their previous home training'. The Headmaster had already commented, in his 1876 report, on the friction that had been caused by 'the introduction of the new element - paying boarders'. He was quick to point out, however, that the trouble had entirely stemmed from one source - 'the ill feeling and unkindness manifested by the old foundationers towards the newcomers'. He had found no instance of 'a paying boy acting unkindly or otherwise improperly towards a foundationer'.

Faced with this worrying situation, Mr Hancock launched a sustained campaign to bring about reform. First of all, he determined to root out troublemakers. For instance, those boys who had been drinking in The Bell in 1872, were beaten and deprived of all holidays until further notice; five boys were first suspended and then expelled for poor work and behaviour in 1876; while Alfred Wilson was expelled for theft and Malcolm Thompson for persistent disobedience in 1880. Secondly, he exerted steady pressure on the Governors to recruit more fee payers and to seek a change in the leaving age from the Charity Commissioners.

He argued that the fee payers, whose attitude was much more positive in general, tended to be swamped by the greater number of exhibitioners. There was, therefore, a strong case for equalising the numbers and ensuring that the fee payers were given time to reach the top class (many did not join the school until they were twelve and were forced to leave as soon as they reached fifteen). 'Their example and influence would greatly benefit the moral tone and discipline of the school, if they could remain long enough to become prefects', he argued.

Mr Hancock set great store on the leadership of older boys, regretting each year the loss of his 'leading boys' just as they were beginning to exercise responsibility. 'There is no boy whose age or influence will fit him to succeed the present Head Boy', he lamented in 1881. Although a system of Monitors under a Head Monitor had operated during Mr Rowlatt's headship, the term 'Head Boy' was introduced by Mr Hancock in 1871, along with the term 'Prefect' (though these titles often remained interchangeable with the term 'Monitor'). By 1894, there were eight Monitors, including a Head Monitor, a Captain of Football, a Captain of School, a Senior Librarian and a Custos of Games. Furthermore, the Number '76' was no longer given to a boy on admission, but (from 1889) granted as a reward to a boy who had already proved himself worthy in both behaviour and example - normally the Head Boy or another Prefect/Monitor.

The Headmaster's main concern, therefore, was to improve the school by attracting more of the better quality fee payers. He therefore wanted to ensure that they had time enough at Colston's to develop their own potential (which was often greater than that of the exhibitioners) and to improve 'the moral tone' by exercising a strong leadership role within the school. The Management Committee supported his request in 1878 to increase the size of the school to 200 (thus catering for 100 fee payers), but reluctantly was forced to postpone the implementation of the plan. It concluded that the funds at the time would not permit the building of the extra accommodation required, including a new dormitory, a large schoolroom and a science laboratory. Indeed, the goal of achieving 200 pupils in the school was not to be achieved until much later. Meanwhile, the Governors decided instead to spend what money they had on providing more attractive facilities for the 150 boys who could already be housed (including improvements to the dormitories, better toilet facilities, central heating in all the rooms and a decent fresh water supply) and a new advertising campaign to boost the recruitment of fee payers.

This policy met with initial success. In 1884, for instance, 157 pupils were on the school roll (the highest number ever reached to that point), including 85 exhibitioners and 72 fee payers. The Headmaster's dream of equalisation was apparently well within his grasp. Any optimism, however, proved to be short-lived. By 1889, the total had dropped to 135 (with 89 exhibitioners and 46 fee payers) and by 1893, it had slumped to 119 (including 89 exhibitioners and just 30 fee payers). It is also worth noting that the school, during the first twenty-five years of the New Scheme, never once reached its allocation of 100 boys on free places. The policy of seeking to achieve a more equal balance between exhibitioners and fee payers was not achieved until after 1910, when a further scheme for the management of the school, drawn up by the Board of Education (see Chapter 8), lowered the maximum number of exhibitioners to 75, thus opening the way for a sizeable increase in fee payers.

William Proctor Baker, Chairman of Governors, 1875-1907. (SMV Archive)

Mr Hancock did, however, manage to achieve one of his stated ambitions some years before his retirement. In 1883, the Governors were finally persuaded to seek permission from the Charity Commissioners to amend article 75 of the New Scheme, which stipulated that no boy could remain in school after he had reached the age of fifteen. The Governors applied 'for leave to retain twenty boys in the school until the end of the term in which they attained the age of *sixteen*, and five of this number until the end of the school term in which they attained the age of *seventeen* years'. The commissioners agreed - but only with regard to fee paying pupils. Exhibitioners were still bound by the previous restriction, which limited their free places to five years duration. When, therefore, the Headmaster made his annual request to the Governors for specified boys to be allowed to remain in the school 'after the usual leaving age', the rider was always added to the minute that 'no free place boy could stay for more than five years'. Nevertheless, it was technically possible to circumvent this ruling, as an exhibitioner named Goodwin discovered in 1889. Although he had been at the school for five years, his mother was so keen for him to stay on until he was sixteen that she agreed to pay the cost of the extra year herself. This was accepted.

A 'Mutinous Spirit', 1889-91

From the time of his appointment, Mr Hancock had been deeply critical of the 'moral tone' within the school and, although occasionally noting 'some improvement' in his annual report to the Governors, he frequently suggested that the situation was unsatisfactory. He blamed in turn the New Scheme, which ensured that his best boys were forced to leave before they became prefects; the unprincipled background from which the exhibitioners were drawn; and the untruthfulness of those who had supplied character references prior to a boy's admission. He failed, however, to blame his own shortcomings - his low expectations of the boys entrusted to his care, his pessimistic view of human nature and his failure to provide a positive lead to masters and boys alike.

Nor was the Headmaster alone to blame for the distinct change of atmosphere, which had been witnessed in the school since the time of Mr Rowlatt. The minute books of the Governors and Management Committee no longer bristled with excitement and a sense of fun. There were no more lively excursions to Badminton or Weston-super-Mare involving the whole school (and organised by individual Merchants or Nominees) - or, if there were, they were not considered to be of sufficient importance to be noted in the minute books. Of even greater significance was the fact that the Management Committee usually met at Merchants' Hall in Bristol and not at the school in Stapleton (except, that is, when a crisis had occurred or the fabric needed inspection). Whereas the old Visiting Committee and the former Nominees had always met on the site and had become personally involved in the everyday life of the school through frequent visits to lessons and pep-talks to boys, the new Governors (with a considerable element of representatives from outside bodies) became much more remote. Furthermore, although in theory the new entrance examination was a sensible reform in itself, the school lost one main benefit of the old system - namely that it relied on the individual nomination of boys by Merchants and Nominees based on personal knowledge. References supplied by outsiders proved to be much more unreliable, as Mr Hancock had found to his cost.

Serious disciplinary cases abounded. In May 1876, for instance, five boys were suspended and later expelled for gross insubordination and dishonesty, after 'a series of petty larcenies' in the masters' dining room. They had apparently raided supplies of bread, butter and sugar during the night on a number of occasions, opened two staff lockers 'with a false key' and 'regaled themselves with biscuits, cocoa and methylated spirits under the supposition that it was gin'. Furthermore, 'their carousels were also enhanced by the smoking of cigars and cigarettes', the latter stolen by a young new boy from his mother's shop, after he had been 'induced' to do so. No sooner had the Headmaster 'obtained a clue', which directed suspicion towards the five boys, than the two ringleaders absconded in the hope of escaping abroad by ship from Cardiff. The Headmaster's distress over this disgraceful episode was compounded by the fact that several other boys 'had subscribed money towards the elopement of the two ringleaders' - another example, he was quick to stress, 'of the low moral tone of the school'.

Although the Headmaster had, in 1883, secured an extension of the leaving age for his better boys (which he had promised would transform the 'moral tone'), within five years the situation had deteriorated even further. A most serious crisis hit the school in 1888, which was to have an adverse effect on performance, morale and recruitment over the next few years. In February, the Management Committee was informed that three boys had run away. Their ringleader, when caught, was duly expelled as an example to others. Shortly afterwards, however, the committee received a letter from the father of one of the other boys involved, alleging that his son had previously been ill-treated by two masters, Mr Hamilton (the Fifth Master) and Mr Evans (the Junior Master). When interviewed, they were severely reprimanded for pulling the boy 'by the ears and hair' and reminded that corporal punishment 'of any kind and degree' was reserved for the Headmaster. Worse was to follow. Shortly after this episode, the committee went out to Stapleton to investigate why two other boys had run away during the night. It duly interviewed a number of pupils, including several reliable monitors, and discovered that the runaways had left a note for the Drill Sergeant, alleging that one master 'had been down on them'. The Governors present then interviewed Mr Charles (the Third Master) and decided that he should be dismissed.

By April, the Headmaster had reported that Mr Evans (the Junior Master, who was reprimanded earlier) had resigned and that it had come to his knowledge that 'the moral character' of the Reverend A.D. Sylvester, his Second Master, was so 'bad' that he had requested his letter of resignation. Meanwhile, the Management Committee had been drafting a letter of their own to Mr Hancock. They had been deeply disturbed by their visit to the school, which had 'disclosed a complete absence of sympathy between the assistant masters and the boys, and many causes of reasonable discontent on the part of the latter'. They were astounded that the Headmaster had been aware of the matter for at

To the Governors of Colston's School

My Lords & Gentlemen,

I have the honour of laying before you the following brief statement respecting the School, for the year ending April 24 1884.

The numbers on the Registers at the Commencement of the School year [Ap.l 28. 83] were as follow:—
Nominated Scholars 92; Paying Scholars 49: Total 141; and the following Changes occurred:-

Admissions	1st Term	2nd Term	3rd Term		Totals
Nominated Scholars	0	10	0	=	10
Paying Scholars	8	11	6	=	25
Total —	8	21	6	=	35

Withdrawals	1st Term	2nd Term	3rd Term	Totals
Nominated Scholars	5	6	7	18
Paying Scholars	6	6	6	18
Total	11	12	13	36

The numbers on the Books therefore at the end of the School year [Apl 24.84] were Nominated Scholars 84; Paying Scholars 56; Total 140.

The health of the boys during the last two terms has been on the whole very satisfactory. The epidemic of Scarlatina to which I called the attention of the Governors in my last report persisted more or less to the end of the first term and into the first fortnight of the Summer holiday.

The work of the School has I fear been a little arrested by the somewhat wholesale change of masters in the Summer; and again last term by the illness of one of the Assistants. Except for this I think I should have had the pleasure of reporting a somewhat higher standard of work.

In the moral tone of the School I may venture to report some improvement. I hope, however, to see a still further improvement. The permission for boys to remain at School a year longer, judiciously granted, will, in addition to other advantages, be a great help towards maintaining this improvement. Nine of our elder & better boys have already availed themselves of the privilege. I beg to take this opportunity of thanking the Governors for obtaining this great boon from the Charity Commissioners.

Extract from the Headmaster's report to the Governors in April 1884 on the latest numbers, health of the boys, work in the classroom, the wholesale turnover of staff and 'the moral tone of the school'. Mr Hancock was famed for his copperplate handwriting. (SMV Archive) least a year, judging by a circular he had sent to the masters on this subject, and that the had failed to inform the committee. The actions he had taken to remedy the problem had been largely ineffective and showed a total lack of leadership. Furthermore, they had unearthed the fact that 'many and heavy complaints of improper forms of corporal punishment' had been made by boys and parents for some time; that there had been 'a laxity of behaviour and a neglect of discipline among both masters and boys'; and that Mr Hancock had refused a recent request from a parent to investigate a complaint by his son against a master. The Headmaster was duly reprimanded and warned by the committee that they wanted 'a more friendly feeling' to be cultivated within the school.

Before the summer was out, Mr Hamilton (the Fifth Master, who was reprimanded earlier) had resigned; Mr Robinson (the Fourth Master) had left - presumably in despair; and Mr Brown (the new Second Master appointed to replace Mr Sylvester) had moved on to a Headship within just two months of his appointment at Colston's. By December, M Lestang (the French teacher) had also resigned - and two more boys had been expelled for theft. The whole teaching staff (apart from the Headmaster and the Singing Master) had therefore left the school, much to the disruption of its academic programme. The Headmaster was quick to take up this theme in his next annual report (July, 1889), preparing the Governors no doubt for some poor examination results. The effect of losing five masters so quickly, he said, was 'disturbing to the discipline of the school and the cordiality which ought to subsist between masters and boys'. The inevitable result was 'friction'. He went on to launch his usual diatribe against the 'moral tone' of the school: 'Almost daily we have to contend against falsehood, fraud, selfishness and dirtiness in some form or other. These seem to be characteristic propensities of the majority of the boys who come into the school'.

The Governors reacted sharply to this pessimistic report, discussing 'at some length the unsatisfactory state of the school, which it appeared to disclose'. The Chairman wryly pointed out that, 'although the tone of the school was low when he was appointed Headmaster nineteen years ago, the Governors had hoped that he would have raised it to a much greater extent than seems to be the case'. While Mr Hancock was quick to take the point and actually avoided any mention at all of the 'moral tone' of the school in his next report (January 1891), the problem of establishing a settled staff still remained. By the time he delivered his report, the replacements appointed as Third and Fifth Master had already left and, by July, the new Second Master (Mr Searle) had been asked to resign. This followed the discovery that 'a mutinous spirit appeared to exist in the school against Mr Searle, who was not popular among the boys by reason of his supposed unfairness'. On a brighter note, the Headmaster was able to announce that two former pupils had been appointed to fill the vacancies - Mr Clevely as Third Master (who had been in the very first batch of boys recruited under the New Scheme) and Mr Crouch as Fifth Master (who had been one of the first boys at Colston's to be awarded a leaving exhibition, tenable at Bristol Grammar School). Mr Hancock felt that these former pupils would at least feel 'more at home' in the atmosphere of the school!

Sadly, the arrival of these staff reinforcements made little apparent difference to the behaviour of some of the boys. Expulsions continued. In 1892, therefore, three boys were excluded because they were 'idle and materially below the standard of position and attainments proper to their age; in 1895, Sydney Tinklin for theft and 'general bad behaviour'; in 1897, William Bruton 'on account of his extremely filthy habits'; in 1898, Sidney Goodwin for 'idleness' and dismal performance; and in 1901, William Batman for disgraceful behaviour, his guardian being sent 'a copy of a letter written by Batman and of a shockingly indecent character'. Nor did changes to the composition of the staff bring about an improvement in the conduct of the masters. In 1897, Mr Calway (the Fourth master) was found 'guilty of indecent conduct with one of the boys' and dismissed without notice; and in 1900, after Mr Christie (the Second Master) and Mr Williamson (the Third Master) had lodged formal complaints against each other, it was decided that it was 'not for the good of the school' that either should remain. They were therefore removed. In all, there were no fewer than nine staff changes between 1897 and 1901 - a massive turnover in such a small school.

Life at Colston's, 1873-1901

The appointment of a new Headmaster in 1871 and the increased scrutiny of the school by government commissioners had combined to bring about a number of changes to life within the school. Shortly after his arrival, Mr Hancock had requested permission to amend the rule stipulating that each boy should be in bed by 8.00 pm. There were two serious disadvantages to this system, he explained. First, by the time the boys had finished their lessons at 5.00 pm, had had supper, cleaned their boots, brushed their clothes and said their prayers, there was only half an hour left for the preparation of next day's lessons. This was inadequate for the older boys who, furthermore, found it impossible to sleep at such an early hour. There was therefore, much 'surreptitious carrying to bed of schoolbooks'. He was keen to provide the boys with the opportunity for 'real learning and study' on their own. Bedtime was therefore extended for the older boys (at the Headmaster's discretion) to 9.30 pm at the latest.

School meals were also reviewed. By 1875, when the Governors re-examined the boys' diet, improvements had already been made to the weekly menu, which had been established in 1837 (see pages 61-62). Breakfast now included dripping or treacle, to accompany the bread and butter, and coffee with sugar and milk. The main midday meal (dinner) now always consisted of a meat ingredient (boiled or roast beef, roast mutton, hashed meat, pea soup with meat etc.) with either bread or potatoes and fresh vegetables. Broth and plum pudding were no longer in fashion. Desserts, too, had made their first appearance, including suet pudding, rice with sugar, fruit and jam tart. Although supper continued to consist essentially of bread and cheese, the boys were now also offered coffee or cocoa with milk and sugar - with a special treat of bread, jam, cake and tea on Sundays. The Governors decided to make further improvements to this diet (although these are not specified in the minutes) - a move which enabled them to boast in their new prospectus that 'the dietary is substantial and abundant'.

The school uniform was another aspect of life to experience change during the last quarter of the nineteenth

Colston's Hospital, Stapleton

LIST OF ARTICLES TAKEN HOME BY
.... No. ....

....

2 Coats, 2 prs. Breeches, 1 Vest, 3 Shirts, 2 prs. Stockings, 2 Bands 1 pr. Drawers, 3 prs. Shoes, 1 pr. Slippers, 2 Caps, 2 Girdles, 1 Bag containing 2 Combs & 2 Brushes.

Parents and Guardians are requested to take notice that every article taken home must be returned *clean and mended*, and if damaged or lost must be made good.

It is expected that Boys' *Best Clothes* will be restricted to Sunday wear only ;—it is on this condition that they are allowed to be taken home.

The School will re-assemble on

....

and every boy must be in his place, without fail, not later than Eight o'Clock in the evening.

JNO. HANCOCK,
Head Master.
187

List of clothing taken home by boys at the end of a term - issued by Mr Hancock to parents during the 1870s. Note that boys were permitted to wear these items while on holiday, although this agreement was ended in 1885. (SMV Archive)

century. In 1875, the Management Committee, after viewing sample materials, decided to 'modernise' the dress by introducing a number of modifications to the traditional Hospital uniform. The long blue tunic was replaced by a blue jacket with silver buttons - and the tight breeches by loose-fitting blue knickerbockers with red piping; and the soft, flat cap by a 'kepi' (i.e.. a cap with a horizontal peak). The original bands were discarded; a leather belt took the place of the girdle; and boots were issued instead of the brass-buckled shoes (see photograph below). Old Boys were to look back later with affection to this 'striking costume, somewhat like the uniform of a French soldier of the period'.

The Committee issued their 'New Clothing Regulations' in 1877, requiring parents to sign an agreement with the school. For the first time, all parents were charged a clothing fee of £5 per annum, though the

G.W. Pearce in 1885 (aged 13), wearing the revised uniform (which had been introduced in 1875) just before it was discontinued. Note the jacket, silver buttons, loose-fitting knickerbockers, leather belt, boots and kepi. (SMV Archive)

Governors were empowered to remit this 'in special cases of poverty' - and often did so, in fact, for several exhibitioners each year. In return, the school provided each boy with 2 blue tunics, 2 pairs of knickerbockers, 1 leather belt, 1 kepi, 2 pairs of boots, 6 pairs of boot laces, 1 pair of leather slippers, 4 pairs of scarlet woollen stockings, 4 day shirts, 2 night shirts and 3 pairs of drawers. The life expectancy of each item was clearly stated (ranging from 9 months to 3 years). The clothes were to remain the property of the Governors, who would reallocate them to other boys as and when necessary (although, from 1872, they had agreed to 'disinfect' the clothes before passing them on and to use 'a travelling tailor' for repairs). For their part, the parents agreed to provide 2 under-flannels ('if worn'), 6 handkerchiefs, a pair of garters, a pair of braces, 2 combs, a hair brush and a tooth brush.

This uniform, however, was again substantially modified in 1885, when the tunics and knickerbockers were replaced by blue patrol jackets (which were braided and fitted with hook-and-eye fasteners up the front and high collars) and short trousers; the kepis by 'polo caps' (i.e. round forage caps with chin strap fastenings); and the scarlet stockings by blue ones. In future, boys would not be permitted to wear their uniform during the holidays or when working either as messengers or shop assistants. Three years later, it was decided that a dolphin badge, stamped out of 'white metal' and 'the size of a florin', was to be worn on the cap. In 1890, finding through experience that the blue dye of the boys' stockings was 'not a fast colour', the Governors agreed to substitute a heather mixture instead. This new uniform, which proved to be unpopular, uncomfortable and unattractive, was widely criticised at the time by Old Colstonians, the citizens of Bristol and the local press.

Although clubs and societies did not really operate to any great degree until after Mr Hancock's retirement in 1901, the school band continued to flourish, as did the school choir - although, from 1891, it was decided that the choir should no longer sing at Sunday services in Stapleton Church (which had been the previous practice), but only on 'Red Letter Saints' Days'. After conducting a survey on the amount of time spent by boys on both singing and practices, the Headmaster concluded that their work was suffering. The musicians, however, normally combined for an annual concert in the dining room in December, followed later by a carol concert just before Christmas. The cause of music was enhanced in 1878 by the introduction of voluntary piano lessons paid for by parents. Apart from these activities, there was very little entertainment provided - although a 'magic lantern' was purchased in 1890 for slide shows of an educational nature during winter evenings.

Nevertheless, the boys were always ready to compensate by

The School Band in 1894, wearing the new uniform which had been introduced nine years earlier. Note the the patrol jackets with high collars, the short trousers and the round forage caps with chinstraps and dolphin badges. (SMV Archive)

providing their own amusements. By 1899, for instance, there were five school 'newspapers' in circulation. They also had a lot of fun in the playground. One prank involved the induction of new boys into the mysteries of the Stapleton site. Central to the joke was the old 'Tulip Tree' (a species of magnolia, properly named *liliodendron tulipifera*), which stood outside the dining room at the edge of the parade. Gullible new arrivals from the wilds of Wiltshire were easily persuaded that the tree (which was also nicknamed the 'Bacon Tree') not only grew tulips, but also produced the rashers of bacon served at the masters' breakfast table each morning. It was then but a small step from this fiction to a belief in the 'Cocoa Mine', which supplied the masters with their mid-morning drink. Curious first formers were shown its entrance, which was located in the basement - namely, the door leading into the boiler room. Many Old Colstonians were understandably saddened when the moribund Tulip Tree was finally uprooted in 1908.

The boys of this period also had their own highly-complex vocabulary for use on the playground - a mixture of jargon and slang (some of it unique to Colston's), which was recalled in *The Colstonian* magazine of 1907. The words and expressions included 'to bung' (to push in), 'dolphers' (the silver buttons on the uniforms), 'gunger' (rubber), 'moater' (one who funked at the swimming bath, keeping close to the wall), 'muggety' (stingy), 'nobs' (apples), 'pur' (a prefix meaning passably - as in 'pur-good'), 'scrummy handed' (left-handed), 'skeem' (to shirk any duty or punishment), 'timmy' (a stick), 'toe ball' (football), 'Joe' (a friend), 'stuff' (tuck), 'friends' (relatives), 'stally' (jam tart - the usual dessert on Sundays), 'noggy' (fat meat), 'sap' (a simple fellow), 'sappy' (an easy lesson), 'mall' (drill) and 'marks' (the pigeon holes for clothes, which were marked with the boys' numbers).

Although, with increased exercise and better diet, the school essentially remained a healthy place, there were occasional outbreaks of 'scarlatina' or scarlet fever (13 cases in 1885), measles (1889), German measles (17 cases in 1891) and playground accidents (a broken arm and a broken thigh, for instance, in 1889). These were always treated competently by Dr Bernard, the school doctor (or 'medical attendant') who, on his appointment in 1872, began the practice of examining every boy on return from the holidays 'to see that he brings no infectious disorder'. After the outbreak of scarlet fever in 1885, the Management Committee ruled that all boys were to be vaccinated, that clothes were not to be washed in future at private laundries and that parents were to certify at the start of each term that their sons were 'not likely to bring back with them the seeds of infection or contagious diseases'.

The problems of hygiene and effective sanitation, however, continued to cause alarm. In 1877, Dr Bernard alerted the committee to the total inadequacy of the boys' washing and bathing arrangements. He reported that 'the boys are bathed weekly in a bath in the basement' holding 1,300 gallons - but that all the 150 boys bathed 'in the same water'. Furthermore, the dressing room, measuring just thirteen feet by nine feet, was totally inadequate, as was the washroom. The 130 older boys went down from their dormitories to the basement 'for their daily ablution partially dressed - only to queue for a long time for a turn at one of the thirty basins. The Governors were stung into action, although their plans to install lavatories and baths alongside the dormitories were shelved in view of the cost. As a compromise, they arranged for 20 individual baths to be placed in the basement together with a much larger changing room.

The problem of sanitation, however, still remained. The school's external examiner (Mr G. Fox) had, for instance, reported in 1886 that the arrangements for the boys' lavatories were 'far below' what was expected. In 1891, The Management Committee called in expert advice to investigate 'certain fouls smells in the house'. The subsequent report highlighted various faults with blocked drains, cracked sanitary pipes and an irregular system of flushing WCs by 'an attendant' using buckets of water. The Governors did what they could, but could not afford what was recommended - new WCs, each with its own cistern and chain pull. The foul smells, therefore, continued.

By 1890, the pattern of school holidays had been further modified from that established in 1862 (see Chapter 6). Although the Christmas holidays continued to consist of four weeks from about 20th December, the summer holidays had been extended to six weeks (usually from the beginning of August to the middle of September) and the Easter holidays had been increased from a mere four days to three weeks. Half-term holidays now consisted of four days in October and two days in the summer. Perhaps to compensate for this, few extra holidays for excursions or special events were recorded - apart from a day in Bristol for the whole school in December 1899, when Queen Victoria visited the city. For this, the Management Committee actually authorised the sum of £34 10s 0d to be spent on 'the erection of a stand' so that the boys and girls from their two schools could have a better view of the procession. Nevertheless, whenever events of interest took place they

The School Chapel in 1891. Previously the private chapel of Bishop Monk, it was refurbished in 1873 for the boys' daily services and later converted into the Staff Common Room. (SMV Archive)

were faithfully reported in school magazine, *The Colstonian*, which was launched in February 1894 and published twice a term initially (although this policy was changed to once a term from 1901 in view of the cost).

One other element of school life should also be mentioned. The practice of holding morning and evening prayers (as stipulated by Mr Colston) continued throughout all the changes that had taken place since 1861. By 1873, these services were being held in the dining room. In that year, however, the then Visiting Committee agreed to provide the old private chapel of Bishop Monk (which was situated inside the school and had already been reconsecrated at the official opening of the school's new Stapleton premises in 1862) with 100 chairs, a lectern and a reading desk. The Society of Merchant Venturers donated a harmonium. After the walls had been suitably decorated and the altar furnished by the masters of the school and their friends, the Chapel was formally opened with a service and then used on a regular basis for both daily prayers and a special service at the start of each term.

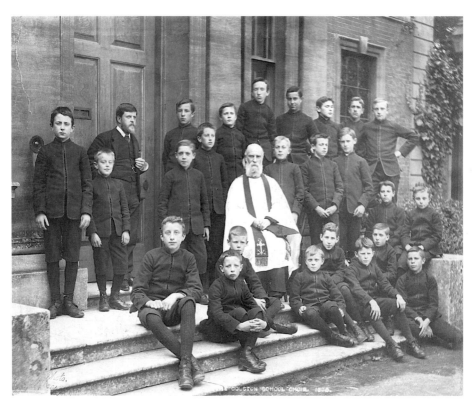

The School Choir in 1896 with Mr Hancock (who had been ordained in 1880) outside the School Chapel. (SMV Archive)

Five years later, however, the new Governing Board - in an attempt to create a much-needed large teaching space - decided to revert to the old idea of using the dining room for prayers. The Chapel, therefore, was briefly converted into a lecture room and library, although by the early 1890s it had been restored again to its former state. By then, the Headmaster, who had been ordained in 1880 and was already assisting with services at Stapleton Church, had been licensed by the Bishop to officiate as School Chaplain - and Mr Christie, the Second Master, had been licensed as a Lay Reader to help with chapel services. The Chapel was lavishly refurbished in 1890-91 with a new altar and cross (carved by one of the Headmaster's sons), embroidered frontals, brass candlesticks, wrought iron work for the altar rails and two banners. Apart from the regular services, special services were held on Ascension Day, Empire Day (when Kipling's *Recessional* was sung), every Friday in Lent and every evening during Holy Week. The Headmaster also prepared about twenty boys each year for confirmation and regularly arranged talks on missionary work, including one by another of his sons, who was a missionary in central Africa. In addition to theses activities in the School Chapel, the boys still continued to attend morning and evening services on Sundays at Stapleton Parish Church. A close relationship therefore grew up between the school and the local church.

The Start of Organised Games

Organised games began to make an appearance in life at Colston's during this period. In May 1872, for instance, the Society of Merchant Venturers granted £5 towards expenses incurred at the Stapleton Village Athletic Sports, in which a number of boys were participating. This experience clearly encouraged the Headmaster to organise the school's own Sports Day (the first ever) in the following year (June 1873), an event attended by the Master of the Society, who presented the prizes. This was, thereafter, to become an annual fixture in the school calendar, attended by a large crowd of parents and Old Colstonians. By 1893 the programme had been enlarged to include handicap races over 200 yards and 440 yards, an egg-and-spoon race, a three-legged race, a hurdle race, a cock fight, an Old Colstonians' race and a three-mile cross-country over Purdown. A tug-of-war and an obstacle race were added six years later. Sports Day was a highly popular occasion. In 1895, for instance, it attracted 950 entries and, according to *The Colstonian*, the boys were so keen that the majority of them 'had been training for many a day before the sports'. Indeed, so rapid was its growth that, by 1898, the organisers were being forced to hold heats on the previous day.

Writing in *The Colstonian* in 1897, S.D. Ryall (Old Colstonian)

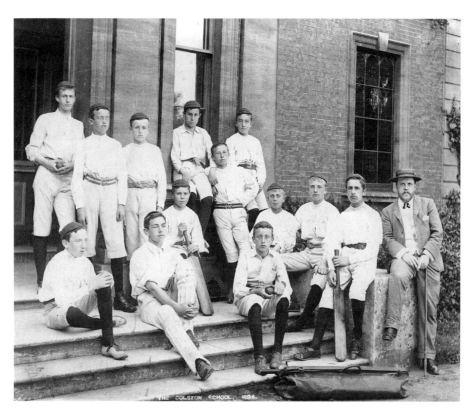

The School Cricket Team in 1894, wearing the 'caps' which were awarded for the first time in that year. (SMV Archive)

claimed that the school's first cricket match had been played against Queen Elizabeth's Hospital on Durdham Down in 1850, when 'a solid india-rubber ball' was used. But although the boys had continued to play scratch games of football and cricket in the playground (forcing the Governors to erect wire netting in 1897 'to keep balls from being sent over the walls'), they badly lacked a proper playing field for matches. By 1891, the school was renting a pitch from the local Stapleton Cricket Club at the cost of £5 per annum, although this arrangement was less than satisfactory. Four years later, therefore, the Governors expressed a wish to find a field of their own - a seemingly impossible task until the Duke of Beaufort (who was himself a Governor) came to their rescue by offering a plot of ground for football and cricket at the foot of Purdown, just five minutes walk from the school. He generously agreed to rent the field on a 60-year lease for just two shillings and six pence per annum. The Governors quickly erected an iron fence around the ground, hired 'a heavy roller' from Gloucestershire Cricket Club to prepare it for play and sold the grazing rights for sheep to Mr Bence, a local farmer, for £12 a year.

By 1894, the school was playing thirteen or so matches a year (increasing to twenty in 1899) with fixtures against such teams as QEH, Bristol Cathedral School, the YMCA, Stapleton Cricket Club and the Old Colstonians (the annual 'Past' versus 'Present' match had been inaugurated in 1893). Until pitches improved in quality, matches were usually low-scoring affairs with bowlers predominating (Rawling, for instance, taking a hat-trick against the YMCA in 1894). 'Caps' were first awarded to outstanding members of the team in both cricket and football from 1894, with special 'colours' also awarded in cricket from 1897.

Meanwhile, by the 1890s, rugby football had started to be played, although (according to *The Colstonian*) it was impossible to raise a good team 'owing to the early age at which boys are compelled to leave'. In 1894, therefore, matches were only played against Bristol Grammar School 2nd XV and Brighton House School 2nd XV, although within two years fixtures against Bristol Cathedral School and Dings Football Club had been added. Nevertheless, the school became affiliated to the County Rugby Football Union in 1896 and rejoiced in the fact that so many Old Colstonians were playing for local clubs - including T.O. Davies, who was captain of Bristol. The match against Dings F.C. in 1896 was actually played 'in the playground' with a number of masters representing the school team 'for the first time'.

Although rugby had made its appearance as a team game first, an 'association football' team was formed in the 1892-93 season 'for the purpose of meeting our old opponents and friends, the City School [i.e. QEH] who, owing to the nature of their playground, are prevented from playing according to the handling code'. Subsequent reports in *The Colstonian* of matches played 'under Rugby Union rules' or 'under Association rules', always appeared under the general heading of 'Football'. The Captain of Football was automatically the captain of both teams.

Association football slowly took hold with additional fixtures arranged with Stapleton Reserves (1898) and King Edward's School, Bath (1900). Blame for defeat in the latter by 4-2 was squarely attributed in *The Colstonian* to Evans, the goalkeeper, who 'stopped some good shots, but allowed some ridiculously easy ones to roll past him'. The boys, however, did not lack encouragement from the staff, a number of whom regularly played in matches or supported from the touch line. One observer commented on one match: 'Fortunately several of our masters were present to cheer and encourage our team - and right nobly the latter responded to every call'. Quite apart from school

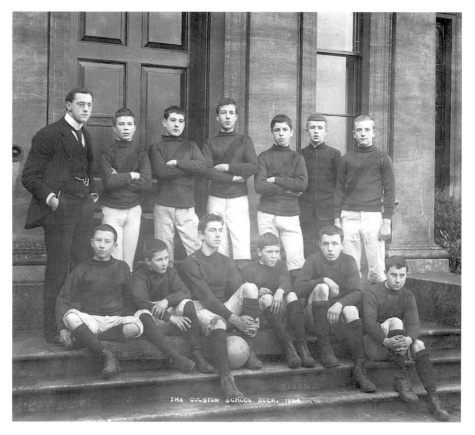

The School Football Team in 1894. The first such team had been formed just two years earlier. Football, however, was abolished as a school sport in 1916. (SMV Archive)

matches, many inter-form games were played in the playground. It was reported in 1900 that 'a great wave of enthusiasm has recently swept over the school, for every form has purchased a football for its own special use, and the number of games to be seen in progress is at times bewildering'.

The swimming bath (or, as the prospectus called it, 'the safe bathing place in the river which skirts the grounds') continued to provide the major source of pleasure, although it was frequently damaged by floods (1889), trespassers (1892 and 1899) and 'roughs coming out of Bristol' (1895). The Governors regularly wrote to the Chief Constable of Gloucestershire and the Watch Committee of Bristol Corporation seeking protection. Police constables were duly instructed 'to make frequent visits'. By 1894, the 'swimming contest' had become an established fixture in the annual programme. Apart from normal races to find the senior and junior champions, there were three handicap races and (from 1896) competitions for 'swimming under water' and 'diving for objects'. Life-saving techniques were also taught and swimming certificates awarded for proficiency. In 1900, a water polo match was organised for the first time. Most boys looked forward to their morning splash in the pool during the warmer months of the year - or at other times, if they could persuade a master to supervise them.

Work in the Classroom, 1873-1901

The New Scheme of 1875 had clearly stipulated the curriculum to be followed by boys at Colston's School. The majority of time in the classroom would still be spent, as it had been for many years, on the basic subjects (reading, spelling, writing arithmetic, elementary mathematics, English grammar and literature, history and geography) with a little singing and drawing thrown in for good measure. For the first time, however, regular space was also to be found for natural science and either Latin or French (or both). From the outset, it quickly became apparent that this curriculum was much too restrictive in relation to any higher ambitions that the Headmaster or Governors might harbour.

The lack of time to develop Latin and the lack of money to develop science, in conjunction with the early leaving age and the failure of the entrance examination to recruit pupils of higher ability, combined to ensure that the majority of boys at Colston's were merely prepared for employment as clerks. Mr G.E. Rees (the school's external examiner in 1890) concluded that, under all these adverse circumstances, the school's limited objectives seemed to be 'the wisest' - namely, 'to make the education in what are called English subjects as thorough as possible'. These sentiments were echoed by the Headmaster in his annual report two years later. Under present conditions, he said, as the school could never become 'a classical school', work in English was to be regarded as the '*raison d'etre*'. It is perhaps significant that, in 1887, a Mr Evans was employed to teach shorthand in after-school lessons.

Nevertheless, the Governors did what they could to develop the new subjects permitted by the Scheme. The teaching of French was extended to the whole school in 1876, as was Latin one year later. It has to be said, however, that this policy met with limited success, judging by the reports submitted by examiners after their annual visit to the school. In 1878, for instance, Mr Henry Foster noted that Latin was 'very meagre in quantity and not very superior in quality'. In 1882, the Reverend W.S. Grignon commented that 'the whole school without exception had failed in French', in which subject they had clearly been 'untaught or mistaught'. He recommended that Latin should be dropped, so that more time could be devoted to French - an idea echoed in 1893 by Mr C.A. Buckmaster, who doubted 'how far the continuance of Latin in the school course is of any great value'. Performance in both subjects was regularly classed as 'weak'.

Science, too, came in for criticism. Mr Buckmaster, in advocating the extension of the subject to include physical science in 1893, also noted 'the entire want of facilities for giving such instruction'. He castigated the Governors' spending policy on new buildings, pleading for the provision of a science classroom. Reacting somewhat slowly to this advice (for reasons explained below), the Governors finally resolved in 1899 to investigate the cost of providing equipment for 'the effective teaching of natural science in the school', although nothing was actually achieved in this sphere until after Mr Hancock's retirement in 1901.

Boys were taught initially in five classes, according to ability rather than age, although a sixth class was formed in 1877 to cater for a sudden influx of numbers. The top class was originally labelled the 'first class', but by 1885 was being described as 'the sixth form'. By then, of course, the Headmaster was able to strengthen the top end of the school by recommending specific pupils to stay on for an extra year (as authorised by the Charity Commissioners in 1883). Within the first two years of the new arrangement, no fewer than 24 boys had availed themselves of the opportunity - a clear indication that, in spite of the mediocrity of many of the pupils, a significant number were keen to progress. Nor could they now rely on apprenticeships being found for them and financed by the school (which had been one of Mr Colston's chief concerns). That system had ended in 1882, when the last boys to have joined the school under the old arrangements (i.e. before the start of the New Scheme in 1875) finally left.

Those with ambitions, however, worked hard to win one of the new leaving exhibitions, which would enable them to progress up the educational ladder. The system worked extremely well, in spite of the Governors' difficulty in funding it. A start was made in 1877, when the Management Committee proposed the award of one exhibition of £25 a year, based on the Headmaster's recommendations in the light of success in the summer examinations. This would be tenable for three years at a grammar school or other place of 'liberal or professional' education' and was dependent on 'good behaviour'. Awards were therefore made regularly from 1878 onwards, with Colston's boys going on to such places as Bristol Grammar School, Wells Grammar School, Llandovery College, Monmouth Grammar School, the Bristol Trade and Mining School, the Westminster Hospital Medical School and Denstone College. Some former Colston boys then went on from these schools to university, like W.A.T. Jarrett, who entered Hertford College, Oxford in 1898 from Denstone.

In 1883, however, the Charity Commissioners refused to permit the Governors to continue their practice of limiting the number of exhibitions to just one a year, insisting that they should adhere to the allocation of £100 per annum from their funds for this purpose, as specified by the New Scheme. Three years later, therefore, it was agreed to offer four exhibitions a year, including two which would be tenable at the old Bristol Trade and Mining School (which had just been taken over by the Society of Merchant Venturers). There is no doubt that some boys greatly benefited from the opportunities thus provided. For example, N.G. Veale (the first boy to be awarded a leaving exhibition) eventually gained a degree at Oxford in 1885, while E.I. Phillips (who was awarded a leaving exhibition in 1885) was 'classed among the Wranglers in the mathematical tripos at Cambridge' in 1892 (i.e. he obtained a first class degree).

In an attempt to check on educational standards, the New Scheme had insisted that all the boys in the school should be formally examined each year by a paid external examiner, who would then submit a written

The whole school taken between 1885 (when this new uniform was introduced) and 1888 (when the dolphin badge was added to the polo cap). The Headmaster, Mr Hancock (with the white beard) is seen on the back row. (SMV Archive)

report to the Governors. Mr Hancock was keen from the outset that these examinations should be conducted by an established examination board. In 1874, therefore, he wrote to the secretaries of three boards, including the Cambridge University Local Board, which offered a five-day examination for a fee of £16. The Governors, however preferred at first to appoint their own individual examiners from the locality, partly in an attempt to save money. A number of individuals therefore assisted in this way, setting written papers for each class in the whole range of subjects, as well as oral examinations where relevant - the Reverend Taylor, curate of St Mary Redcliffe (1876), Mr H.W.L. Tanner, a master at Bristol Grammar School (1883) and Mr C.A, Buckmaster, an Oxford graduate (1885, 1893-97 and 1899-1900). Latterly, however, the Headmaster managed to persuade the Governors to employ the Examination Board of the Diocese of Gloucester and Bristol (1887), the Oxford and Cambridge Local Examination Syndicate (1889 and 1891) and the Oxford Local Board (1890 and 1892).

The reports on these three-day examinations were largely favourable, although the examiners tended to take into account the modest level of ability within the school. Mr Buckmaster, the examiner in 1885, for instance, informed the Governors that he had 'lowered the difficulty of the questions in the written papers, and the results obtained are such as to fully satisfy me of the wisdom of the alteration'. Criticisms were of course made of specific weaknesses. In 1878, the mathematics examinations showed that there was 'no boy who had greatly distinguished himself'; and, in 1886, the papers were 'carelessly written', 'untidy' and completed 'regardless of punctuation'. In the main, however, the examiners praised the punctuality, behaviour, appearance and discipline of the boys.

On the academic side, Mr Buckmaster's comments in 1893 were typical of many: 'The boys have done decidedly well in all the subjects of the examination (with the exception of Latin) and the school deserves congratulation for the ability shown'. These judgments, however pleasing to the Governors, were nevertheless all relative. The fact remained that the standard of work in the school was now much lower than before and that Mr Hancock did not feel able to enter any boys for *external* examinations until twenty years after the start of the New Scheme. Whereas, up until 1874, individual pupils had regularly been entered for the examinations of both the Cambridge Local Examination Board in Bristol and the Science and Art Department (see Chapter 6), this practice was not revived until 1894, when a few of the most able boys were entered for the Oxford Local Board examinations. This policy then continued over the next few years.

The limited horizons and restricted opportunities of most boys in the school were highlighted by Mr Hancock in his annual report in December 1899. Of the eighteen boys about to leave, he said, 'Castles is ultimately bound for the Navy; Pain is a medical in embryo; Drew and Thompson passed the Bristol School Board Pupil Teachers' Examination; Brown is engaged in helping to carry on the work of the Great Western Railway; Rudge intends to devote himself to banking; Watts has entered the office of the Bristol Sanitary Board; Hood is absorbed in business; Morgan has turned his attention to drapery; Challenger is in a ship builder's office; and Laurence is interested in the Taff Vale Railway Company'.

A Financial Crisis, 1879-1901

From 1873, a great depression hit English agriculture, which was to last until 1914. There were many reasons for this - a series of bad harvests between 1873 and 1879, the importation of cheap American wheat (made possible by the development of railways across the prairies, combine harvesters and steamships), cheap refrigerated meat and frozen butter from New Zealand and high class merino wool from Australia. Between 1880 and 1892, rents of agricultural land fell by one-fifth as the depression hit the countryside; by 1900, they had fallen by a half. These developments were to have a serious impact on the state of the school's finances and its ability to expand facilities and raise the level of its educational provision.

In 1881, the Governors were presented with a disturbing report on the financial state of the Colston Hospital Trust. Their estates in Somerset, which provided a large part of the income, had been hit by the depression, making it difficult for their tenants to work at a profit. The Society of Merchant Venturers (the trustees) had, therefore, been 'compelled to return part of the rents' in line with the policy adopted by neighbouring landlords. In 1879, 10% of the rents had been returned; by the following year this had been increased to 20%. In view of these facts, the Society calculated that they should expect a permanent diminution in the revenues of the manors of Beere and Monkton of about 20% - or, in other words, an annual loss of about £385. The accounts show that, whereas the income from all rents and dividends had totalled £4572 in 1878, this figure had dropped to £3515 in 1880 and £2784 in 1883. The 'balance in hand' had been reduced from £798 in 1874 to £251 in 1880 and £115 in 1881. Nor did the crisis abate. In 1893, the Management Committee heard a report from the Clerk of the trust that the trust's income during the year had fallen short of expenses, leaving a deficit of several hundred pounds 'owing to the depressed state of agriculture and the necessity of making large returns

The main entrance of the school in 1896, showing the monkey tree, which was damaged by a bomb in the 2nd World War and pulled down in 1943. (SMV Archive)

of rent, if the tenants were to be retained'.

This dire financial situation goes a long way to explaining why the years 1873 to 1901 were years of stagnation for the school. The trustees, of course, were responsible - under the terms of the New Scheme - not only for funding Colston's Boarding School for boys, but also for establishing Colston's Girls' School for 200 day pupils by January 1883 and for taking over responsibility for the Bristol Trade and Mining School. This proved in total to be an impossible task. In 1877, therefore, the trustees sought leave of the Charity Commissioners to postpone the establishment of Colston's Girls' School 'for so long as the Governors might find it necessary'. Although the commissioners agreed to an extension to 1883, the Governors again appealed for more time in 1882 and were given a new date of 1886. The date again slipped, however, and it was not until January 1891 that the school was finally opened. Even then, it had only become possible through a generous decision of the Society of Merchant Venturers in 1885 to take over financial responsibility themselves for the Bristol Trade and Mining

School. This freed the Colston Hospital Trustees from that particular burden and enabled them to invest their remaining resources in the Girls' School.

Meanwhile, it was hardly surprising that the Governors of Colston's School were in no position to fund the Management Committee's proposals for enlarging the school in 1878, implementing a new system of sanitation as recommended by experts in 1891 or building a new gymnasium as advocated in a committee report of 1890. This latter facility was not in fact achieved until 1926. In the light of comments made by examiners, the Headmaster warned the Governors in 1891 that, as Colston's was 'behind schools of a similar kind' in terms of facilities, the school could 'hardly hope to compete successfully for paying scholars'. The Governors, alas, were powerless to act. Mr Hancock's comment on the lack of paying scholars, however, touched a raw nerve.

Two years earlier, they had called the Headmaster's attention to 'the steady decrease in the number of paying boys' in the school. Numbers of fee payers had in fact slumped from 68 in 1885 to a mere 30 in 1894. So concerned was he that, in 1893, the Chairman of Governors (Mr Proctor Baker) presented a paper of his own to explain 'the great falling off in the number of paying scholars'. After sending out a questionnaire to parents, he had discovered that almost half of the boys had been introduced to the school through friends or local knowledge; that, apart from adverts placed in two London papers (*The Telegraph* and *The Standard*), advertising had been noticeably unproductive of recruits. Indeed, only five out of the twelve county papers used had produced any boys at all in the survey.

He believed that one crucial factor in the decline of numbers had been the establishment of technical schools throughout the country, after the passing of the Technical Instruction Act of 1890. Scholarships which had been created for these schools, were not tenable at schools like Colston's - a fact which effectively removed many potential recruits. He failed to mention another important element in the decline - the impoverishment of many local farmers, who had previously been an important source of supply for the school. The Chairman concluded that, rather than spending more money on advertising, they needed to 'make the excellence of the school more widely known' in other ways. The Headmaster was instructed to draw up 'a list of honours obtained by the school in recent years' and to arrange for the school to be examined again by a reputable public body (i.e. the Oxford Local Examination Board). Although this was put into effect, the number of fee payers remained disappointingly low with just 30 again recorded in 1898. By 1902, the number had plummeted to 27.

The lack of anticipated fee income seriously exacerbated the financial crisis. When, therefore, Mr Crouch (the Fourth Master) resigned in 1893, the Governors decided that he would not be replaced 'as the numbers of the school have diminished of late'. Similarly, Mr Greenwood (the music teacher) was not replaced in 1894, his duties as organist and 'choir master' being taken over by the Second Master with an increased allowance of £10 per annum. Although these cuts brought about useful savings in salary, they further undermined academic performance - a fact which was quickly pointed out by the Headmaster in his 1894 report. He complained that the decision, considerably affected 'the working and teaching of the school', especially in view of the fact that the number of classes which were taught remained exactly the same. Remuneration to staff was inevitably kept to a minimum - a point made by inspectors from the Board of Education in 1905, when they remarked that 'the salaries of the assistant masters are low'. This made it very difficult to recruit teachers of high calibre. Furthermore, the minute books record an endless procession of masters requesting increases in salary during these years -

The Reverend John Hancock, Headmaster 1871-1901. (SMV Archive)

requests which were normally refused, as the Headmaster himself found to his own cost in 1893. Furthermore, the Governors ruled in 1898 that no assistant master was to take on any work outside school. A few had apparently been supplementing their meagre salaries by teaching at evening classes in local schools. Given this background, it is hardly surprising that staff morale was often low and resignations frequent.

The Resignation of Mr Hancock

In December 1900 the Headmaster, the Reverend John Hancock

informed the Management Committee that he had received an offer of a living at the parish church of Horkstow in Lincolnshire with a stipend of £150 per annum. Bearing in mind that he had little by way of private means, the Governors agreed to supplement his future income by granting him a pension of £60 a year. He therefore retired from Colston's at the age of sixty-seven in July 1901, somewhat disillusioned and no doubt relieved that his years of frustration were at an end. He had battled for three decades with the thankless duty of implementing the New Scheme (which he believed to be flawed) with inadequate resources in the middle of a depression; and had struggled endlessly with the seemingly impossible challenge of raising the 'moral tone' of the school. In spite of his own inadequacies as a leader and the lack of inventiveness he brought to school life, he had stuck loyally to the task and had steered the school through one of its most difficult periods.

At a farewell presentation organised by the Old Colstonians, Mr Hancock admitted that, in some ways, he would like to have continued - 'but the work of the school became very distressing, not so much to him as to Mrs Hancock'. The Old Boys paid glowing tributes to his personal qualities ('he had been to all the boys in his school a guide, philosopher and friend'); his hard work ('his career at the school had been one of unremitting toil for 30 years'); his modesty; his organisational skills and his legendary reputation for punctuality. He was 'a really God-fearing man, a scholar and a gentleman'. After his death in 1921 at the age of eighty-seven, his obituary in *The Colstonian* emphasised the reality of his deep personal faith, concluding that, to the end, he had 'charmed all who knew him by his simple saintly life'.

Sources used in Chapter 7

D.J. Eames, *The Contribution of the Society of Merchant Venturers to the Development of Education in Bristol* (unpublished MA thesis for the University of Bristol, 1966), pp 167-200
Society of Merchant Venturers Archive:
   The Hall Book of Proceedings, vol.25 (1870 -75)
   Visiting Committee's Minute Book, 1870 -75
   Colston Hospital Trust:
      Governors' Minute Book, 1875-1934
         Management Committee's Minutes, vol. 2, 1887-1923
   Headmasters' Letters and Reports, 1870 -1921
   Admissions Register - Paying Scholars, 1875 -1926
   Admissions Register - Nominated Scholars, 1875 -1926
   Box of Appendices -
      Bundle 16 (Mr Hancock's application; Oxford Local

Examinations, 1874; school prospectus; report on the financial position of the Trust, 1877; letters and reports, 1880 -1912; examination reports, 1890, 1892, 1893)

The Colstonian, vols. 1-7 (February 1894 - July 1901)

SPORT AT COLSTON'S IN THE 1880s

An Old Colstonian

Both cricket and football were very differently looked after to what they are now. Cricket being confined to two matches, one out and one at home, with the Q.E.H., and two with Stapleton each year for the first XI; and, for the second XI, to two matches with the Cathedral School.

As to football, we played no matches at all; in fact it would have puzzled an expert to decide as to what game we played, as it was such a glorious mixture of both Association and Rugby.

I know it was Association, because to score it was necessary to put the ball under the cross-bar; also, opposing players could charge each other and were not allowed to handle the ball; but, as it was possible to score a try if the ball was kicked outside the goal posts (in which case it was brought out and placed for a kick over the bar - and also we used to make a mark for a fair catch), I consider there was at least more than a dash of Rugby in it.

To further complicate matters, we used an Association ball and the number of players on each side was unlimited; also we scorned to play two halves of 35 or 40 minutes, but used to commence first thing in the afternoon and kept it up till tea time, during which time it was nothing unusual for twenty or thirty goals to be scored.

There was an offside rule too, but I do not think more than one or two claimed to understand it - and even they used to disagree about it. For my part, if the ball came my way, I kicked it and chanced my luck.

There was certainly once an attempt to organise a sports day, but it was entirely unofficial - and in connection therewith hangs a tale. It was the year 1882 that this occurred, the idea arising from the appearance in that year of a certain story in the *Boys' Own Paper* entitled 'The Fifth Form of St Dominic's', wherein mention was made of a Sports Day being held at St Dominic's. Whatever the St Dominicans did, the Colstonians followed. Hence the origin of the 'Sports Day'.

Also in this story, a school newspaper, *The Dominican*, was published and, of course, we felt we must do likewise. It was 'Spider' Mayne (Pupil No. 94) who suggested it, and the idea caught on. Once a week this paper was issued. Spider, who wrote a very neat, small hand, transcribed the matter on a very large sheet of drawing paper - six or eight columns of it, and the heading, *The Colstonian*, was printed in Old English letters by hand.

A committee was formed for the Sports Day, Spider being the leading spirit, and a programme was made out, all of which was duly chronicled in *The Colstonian*, which, by the way, was tacked on a special board and hung up in the shed, there being, of course, only one copy. The entrance to the various items was by payment of sums of money, a penny or two pence, and the prizes were also to be in cash. Fancy Colston's school going *en bloc* into professionalism!

Well, we all went into training, which consisted of trotting around the playground each half-holiday. The great day came, wet and dismal of course. No one would hear of postponement, and an attempt was made to carry out the programme. I say an attempt, because when the first race was run, the winners waited on Spider for their prizes. Now there was a great shortage in the money market of the school, for the greater number of contestants had entered 'on the nod', so that prizes were not readily available.

But the winners were obdurate; and those who had actually paid their entrance into other races, becoming alarmed, joined in the cry. The last scene of that day was poor Spider in the corner of the shed, surrounded by an angry, clamouring mob demanding their cash.

The whole thing therefore failed ignominiously, and its failure brought down *The Colstonian* with it, for it did not appear again.

(From The Colstonian, *August 1903)*

CHAPTER 8

Years of Progress, 1901 - 1922

'The Governors congratulate Dr Finn upon the brilliant success of the school and assure him that they appreciate highly the ability and good work on his part, without which this success could not have been achieved'. (Governors' Minute Book, December 1915)

A Change of Headmaster, 1901

Advertisements were immediately drawn up for Mr Hancock's successor. The job description stressed that the new Headmaster would be responsible 'not only for the teaching, discipline and moral welfare of the school, but also for the whole of its domestic economy...Careful administration has become a matter of the first importance, owing to the falling off, through agricultural depression, of the revenue derived from the endowment'. The successful candidate, it went on to state, would be a graduate and member of the Church of England, aged between 27 and 37, who was also an experienced teacher, 'able to maintain authority', with personal knowledge of a school offering science. By May 1901, 48 applications had been received from qualified candidates, of whom three were short listed for interview with three more named as 'reserves'.

The man who was eventually offered the job was Dr Anthony Finn, but on the firm understanding that his wife would undertake the duties of Housekeeper. A graduate of Trinity College, Dublin, he was at the time of his appointment an assistant master at Birkenhead School, having previously taught at Darlington Grammar School. He was offered an annual stipend of £225, plus £1 per annum for each fee paying pupil and one quarter of any future grant awarded annually by the Board of Education (see below). He would be provided with six unfurnished rooms (free of rates and taxes), coal, gas and food for himself and his family.

At first sight, Dr Finn's inheritance was both poor and unpromising. The school's finances were in a desperate state; pupil numbers were critical, (with only 114 on the roll, instead of the 150 that had always been envisaged); the quality of academic work was dire (much worse, in fact, than it had been before 1875); and staff were difficult to recruit and impossible to retain. This situation in itself was depressing enough, but the new Headmaster was soon to discover that things were even more worrying beneath the surface. At the end of his first year (in July 1902), he presented the Governors with a detailed report on the level of dishonesty within the school. He had discovered systematic cheating on a major scale from the first form right up to the sixth form. The boys, for years, had apparently been adopting a number of methods to avoid the pain of personal study - the surreptitious looking at a book during tests; copying work from a neighbour during supervised evening prep; taking an exercise book from a boy's desk during play hours and 'copying written work from it'; 'bigger boys getting smaller boys during play hours to copy written work for them from another boy's book'; 'calling out a higher number of marks than those honestly obtained to the master, when entering the marks in the register'; and awarding incorrect marks quite deliberately when boys exchanged papers at the end of a test.

There was no doubt in his mind that very much of this represented 'an organised scheme' of dishonesty - a fact confirmed by the evidence of an exhibitioner (Edgar Stanford), who was dragged reluctantly before the Headmaster by his father. He told how he had been desperately unhappy in the school for four years at the systematic cheating, 'which he had been morally compelled to take part in against his will'. Dr Finn assured the Governors that he was adopting a tough line on this, with 'every boy in future regarded as suspicious'. He would therefore be exercising tight control, until 'a better moral tone' prevailed, although recent statistical evidence suggested that he was now well on

Dr Anthony Finn, Headmaster 1901-1922. (SMV Archive)

top of the problem. Whereas, in his first term, he had beaten 28 boys for cheating and dishonesty, he had chastised only 20 boys in this way during the second term and just 11 during the third. He was utterly convinced that this problem, more than any other, had undermined the academic performance of the school over a long period. The new Headmaster had quickly demonstrated his determination to succeed.

Old Colstonians later recalled the strict, but fair disciplinary regime, which operated under Dr Finn. A.J. Brown (1900-1905) remembered being told that boys should never lock their boxes of possessions, 'because to lock them was to imply that there were thieves about - and there were supposed to be no thieves in the school'. However, on one occasion, 'a boy complained that he had lost a shilling out of his box. The school didn't half suffer for that. For two days we were not allowed to play games, until the boy confessed. When he did so, a dreadful scene followed, because he was publicly birched in front of the whole school. A shocking experience, which I shall never forget and never saw again'. Finn himself was a compassionate and sympathetic man, but he was determined from the outset to set standards of the highest order. This public birching, therefore, was an exceptional occurrence, although ordinary caning continued to be used as a deterrent. Arnold Stock (1914-18) recalled that, on the rare occasions that boys were allowed to go out of school on their own, they were 'only permitted to go one way - which was in the direction of Frenchay'. Bell Hill, he said, 'was out of

The school assembled on The Parade in c.1903. Note that peaked caps with badges have replaced the polo caps. The School Sergeant is standing in the background in front of the gymnastic equipment. The confined nature of the playing field beyond is also visible. (SMV Archive)

bounds and any boy found guilty of breaking this rule was duly punished by six strikes of the cosh from Joey' (i.e. Dr Finn).

Norman Emmerson (1916-20) vividly remembers how Dr Finn 'ruled with a rod of iron'. Although he undoubtedly 'a learned man', he was 'far too harsh and rough with the boys'. All misdemeanours were recorded by masters on the weekly mark lists, which were read out before the whole assembly on Monday mornings. Boys who had been graded 'C' were instructed to join the line which was forming behind the Headmaster and to follow him into the Committee Room, where he 'brought out a selection of canes'. Each boy then in turn held out both of his hands to receive strokes of 'the cosh' in multiples of two, according to the gravity of the offence.

Norman Emmerson also recalls the military-style regime which prevailed under the tight control of the Sergeant-Major. The boys, who were summoned by the Sergeant's bell and marshalled into forms on The Parade, 'marched everywhere' - into class, into church, into chapel and into the dining hall. At the end of each meal, the Headmaster would ring a bell, the boys would stand, grace would be sung, a second bell would sound and the boys would step carefully over their benches before marching out to the Sergeant's instructions. If, however, a bench was knocked over in the process, the six culprits would be ordered to stand in front of the Headmaster. A prefect would then be detailed to supervise the usual punishment on the field outside. Two of the boys would be made to carry the offending bench round the field, before handing it over to the next two and so on.

In the eyes of a young boys, the school was 'like a sealed unit' once term had started with each pupil 'more like a prisoner'. As classrooms were out of bounds, boys were often set the task after church on Sunday mornings of digging up a given number of weeds or picking up small stones from the field; Sunday afternoons were simply devoted to writing letters and walking around the grounds. Permission to visit parents was seldom given - so boys often took the law into their own hands. Mr Emmerson confesses that he and his brother frequently broke bounds by moving stealthily across the playing field, climbing through the hedge and escaping to their Bristol home where supplies of food were eagerly taken on board. Only once were they caught when the Sergeant's wife spotted the break-out and reported it to Dr Finn, who immediately ordered a roll call to identify the culprits. They were duly 'coshed' on their return.

A Change of Fortune, 1900-1903

In the country at large, great strides had been made to set up a national system of education. The Local School Boards, which had been established in each district by the Education Act of 1870, had built many new elementary schools to supplement the work being undertaken by church parochial schools. Such was the success of this policy that, by 1880, school attendance had been made compulsory for the first time for children between the ages of 5 and 13 and, by 1891, education was being offered free of charge in all Board Schools. The Education Act of 1902 (Balfour's Act) abolished School Boards and established Local Education Authorities, which became responsible for coordination of all elementary and secondary education in their areas. They were also given power to build and control grammar schools of their own - not to mention the technical schools, which had been set up by the Technical Instruction Act of 1890. In the face of all these developments, which offered free and widely-available state education to all children, old endowed schools like Colston's discovered that they had finally lost their monopoly.

There was, however, one other development at the turn of the century, which helped to salvage the school's rapidly diminishing fortunes. In an attempt to bring the old endowed schools within the national framework of education, the Education Act of 1899 (based on the report of the Royal Commission on Secondary Schools in 1895) had set up a central Board of Education to take general responsibility for all aspects of education. Endowed schools like Colston's, therefore, passed from the control of the Charity Commissioners to the control of the Board and became subject to official inspections (which took place at Colston's, for instance, in 1901, 1904 and 1905). Although the inspectors' reports were purely advisory in nature, substantial benefits in the form of grant aid awaited those endowed schools which applied for 'recognised status'. Such a step did not mean the surrender of a school's independent authority, but it did involve the modernisation of both buildings and teaching methods, together with the acceptance of 'free place' boys from the Local Education Authority. The latter stipulation, of course, would present no problem at Colston's, where up to 100 boys were already being taken in from elementary schools on exhibitions.

The Governors therefore decided, wisely enough, to apply for 'recognised status' at the first available opportunity. When this was granted in April 1900, the school received its own distinctive registration number of '1309' and the right to earn grants from the Board of Education, based on successful examination results. Under these circumstances, it is hardly surprising that the new Headmaster quickly revived the lapsed former practice of entering his most able pupils for the Science and Art Examinations, which were still organised at South Kensington (but now under the control of a department of the Board of

Education). In 1901, twenty Colston's boys gained certificates in those examinations; in 1902, the total had risen to forty-five.

Events now moved on rapidly. The Governors, desperately anxious to develop and expand the school, had already gained estimates in March 1899 for the cost of providing equipment and facilities for 'the effective teaching of natural science'. In spite of the serious financial state of the Colston Hospital Trust, detailed plans were drawn up for science rooms costing £2,337. Unable to fund this development out of income or cash reserves, the Governors applied, in June 1901, to the Charity Commissioners (who were still, of course, overseers of the endowment) for permission to sell as many of the consols (i.e. government securities) held by them as needed to cover the cost. A month later, a report of the Board of Education's inspector lent weight to their case by drawing attention to the lack of 'proper apparatus for science teaching at the school and the insufficient accommodation for the various classes'. As a result of this, the Charity Commissioners agreed both to the selling of investments for the provision of science facilities and to an amendment of the New Scheme of 1875 which transformed Colston's into a 'school of science'.

All this had been agreed in principle by December 1902, although it took another year (until December 1903) for the Board of Education to give its formal recognition to the school as a 'Secondary School in Division A' (i.e. a school offering more advanced courses in science and eligible for direct government grants). As part of the deal, the Governors were obliged to promise that a fair proportion of the older boys would take the advanced course, which was normally of four years duration from the age of thirteen. To make this possible, the Board agreed that, from 1902, up to 20 boys each year (nominated by the Headmaster) would be permitted to remain in school until the age of eighteen - although the anomaly still remained that no exhibitioner (now renamed 'free scholar') could stay in the school for longer than five years on his free place. Nevertheless, it was with a sense of great pleasure and relief that the Governors invited the Lord Bishop of Bristol to open formally the new science rooms on 18th May 1903. This enabled them to boast in the new prospectus, published shortly afterwards, that 'the science buildings (consisting of chemical and physical laboratories and a science lecture theatre) form one of the most complete school laboratories in the country'. The Board of Education inspectors agreed, pronouncing them as 'excellent'.

Colston's had at last shaken off its image of being little better than an elementary school. Grants from the Board of Education would help to ensure that facilities could be further upgraded, while the prospect of a later leaving age and more advanced courses held out a hope to the boys

The 'Chemical Laboratory', which was opened in 1903 as part of the new science block. (SMV Archive)

of progressing to university straight from their own sixth form. Whereas, in 1901 (according to Dr Finn's first annual report), the majority of school leavers had 'obtained posts in good business offices' or had 'become pupil teachers' in schools under the Bristol School Board, by 1903 a higher ambition was beginning to stalk the corridors at Stapleton. Indeed, the new prospectus stressed that boys were now prepared for the 'Civil Service' and the 'scientific professions', as well as for commercial, mercantile and manufacturing occupations.

The Rapid Growth of Sport

From the start Dr Finn had been particularly active in encouraging team games. In 1901 he had divided the school into four sections (North, South, East and West) and had organised junior and senior inter-section competitions in both rugby and association football with each team playing the other teams twice on a league basis. Challenge shields, which had been bought from donations subscribed by masters and boys, were awarded at the end of each term to the winning teams. The purpose of all this, Dr Finn explained to the Governors, was 'to prevent loafing in the playground'. The policy, he said, had been an outstanding success, 'since one term's competition during the football season involved 48 games, so there was not much opportunity for loafing'. Similar competitions were organised in cricket and athletics (from 1902) and in tennis (from 1904).

To create more interest in the cricket competitions, sectional averages were published in *The Colstonian* magazine and prizes awarded for the best batting and bowling performances. The sectional matches were played on Tuesday, Thursday and Saturday afternoons - a fact which emphasises the increasing role of sport in the life of the school. The sections (later to be called 'houses') were distinguished by a colour - light blue (North), red (South), orange (East) and green (West). The appropriate colour for an individual boy would then be displayed in two ways - in the dolphin on his school cap and in the border of his dark blue games jersey, which had been introduced in 1903. With the rapid expansion of sports in so many ways, all boys were expected to contribute a subscription of one shilling per term to the 'Sports Fund'.

The annual athletic sports continued as a popular annual event, which was switched to Easter Monday in 1904. Although a 'pillow fight' was substituted for the obstacle race in the same year, the events became much more serious in nature. The mile race (1908) and the relay (1912) each made their appearance and a Challenge Bowl was warded for

Sports Day winners in 1903 with their prizes. The Headmaster, Dr Finn (wearing a mortar board) is in the doorway. (SMV Archive)

for first time in 1908 to the boy with the most points gained in the scratch events (i.e. a *victor ludorum* trophy). By 1914, all the original 'fun' events had been withdrawn and, by 1916, medals and certificates had been substituted for prizes. In the cause of fitness, Mr Beckett organised paper chases in 1914 as training for the cross country race, while gymnastic equipment was always available in the field outside.

Start of the Five Mile cross-country race in 1914. This race, together with the Three mile race, had been featured as part of the annual Sports Day programme from the late 19th century. (SMV Archive)

At the same time, swimming in the bath by the river continued to be popular with all boys encouraged to qualify for proficiency certificates. Mr G.H. Kinchin, who joined the school as a handyman in 1920 and went on to complete 50 years of service, described later what the bath was actually like:

> The pool was down Wickham when I came - an open air swimming bath from the river in what used to be a disused mill pond. It was laid out as a bath, paved out at the bottom and all around the sides. It was quite a pleasant little place and it wasn't cold. The river was originally what you might call a pure river, more of less fresh from the springs. It became disused because they were repairing the sewers right along the Frenchay Road and I think the river became

contaminated when the sewers got broken from time to time.

An Old Colstonian, writing in *The Colstonian* in 1953, also described what the bath was like in 1918 when he arrived at the school:

> For swimming we went out of the gates and turned right down towards the Frome, down a narrow lane and through a padlocked gate into our own Big Bar [the boys' slang for the bath]. We undressed on the grass and stepped on old paving stones. The water was as black as that of the river, but none of us got typhoid.

The accumulated silt in the bottom of the bath was scraped out by a fatigue party twice a year at low tide.

Tennis, which was introduced in 1904, quickly became a very popular sport with tournaments and singles championships organised on a regular basis. Nevertheless, cricket remained the major summer game. The fixture list expanded so rapidly that, in 1910, the 1st XI played eighteen matches and the 2nd XI six. Whereas the opponents initially had included such teams as Imperial Tobacco Juniors, Swindon Engineering Students, Bristol Clergy, the Staff and the Asylum Cricket Club, by 1921 more familiar local schools had been added - St Brendan's, Bristol Grammar School 2nd XI, Cotham Grammar School, Kingswood and King Edward's School, Bath. Matches were also played against the Old Colstonians, Stapleton Cricket Club and Bristol University 2nd XI.

The cause of cricket had been greatly assisted by the creation of a new games pitch on the school site. The field, which had been provided at Purdown in 1895 by the Duke of Beaufort, had proved itself to be reasonable for football, 'but little or no use for cricket'. As a result, the Society of Merchant Venturers most generously agreed to the Governors' request in 1910 to provide over four acres of their adjacent field at Stapleton on a seven-year lease at £15 per annum. Out of this new land, it became possible to construct a proper cricket pitch by removing a large tree, which stood 'in the way of the game', and re-turfing a sizeable area. It was also large enough for the establishment four practice nets. The school's lease on the Purdown field, which was now largely redundant, was eventually sold in 1919 for £200. An Old Colstonian later described what the fields were actually like in 1918:

> The boundaries were different from those of the modern school - for, before the widening of Bell Hill, we had a strip of land behind the changing rooms [which later became the workshop] and the bottom wall to the field was much closer to the main building. The cricket field in front of the school was small. A path ran round it, on which we used to walk indefinitely in the days when

there were no dayrooms - and classrooms out of school hours were forbidden. At the opposite side from Bell Hill was the narrow strip of the Headmaster's orchard and fowl run, together with the rifle range (which had to be abandoned later, when a lady living on the opposite side of Bell Hill noticed bullets whizzing through her garden). Beyond this strip lay the Orchard Field with its top and bottom pitches for rugger and five division pitches for cricket.

The Merchants again came to the rescue of the school in 1917 when Bristol Corporation (in response to the government's call for all local authorities to build 'homes fit for heroes' at the end of the war) threatened to schedule the Society's field next to the school for the building of between 600 and 800 workmen's dwellings. In a memo to the Chairman of the Governors, the Headmaster emphasised the importance of the field for further games provision (with additional space needed for five simultaneous games of rugby - not to mention cricket) and the erection of a new boarding house and gymnasium. After urgent consultations with Bristol Education Committee stressing the educational importance of the land, the Governors asked the Merchants to grant a lease for a further six acres of that field. This was hurriedly enacted in 1918 and the crisis averted.

Meanwhile, football in both its forms continued to thrive, although the players sometimes became confused about which code they were

The school rugby team in 1905 (SMV Archive)

playing. *The Colstonian*, in reviewing the 1903 season, complained that 'our association play suffers chiefly from congestion. Our forwards don't keep their places, but gravitate towards the centre of the ground with the result that there is a perpetual loose scrum going on'. It was perhaps with this in mind that the school accepted an invitation in 1904 for all the boys to watch the match between Bristol Rovers and West Ham - just to see how the game should really be played!

But although the school was managing to put out two association football teams by 1910, success was not always forthcoming. The 1st XI, which played difficult matches against the Pupil Teachers' Centre and Bristol Medical Students, lost 12-0 to Bristol University in that year. Indeed, it became increasingly difficult to run teams in both codes -

a problem exacerbated by the establishment of a strong cadet corps in 1914, which competed for the limited amount of free recreational and leisure time. It was therefore no great surprise when the Governors made the decision in 1916 that 'soccer' or association football would cease to be played at school level. Rugby had therefore emerged as the main winter game.

Nevertheless, the rugby teams had also experienced difficulty in finding sufficient rugby-playing schools for their matches. Their fixture list had therefore included games against Bristol East Old Boys, Fishponds Church Lads' Brigade, Holy Trinity, J.S. Fry & Sons, Bristol University Medical Students and the Police. Gradually, however, some local schools began to make their appearance so that, by 1922, Kingswood 2nd XV, Bristol Cathedral School, St Brendan's, Bristol Grammar

Henry Shewring, the first of several Old Colstonians to play rugby for their country. He represented England ten times between 1905 and 1907. (SMV Archive)

School, Clifton College 3rd XV were all featuring as opponents. Although the First World War was seriously to curtail the number of matches played, a 2nd XV and a Junior XV had been formed by 1915. Such was the growth of the game that the 1st XV played no fewer than fourteen matches and the 2nd XV nine during the 1920-21 season.

Motivation continued to be provided by the award of 'caps' to the best performers (redesigned in 1922 as a dark blue cap with the school crest in the form of a shield) and by the example of some of its former pupils, a number of whom played for local clubs (including Bristol). Great excitement was aroused in 1905 when H.E. Shrewring was selected to play rugby for England against Ireland at centre. Five years later, the school's rugby tradition was further enhanced when W.E. Johnston, the captain of Bristol, played at fullback for England against the other three home nations - with another Old Colstonian, J.A. Spoors selected as reserve three-quarter. Spoors later joined Johnston that year on the 'British Lions' tour of South Africa.

The Rapid Growth of Societies and Activities

Dr Finn was determined not to confine the boys' leisure activities solely to sport. Keen to increase the enrichment of their personalities in as many ways as possible, he brought his own energy and vision into the creation of a burgeoning programme of cultural and recreational pursuits. Chess, draughts and bagatelle competitions were started in 1901; 'ping-pong' became the craze in 1902; a Camera Club was inaugurated in 1904, complete with a fitted dark room and a 'silver medal prize' competition; a Gardening Club commenced in 1905 with prizes for the best flowers raised on the plots allocated to individual boys; model yatch building became a new hobby in 1905; a Sketching Club was formed in 1906, its members taking tea in the adjacent fields to avoid interrupting their work; a fifth form magazine was launched in 1915; a Geological Club commenced in 1920 with field excursions to Weston-super-Mare and Wootton-under-Edge; and historical excursions by bicycle were organised by Mr Mott for fifth formers from 1920 to such places as Bradford-on-Avon and Wells.

The Headmaster's enthusiasm was infectious and he quickly gained the wholehearted involvement of other members of staff. By 1913, a programme of carefully chosen activities was being organised on Tuesday, Thursday and Saturday evenings following the afternoon games sessions and 'prep' (which was brought forward to 4.30 pm, instead of 7.00 pm). These included debating, lantern lectures, musical evenings (with a mixture of solos, quartets and poetry readings) and meetings of the various clubs and societies.

Prominent among these new societies was the sixth form Debating Society. Launched in 1905, it usually held seven debates a term and was

The cast of Le Bourgeois Gentilhomme *in 1912, one of a series of French plays staged by the Literary Society. (SMV Archive)*

attended by about fourteen members, including Mrs Finn and one or two Old Colstonians. The Literary Society, which was started in 1910 for boys in the fifth and sixth forms and supported by Mr and Mrs Finn and a number of masters, held regular readings of Shakespeare's plays. As it extended the range of its activities, it began a series of costumed performances of French plays with *Le Barbier de Seville* in 1911 and inaugurated a literary competition in 1915. The society must also take credit for staging the first real school play in 1920, when *The Rivals* was performed by its members. Their growing confidence in public speaking also encouraged the boys to organise the school's first mock election in 1920, when 'The By-Election at Coulstone' was undertaken, ending in a Unionist victory!

On his appointment as Headmaster, Dr Finn quickly revived the tradition of the Christmas concert, which had lapsed in Mr Hancock's latter years. In 1901, therefore, a choir of 36 boys under the music master, Mr W.S. Calway, performed alongside the band of 25 musicians conducted by Colour-Sergeant R. Evans, who had composed a special march, *The Colstonian*, for the occasion. Given the new wave of enthusiasm within the school, it is hardly surprising that membership of the band quickly grew - encouraged partly by the award of badges for proficiency (a harp surrounded by a wreath and worn on the right arm). Sergeant Evans, supported by four masters who each became responsible for a particular instrument, advertised the formation of a 'supplementary' or training band. Inundated by the 65 volunteers who quickly appeared, he decided to form a drum-and-fife band and a bugle band in addition to the training band.

By 1905, therefore, there were four bands in operation - plus a string orchestra, which began to perform at school concerts. Between 80 and 90 boys were now receiving special music training, including 32 who were learning the piano and others who were receiving lessons in violin, brass or wind. Nevertheless, such was the dramatic rise of the bands that, by 1910, Dr Finn had become so alarmed that he actually proposed their abolition to the Governors. 'The existence of the school band', he said, 'interfered seriously with the education of the boys now that many more subjects were required to be taught than were required when the band was instituted'. The Governors wisely urged him to give the matter further thought and he later withdrew his request. By 1918, boys were being entered for the examinations of the Associated Board of the Royal Academy of Music and the Royal College of Music.

The choir, too, continued to blossom and played a prominent part in the carol concert, which became a regular feature on the last Sunday of the Christmas term. Mrs Finn showed her appreciation of their commitment in rehearsals by giving members of the choir a special tea in December 1902. By sheer coincidence, however, the rugby team - returning to school after a victory - showed that sense of timing, which is so essential in sport, by just happening to appear at the very moment when tea was being served. They were invited to stay by a Headmaster's wife who was becoming deeply involved in the life of the school. Encouragement was also given to all musicians from 1904 through the annual award of the Band and Choir Challenge Cup to the most successful member; and by the introduction of the house music competition in 1919 for choirs, vocal quartets and instrumental solos.

The choir and bands gave many public performances. In 1904, for instance, the choir took part with eight village choirs in a choral festival at Stapleton Church, while the brass and bugle bands played at College Green railway station for the visit of Her Royal Highness Princess Henrietta of Battenberg. At the same time the annual December concerts became more and more ambitious. In 1907, the main item was Parry's *The Pied Piper of Hamelin*; in 1908, Dr A.H. Brewer, organist at Gloucester cathedral, was invited to conduct one of his own works for soloist, choir and orchestra; and in 1909, a programme of 17th century music included a performance by the choir of Purcell's opera, *King Arthur*.

One other activity made its appearance in 1907, when the Rifle Club was formed. The Governors had agreed to the installation of a 'Morris

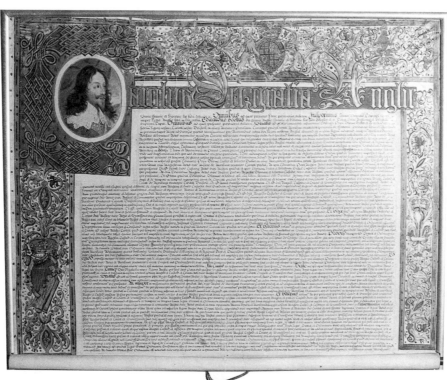

The new charter granted to the Society of Merchant Venturers, Bristol in 1639 by King Charles I. (By courtesy of the Society: photograph by Bromhead Photography)

A drawing by Edward Cashin in 1824 of The Great House in St Augustine's Back in Bristol, which became home to the boys of Colston's School from 1710 to 1861. Note the two boys in traditional dress by the gate, who were on duty as 'doorkeepers'. (By courtesy of the Bristol Museums and Art Gallery)

The School Chapel Choir, conducted by the Director of Music, Ian Holmes, at the Charter Day Service of the Society of Merchant Venturers in Bristol Cathedral in 2000. (Photograph by Martin Chainey)

Presentation of Bibles to Upper Sixth Leavers in 2001 by the Society of Merchant Venturers - a tradition which dates back to 1842. Seen here are Ben Burton (Head Boy), Mr Geoffrey Matthews (Master of the Society) and Rachael Walker (Head Girl).
(Photograph by John Wroughton)

Presentation of buns to the pupils by the Society of Merchant Venturers after their Charter Day Service in November 2001 - a tradition which dates back to the 19th century and is based on a custom at Christ's Hospital in London. Seen here (from the left) are Natasha Woodward (partly hidden), Edward Fursdon, Edward Gallimore, Amy Nommeots-Nomm and Mrs Geoffrey Matthews, wife of the Master of the Society.
(Photograph by Martin Chainey)

The Colston Day Parade in November 2001 to Colston's tomb in All Saints' Church, Bristol. Seen here are (front) Samantha Poulson of Colston's Collegiate School (the Lord Lieutenant's Cadet) and the Head Girl of Colston's Girls' School; (2nd row) Ashley Lowndes and Kelly Harrison (Head Boy and Head Girl of Colston's Collegiate): followed by members of the Dolphin Society (1749), the Grateful Society (1759) and the Anchor Society (1769), which were formed to honour Colston's memory. (Photograph by Steve Waters)

The statue of Edward Colston, designed by John Cassidy, which was erected in the city centre in 1895. The school has traditionally placed a wreath here to commemorate Colston's birthday on 13th November. (Photograph by John Wroughton)

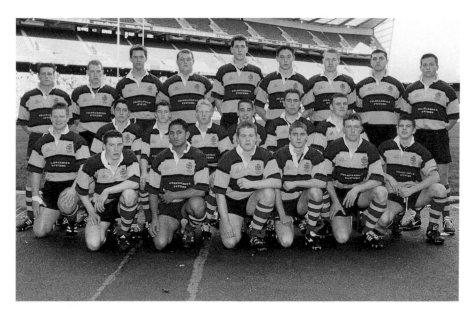

National Champions. Colston's 1st XV in 2000, after winning The Daily Mail Cup *for the sixth successive year. Oliver Barkley, who captained the side (middle row - 3rd from the right), gained a full England cap in 2001.*

(Photograph by courtesy of www.kickphoto.co.uk)

National Champions. Colston's Under-11 rugby team, which won the Preparatory Schools' Rugby Tournament in 1999, seen here with Roger Uttley, the former England international and coach.

Stephen Pritchard's production of The Oresteia *in 1999. (Photograph by courtesy of Mr & Mrs George Phillips)*

The Annual Dinner of the CCF, 2001. From the left: Mr David Crawford (Headmaster); Hannah Coller, Samantha Poulson & Dana Drake (all of whom are members of Colston's CCF); David Faulkner (President of the Society of Old Colstonians) and Brigadier Hugh Pye (Chairman of Governors). Photograph by Clive Warren.

Joe Wakley, Cameron Bracewell and Jamie Doubleday learning the art of survival at the Lower School's summer camp in Pembroke, 1999. (Photograph by Keith Watts)

tube range' and the purchase of War Office miniature rifles at a total cost of £52 12s 0d (raised partly with the help of subsidies from the Society of Merchant Venturers and the National Rifle Association). The club, which grew rapidly in popularity, organised an annual competition for the Donegall Badge and shooting matches for the sections within the school. Quite apart from the club's matches against other schools (including those at Malmesbury and Olveston), affiliation to the Bristol and District Rifle Clubs' Association enabled it to compete with local clubs in the Stansfield Cup Competition and the Miniature Bisley Open Competition at Eastville organised by the *Daily Express*.

The Expansion of School Life

Dr Finn was not only a man of high expectations, firm discipline and abundant enthusiasm, he was also a man of great human sympathy. He and his wife were determined to make school life a happy and enjoyable experience for the boys entrusted to their care. The place therefore became much more civilised and conditions far less spartan under the new regime. Reveille, for instance, was changed from 6.00 am to 6.30 am (and 7.00 am on Sundays); an additional light supper of cheese and biscuits was served later in the evening; 'orderly duty', which had seen the boys undertake a whole range of domestic chores, was abolished in 1905; a drinks fountain was placed in the playground in 1910; and afternoon school was fixed to start an hour later in winter to give more time for outdoor recreational activities. [By 1904, lessons during the summer were taught in the mornings between 9.00 am and 12.55 am with two ten-minute breaks; and in the afternoons between 2.35 and 5.00 pm]

Some welcome refinements were introduced to meal times, as one Old Colstonian later recalled: 'Mugs and urns gave way to teapots, sugar basins, milk jugs, spoons and knives - so the place became more like a home and less like a barracks'. The staff, too, became less remote. A 'high table' was instituted on the platform in the dining room, enabling the Headmaster, staff and prefects to dine together in the presence of all the boys (the staff had always eaten separately before). Parents, too, were made much more welcome in the school, attending prize givings, concerts and athletic sports. From 1907, the Headmaster and his wife gave an annual Garden Party in July for parents and friends of the boys with the school band providing background music.

Dr Finn also realised the importance of the tuck shop to the morale of the boys. This had been run since the late 1870s by Miss Lake, whose father had been the school's drill sergeant. An Old Boy, writing later in *The Colstonian*, recalled 'old Mother Lake' and her mobile shop

The School Dining Room in 1905, illustrating Dr Finn's 'homely reforms' with the introduction of tablecloths, proper crockery and cutlery, water jugs etc. Note also the High Table, where Headmaster, Staff and Prefects dined in the presence of the other boys. The clock and portrait of Colston are still in place in 2002. (SMV Archive)

in the covered shed: 'One hundred and twenty hungry boys awaited her arrival as she entered the gate armed with her two baskets of goodies; and one may conjecture why poor old 'Ma' was not crushed to death with monotonous regularity twice a week'. By 1903, she was already elderly and her visits, which provided an income for her upkeep, became less frequent (especially in bad weather). A.J. Brown, who was at Colston's between 1900 and 1905, later recalled how Miss Lake's services were eventually taken over on Wednesdays and Thursdays by 'a shopkeeper, who would come up from the city and set up a trestle table and exhibit things for sale - fruit, apples, oranges, tins of sardines, tins of anchovies, small pots of paste, fish paste and several things like that'. He went on to say that, although very few boys had pocket money in those days, those who did have cash (Brown himself had twopence a week) readily spent it on items of food to improve the quality of their tea. In 1912, the school decided to open its own tuck shop. Profits were used to finance the growing range of activities, including the hire of lantern slides, costumes for the French plays and sheet music; the fares of boys travelling to away matches; and the cost of sports equipment.

The Headmaster's success in creating a much happier and more homely atmosphere within the school is confirmed by the fact that very few boys were expelled during his twenty-one years in charge. Discipline improved out of all recognition. Furthermore, there were hardly any cases of boys running away in a state of misery, although two new boys did leave in 1904 right at the start of Dr Finn's headship - Howard Gregory ('on account of his homesickness') and Harold Evans (who 'absconded on the first day of term'). On the other hand, Thomas Pope left in 1909 on a matter of principle - 'because football is compulsory'.

Nevertheless, Mr Kinchin, the handyman who joined the school in 1920, later made the point in *The Colstonian* that, in spite of the reforms, the boys at Colston's were still subjected to a a fairly severe regime:

When I came here, it was just naked gas lights in the changing rooms and toilets. Someone had to go round to light them all: the gasboy, they used to call him (a middle school boy or something of that sort). There was no heating anywhere then; and they had to get up at 6.30 in the morning. There was no hot water...cold water was piped from a huge tank on the main roof, which was filled with rain water. Often, in summer, larvae could be seen swimming about in the bowls. Every boy was inspected very thoroughly; far more discipline then than there is now. They were all inspected - the juniors behind the ears - and the Prefects used to yank them over to the Changers [slang for changing rooms]. Nail brushes and all sorts were used - I've seen it done. Everyone fell in to the drum and bugle; parade three times a day - extremely strict. Chapel first of all [at 7.15 am] - and then woe betide the boys who had to have the cosh [slang for the cane]; that came next. They were coshed by the Headmaster after chapel and before breakfast. Every morning there were some for coshing; I've seen as many as eight. The then Headmaster (Dr Finn) used to lay it on well and proper. I almost hesitate to say how many he used to lay on - but it often ran into double figures.

An Old Colstonian later described his own experience of discipline as a new boy in 1918:

Our discipline was hard enough if one can judge by the reaction when we were released from it. I remember the last day of my first term. Those boys who had caught trains had gone off to the stations. The hundred or so of us who lived in Bristol remained waiting for the signal, when the Head suddenly noticed that two of us were missing. We were paraded, the roll was called, the names of the absentees taken and two Prefects were sent off to bring them back. Meanwhile, the rest of us innocents waited two hours until the culprits returned.

When we did get off at last, it was to one of the happiest days of my life. I still remember the joy of going off to do Christmas shopping with my family. I was rich with 4s 6d, for in those days boys below the fifth form were not permitted to keep a farthing of money - so our Colston and Charter Day shillings (along with 2s 6d kindly left by two Old Boys called Philip Jones and Philip Vaughan) were in our pockets, and thirty-five years ago [i.e. in 1918] that sum was wealth.

Perhaps one of the most popular reforms introduced by Dr Finn was that of a new uniform in 1908. The previous one, which had been brought into use in 1885 (see page 148), had been widely criticised and greatly disliked. The Bristol *Mirror and Times* had commented in 1903: 'What a pity the dress of the Colston boys was ever altered! The modern tight-fitting jacket and knickerbockers of sombre blue, unrelieved by a touch of colour, have their ugliness completed by the odd-shaped boots'. An Old Colstonian, writing in the *Western Daily Press*, was even more scathing as he highlighted 'the uncomfortable and irrational uniform', which was 'ugly and meaningless', and the 'ridiculous pill-box cap'.

The Governors gave careful consideration to the alternatives on offer by parading four boys at their July meeting in 1908, each wearing a different sample. They finally selected a dark grey Norfolk suit. With the jacket, boys who were over 14 would wear long trousers, boys over 12 short trousers 'banded at the knee' and boys under 12 short trousers

A coach taking boys to the railway station at the end of term in 1908. (SMV Archive)

open at the knee. The younger boys also wore white Eton collars, while the peaked blue school cap with a dolphin badge was compulsory for all (although the prefect's cap consisted of a full shield with two dolphins and an anchor). By 1912, shoes had replaced those 'odd-shaped boots'. The clothing inventory, sent to parents in 1920, also included an overcoat or mackintosh and the appropriate sports gear (whites for cricket and dark blue jerseys and shorts for rugby). [It is interesting to note from surviving photographs that Dr Finn had clearly introduced a school cap early in his headship to replace the much-disliked polo cap with chinstrap. Nevertheless, the latter was apparently still used on occasions, until 1908, both by the band and by boys drilling with their newly-acquired carbines - see page 197.]

Health and safety also received a much higher priority. A 'nurse-matron' attended the sickroom (used for ordinary illness) and the sanatorium (brought into use for isolation purposes), while the school doctor (or 'surgeon') attended the school twice a week. Dr Bernard, who

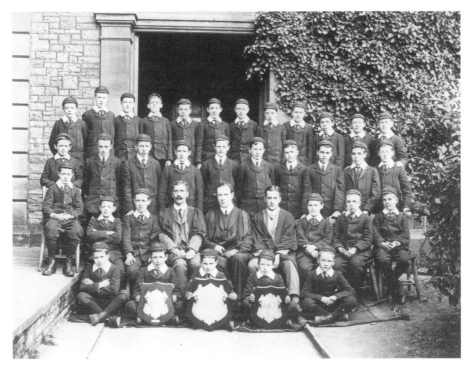

West House in 1910, showing boys in the new uniform (introduced in 1910) of grey Norfolk jackets, trousers (banded at the knee for younger boys, who also wore the white Eton Collar) and caps. The Headmaster (holding a mortar board) is seen on the second row with the Housemaster, Major G.R.A. Beckett, on his right. (SMV Archive)

had been appointed to the job in 1871, actually retired in 1905 - but was immediately succeeded by his son! One complete innovation caused a stir in December 1903 with the introduction of fire drill for the boys and the installation of 'life-saving' fire appliances. Earlier in the year, the Headmaster had consulted with the Chief Fire Officer, who had recommended 'canvas shoots to be fixed to certain dormitories' as fire escapes. Apart from the cost involved in this scheme (£50), the Governors also invested further in safety by instructing the Bristol Water Company to lay 'a three-inch special fire main' to the main entrance of the school 'with one of the company's new fire hydrants fixed at the end'. The prospectus, however, revealed the main weapon in the school's armoury for fighting fires, when it announced that a number of the boys had formed 'a fire brigade'.

A dormitory c. 1905-1910. (SMV Archive)

Dr Bernard coped admirably with the epidemic of mumps in 1906, the outbreaks of influenza and mild diphtheria in 1907 and the more serious outbreak of scarlet fever in 1909, which caused all exeats to be suspended. The more professional approach to health was illustrated in 1909 by the purchase of 'a weighing machine' and 'register book' in which could be recorded 'the physical progress of the boys'. The vexed question of sanitation, which had exercised both doctors and governors for decades, finally neared a solution in 1907, when it was agreed to abandon the old system of drainage linked to the cesspool and to lay down a new system linked to the main sewer 'recently constructed in Bell Hill'. This would incorporate manholes, inspection chambers and air vents. At the same time, an automatic flushing tank was installed to the boys' urinals.

Hygiene, too, was given a much greater priority, although boys still found conditions somewhat spartan for their early-morning wash. A.J. Brown recalled that, when he was at school between 1900 and 1910, the washroom contained 'numbered hooks on which our towels were hung - and a number of basins filled with cold water'. This had been placed in the basins by the maids on the previous evening - and, according to Brown, on several occasions in winter time they 'had to break the ice on the top of the water' before they washed. In addition, however, all boys were expected to have a hot bath several times a week. The baths were organised by prefects in the period between lunch and the resumption of classes at 2.30 pm., boys being taken into the bathroom by 'tables' (i.e. the groups allocated to tables in the dining room). 'There were about thirty baths all round the room', said Brown. 'The prefect saw that every boy had a bath and they didn't waste hot water and soap. It was supposed to take us twenty minutes or so - and, as soon as we had finished, another table would be coming through'.

On a brighter note, the boys did enjoy a number of special events. In 1908, for instance, the school attended the visit of the king and queen to open the King Edward VII Dock in Bristol. They were transported by horse-drawn brakes and presented later with a box of chocolates by the Lord Mayor as a memento. In November 1919, they were invited (together with Colston's Girls' School and the Merchant Venturers' Secondary School) by the Society of Merchant Venturers to a programme of entertainment in the Victoria Rooms to celebrate the country's victory in the Great War. Some 1,500 boys and girls were present, each receiving a gift of chocolate from the Merchants. Peace Day celebrations on 19th July, however, were largely ruined by heavy rain. The planned programme of activities at school (including sports, conjuring entertainment, fireworks and illuminations) was seriously curtailed - and the boys quickly found themselves back in the classroom.

Dr Finn also tried to inject something of a school spirit and pride into the Colston tradition. A school song, *O Stand We Together*, was composed (1902) and sung at various functions; the statue of the founder was renovated and sited in the entrance hall (1904); and, following a collection in support of the British Antarctic Expedition in 1910, a request was made that the dog, which the school had purchased for Captain Scott, should be named 'Colston'. The school still attended the two annual services in November (Charter Day and Colston Day)

Boys processing to the Cathedral for the Colston Day Service, sometime after 1908.
(SMV Archive)

- a period which was increasingly referred to by Old Boys as
'Colstontide'. However, with the reduction in the number of
foundationers to 75 in 1907 (see page 204), it now became possible on
that occasion to present *each* boy in the school with the two new
shillings funded by the endowments for Pupils numbered '49' and '76'.
The latter was now nominated for one year only by the Headmaster in
consultation with the staff. The award, which was announced at Prize
Giving, went to the boy judged 'most worthy' - normally the Head
Prefect or one of the other prefects.

A major opportunity for instilling pride in the school's long history
presented itself in July 1910 with the bi-centenary of its foundation. As
early as January 1907, the Old Colstonians had proposed the building of
a Memorial Chapel to celebrate the event, particularly as the present
School Chapel was no longer large enough to accommodate all the pupils.
By the end of the year, however, the idea had been dropped for fear of
infringing the new Board of Education regulations concerning
denominational schools (particularly in view of the fact that by 1907
over 25% of the boys were nonconformist in religion). A Memorial
Library was now proposed instead on a site immediately adjacent to the
new science building. The Old Colstonians raised over £600, with the
boys themselves donating a further £100, towards the eventual cost of
£949. Some money was raised from an old stock of the large circular

Laying the foundation stone for the Bi-centenary Memorial Library, 9th July 1910. The science block is visible in the background with work nearing completion on a new upper floor on half of it to provide a art room and an additional classroom. (SMV Archive)

dolphin badges, which had been worn on the original school uniform. These were framed in wood taken from the old much-loved Tulip Tree and presented to Old Colstonians who had contributed £5 to the Library.

The celebrations, which took place on Saturday 9th July 1910, commenced with the placing of a laurel wreath on the statue of Edward Colston in the city centre (which had been unveiled in 1895), where the school band played *The Last Post*. The boys then marched in procession with the Merchants, Governors and Old Colstonians' Society to Merchants Hall and then on to the Cathedral for a service in which the bishop took as his sermon text, 'Go and do thou likewise'. At Stapleton in the afternoon, the foundation stone for the Memorial Library was laid by Edward Colston (a member of the founder's family), presided over by the Chairman of the Governors, Mr W.W. Jose, who had first joined the Governing Board in 1859. A record of the ceremony was inscribed on vellum and sealed in a bottle, which was placed under the stone. After the ceremony, a 'Past v Present' cricket match was played and, to complete the celebrations, the Old Colstonians held their own service

An artist's impression of the Memorial Library, opened in 1911. The science block behind shows new upper floors for both its wings. However, although half this project was completed in 1910, the remainder was postponed until 1927. (SMV Archive)

next day in Stapleton Church.

It was firmly resolved to observe 10th July each year in future as 'Commemoration Day' and to organise a series of events on the nearest weekend. This quickly became a tradition. It was perhaps appropriate that the preacher at the Commemoration Day service in 1912 was the Reverend James Jones, a former pupil who had become Head Monitor and then the Pupil Teacher under Mr Rowlatt, before eventually rising to Second Master under Mr Hancock. He had later become Headmaster of the Town School at Ventnor in the Isle of Wight, prior to his ordination for parish work in Birmingham and Rushbury. In his sermon, he acknowledged his 'lifelong gratitude for the bounty of Edward Colston', for it was, he said, 'now 54 years ago that a poor, tired mother and her son stood in the Hall of the Merchant Venturers' Society in King Street and heard the welcome decision that the boy was elected to enter Colston's Hospital'. He concluded in these words: 'The voice of our great Founder and, above all, the voice of our Blessed Redeemer Himself calls individually and insistently to us today, saying 'Go and do thou likewise'. The Memorial Library, housing 3,000 volumes, was eventually opened in January 1911 by Mr Edward Colston, the boys singing hymns and, finally, the School Song.

The Rise of the Old Colstonians

The Colston Fraternal Association, which had been founded in 1854 at the prompting of Mr Rowlatt, never regarded its chief purpose as that of staging reunions for Old Boys of the school. Its aim was primarily to support boys in need when they left school and on occasions later in life when they ran into difficulties. The association's funds had built up substantially over the years, partly as a result of the contributions made by the boys themselves while still at school through the donation of one of the two new shillings given to them annually at the 'Colstontide' celebrations in November. By 1905, the association held a balance of £4,300, in spite of generous payments made each year to school leavers (see pages 116-117).

By the 1890s, many Old Boys were taking a much closer interest in the school, attending events and listening with enthusiasm to the Headmaster's reports at both Prize Giving and the annual general meeting and dinner of the Fraternal Association. As a result of informal discussions on those occasions, the idea emerged of staging an Old Colstonians' reunion and dinner. This eventually took place on 12th November 1894 as part of the Colstontide programme. Those present took the opportunity of subscribing for two memorial brasses to be fixed on the wall of the School Chapel in memory of Mr Rowlatt (the former Headmaster) and Mr Greenwood (the former music master), both of whom had recently died. The reunion dinners quickly became popular, with almost a hundred attending the 1898 event held at Stuckey's Restaurant. By then a committee had been formed, which also organised a series of 'musical reunions', plus a number of informal get-togethers at the Crown and Dove Hotel.

Events moved rapidly on. In 1898, the Old Colstonians' Cricket Club was formed, with the Duke of Beaufort as its first president. During its initial season it ran two teams on the Eastville Rovers football ground, the 1st XI playing twenty-seven matches and the 2nd XI twelve. Sadly, the club broke up in the following year due to the difficulty in finding a permanent ground, although the fixture against the school was revived in 1907. On the other hand, an Old Colstonians' Rugby Club had been established 1902, while the continuing interest of the Old Boys in sport was sustained by the offer in 1898, which enabled them to purchase replacement 'caps' for those previously awarded - or to obtain them for the first time, if they had regularly played rugby or cricket for the school in years before caps had been awarded.

In 1903, the logical decision was taken that the Colston Fraternal Association and the Old Colstonians' Reunion Society should combine for both their annual dinner in November and the 'smoking concerts'.

Two years later, the number attending the dinner had reached 126. By then the society was also organising an annual outing to such places as Badminton, Berkeley Castle and Bradford-on-Avon and an annual service in Stapleton Church in May. A further important development took place in March 1908, when the society staged its first-ever London dinner at the Holborn Restaurant, having contacted over 100 London-based Old Boys. The aim was twofold - to raise money for the bi-centenary Memorial Library and to establish a London branch of the society. The latter objective was achieved one year later, when the Society of Old Colstonians in London held its inaugural dinner at the Trocadero Restaurant. The sixty members who attended unanimously elected Dr Finn as their first president.

Annual dinner of the Society of Old Colstonians in London, 1919 (SMV Archive)

Meanwhile, another significant step had been taken in 1907 with the formation of the Colstonian Guild. This firmly emphasised the nature of the school's original foundation and the continuing strength of Christian belief among many of its former pupils. Members of the guild promised to pray for Colstonians each day, to receive communion regularly and, on three specified Sundays each year, to join in the 'Guild Corporate Communion' wherever they were in the world. The idea, according to one organiser, was 'the natural outcome of the way in which church teaching and working has ever been interwoven with the life at Colston's School'. With Dr Finn as its president (enthusiastically supported by the Reverend John Hancock) 40 members - including some boys - took their first communion together on Charter Day in November 1907. Membership rapidly grew, reaching 89 by 1910, 180 by 1914 and 330 by 1919.

The guild soon played an important part in the annual programme of Old Boys' activities, which centred increasingly on two months in the year. From 1910, the Old Colstonians' summer festival was held over a weekend in July to coincide with Commemoration Day. After a garden party and a cricket match against the school on the Saturday, the Colstonian Guild held its communion on the Sunday morning in Stapleton Church (attended also by boys who had been recently confirmed), followed by breakfast. The annual Old Colstonians' service, supported by the school choir, was then held in the afternoon, followed by tea at school. The other main month for reunions was November, when Colstontide was extended to include (in addition to the two services) the Old Colstonian Society's annual dinner, a corporate communion of the Colstonian Guild and (by 1920) a rugby match between the Old Boys and the school.

The Colstonian Guild after their corporate communion at Stapleton in 1919. Dr Finn is in the middle of the third row with a number of boys in the front.(SMV Archive)

Old Boys of the school were increasingly playing an active role in the business, commercial and professional life of Bristol and beyond. By the outbreak of war in 1914, no fewer than 118 Old Colstonians were listed as living and working abroad. It is true that few had become really famous in the wider world. Nevertheless, apart from Thomas Chatterton (see Chapter 5), the school could boast Sir Francis Freeling (1764-1836), who had become Secretary of the General Post Office; Sir Stanley Reed, who became Editor of *The Times of India* in 1907 and who accompanied the Prince and Princess of Wales on their tour of that country; and C.R. Penrose who, by 1907, was a most distinguished HM Inspector of Factories. Several former members of staff had also gone on to headships, including E.I.A. Phillips (Kelly School, Tavistock), E.T.S. Tadman (King Edward VI School, Macclesfield), L.J. Calway (All Saints' School, Clifton), C.P. Rosling (Horwell End School), H. Baxter (King's College School, Peterborough), J. Jones (the Town School, Ventnor) and H.H. Hutchinson (Rugeley Grammar School). In 1921, the first Old Boy (Mr Fred Organ) was appointed to the Governing Board of Colston's School.

The Cadet Corps and the First World War

The school's long tradition of drilling the boys under the command of a drill sergeant extended back to 1843 (see page 71). Against the background of the Crimean War (1854-56), this activity became even more fashionable in many public schools throughout the country as the century progressed. By 1900, therefore, the boys at Colston's were very accustomed to marching in step behind the band to the Colstontide services in November and on other major occasions. In 1905, the drill took on a more military aspect when (this time against the backcloth of the Boer War) the Governors authorised the purchase of 'about 40 old military carbines' at 1s 6d each for use in musketry drill. They were keen to stress, however, that these were 'not for firing'. It should be noted that many public schools seized this moment to establish a cadet force - that at King Edward's School, Bath, for instance, was founded in 1900. The question was not really discussed at Colston's until 1914, following the outbreak of war.

At their meeting in December of that year, the Governors considered a memo which had been received from Field Marshal Lord Kitchener, regarding 'the country's need for young men fit to become potential commanders of men'. They decided to apply immediately to the War Office for permission to set up an Officer Training Corps and to the Society of Merchant Venturers for funding. The Headmaster hurriedly penned a letter to the War Office in support of this application, realising

Boys in normal school uniform, drilling with their newly-acquired carbines (purchased in 1905). The Cadet Corps was not established until 1915. (SMV Archive)

that the school's case was not strong. He accepted that only one former pupil had obtained a commission in the army prior to the outbreak of the war, but explained that the situation had now been changed by the raising of the leaving age to eighteen. With 21 boys now in the sixth form, he was confident that 'a sufficient number would seek commissions in the territory forces to justify the formation of an Officer Training Corps'.

The application, however, was refused - the War Office judging that Colston's was more likely to produce recruits for the ranks than officers for the regiments. Permission was therefore granted instead to establish a Cadet Corps, which would be attached to the 4th Battalion of the Gloucestershire Regiment. By April 1915, the Merchants had generously voted a grant of £100 towards the setting-up of the corps with a promise of a further £100 on loan should this become necessary. As the initial cost of uniform and equipment for just 60 boys had been estimated at £165, the loan was quickly taken up.

The Headmaster was duly appointed commander of the corps with the rank of captain. The cadets (the number of whom had risen to 125 by 1917) were divided into four platoons, which corresponded with the four boys' houses within the school. These were organised by three other members of staff, who were too old for active service, but who had enrolled as volunteers - Mr S.V.R. Drapes (the Second Master), Mr S.N. Player and Mr W.S. Calway. A silver challenge cup was provided by the Society of Merchant Venturers for inter-platoon competitions. The boys, who according to regulations were all over 13, wore uniforms bearing a dolphin badge, paraded twice a week, undertook periodic route marches and attended both field days and camps. Part of the old coach house was converted into their armoury. Boys who opted out of joining the cadets were normally sent to work in the school garden instead.

COLSTON SCHOOL CADET CORPS. STAPLETON. 3.

The Cadet Corps on parade shortly after its formation in 1915. Note the old open-sided 'shed' in the background on the left, which was replaced in 1928 by a colonnaded covered way built in brick. (SMV Archive)

Needless to say, the school was seriously affected by the war. As hostilities continued, so it became increasingly difficult for the Headmaster to obtain supplies of clothing, to get boots repaired, to find domestic servants and to maintain the normal diet. In December 1916, the Dr Finn had reassured the Governors that, if the government ordered 'meatless days' throughout the country, no difficulty would be experienced in providing the school with adequate substitutes. By April 1918, however, he was facing the harsh reality of a wartime rationing scheme which had been imposed in Bristol. The school's weekly allowance of meat and margarine had been cut by half, tea by a third and sugar by a quarter. Nevertheless, he was able to reassure the Chairman of Governors in a memo that he had compensated for the losses with beans, peas, lentils, rice and syrup. The boys, too, had helped the situation by growing potatoes in the kitchen garden. Then, in a dramatic use of statistics, he showed that the boys had not suffered at all from the shortages, because 'their total weight increased during the Christmas term by over 12 hundredweights'. The newly-acquired 'weighing machine' had been useful after all! Nevertheless, Norman Emmerson (1916-20) recalls how he was 'always hungry' during his time at school.

Teaching resources were also badly stretched. From December 1914, the Governors' minutes are dotted with reports on the latest staffing situation. During the Christmas Term of that year, no fewer than three of the masters had left for military service, followed by two more in the Spring Term of 1915. By 1917, six of the eight resident staff were on the front line and were soon joined by the school doctor and the school gardener. By the end of the war, nine teachers had seen service in all (seven of them with commissions). The Headmaster did what he could to find temporary replacements. He used a total of sixteen in all, including a local clergyman, Mrs Finn and four other ladies. [Colston's first female teacher, in fact, had been Miss Norah Fry, who had been appointed in 1909 to teach art on a part-time basis.] For their part, the Governors did their best to reassure those masters who were serving their country - partly by making up the difference in salary in 1915 for three whose army pay was lower than that provided by the school; and partly by ensuring that, on their return from active service in 1918, their salaries took account of their years in the army.

The Governors also heard with great sadness of the death of three of their former teachers on front line duty - Captain G.C. Watson of the Devonshire Regiment in Mesopatamia (1916); Lieutenant S. Warburton of the Lancashire Fusiliers in Salonica (1916); and Lieutenant W.A. Wildblood of the Royal Army Service Corps in Flanders (1917). They were gradually informed, too, of the loss of 77 Old Boys in the fighting out of a total of 510 who served. It is interesting to note that, out of this number, no fewer than 95 had been awarded commissions - an indication, perhaps, that the War Office had got it wrong in 1914 over the formation of an Officer Training Corps at the school.

A further indication of this was provided in 1915 by the exciting news that three Colston's boys (K.A.T. McLennan, H. Munden and G.N. Wood) had been placed 1st, 2nd and 3rd respectively out of 340 candidates in the examination for admission to the Royal Military Academy, Sandhurst - each gaining a Prize Cadetship of £107 10s 0d. Furthermore, M.W. Hemingway had been successful in the entrance examination for the Royal Military Academy at Woolwich. The Headmaster was rightly proud of these achievements which 'no school had ever emulated'. The Governors, in a rare burst of uncharacteristic

Harold Hayward, who played for the 1st XI cricket team in 1912. Having joined the Welsh Regiment during the 1st World War, he was awarded the Military Cross in 1918 for continuing to direct his platoon after being wounded in action. He was praised for his courage and inspirational leadership in capturing two machine-gun positions following heavy hand-to-hand fighting. (SMV Archives)

praise, resolved that they should 'congratulate Dr Finn upon the brilliant success of the school and assure him that they appreciate highly the ability and good work on his part without which this success could not have been achieved'. It is interesting to note that McLennan, who served with the King's Own Scottish Borderers, retired in 1947 as a Brigadier, having been awarded the Military Cross; Munden transferred to the RAF, after serving with the King's Flying Corps in the First World War and winning the DFC; and Wood, who served with the Dorset Regiment, rose to the rank of Major General and was not only awarded the DSO and MC, but was also appointed CB and CBE.

After the war, the Old Colstonians' Society was very keen to establish a suitable memorial to those Old Boys and staff who had died in the conflict. In 1919, therefore, they put forward a further plea for the building of a Memorial Chapel, commissioned an impressive design, gained an estimate of £5,000 and launched a subscription fund. When, however, the fund fell far short of the intended target, the plans were quickly changed. Their 'Memorial Committee' eventually submitted a scheme to the Governors, which finally cost £2,020, for a War Memorial to be sited in the Dining Hall. The plan involved enlarging the dining space by removing the wall between the Dining Hall and the lower hall, panelling the room in English oak 'in the style of the early Georgian period' and creating a memorial around the doorway leading into the Headmaster's house. The school arms and motto were to be displayed over the centre with a memorial inscription on a frieze below; the arms of both the Society of Merchant Venturers and the See of Bristol incorporated in the two mantelpieces; and the names of the fallen inscribed on the two side panels. Above the doorway would hang the portrait of the founder, as stipulated in his will - i.e. that 'his picture' (which had hung in his drawing room at Mortlake) should be sent to Bristol and 'set up in the schoolroom of his Hospital'. The Memorial was officially opened in 1922 by Lord Roundway (a member of the founder's family) with *The Last Post* played by buglers from the school band and the dedication given by an Old Colstonian, the Reverend James Jones, who, as Head Monitor in 1861, had been the first boy to enter the Dining Hall.

The Reverend James Jones, former pupil (1858-65), teacher and Second Master at the school. A frequent visitor to Colston's in later years, he had preached at the Commemoration Day service in 1912 (see above) and made the dedication of the War Memorial in 1922. (SMV Archive)

A Fine Balancing Act

Dr Finn had brought much-needed energy and vision onto the scene. His infectious enthusiasm, unstinting effort, single-minded determination and human sympathy had quickly endeared him to the Governors, who were swept along by his ambition both for the school and for the individuals who were committed to his care. There is no doubt, too, that he was greatly assisted in his plans by a sudden surge of support from the Old Colstonians and by the reports of visiting inspectors, who lent weight to his arguments for improved facilities.

Nevertheless, when Dr Finn commenced his duties in 1901, the Governors and Headmaster together faced a most challenging future of mounting costs, rising prices, diminishing assets and government legislation, which was to impact seriously on the school's finances.

Against this background, they were confronted by three serious problems, which required immediate attention - the need to improve and expand facilities to cater for the rapid rise in numbers; the need to improve staff conditions, including salaries and pensions, thus ensuring that masters of high calibre could not only be recruited, but also retained; and the need to expand the curriculum in a way that would prepare boys for university.

The story of the years 1901-1922 is therefore the story of how the Governors managed in a most skilful manner to achieve a fine balancing act between insolvency and prosperity. Whereas capital was always needed to fund the Headmaster's plans and to tackle the problems outlined above, the finances of the Colston Trust were in a perilous state, the Board of Education was always reluctant to authorise loans and, in the face of escalating costs, the annual accounts were normally in deficit. On the other hand, they feared that raising the school fees would seriously reduce pupil numbers, thus threatening the very life-blood of the school; and trimming the Headmaster's ambitions could relegate Colston's once more to a position of mediocrity.

(a) The Rapid Rise in Numbers

Dr Finn, fully aware of the need to boost the number of fee paying pupils, set great store on the effectiveness of the new prospectus, which he had designed. Published in July 1903 and illustrated for the first time with photographs, it had a print-run of 2,000 copies, which were distributed to the clergy, hotel keepers and other influential groups in Bristol and the neighbouring counties. It was supported by a special information sheet for 'free scholars' and a large advertising campaign (costing £50) in 30 weekly papers and 10 daily papers. The Headmaster was gratified by the results of the campaign. In a note to the Chairman of Governors in September 1903, he claimed that he had already received twenty-three requests for the prospectus (compared with just three at the same time in the previous year) and nine new fee paying pupils had already enrolled. 'This shows pretty conclusively what advertising can do', he concluded.

Entry into the school was still gained through an entrance examination, although English grammar and geography had now been added to reading, writing and elementary arithmetic as the subjects tested. One other important change occurred, which would not have pleased Mr Colston or his former Nominees. On the Headmaster's advice, the Governors abolished the requirement that candidates be examined in the church catechism. He believed that it was a meaningless exercise, because 'a large proportion of them merely crammed it during the few days after their entering for the examination'. Nevertheless, the Governors ensured that all candidates were informed that the religious education in the school was 'in accordance with the doctrines of the Church of England'. Boys admitted on free places under the endowment were in future to be called 'free scholars', rather than exhibitioners or foundationers. Fee levels remained the same as they had been in 1875, paying pupils being charged £31 per annum (for tuition, books, board, lodging and clothing) and free scholars just £5 a year for clothing.

The rise in numbers during Dr Finn's Headship was remarkable. Aiming initially at a total of 150 boys (including 100 free scholars and 50 fee payers), he found initially that numbers had dropped to 108 by 1903 (with 85 free scholars and just 23 fee payers). The following table charts the school's subsequent growth.

Date	School total	Free scholars	Fee payers
1903	108	85	23
1904	145	89	56
1905	151	92	59
1907	147	75	72
1911	172	71	101
1914	177	72	105
1915	161	68	93
1916	149	61	88
1917	181	67	114
1920	198	69	129
1921	181	74	107

During the same period, the number of boys applying for free places rose from 74 (for 15 vacancies in 1905) to 281 (for 18 vacancies) in 1917. 'Waiting lists' of boys who had passed the entrance examination now became a regular feature - as did candidates from overseas. In 1910, for instance, two boys were admitted from Jamaica, two from Mexico and two from New Zealand on a fee paying basis. Arnold Stock, who was at school between 1914 and 1918, could remember boys at Colston's who came from India, South Africa, Canada, Mexico, Spain, Gibraltar, Italy and France. Those unable to travel home for the holidays (and without relatives in England) were accommodated by Miss Messenger, whose brother (Harry) was chairman of the Colston Fraternal Association.

A number of points should be noted from the above table. In 1907, at the suggestion of the Board of Education and in the light of the Colston Trust's diminishing income, the number of free scholars (now to be called Colston Scholars) was reduced from 100 to 75. This therefore enabled the Governors to admit more fee paying pupils, thus bringing considerable benefit to the school's finances. At the same time, the Governors asked the Board of Education for two further amendments to the New Scheme of 1875 - namely, the removal of the restriction which had limited the free scholars to just five years in the school (thus denying many of them of the chance to undertake the new advanced courses); and the extension of the leaving age to eighteen for all pupils (and not just the twenty nominated by the Headmaster). All these proposals were incorporated in an amended scheme for the school, published in February 1910 - changes which greatly raised the school's potential for increasing its numbers.

The school roll decreased quite significantly in 1915 and 1916, thanks largely to the impact of the outbreak of war. As the Headmaster explained to the Governors, the steady diminution in numbers was 'due entirely to boys leaving prematurely to fill up the gaps created by the rush to arms during the first year of the war'. Local businesses in particular were recruiting boys to cover the emergency. Later in the war, numbers recovered, before reaching a peak of 198 in 1920. It was at this point, however, that the Governors, realising that the school's accommodation was now badly overcrowded, took a decision to reduce numbers to 175 (hence the drop in 1921). Nevertheless, with 30 qualified candidates on the waiting list, the Headmaster expressed the hope in his annual report that the school would eventually rise to 250. It is also worth noting that, in spite of Dr Finn's assertion in 1903 about the power of advertising, the school had not advertised at all since 1914. Success, as always, breeds success.

The growth in numbers did, of course, bring financial benefit to the school in both increased fee revenue and increased government grants. As a school of approved status in Division A, Colston's qualified for annual grants for all those pupils taking the four-year advanced course from the age of thirteen - with (in 1903) £4 per boys available for those in the first year of the course, rising to £10 per boy for those in the fourth year. The total grant therefore grew from £248 (for 62 boys) in 1903-4; to £642 (for 138 boys) in 1907-8; and to £754 (for 161 boys) in 1912-13. By 1919, the school was receiving £1,300 a year in grants.

(b) The Need to Enlarge Facilities

As numbers increased, so the need for additional accommodation became a matter of urgency. Although the opening of the new science block in

The Main Schoolroom in 1905 (before it was partitioned in the following year), showing no fewer than four teaching desks. (SMV Archive)

1903 had provided some welcome relief, in most respects the school was still only capable of housing 150 pupils. The seriousness of the problem was raised in a Board of Education report in 1904, following an inspection, which highlighted the fact that three classes were actually being taught in the main schoolroom at the same time due to the lack of classroom space. In view of the damaging impact of this on the quality of teaching, the report recommended the construction of two more classrooms, including one to be used exclusively for art. A year later, however, the Board amended its recommendations, following another inspection which had noted the boys' cramped sleeping accommodation. It now suggested dividing the main schoolroom with two sliding partitions and the building of one new classroom (costing £608) and a new dormitory for 34 boys with two masters' bedrooms and a number of WCs (costing £1,800). The Governors acted quickly to put these plans into operation, the classroom for sixth formers and the partitions being completed in 1906 and the dormitory in 1907.

Nevertheless, the Governors (prompted as ever by the Headmaster) were only too well aware of other inadequacies on the site. In 1909, with numbers poised to breach the 150 mark through the rapid expansion of the fee paying intake, their Management Committee drew up a report on the school's overall needs. It recommended a new wing for the Headmaster's house, a new floor on top of the science block (to house three new classrooms and an art room), a new changing room block with showers, new boys' latrines and a newly-created room for 14 baths and a number of WCs adjacent to the dormitories.

Having estimated that the package would cost at least £6,625, the Governors then applied to the Board of Education for permission to raise a loan of £8,000. Although the budget for that year was predicting a slight surplus, the Board refused this request in view of the precarious state of the school's finances, agreeing instead to a reduced loan of £4,000 (later increased to £5,000). Faced with this situation, the Governors modified their original scheme, partly by omitting two of the classrooms and the bathroom block and partly by reducing the specification on the remaining items. A loan was duly taken out with the Sun Insurance Office at 4% interest and the work completed in 1910.

The new Art Room opened in 1910 on the upper floor of the Science Block. (SMV Archive)

Two years later, an attempt was made to revive the remainder of the scheme, including the other two classroom on top of the science block. However, although the Board of Education approved the plans in principle, they refused - against the background of a budget deficit - to grant the Governors authority for a further loan of £2,450 to cover the cost. By 1913, the Governors themselves had abandoned the scheme, following a further budget deficit in that year. As the financial crisis deepened in the face of roaring inflation and escalating costs (see below), the Headmaster's other ambitions for expansion were systematically deferred.

By 1914, for instance, rising numbers (totalling 177 at that point) had put the kitchen under serious strain. A proposed enlargement at a cost of £337 was, however, postponed by the Board of Education after yet another budget deficit. In the same year, rising numbers had also given further urgency to the school's long-held ambition for a gymnasium - but, although some old stables next to the school were now earmarked for conversion, finance for the project remained elusive. By 1919, with numbers reaching a new record of 195, there was a serious shortage of sleeping accommodation. The Governors were sorely tempted to buy a large house, which had come onto the market in Stapleton and was capable of taking 60 boys - but drew back on financial grounds.

In view of this desperate situation, the Governors were reluctantly forced plan a gradual reduction in the size of the school roll to 175, starting in 1920. Their ultimate aim to expand Colston's to a size of around 250 had, therefore, been thwarted - at least for the time being.

(c) The Need to Improve Staff Conditions

It has already been shown in Chapter 7 that the morale of the staff was exceptionally poor by the time of Dr Finn's appointment, with frequent resignations, low salaries and weak discipline. In 1901, the new Headmaster had inherited a staff of six full-time masters - Mr S.V.R. Drapes (Second Master at a salary of £105), Mr S.N. Player (Third Master, £85), Mr W.G. Humphries (Fourth Master, £70), Mr W.S. Calway (Fifth Master, £60 plus £10 for music teaching) and J.D. Harris (Junior Master, £30). There were also two part-time teachers to cover art and French. From the outset, the new Headmaster showed himself much more supportive towards the needs of his teachers, frequently recommending individual increases to the Governors for good service.

After criticism for the Board of Education inspectors in 1905 that the remuneration at Colston's was distinctly low, the Governors drew up a new scheme of salaries in 1908, which was much more generous. In future, graduates would commence at £100 per annum and would then rise by six increments of £10 to a maximum of £160, while the Second Master's salary was fixed at £180. Then, with galloping inflation throughout the country during the First World War, the Board of Education increased their grants to schools in 1917, so that they could improve their salary scales accordingly. Graduates at Colston's therefore were placed on a new scale, starting at £140 per annum and rising in six increments to £200 (with the Second Master fixed at £220). However, just one year later, the Board of Education published a report on salaries in secondary schools, which stressed 'the general feeling that capable men will not be attracted to the teaching profession' until remuneration improved.

In 1918, therefore, Colston's adopted the revised local authority scales, which had established a pay spine commencing at £160 and rising to £360 (or even £400) after 21 years at the age of 42. The Second Master's scale was to rise from £240 in four instalments to £320 and retirement age was set at 60 years for all staff. The Governors estimated that the cost of salaries under this plan would rise (without further inflation) from £1880 in 1919 to £2670 in 1940. These figures, however, were quickly made obsolete by the introduction of the government's new Burnham Scale in 1920. After adjustments had been made to adapt the scheme for resident staff (i.e. by deducting £75 per annum to cover the cost of board and lodging and by adding £1 per night for boarding house supervision), the salary of the most junior master was to rise from a new level of £200 in 1920 to £345 by 1925, that of a senior master from £360 to £458, and that of the Second Master from £400 to £508. The impact of all this was to increase the salary bill from £2,600 in 1920 to £4,066 by 1925.

Meanwhile, the Headmaster's salary had also undergone major revisions - partly, of course, due to the Governors' delight at his outstanding performance. He had been appointed in 1901 at a salary of £225, plus £1 per annum for each fee paying pupil and one quarter of the government's annual grant. In 1907, his basic salary was raised to £275 (and to £300 in 1909) and his capitation fee to £2 for each pupil over the total of one hundred (increased to £3 in 1909) - in return for the surrender of his right to a percentage of the government grant. Then, as staff salaries escalated, his remuneration was enhanced to £500 per annum in 1918, plus a further fixed sum of £300 per annum in 1920 in return for the surrender of his capitation fees - making a total of £800 in all. Costs associated with the Headmaster's office had been increased further in 1911, when Mr W.S. Calway, having resigned his position as Fifth Master, was appointed as the Headmaster's first-ever secretary (although he also agreed to a little part-time teaching in addition).

The Governors found increasingly that they were no longer able to dictate the conditions of their staff in isolation. These were the years of major social reform, largely inspired by Lloyd George and the Liberal government (1905-1914). National insurance, old age pensions and fair wage settlements were just a few of the policies implemented at Westminster, which had serious repercussions at Colston's. In 1907, for instance, the Governors decided to obtain insurance cover (following the Workmen's Compensation Act of 1906) for the 25 school 'workmen', including cooks and domestic servants. This was largely prompted by a

The Staff in 1919. Back row (left to right): *S.V.R. Drapes, M. Bouchard, Sergeant Higgins, J. Gray.* Middle row: *G.R.A. Beckett, H.H. Hutchinson, J. Noddle, W. Griffiths, W. Davies.* Front row: *W.S. Calway, Mrs Finn, Dr A. Finn (Headmaster), Miss Prosser (drawing), ...?, Nurse Whitting (matron). (SMV Archives)*

claim for compensation from the school's former Porter, Sergeant J. Walsh, following an injury sustained at work which had left him incapacitated. Although the Governors rejected his claim, they quickly took out an insurance policy with the General Accident, Fire and Life Assurance Company.

In 1904, they also requested permission from the Board of Education to extend their pension scheme, which had only been established for the Headmaster, to assistant masters as well. [Dr Finn was paying £25 a year into his scheme - with a matching amount paid by the Governors - to produce a pension of £125 per annum or a lump sum of £1,350 at the age of 55]. A local scheme was eventually set up for the other masters in 1909 with the Norwich Union, which enabled senior staff to match the Governors' own contribution of £7 10s 0d per annum (junior staff £5 per annum) to produce either a pension or a lump sum (the size of which to be dependent on the age at which they were first insured). In 1918, at their own request, the teachers transferred to the official Teachers' Superannuation Scheme, which had been established by the 1918 Act.

The combined extra cost of increased salaries, workers' insurance and teachers' pensions was to place considerable strain on the school's brittle finances (see below). Meanwhile, the staff itself had been expanded to reflect the larger school roll with the appointment of two additional masters - a classics master in 1908 and a mathematics master in 1909. This brought the total (excluding the Headmaster) to 8 resident full-time staff and two part-time staff - a total which still prevailed in 1920, although a further full-time mathematics master was appointed one year later. Almost all the staff appointed during this period (with the exception of the temporary war-time appointments) were graduate specialists - a further burden on the salary bill.

(d) The Need to Offer New Courses

Specialists teachers were, of course, needed to run the new advanced course in science, which had been agreed with the Board of Education in 1903 - but they were also required increasingly in other areas as the school set its sights on preparing boys for university in a whole range of subjects. By 1903, the curriculum had been expanded to take account of the school's new status as a secondary school. Reading, writing, English grammar and literature, history, geography, mathematics, French, drawing and singing had all been retained from before. Science, however,

The Workshop during Dr Finn's period in office. (SMV Archive)

had now been expanded to include chemistry, physics, mechanics and geometry, while German had been added to French as modern languages 'taught on the newest methods, instruction being given at each lesson in the spoken language'. Latin (which the Headmaster had suggested should be abandoned in 1902) was in fact retained up to fourth form level, but then made an optional subject in the fifth and sixth forms alongside shorthand, bookkeeping and commercial correspondence. The other new subject was woodwork. Dr Finn had successfully persuaded the Governors to set up a 'carpenter's workshop' and pay a well qualified man already on the staff an extra £5 a term to act as an 'instructor in woodwork' outside normal school hours. All boys in the four highest forms (i.e. those involved in the new advanced course) had 3 hours of practical work in the science laboratories each week and 1.5 hours in the carpenter's shop.

Although Greek had been added to the curriculum in 1910 'for those who would benefit', major new changes were made in 1917-1918, which were to have cost implications for the future. With the maximum leaving age for all boys now raised to 18, the Headmaster was keen to encourage as many boys as possible to stay on into the sixth form as a prelude to university entry. As early as 1912, he had written in the school magazine that 'we hope in future to send at least one boy a year to university'. Although at present, he said, large numbers leave school at 16 for a career in business, the boy who does so 'may be doomed to spend most of his life doing uncongenial work'. Wishing, therefore, to expand the options available in the senior forms, he gained permission from the Board of Education in 1917 to offer an additional advanced course in modern studies (including French, history, Latin, English and, later, German). Although the implementation of this was postponed due to war-time disruption, German was commenced as a serious subject at fourth form level from 1918 as preparation for the introduction of this course.

In 1918, the national examination system was changed with the introduction of the School Certificate for pupils at fifth form level and the Higher School Certificate to be taken two years later. The examinations were run by various universities throughout the country, Colston's opting at first for papers from the Cambridge Board, but switching to Bristol University from 1919. Pupils who gained 'credits' in School Certificate in all three groups of subjects (i.e. the English, foreign language and mathematics/science groups) were awarded their 'matriculation' (which was the basic qualification for university entrance); pupils who gained the Higher School Certificate (HSC) were enabled to start university 'at a higher level'. The examination boards offered four courses at HSC in classics, modern studies, mathematics and science - a situation which caused the Headmaster to split the sixth form in 1920 into 'literary' and 'scientific' divisions.

His policy of encouragement to both boys and their parents to raise their ambition - coupled with the rising standard of teaching in the school - resulted in a most noticeable surge in academic success. Whereas in 1911 just six pupils had passed the old Cambridge Local Examinations at fifth form level, in 1920 18 boys gained the Bristol School Certificate (13 with matriculation) in the nine subjects on offer. Furthermore, E.E. Rich distinguished himself by gaining nine credits - the only boy to do so out of 344 candidates with the Bristol Board. Of even greater significance was that ten of those boys stayed on into the sixth form to take their HSC. Dr Finn soon emerged as one of the early pioneers in the use of statistics to impress both Governors and parents alike. In 1921, therefore, he pointed out that the school had achieved an 82% pass-rate in School Certificate, compared with a local average of just 64% and that 70% of their boys had matriculated, as opposed to a mere 28% of the other candidates. He even went on to analyse the pass-rate in each subject, with religious knowledge (100%) appearing at the top of the list.

Gradually, more boys began to take the HSC - Kenneth Duffield, for instance, passing the classics course with distinction in 1918 (the only boy in the country, in fact, to choose that option!). He went on to gain a scholarship at Brasenose College, Oxford with the help of one of the Governors' leaving exhibitions, which were still in operation. Many parents, of course, needed a financial incentive like this to permit their sons to proceed to university at all. Other leaving exhibitions were granted to T.F. Rodgers, who gained a classics scholarship at Merton College, Oxford in 1916 (the first boy ever to secure an Oxbridge place while still a pupil at Colston's School), before eventually gaining a first class degree; F. Britton, who was first in order of merit for a mathematical scholarship at Queen's College, Cambridge in 1921; and H.T. Woods, who won a similar award at Brasenose College, Oxford in 1922.

By 1920, the Headmaster was able to announce that there were now ten Old Colstonians at university, the same year in which *The Colstonian* began to feature 'letters' from Old Colstonians in residence at the universities of Oxford, Cambridge and Bristol. This increase had been stimulated partly (from 1911) by the newly-created Proctor Baker Scholarship of £30 a year, awarded after examination to candidates 'of great promise and slender means' for use in the faculty of engineering at Bristol University. They had been established in memory of William Proctor Baker, who had died in 1907 after 32 years as Chairman of Governors.

To stimulate and support this growth in academic achievement, the

Headmaster had encouraged the development of the library (even in 1903, it was estimated that three out of every four boys borrowed at least one book each week); visits to the theatre to see plays which were being studied for examinations by senior boys (*Julius Caesar* and *Macbeth* in 1903, for instance); specialist 'subject' prizes awarded at 'Speech Day' (so called for the first time in 1905); and competitive 'Honour Essays' written on a weekly basis by each boy in the school, with awards given for each form and listed in *The Colstonian*. Much of this success was clearly due to the energy, drive and vision of the Headmaster.

(e) The Need to Manage a Financial Crisis

The financial situation which faced the school throughout Dr Finn's headship required the most skilful management. Although some of the pressure was created by internal ambition (i.e the need for better facilities and a more modern curriculum), most of the difficulties were imposed by outside forces over which the school had no control (i.e. rising inflation and government legislation over insurance, pensions and pay). Colston's was therefore fortunate that it could draw on the expertise of a highly experienced Governing Board, the constructive advice of a most supportive Board of Education and the sensible restraint of a Headmaster who could always appreciate the wider picture.

The Governing Board contained a number of men of immense wisdom and judgment. Mr W. Proctor Baker, who was Chairman until his death in 1907 (a position he had held for 32 years since the formation of the original Governing Board), was succeeded by Mr W.W. Jose, whose involvement in the management of the school went back to 1859. The amended scheme for the school, which was drawn up by the Board of Education in 1910, still gave the Society of Merchant Venturers a majority interest on the Governing Board. Out of 23 members, it had 13 places - the remainder consisting of 2 ex-officio members (the Bishop and the Rector of Stapleton), 5 local authority representatives (i.e three from Bristol and one each from Gloucestershire and Somerset) and three co-optative governors appointed by resolution of the board.

The situation was again modified, however, by the Board of Education in 1920, when the Society's representation was reduced to 10 and that of the local authorities increased to 8 (including five for Bristol and one each for Gloucestershire, Somerset and Wiltshire). This meant, at least in theory, that the Merchants could now be outvoted, if all the other members joined forces against them. On the other hand, it should be remembered that the local authority representatives could be extremely useful in interpreting the mass of new legislation and representing the school's interests on local councils.

As early as 1905, the Board of Education suggested to the Governors that they should consider increasing the school fees (especially the boarding element). This advice was eventually taken as they faced up to the cost of funding salary increases, pensions and new buildings - particularly in view of the fact that the total fee of £31 per annum (which included £20 for board and lodging, £5 for tuition, £5 for clothing and £1 for books) had not risen since it was first set in 1875. Although fees were therefore raised to £34 in 1909, £37 in 1910 and £39 in 1913, parents were advised that, for the first time, these figures would include the cost of the games fund, examination fees and the school magazine. Fees did not increase again until 1920 (see below).

Meanwhile, the overall financial situation had deteriorated. After two successive budget deficits, when surpluses had been predicted (1912-13), the Governors appointed a sub-committee to examine the whole financial picture. [This Finance Committee now took over, in effect, from the Management Committee, which had previously been responsible for the detail of school affairs.] Its report in July 1913 made gloomy reading. Over the previous year, income had fallen by £110 (largely due to a steady decline in revenue from their estates) and expenses had increased by £150. To avert a huge deficit, therefore, the Headmaster was asked to effect considerable savings - by, for example, using 'a different class of butter', dispensing with one servant during the summer, appointing less expensive staff and amalgamating classes. To his credit, Dr Finn did actually manage to achieve a saving of £186 during the following Christmas Term, a fact which contributed to a small surplus in the accounts for the year ending March 1914.

Nevertheless, in spite of their endeavours, other forces outside their control were quickly coming into play and, by the end of 1914, a deficit of £386 was being predicted. With the outbreak of war, rampant inflation had set in, causing the Headmaster great difficulties in purchasing supplies. He later reported his analysis to the Governors, showing that, between 1916 and 1919, total expenditure on all items of food, clothing, books and servants' wages had risen by 70%, whereas the number of boys had only increased by 21.5%. Within that total average, however, some individual items had risen most alarmingly - milk by 164%, books and stationery by 170% and clothing by a staggering 205%. Little wonder that the Headmaster confessed to the Governors in 1920 that he had overspent his clothing budget by £828! It was against this background that all further building developments were suspended.

By 1919, the situation had become so desperate that the Governors (in conjunction with the Merchants) had agreed in principle to sell off their estates at Locking, Beere and Monkton and to invest the proceeds 'in more liquid securities', which would 'materially increase the income of the Trust'. As a first step, permission was gained from the Board of Education to dispose of Locking Manor, a sale which produced over £62,000. This did not in itself produce an instant solution to the school's mounting problems. By 1920, the total debt of the school had risen to £1,736.

It is hardly surprising, therefore, that the Governors had been forced to take - with great regret - a most difficult decision in the previous year. They were informed by the Board of Education that they would need to abrogate Clause 25 of the 1875 New Scheme (as a result of new legislation), if they were to retain their recognised status. This clause had specified that the Headmaster should always be a communicant member of the Church of England - one of the most crucial points established by Edward Colston in his original settlement. The Governors were most reluctant to agree; submitted a strongly-worded protest; but, in the event, quickly acquiesced - for at stake were the annual government grants, which then amounted to £1,300 per annum. Although, under the circumstances, they probably had little choice, the fact remained that the religious aspects of the school's foundation were gradually being eroded.

By 1920, the Governors had decided that strong action was needed to set the finance on a more even keel. They therefore agreed, with the permission of the Board of Education, to abolish the clothing fee (£5) and the fee for books (£1) and to make the parents responsible for buying these items in future (items which, of course, were running at a colossal rate of inflation). At the same time, the boarding fee was increased to £35, thus making the total fee £40. They did agree, however, to remit the increases to 'needy' parents, to give credit for books returned in serviceable condition and to permit boys at present in school to retain their existing clothing. A notice was duly sent to parents, explaining that 'during the war and since, the school has carried on under great difficulties and with great loss, without any increase of fees, in spite of the steady increasing cost in every department'. Later in the year, the Headmaster reported back that the parents had accepted the increases 'as inevitable'.

Within a year, however, the situation had deteriorated even further, with a total debt now revealed of £3,674. The Governors therefore, felt obliged to raise the fees yet again from January 1922 - this time by putting an additional £15 per annum on the tuition fees (largely as a result of the new Burnham Scale). The total school fee had therefore risen from £31 in 1903 to £55 in 1921 (with parents additionally responsible now for buying both uniform and books). Nevertheless, in his 1921 report to the Governors, the Headmaster was able to state that

the increases did 'not appear to have had any effect upon the
applications for admission' - indeed, he continued, 'the school will still
be one of the cheapest in the country'. One year later, in 1922, the
predicted debt of the school had risen to £3,964!

The Sudden Death of Dr Finn

At the Speech Day in October 1921, Dr Finn - after giving his annual
report on another outstandingly successful year - looked back over the
twenty years of his headship, highlighting a remarkable range of
achievements and paying a heartfelt tribute to the support he had
received from the Society of Merchant Venturers. Little did he realise
that this was to be his last major school occasion.

His health in fact had been deteriorating over a number of years.
Early in the war, his friends had noticed that he had become thinner, but
attributed it to the wartime food. However, the condition persisted after
the war and, by February 1922, he had become so seriously ill that the
Governors had appointed Mr Drapes, the Second Master, to take over
as Acting Headmaster until the end of term. Although his health had
improved by Easter, the doctors advised that, for a full recovery, 'he
should be given a complete rest for not less than three months and, for
this purpose, he should go on a sea voyage'. The Chairman of
Governors, Mr Mervyn King (who had been elected to the office on the
death of Mr Jose in 1916), made arrangements for Dr Finn to go on a
trip to New Zealand and, 'having regard to the great services he had
rendered the school' agreed that the Governors should 'bear the cost of a
second class return ticket (£217)'. When the ship eventually docked, he
managed to spend four happy days in Christchurch with the family of
his brother, John (who had died in 1917, after emigrating to New
Zealand nine years earlier).

When he returned at the end of August, Dr Finn had apparently
made a full recovery from his illness. Sadly, however, he died suddenly a
few days later (at the age of 53) from 'a haemorrhage of the lung'. His
niece, Miss Nora Finn (who, as a little girl had met him in New Zealand)
has since indicated that he had been suffering from tuberculosis at a time
when it was not possible to benefit from insulin. His funeral was held in
a packed church at Stapleton, followed by burial in Frenchay
churchyard. At their emergency meeting in September, the Governors
paid tribute to 'the great services rendered by Dr Finn to the school
during the twenty-one years of his headship'. Mr Drapes was again
appointed Acting Headmaster and Mrs Finn was asked to continue as
housekeeper until the end of term.

There is no doubt that the years of Dr Finn's headship had been most stressful. He had battled against the pressures of a poor inheritance, a brittle financial base, a period of great disruption during the war and a constant flow of new legislation. Totally dedicated to the job in his determination to transform the school, he had worked incessantly hard without regard for his health. Mr Harry Messenger, the Chairman of the Colston Fraternal Association, had no doubt that the strain of overwork and 'his neglect of his doctor's advice' were largely responsible for his early death. Nevertheless, he said, Dr Finn had 'brought into Colston's the inspiration and energy for which we had long been waiting'.

The *Penrith Observer* commented that his career 'was a remarkable example of what can be done by strenuous effort, coupled with great natural abilities'. *The Bristol Daily Press* added that 'he was one of the new, broad-minded school of masters, who realised that clean, healthy sport was as essential to the mind and body of a growing boy as intellectual striving'. An obituary in *The Colstonian* paid tribute to his personal qualities - 'a man of fine presence and dignified bearing; firm and steadfast in purpose and devoted to duty' - before concluding that 'he was in truth a very great headmaster and a very perfect gentleman'. Mr G.F. Eberle went even further by saying that 'his early decease had robbed England of one of its finest public school headmasters'.

His achievement at Colston's was immeasurable. He had transformed an institution with low expectations, poor morale, narrow outlook and mediocre standards into a school which was ambitious, energetic, civilised and successful.

Sources used in Chapter 8

Scheme for Public Secondary Schools for Boys and Girls, 19th February 1910 (printed in Eames, op. cit., Appendix 2)
Society of Merchant Venturers' Archive:
    Colston Hospital Trust :
        Governors' Minute Book, 1875-1934
        Management Committee Minute Book,1887-1923
    Admissions Register - Paying Scholars, 1875-1926
    Admissions Register - Nominated Scholars, 1875-1926
    Headmasters' Letters and Reports, 1879-1921
    Box of Appendices
        Bundle 4:   *Mr Finn's Correspondence*
                   School Prospectus, 1903
                   Submission to B. of E., 1904
        Bundle 16:   *Letters and Reports, 1890-1912*

The Colstonian, vols. 8-30 (August 1901 - Autumn 1922)

Volume of Newspaper Cuttings, 1901 - 1922

Cribsheet (The Old Colstonians' Newsletter), October 1986, January 1993, January 1994

Personal interviews and written submissions (as acknowledged in the text)

John Wroughton, *King Edward's School at Bath, 1552-1982* (1982), pp 118-124

MEALTIMES, 1919-23

James Gidley *(Old Colstonian)*

I started as a foundationer or scholarship boy in September 1919. Besides myself, there were fourteen of us in that batch. After tea, that first night, we idled around until nine when we again entered the diners [i.e. the dining room] for mugs of thick cocoa and hard biscuit - after which Joey [i.e. Dr Finn], awesome in cap and gown, appeared on the dais and helped us to sing 'Lord keep us safe this night'. With that over, we trooped up the broad stairway in the Georgian building to our dormitories.

At first I slept in a small room under Prefect Bernard. I was soon shifted to a large one above the dining hall. I recall the prefect telling us to kneel down beside our beds for a minute or two, whether we wanted to pray or not. We wore night gowns and there were chamber pots under the beds, both going out of fashion during my stay at the school.

Before going into breakfast, you were expected to clean your shoes. To that end, a mixture of blacking and water was set out for us in the changing rooms. The best way of getting a shine was by applying it, walking to and fro on parade till it had dried, then brushing vigorously. About the first thing we wrote home asking for was proper boot polish. We lined up on parade by tables [i.e. the table groups in the dining hall], each with its prefect, before entering the diners, the school Sergeant inspecting us and perhaps scanning our heads to see if we wanted haircuts. The prefects ate at 'high table' at tea time - and the assembled masters, the Head, his wife and two privileged prefects had dinner there. Our diet was a constipating one, or for me it was until I started getting parcels from home.

We lined up in 'tables' before going into dinner and marched in to the tune of our bugle band. We marched past the arbutus tree by the lawn railings. Inside, on the right as you entered, a joint of meat lay on a table, the porter standing near with a carving knife and fork ready to cut off slices. On the table were plates with the potato and cabbage upon them. You took turns with the boy next to you carrying a couple of plates for portions of meat. We disliked the fatty bits. Sometimes, however, we had pratty pie, a mixture of potato and minced beef, served out by our prefect at the table head. For dessert we ate rice, rice and rice. We got so tired of it that we asked the prefect to dob only one large spoonful on our plates so that it could be messed around to seem as if a lot had been eaten.

Then Joey got to know and his wife, 'Maffs', came down from the dais one day and dished it out, sitting in the prefect's place and ate a double helping just to encourage us. Towards the end of my stay, the food began to vary a little more. We had spotted dog and jam tart - as well as rice.

Two prefects usually sat at 'high tab' with the masters and the Head - they said the food was no better. We sang a Latin grace before and after dinner, *Benedic nobis domine et omnibus donis tuis* and then *Nomen sanctum tuum laudamus*. No doubt our Bristolian voices sang 'chew-um' for the Latin word!

Tea was the only meal we looked forward to, for we were then able to utilise the marmite, jam, butter and other spreads sent from home and partake the cakes, biscuits, sardines and tinned fish coming in our parcels. The prefects then being at high tab, we could talk bawdy and swear pretty much as we pleased. One swear word we never used at Colston's: one reflecting on your parentage. [A fairly high percentage of the foundationers were 'fatherless boys' or orphans].

(From Cribsheet *January 1993)*

James Gidley sent these reminiscences from his home in Sydney, Australia

DISCIPLINE IN 1920

James Gidley *(Old Colstonian)*

[Major G.R.A. Beckett, MC, MBE, MA, who was a master at Colston's for 41 years between 1904 and 1945, eventually took over as both Second Master and Housemaster of West House. Having served in the First World War, during which he was awarded the Military Cross, he commanded the cadet corps on his return to the school. A fierce disciplinarian, he was not altogether the most popular member of staff).

We now come to Pop (the Major) - not an inappropriate name for he was always about to pop over. Even Liddington, who rarely bore anyone a grudge, detested Major Beckett. There were never enough rules at Colston's for him to catch you breaking - and when unable to find you fracturing them, he would get at you some other way. He wanted to turn the Crib into an army barracks. I loathed his bushy brows and glaring, suspicious eyes and the green suit that he was fond of wearing (made out of a *Sports Times*, they said). I was in the Caddy Corps to begin with, but left later. It was enough having to put up with Pop in the classroom. I don't doubt his being an efficient, capable soldier - but Captain Bligh was an efficient navigator.

In summer, we liked having feasts, clubbing together the contents of parcels sent from home. A favoured spot was behind the changing room, between them and the school wall. Pop nabbed one of the fourth forms at it and confiscated the food - home-made cakes and pastries, tinned herrings, butter, scones, biscuits and even strawberries and cream. Any other master, mindful of the diet of the Crib, would have taken no notice - even Acki [Mr W. Davies, the then geography master] contenting himself with a few sarcasms before passing on.

Pop once slippered Harrington and me. In the fifth form, we used to go into the art room to play ping-pong. Our own desks were too sloping to make good tables, but the flat-topped art room ones were excellent. Pop, coming up the stairs unexpectedly, found a dozen of us there playing and forbade it in future. Harrington and I argued that, by shifting art room desks into the fifth form room and playing on them there, we were not breaking the Major's decree. He discovered us at it, claiming that we had deliberately disobeyed him and asked if we would rather be punished by him or be taken along to 'Dads' [the Headmaster]. Like fools we said 'him'. After whacking you, it was Pop's trick, a couple of days later, to send you on an errand, as if conferring a favour. A lesser military man, Napoleon I believe, pursued the same practice and Pop wanted to be sure the great general and he thought alike.

[John Quayle, who was at school between 1929 and 1934, also recalled the Major)

He was probably a very good schoolmaster and ran West House very well. He was a stern disciplinarian. I remember as a senior boy without office being upset by a decision he made not to allow any swimming in the new pool for boys who had failed on one occasion to turn up for an earth-moving exercise. I had not appeared on that isolated occasion in order to go down to the nets for cricket practice. A keen swimmer, I was sufficiently enraged to tackle the formidable Major in the Masters' Common Room on the unfairness of his general decision. I believe it nearly cost my place in the school. The Headmaster, A.R. Millbourn, 'saved my bacon'.

(From *Cribsheet*, January 1994, January 1998)

CHAPTER 9

Years of Consolidation, 1922-1939

The general note of a Speech Day report seems to be one of steady, if uneventful activity. I believe this to be a healthy sign. The machinery, if it functions quietly, is most probably functioning efficiently. (Headmaster's report to the Governors, October, 1931)

Change and Stability

This period was to witness nationally the post-war depression, the General Strike of 1926, the first-ever Labour Government in 1924, the economic slump of the 1930s, widespread unemployment, the growing threat of German expansion and the outbreak of the Second World War. Education in the country at large began to develop a distinctive shape, especially after the publication of the Hadow Report of 1926, which outlined an ambitious plan for the future. Secondary education was to be made available for all children in 'grammar' schools, 'modern' schools, 'senior classes' or 'junior technical schools'. The Education Act of 1936 did its best to assist in the reorganisation of schools along these lines, but it was not until 1944 that theories were effectively put into practice. Nevertheless, the threat of an uncertain future hovered over the Governors and the Headmaster at Colston's throughout the 1930s.

At first sight, therefore, the prospects for success did not appear too promising for Dr Finn's successor, when he eventually took over the Headship in January 1923. Nevertheless, one important human factor was to work in his favour over the coming years - namely the marked continuity in membership of both governors and staff. For instance, Mr Mervyn King (chairman between 1916 and 1929) had actually served as a governor of the school for 62 years, when he died at the age of 89 in 1934. Mr W.W. Ward, who died in 1932, had served on the governing board since 1898, while Mr A.C. Powell did so between 1909 and 1949 and Mr Fred Organ between 1920 and 1950. On the teaching side, Mr S.V.R. Drapes was Second Master for 29 years until his retirement in 1929. He was succeeded in that office by Major G.R.A. Beckett, who eventually retired in 1945 after 41 years in the school. Mr W.H. Davies worked as an assistant master for 30 years, while Mr W.S. Calway eventually resigned in 1926 after working for 27 years as both music master and Headmaster's secretary. When Dr Claude Bernard retired in 1936, he had been school doctor for 30 years - just two years fewer than

Sergeant Higgins (the school sergeant), who finished work on health grounds in 1942.

After Dr Finn's sudden death in August 1922, Mr Drapes had been appointed Acting Headmaster for one term (with Mrs Finn continuing as Housekeeper) while the Governors advertised for a successor. By December, they had shortlisted six candidates out of an application list of 126. After two secret ballots at their special selection meeting, the Governors eventually appointed Mr A.R. Millbourn, MA, to the Headship with his wife as the new Housekeeper and Matron. His salary was to be £600 per annum, rising to £800 by yearly instalments of £25.

The Staff in the early 1920s. The front row (from the left) consists of F. Noddle, S.V.R. Drapes (Second Master), Mr Millbourn (Headmaster), Major G.R.A. Beckett and W.S. Calway. (SMV Archive)

A Mounting Financial Crisis, 1923-1934

Within months of his arrival at Colston's, Mr Millbourn was to discover the desperate state of the school's finances. Although the accounts for the year ending March 1923 were to show a profit of £800, the governors acknowledged that this was a misleading figure because, in view of the high price of food, they had been using their existing stock without renewing it in the forlorn hope that prices would fall.

Furthermore, they stated, 'other economies had been effected which would not be repeated'. By July, therefore, the bank account showed a deficit of £6,643. Within a year this had increased to £8,020 and by July 1925 it had risen further to an alarming £8,699. The Treasurer of the Society had pencilled into the margin of the accounts his explanation of the 'abnormal expenditure' during the last term (i.e. a sudden increase of six new pupils to feed, the cost of food continuing to escalate and 'boys eating more').

It was at this point that the Chairman of Governors (Mr Mervyn King) took personal control of the situation and, by dynamic intervention, saved the school from bankruptcy. At the board meeting in June 1926, he announced that he was in the process of collecting subscriptions, after a personal appeal to friends and colleagues, with the aim of raising a sufficient sum to liquidate the school debt and, at the same time, to provide funds for additional buildings and facilities. He had already raised £9,000, of which £6,000 had immediately been applied to erase the deficit. By December, the total figure had reached £13,470 (eventually increased to £13,808) in what was effectively the school's first-ever

Mr Mervyn King, Chairman of Governors 1916-1929. (By courtesy of the Society of Merchant Venturers)

'development appeal'. The list of subscribers included Sir George Wills (£2,000), Mrs Yola Richardson, who was a member of the Wills family (£2,300 - earmarked for a new gymnasium), Mr Mervyn King (£1,000) and the Society of Merchant Venturers (£2,000).

Given this huge injection of cash, the bank deficit gradually reduced to £2,137 in December 1926 and to a mere £375 in December 1927. By the mid-1930s, the school was regularly in credit - £761 in July 1934, rising to £3,149 by July 1939. There is no doubt that Colston's owes an enormous debt of gratitude to Mr Mervyn King's decisive leadership throughout these difficult times. When he died in 1934, after an incredible 62 years as governor of the school, the governors paid tribute to this man who 'had rendered such loyal service and had been untiring in his personal efforts to promote the interests of the school and to bring it to a sound and solvent financial position...The increasing prosperity of the school will ever serve as a memorial to his prudent wisdom and foresight'.

Colston's School, of course, was not alone in facing these difficulties. Indeed, the government had set up a committee under the chairmanship of Sir Eric Geddes to investigate the growing crisis in the nation at large. Its report, which recommended an economy drive to help solve the country's problems, led to a series of cuts in expenditure - including teachers' salaries. Direct Grant Schools [i.e. those schools receiving a grant from the Board of Education rather than the Local Education Authority] were expected to fall into line. When, therefore, the Bristol Education Authority requested Colston's to follow their own policy by reducing staff salaries by 5% from 1st April 1923, the governors reluctantly complied after seeking agreement from staff. The teachers accepted the reduction on the strict understanding that it 'was a special contribution made for one year only'. Twelve months later, however, they were forced to sanction the cut for a further year.

Although full salaries were restored on 1st April 1925, they were again cut from October 1931, as the economic slump of the 1930s began to bite. This time, however, they were reduced by 10%, enabling the Board of Education to lower its yearly grant to the school from £9 to £7 7s 0d per pupil. The governors did their best to lighten this further blow to the income of staff by offering a 10% reduction in the charge made to resident staff for board and lodging and by abolishing the charge made to non-resident staff for daily lunch. The Board of Education restored 5% of the salary cut in July 1934 (increasing at the same time the per capita grant to the school to £8) and restored the remainder a year later, when the direct grant was raised to £8 13s 0d and an additional sixth form grant introduced for the first time.

By 1934, therefore, the school's finances were on much more of an even keel, even though times generally were still difficult. The governors continued to face the challenge of extra demands on their budget - in 1928, for instance, the local rates assessment on the school's buildings was increased from £291 to £633 (reduced to £575 on appeal); and in 1927, the era of parental claims against the school began. A fee-paying pupil (R.J. Pratt) had been removed by his father, who asked for a remission of the term's fees on the grounds that the quality of the food provided was not, in his opinion, 'up to the standard promised in the prospectus'. After investigation, the finance committee rejected the complaint on the grounds that 'in their opinion the removal of the boy after an experience of school life of less than four days was improper and unwarranted'. They nevertheless felt it wise to remit the fees and so 'conclude the matter'. This desire to avoid bad publicity was again evident in 1930 when Mr Mahoney, the father of a foundationer, claimed for the cost of his son's new coat which 'had been damaged beyond repair by mice'. The governors again complied.

Academic Improvements

Mr Millbourn was determined from the outset to increase the number of boys being entered for the First School Certificate, which was taken after four years in the school. In a memorandum to governors in February 1926, he outlined his plan for the restructuring of school classes (see page 244), which was to give all boys the opportunity to proceed into the fifth form. Whereas previously members of the 'b' stream had remained in 4b for their final two years without taking a leaving examination, from 1927 all boys were permitted to progress into the fifth form, thus enabling them to take the School Certificate.

This policy was quickly justified. In 1924, for instance, just 13 boys had been successful in that examination. From 1928, however, an average of 25 pupils passed each year (with a peak of 34 in 1938) out of a total fifth form of about 40 boys. Of these successful candidates, something in the region of 65-75% gained matriculation (i.e. they proved themselves of a sufficient quality to join a university course without the need to take any further entrance examination). What was particularly pleasing was that many 'b' formers rose to the challenge. In 1929, for instance, nine out of the twenty pupils in 5b passed, including two who gained their matriculation. A year later, one 'b' former actually gained the maximum number of eight credits - a notable achievement. It is true, of course, that teaching methods were often uninspired with a considerable degree of learning by rote. Roger Newport (1930-37) recalls that W.H. Davies regularly made the boys in geography lessons chant out loud all the railway stations between Bristol and London.

At the annual dinner of the Old Colstonians in 1929, the Headmaster made the point that schools were now judged on their examination results and that this was 'a necessary evil'. He went on to claim that 'the standard achieved by Colston's School bore comparison with that of any other school in the West of England'. However, although Mr Millbourn drew great satisfaction from the performance of his pupils at School Certificate level, he was undoubtedly disappointed by the reluctance of many boys to enter the sixth form and to proceed to the Higher School Certificate (HSC). In spite of the fact that total numbers in the sixth form had risen to 13 by 1927, the number taking HSC remained small throughout the inter-war years. In a typical year, no more than 3 or 4 boys were successful out of the 5 or 6 who took the examination.

Many boys had in fact no ambition to go on to university at all. In his report to governors in 1938, the Headmaster listed the destinations of some of his leavers - one boy had been articled to the Town Clerk of Clevedon, another to the City Surveyor in Oxford; two boys had entered the Civil Service; one had gained a short-service commission in the RAF; another had gained entry to Sandhurst; and several boys had taken up clerical posts in Bristol, thanks to help provided by the local Schools' Careers Council. A number of boys had previously done well in entrance examinations for the Civil Service - in 1929, W.F. Woods was placed 50th out of 700 candidates for executive appointments; in 1937, E.R. Gunstone was 6th in the whole country for an appointment with Customs and Excise; and in 1930, K.A. Haddocks (with three distinctions in HSC) rejected a chance of a university place in favour of an executive appointment with the Admiralty.

Nevertheless, two or three boys did proceed each year to university. Bristol University proved to be by far the most popular choice over a wide range of subjects. In 1937, for instance, Old Colstonians were between them reading zoology, medicine, dentistry, engineering, science, mathematics and history at Bristol. At the same time, a few boys distinguished themselves by gaining scholarships or exhibitions at Oxford or Cambridge - in 1923, E.G. Rich (history) at Selwyn College , Cambridge and D.S. Simmons (history) at Queen's College, Cambridge; in 1925, E.J. Taylor (history) at Sidney Sussex College, Cambridge; in 1934, K.A. Bewell (mathematics) at St Catherine's College, Oxford; in 1938, I.H. Williams (history) at Oxford and A.G. Harding (history) at St Catherine's College, Oxford; and in 1939, A. McColm (English) at Worcester College, Oxford.

A stumbling block to university entrance for many boys at Colston's, of course, was the problem of funding a three or four year course. In 1923, the school had only a small number of leaving exhibitions to offer for such purposes (two of their own, plus the Proctor Baker scholarship established in 1911), while the scholarships won by boys at Oxford and Cambridge (normally worth £60 or £70 a year) were in themselves insufficient to cover the cost of fees together with board and lodging. Topping-up grants were therefore often vital. To their undying credit, the Society of Merchant Venturers usually came to the rescue, if other funds were not available. In 1923, for instance, finding that the governors had already allocated their leaving exhibitions for the year, the Society granted £50 per annum to both D.S. Simmons and E.G. Rich to enable them to take up their places. Further topping-up grants were made to each boy by the Colston Fraternal Association (£25 a year) and Bristol Education Committee (£20 a year). Similar assistance was granted by the Society to W.F. Jones in 1925, after it had discussed with his father how much he could afford to pay himself.

In view of these problems, particularly during years of national depression or economic slump, the Headmaster and governors quickly realised the need to encourage Old Colstonians and individual governors alike to help with the creation of additional exhibitions, which were not too inflexible or restrictive. In 1934, therefore, they persuaded the Society of Merchant Venturers to amend the conditions attached to the Proctor Baker Scholarships, which had not been awarded since 1926. These stipulated that the scholarships were solely tenable in the engineering faculty of Bristol University. In future therefore they would be valid in any faculty at any university - though with a preference for Bristol.

Meanwhile, the Colston Fraternal Association had boosted its existing provision for university grants by establishing an Exhibitioners' Fund in 1930 (see page 239). Four years later, the Rector of Stapleton had generously funded the Peter Huddleston Staley Leaving Exhibition worth £60 a year (with the first recipient named as A.D. Coombs, who had won a place at Pembroke College, Oxford). Then in 1937, Mr Claude B. Fry (the Chairman of Governors) vested a sum of £2,000 to establish a number of leaving exhibitions tenable at Bristol University - to be awarded by the Society of Merchant Venturers on the Headmaster's recommendation. In the same year, the E.W. Allen Scholarships were established from a £4,000 trust set up by the will of this loyal Old Colstonian. Part of the income was again to be donated to leaving exhibitions at Bristol University.

In addition to the increasing availability of these grants, successful university applicants could also benefit from the new scheme of State Scholarships and County Scholarships, which were awarded on the evidence of HSC results. K.A. Haddocks won one of the first-ever State Scholarships in 1930. Even so, to make ends meet, boys were often still obliged to look for funding from several combined sources. In 1931, for instance, R.E.F. Malony combined a Wiltshire County Scholarship (£125 a year) with a Kitchener Scholarship (£45), a Governors' Exhibition (£50) and a Fraternal Association Exhibition (£25) to enable him to take up his place at Jesus College, Cambridge to read engineering.

The school was therefore making steady progress in academic matters during these inter-war years. His Majesty's Inspectors, who conducted a full inspection of the school in 1923, reported that 'the standard of work throughout the school was good and the staff efficient'. They also congratulated the Society of Merchant Venturers, as estate governors, on its foresight in selling off the Colston Trust's Somerset estates and investing the proceeds. The inspectors, who visited the school in 1931, stated that Colston's had shown 'an encouraging record of progress' since the inspection of 1923. Quite apart from official praise of this kind, the school could also be rightly proud of a number of academic distinctions achieved - first class degrees, for instance, were gained at Oxford in mathematics in 1925 by H.J. Woods and in classics in 1923 by T.F. Rodgers, who went on to become Headmaster of King Edward's School, Camp Hill, Birmingham at a very young age in 1930. In the same year, E.G. Rich, who had been granted a special leaving exhibition by the Society of Merchant Venturers in 1923 (see above), was elected Fellow and Director of Historical Studies at St Catharine's College, Cambridge. It was therefore gratifying that the school was now managing to identify, encourage and support academic potential of this quality.

Life Outside the Classroom

Life at Colston's, during the period 1922-1939, continued very much along the lines which had been established by Dr Finn. However, although the programme of extra-curricular activities remained full, there was noticeably less excitement conveyed about them in the pages of *The Colstonian* and remarkably few innovations recorded to the old routine. The Literary and Debating Society, the Cadet Corps and the Geological Club survived the years, while other organisations came and went as whims and fashions changed. The Radio Club (1924), the Art Club

The Cadet Corps Band leading the procession from the Cathedral on Colston's Day, 13th November 1933. (SMV Archive)

(1925), the Glee Club (1926), the Wireless Club (1927), the Botany Club (1927) and the Drama Club (1932) all made fleeting appearances on the scene, whereas the Scientific Society (which was founded in 1930 and featured both Sunday evening talks and visits to local factories) and the Stamp Club (with its own 'school collection') survived to the outbreak of war in 1939. Gardening, too, continued to create an interest for some boys on the small allotments provided for their use - with 'at least thirty per cent' of the flowers used in school being grown by pupils. However, Stanley Bowell (1924-29) has recalled that 'there was not so much to do - boys made their own amusements'. This situation inevitably led some of them into trouble - especially the members of the CCC or Corps' Criminal Club (led by a boy named Corps), who 'got up to hair-raising pranks'. For instance, 'they put things into the flower beds', which could hardly be classed as flowers!

Two Senior Prefects lay a wreath on Colston's Memorial before the procession to the Cathedral for the Colston Day service during the 1930s. (SMV Archive)

The Cadet Corps remained as strong as ever, averaging one hundred or so members throughout the period with three platoons and (from 1927) a signals section. The latter unit became extremely popular with its night exercises and the boys put their newly-acquired skills to effective use from the outset. 'During the flu period', stated their column in the school magazine of spring 1927, 'communication was established between sick signallers and their healthier colleagues by means of the telephones. This enabled anyone who desired to send a message to a sick person to do so at the rate of ten words for a halfpenny'. Proceeds went to the Chapel Fund.

Some of the keenest cadets attended the annual Public and Secondary Schools' Camp, which was normally held in the summer at either Cirencester or Cheltenham, although numbers from Colston's were always disappointingly small. There was great excitement at camp in 1926, when the Prince of Wales honoured the cadets with a visit; and the school corps excelled itself at camp in 1929 when it gained second place in the Walton Shield Competition for musketry and drill. Musketry lessons had in fact been provided at school from 1924, when the cadets had helped to build a new rifle range. The most promising cadets each year were now entered for the War Office Certificate 'A' examination.

A major change occurred in 1930, when the War Office withdrew its support from all school cadet corps - thus ending Colston's longstanding connection with the 4th Gloucestershire Regiment. A British National

The traditional presentation of bibles, prayer books, buns and shillings in Merchants' Hall after a Merchants' Charter Day service in the 1930s. (SMV Archive)

Cadet Association, however, was quickly formed to provide both a national framework and new-style uniforms (which were generously funded, in the case of Colston's, by the Society of Merchant Venturers) - although rifles were no longer available for use by cadets. Nevertheless, one tradition did survive throughout these changes. The corps band still led the procession on both Colston's Day and The Merchants' Charter Day, while at the same time extending its range even further by beating the retreat on the day of the annual inspection and at the Commemoration weekend in July.

J.P. Quayle (1929-34) later recalled his own experience of taking part in those two annual events:

> Twice a year the Corps, led by the bugle band, preceded the rest of the school in a march through Bristol City streets. How we practised - the whole school marching round and round the Parade. On Colston Day the service was in the Cathedral and it was followed by a wreath-laying ceremony on Edward Colston's Memorial. On Merchant Venturers' Day, after a service in a city church, we finished up at the fine old hall of the Society of Merchant Venturers. There, boys who had left the school in the previous year were presented with Bibles and Prayer Books embossed with the crest of the Merchant Venturers Society in gilt.
>
> On both occasions we had buns. They were nicer than the miserable assortment which were brought round on large trays during prep. But with schoolboy ingratitude very many were showered from the buses, which took us back to the school, on ready recipients in the back streets of Bristol. Some of these children were hungry in those days. On both occasions we received a beautiful mint shilling. They would have been worth something now, for their silver if for no other reason. As it was, they were squandered in the 'dug-out' [the cellar in which the tuck shop operated] at the first opportunity.

In addition to the corps, drama also developed into a vigorous activity. At first it was chiefly a matter of sketches or scenes from Shakespearian plays performed either by a mixture of boys and staff or by members of South House, who staged two 'dramatic entertainments' of their own in 1924 and 1926. From 1927, however, the tradition was established of an annual school play in December, staged in the new gymnasium on two or three successive evenings. The productions consisted of either three short plays (as in 1927 and 1929) or a full-length drama (such as *Julius Caesar* in 1928 with 'a professional producer', *St Joan* in 1930 and *Captain Brassbound's Conversion* in 1931). Plays by Shakespeare became a regular part of the programme (including *Hamlet* in 1936), while the first-ever school musical made its appearance in 1927 with the performance of *The Mikado*. This proved

H.W. Phillips as Pooh Bah in The Mikado *(1927)*

SCHOOL PLAYS
(SMV Archive)

L.M. Blanckensee as St Joan
in 1930

*O.J. Thomas as the Lord Chancellor
in* Iolanthe *(1932)*

to be a great success, making a profit of £28 for the Parents' Fund (see below) and receiving a spontaneous accolade from 'a diminutive member of 2B', who was overheard making the comment on leaving the gymnasium that 'it was spiffing'.

By contrast, music in the school suffered something of a decline. Although the house music competition continued and the corps band remained active, both the string orchestra and the other bands, which had been so much in evidence under Dr Finn, totally disappeared. The annual concert consisted therefore of items by the school choir (augmented by the Frenchay Choral Society and accompanied by an adult orchestra), together with quartets and solos by Old Colstonians and other outsiders. A similar combination was used for performances of Handel's *Messiah* (1928), Brahms's *German Requiem* (1929) and *Bach's Passion* (1930) during Holy Week in Stapleton Church.

Nevertheless, there were a few indications of a growing revival in musical interest. In 1929, for instance, a 'gramophone craze' hit the school with the arrival of a school gramophone based in the gymnasium; and musical evenings were again organised, as were visits to concerts by the Philharmonic Society and the Bristol Operatic School. Furthermore, hymn-singing gatherings were held on alternate Sunday afternoons and Mr Saward did his best to revive the school orchestra (with little visible effect, it has to be said). One major innovation, however, did take place in 1936 with the emergence of the second form percussion band, which received an enthusiastic reception at the annual concert. Nevertheless, by 1939, the concerts were still being dominated by adults, who had largely been imported from outside the school.

Two other developments are worthy of mention, including the origins of foreign travel by Colston's boys. In 1925, pupils from the third and fourth forms took part in a Franco-English exchange scheme organised by a outside body. This enabled those involved to stay with French families in Morainville for three weeks, before returning to England with their exchange partners for a similar period. Then, in 1936, a party of boys joined a summer cruise to Scandinavia with the School Journeys Association. The second new development saw the establishment of the Parents' Fund, organised by a small committee, with the initial aim of raising £500 to provide equipment for the new gymnasium, including curtains for the stage.

Their fund-raising activities at first consisted of running the refreshment stall during the Commemoration weekend in July each year, but were later extended to additional areas. In 1937, after their gift of a new school bell, the Headmaster expressed his appreciation of 'the general willingness of parents to work together with the school for the benefit of their sons'. Extra cash for luxuries and other items continued to be drawn from the profits of the tuck shop, which averaged between £10 and £18 a term. The money was used, for example, to finance the adjudicator's fee at the house music competition, to buy new jerseys for the 2nd XV, to purchase a motor mower for the cricket pitch and 'to repair seats in church damaged by the boys'.

The prefectorial system continued to function with the annual appointment of between five and eight prefects and four house captains. Prefects during this period were not permitted to beat boys with 'the dap' (which later became the norm), as Roger Newport (1930-37) recalls. As Captain of North House, he decided to stifle any potential rowdiness during prep by walking around with a master's cane in his hand. His Housemaster later rebuked him, advising him never to make any threat which it was impossible to carry out. Nevertheless, the cane was used frequently within the school, as a number of boys found to their cost on one occasion after breaking out from school on the last night of term. Discovered on their return by the Porter, they were given the choice of receiving six of the best from Major Beckett or losing the first day of their holidays. They manfully chose the former.

The School Prefects in 1927. Back row (from the left): *E. Dewdney, L. Welch, A.H. Hoskins, C. Lawrence (later chemistry master at school).* Front Row: *E. Rich, W.F. Woods, H.W. Phillips. (SMV Archive)*

According the Mr G. Kinchin, the school handyman between 1920 and 1970, Mr Millbourn (unlike Dr Finn, who had reserved for himself the sole right of beating boys) 'only exercised jurisdiction with the cosh [i.e. the cane] on what he regarded as an occasion of such gravity that it called for himself to deal with it'. Masters, therefore, now took over the chief responsibility for administering corporal punishment. The Monday morning assembly, which under Dr Finn had featured the reading of the weekly mark lists and the ritual beating of boys who had fallen from grace, had been quickly abolished by Mr Millbourn. Although school uniform was strictly enforced during this period, the old Norfolk suits were replaced by ordinary grey ones. One further reform, which was undoubtedly popular, was the change in the morning rising bell from 6.30 to 7.00 am. In spite of all this, however, it can hardly be said that life suddenly became soft. Mel Jenkins later confided in Mr Graham Searle (Headmaster, 1975-88) that conditions at school during the 1930s were far harsher than in prison. While incarcerated in a 2nd World War prison camp, the guard had said to him: 'Jenkins, you are a rogue, but I cannot prove it' - to which Jenkins had replied: 'Well, that is a great step forward - at Colston's they didn't need proof to punish you'.

House competitions were still organised in rugby, cricket, swimming, tennis and athletics - with gymnastics added in 1936 (a cup for which was bought one year later out of money given by the Bristol Coronation Celebrations Committee in lieu of souvenir mugs). A challenge bowl was first awarded in 1939 to the 'top house' in all the sports combined; athletics matches were organised against Queen Elizabeth's Hospital from 1930 and the Old Boys from 1932; swimming certificates and life-saving awards continued to be presented; and a first-ever trip to the Varsity Rugby Match was organised in 1932. Furthermore, there were a number of outstanding successes by both boys and Old Colstonians. Two pupils (Roach and Norris) played rugby for Bristol Secondary Schools against the Welsh Secondary Schools in 1930; Ivor Lawrence, O.C., played hockey for both the Navy and England between 1926 and 1931; Tom Brown, O.C., the Bristol fullback, was capped for England at rugby at the age of twenty in 1928; and (more surprisingly) R.C. Williams, O.C., who was working in Paraguay, was capped for Argentina at rugby in matches against both the English touring side and Chile in 1937. It is interesting to note that in 1933 Brown was banned for life by the Rugby Football Union for allegedly accepting money from Rugby League sources - a ban which was finally lifted in 1993 (long after his death), following endless campaigns by the Bristol Club.

However, in spite of all this encouragement and inspiration in sport, the school teams only enjoyed modest success during this period. Although the rugby teams got off to a good start in 1923 (with the 1st

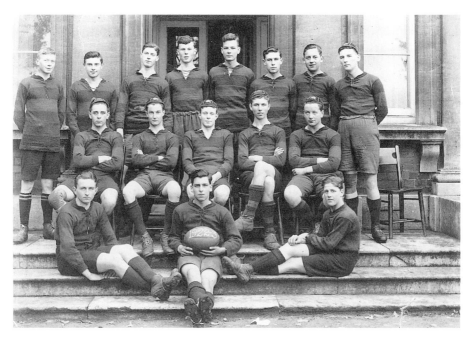

The school's successful 1st XV rugby team in 1922-23, which includes (back row, second from left) Tom Brown at fullback - later to become an England international. (SMV Archive)

XV winning eleven out of its eighteen matches), this achievement was not matched over the next sixteen years. In 1927, for instance, the 1st XV, 2nd XV and Junior XV together won only four games out of the twenty-eight played, whereas the 1st XV managed just six wins out of fifteen in the 1930-31 season and a paltry three out of ten in the autumn term of 1936. The rugby correspondent in *The Colstonian* called it 'a calamitous season' and attributed the disappointing results partly to the fact that the team was 'much younger and lighter than their opponents' and partly to their 'inability to go hard for seventy minutes'. He concluded that 'this is not physical weakness, but mental'. J.P. Quayle (1929-34) later wrote: 'The 1933 1st XV was particularly successful, the whole of the back division being asked to play for a West of England representative side. The 1934 1st XV, however, was disastrous: I played in both years and still feel the shame and the shock of our reversal in fortune'.

It is true that, even by 1939, the fixture list contained a number of matches against adult teams - Bristol University, Clifton Rugby Club, the Old Boys and the Old Colstonians' Rugby Club. Other rugby-playing schools were still in short supply. The same problem faced the

1st XI cricket team, which featured the Welsh Old Colstonians, the Bristol Clergy, the Old Colstonians' Cricket Club, the Society of Merchant Venturers (a team organised annually by the Master of the Society), the Old Boys and the Parents on their fixture list, together with a mere five local schools. Performance in this sport, too, was distinctly patchy - the 1st XI winning just three matches out of eleven in 1923 and six out of twelve in 1938. Nor could boys find any solace in a game of soccer. Association football was completely banned in the school, as J.P. Quayle recalled: 'Soccer was anathema - a score of enthusiasts were actually discovered playing a game of soccer on the Bottom Field. Their punishment was drawn out and merciless. For the rest of the term all their spare time was taken running around the cricket field with a Prefect on Duty carrying a swagger cane to encourage the slow or weary'.

On a more exciting note, interest had been generated in 1929 by the offer from Sir Alan Cobham of a free flight for 18 Colston's boys and 3 members of staff. Occasionally, too, there were opportunities for light relief. A senior pupil recorded in *The Colstonian* his delight in the summer of 1937, for instance, when the boys took part in celebrations to mark the Coronation of George VI - an indication that the spirit within the school remained both friendly and appreciative. 'The whole school and the juniors in particular', he wrote, 'were pleasantly surprised and

The whole school on parade in 1925, wearing the dark grey suits, which had replaced the Norfolk jackets as the uniform. Note in the background the old changing rooms (which later became the workshops) and the site of the pavilion (which was not built until 1934. (SMV Archive)

delighted when, after dinner on Coronation Day, we were set at liberty to roam Bristol. This was not all, for on Friday morning we were taken to the News Theatre to see the film of the Coronation procession, and in the evening for a drive around Bristol to see the illuminations. This was beyond our greatest expectations and, it may be added, that even a special dinner was supplied to celebrate the occasion. The four house captains were invited to be present at the service in the Cathedral on the previous Sunday and the two Senior Prefects to represent the school at the Empire Youth Rally and Service in London on the following Wednesday'. On Coronation Day itself (12th May) the cadet corps had been involved with celebrations in Bristol, while the rest of the school had listened to part of the radio commentary in the morning and the king's address in the evening.

The health of the boys continued to be taken seriously by the school doctor and the matron, particularly during times of epidemic (such as the outbreak of mumps in 1939, which resulted in an early start to the Easter holidays; or the spread of 'a contagious form of verruca' in 1932). By far the worst epidemic during this period, however, was the influenza outbreak in the spring of 1933. *The Colstonian* reported as follows: 'We began the term badly, as the sick room was full by the time we had been back three days; several boys must have come back with influenza upon them; and, although this says much for their keenness,

The Dining Room in 1925 with Prefects sitting at the head of the tables. Note the maid serving the staff on high table and, behind them, the War Memorial which had been erected just three years earlier. (SMV Archive)

the result was disastrous'. Over a hundred boys and a number of domestic staff were affected, with several cases of pneumonia also reported.

Religion remained a prominent feature of life within the school - a fact illustrated by the motto of East House in 1923: *More things are wrought by prayer than this world dreams of*. In the same year, 35 leavers each received a bible and a prayer book from the Society of Merchant Venturers on Charter Day and 15 boys were confirmed by the bishop. The continuing importance of the school's Christian foundation, as stressed by Edward Colston in 1710, was further emphasised with the ordination of the Headmaster in 1929 to enable him to officiate as school chaplain and the ordination of Mr J.R. Sykes in the following year as assistant chaplain.

The Old Colstonians: a Golden Period

The Old Colstonians continued to thrive and expand during the two decades between the wars. The Colston Fraternal Association (which was claimed as 'the oldest Old Boys' society in the country' - except for that of Christ's Hospital in London), maintained its distinct identity and purpose. In 1923, a presidential badge was worn for the first time at the AGM and, by 1926, a membership of 220 had been recruited. But, whereas in earlier years, it had aimed mainly at buying clothes for impoverished school leavers, from 1917 it had concentrated on providing grants for those who were going on to university. By 1930, over £700 had been disbursed in this way. Nevertheless, with the rapid increase in university entry, the Association realised the urgent need to boost its funds. It therefore established an Exhibitioners' Fund in 1930, appealing to those Old Boys who had themselves benefited from such exhibitions in the past to contribute. Within six years, eight such people had come forward to donate a total of £200 to the fund. This continued to grow in such a way that, by 1938, an average of £240 a year was being granted to boys who were either proceeding to university or joining the professions.

In spite of this special function, however, the Fraternal Association increasingly worked in close collaboration with the Old Colstonians' Society. Their joint dinners in November each year continued to attract attendances of over a hundred and they also stood alongside each other on Colston's Day as the two senior prefects from the school placed a laurel wreath on the founder's statue, before joining the procession to the Cathedral. Both groups were also heavily involved at Commemoration in July, including 'the startling alterations' which, according to *The Colstonian*, were made to the programme in 1937.

Aiming to involve parents much more in the celebrations, a gymnastic display was organised for the mothers and a swimming match for the fathers (with teams of pupils, Old Boys and parents in competition). Parents were also invited to the Old Colstonians' service, which was switched from its normal time on Sunday to Saturday evening. For their part, the parents organised a sale of work throughout the whole afternoon in aid of the Bristol Royal Infirmary.

Furthermore, the two societies joined forces to fund a commemorative brass tablet in honour of the Reverend John Hancock, which was fittingly unveiled in the School Chapel at Commemoration in 1924; and a stained glass window (costing £250) in memory of Dr Anthony Finn, which was unveiled in March 1925. Shortly before his death, Dr Finn had written to Mr Harry Messenger (secretary and founder of the Colstonian Guild and driving force behind the creation of the War Memorial), suggesting that as soon as the alterations in the dining room had been completed, it would be a good idea to place a stained glass panel depicting the story of the Good Samaritan in its northern window. That idea was now adopted as a memorial to Dr Finn himself. The panel also incorporated the school motto and four small shields, each featuring a dolphin in one of the four house colours.

Mr Harry Messenger, Old Colstonian, who was a former secretary of the Colston Fraternal Association, secretary/founder of the Colstonian Guild, driving force behind the War Memorial Fund and both founder and first president of the Welsh Old Colstonians' Society in 1925.

(SMV Archive)

Meanwhile, other developments were taking place within the Old Colstonians' Society. By 1938, the London branch had added monthly reunions at the Old Cock Inn in Fleet Street to their highly successful annual dinners and AGM suppers. Even greater excitement was created, however, in October 1925 with the establishment of the South Wales branch, largely at the prompting of Harry Messenger. After a successful whist drive had been organised in February 1926, the first of their annual dinner/dances was held in the December of that year. Although the number of signed-up members was to remain an ongoing problem (with membership averaging a mere 15 to 20 during the 1930s), their highly active committee still managed to raise both rugby and cricket teams for matches against the school, to put on enjoyable social functions (including golf days) - and, more surprisingly, to attract some 90 to 100 Old Colstonians and their guests to the annual dinner/dance.

The Old Colstonians' Dramatic Club was another new feature to make its appearance from 1929. Annual plays were staged initially at the Folk House on College Green, but later in St Saviour's Hall in Redland. Enthusiasm in Bristol itself was maintained, partly through well-supported dinners (113 present in 1936), and dinner/dances (200 present in 1938) - and partly through the sale of Old Colstonians' ties from 1929. The most successful development, however, was the rapid growth of the Old Colstonians' Sports Club. This larger body had developed naturally out of the Rugby Club, which had been formed in 1902. By 1925, the club was enjoying reasonable success with the 1st XV winning 17 out of its 25 matches in that year and the 2nd XV 10 out of

Menu from the first annual dinner of the Society of Old Colstonians in Wales. (SMV Archive)

25 - although the pinnacle of fame was not reached until 1936 when, in 'one of the most successful seasons in its existence', the 1st XV won 19 out of its 22 games. By Christmas 1938, however, the team had slumped to just one win out of the twelve matches played!

During the 1920s, the club's ground, which was at Manor Farm on Horfield Common, boasted a pavilion with a changing room and refreshment area. The rent of £50 a year was largely funded by the annual Christmas raffle. Members raised money with great enthusiasm through whist drives, dances and club suppers - partly to pay for the establishment in 1925 of a cricket section and a tennis section with two grass courts, and partly to build up capital so that eventually they could afford to buy their own ground and clubhouse. However, although their annual dance was attracting some 200 people by 1936, their search for a ground of their own continued in vain. In 1930, the club had moved to pitches at Beverley Road in Horfield and had managed to convert a hut into changing rooms with the help of a £150 loan. Sadly, no sooner had it settled in, when the land was sold for development and the club was forced to move to a new site at Charlton Road, Brentry, where it remained until the war in 1939.

Old Boys who played during this period later recalled their experiences. Frank Taylor, former President of the Society, described the changing room arrangements: 'Although the OCs were lucky to have a good ground, the facilities were very basic - namely, one domestic bath for each team and a lottery whether the water was very hot, tepid or cold. This largely depended on whether 'Jack' (half a crown a match, including tram fare from Knowle) turned up to keep the outside boiler going. If not, it was someone's chore before kick-off and during half time to act as stoker'. The move to Brentry also necessitated moving the pavilion (known affectionately as 'The Shack'). This was eventually re-erected by the members themselves, who turned up for duty on Sundays armed with spades. Those involved in the club took great pride both in its achievements and in the wearing of its blazer and badge, which had been designed in 1926.

In the autumn of 1938, the Sports Club took the long-awaited decision to purchase a sports ground of its own as soon as possible. This had been largely prompted by a most generous bequest in the will of Mr Edward W. Allen to the Colston Fraternal Association, part of which could be earmarked as a contribution towards the sports ground. The committee therefore launched an appeal for donations and interest-free loans to supplement the bequest with the express aim of naming the ground after Mr Allen, who had been a major force in the Old Colstonians' Society for many years. A former President and benefactor of the Sports Club, he had paid £50 in 1931 for a 'laid' cricket square at the Beverley Road ground. Sadly, within a year, the outbreak of the war had intervened and the Sports Club itself was closed down. The proposed new ground did not become a reality until 1956.

Forward Planning (1) and Development, 1926-1930

In 1923, the Chairman of Governors and the Headmaster shared an optimistic outlook for the future and a driving ambition to raise Colston's to even greater heights. Mr King told the Fraternal

Association in that year that the school 'was ripe for development' while the Headmaster assured the Old Colstonians in London that, in spite of hard times, the school had 'turned the corner' and was eventually aiming at a total of 250 boys. Two years later, Mr King declared that he wanted to see the school 'a perfectly equipped second grade school, one of the great schools in the kingdom'.

The Headmaster had already pencilled in a list of improvements to facilities, his case strengthened by the inspection report of 1923, which had highlighted a number of deficiencies in school equipment, including the gymnasium. A year earlier, inspectors had also been critical of the unsatisfactory state of teaching inside the gymnasium. Sergeant Higgins, the instructor, had therefore been duly despatched to St Brendan's School to observe the lessons there. Mr Millbourn made a mental note of all these priorities, but realised only too well the need for patience in the face of their desperate financial position (see above). Nevertheless, some improvements were made between 1923 and 1926, notably the installation of electric light following the extension of the cable to Stapleton (paid for by an anonymous donor, who later emerged as Mrs H.H. Wills); the erection of a new rifle range for the cadet corps; and the refurbishment of classrooms through the provision of new desks and lockers (paid for by a £250 gift from the Society of Merchant Venturers).

Then, during the school year 1925-26, two things happened which were crucial to future development. In the first place, Mr King launched

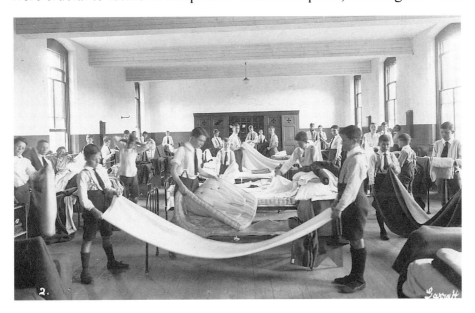

A junior dormitory in the 1920s. (SMV Archive)

his personal appeal for funds (see page 223) and not only cleared the school's bank deficit in the process but also made available some £7,800 for new facilities. Secondly, Mr Millbourn produced the first of three long-term strategies for the school in a memorandum to the governors dated February 1926. His sharp intellect greatly enjoyed the challenge of forward thinking by first analysing the school's problems and then drawing up clear-sighted solutions. 'The clock in my study has to be kept ten years fast', he told the Old Colstonians' Annual Dinner in 1937.

His plan centred on the need to restructure the school. There were, in 1926, six lower forms (2a, 2b, 3a, 3b, 4a, 4b) of 25 boys each, plus one 5th form (the School Certificate class of 20 boys) and two 6th forms (the literature and science groups with a notional maximum of 10 boys in each, spread over the two years of study before HSC). This gave a theoretical maximum of 190 pupils (although in reality it remained at 180). There were, however, only seven form rooms for nine forms, thus leaving the 6th forms with no permanent room of their own. Furthermore, the classrooms were also used as 'living rooms' by the boys during their leisure time. There were only eight full-time staff, each teaching 34 periods a week (normally there would have been nine, but Mr Gray, the mathematics teacher had not been replaced as an economy measure), plus part-time help from the Headmaster (17 periods), Mr Calway (10 periods of class singing) and Sergeant Higgins (6 periods of physical training).

The Headmaster proposed to add an extra 5th form (making two classes of 15 boys) to enable all pupils to progress to School Certificate (see 225), This would also remove the bottleneck caused by keeping 'b' formers down for their final year - '4b has almost become a cul de sac', he argued. 'In the long run boys placed on the 'b' side have tended to form the opinion that they have been classed as stupid' with little chance of promotion. The new structure, which would give an absolute maximum of 200 boys, would require the appointment of two more full-time masters, including Mr Gray's replacement. The second one would cover class music and relieve the Headmaster of some of his periods, thus enabling him 'to deal with administrative work' and 'examine the needs of the curriculum'. Consequently Mr Calway would lose his teaching and secretarial duties, while retaining his private piano pupils. After all, the government inspectors 'had commented unfavourably on the lack of discipline in his classes', while he was 'far from being anything approaching an efficient secretary' Although this would mean the provision of a properly-qualified secretary, Mr Millbourn argued that actual savings on the salary bill could be made through the appointment of younger staff. The two extra classrooms needed could be

The new Gymnasium after its opening in 1927. (SMV Archive)

achieved by purchasing a temporary 'army hut' with a dividing wall at a cost of about £60.

The governors reacted with great enthusiasm to these proposals. Mr Calway duly resigned and was replaced by Mr W.D.E. Havergal to teach music and general subjects; Mr A.G. Saward was appointed as a mathematician to replace Mr Gray; and Miss N. Robinson became the Headmaster's first trained secretary from February 1927. The extra class (form 5b) was created and proved to be an outstanding success (see above). However, the Headmaster's suggestion of an army hut to solve the accommodation problem was firmly rejected - for the governors had decided that they could do much better! As a result of Mr King's appeal there was now money available for an impressive expansion programme. This consisted of two new classrooms built on the top of the science block (costing £4,161 and opened in 1927); the conversion of 'Big School' into 'day rooms' for the four houses (1927); a new gymnasium to double as a concert and assembly hall (funded at a cost of £2,321 by Mrs Yola Robinson, who opened the building herself in July 1927); and the replacement of the old covered shed next to the changing rooms by a colonnaded covered way built in brick and carrying a terrace above (costing £675 and opened in 1928).

Furthermore, the parade, the drive and the tennis courts were all relayed (1928); a motor mower purchased for the playing fields (1929); the central heating system extended to the dining room (1926) and 'a potato peeling machine' bought for the kitchen (1926). Finally, in 1929, the governors seized the opportunity to turn to their advantage the Corporation's scheme to widen Bell Hill (which was to take a thirty foot strip of land from the northern edge of the cricket field). A smart deal with the Corporation and the Society of Merchant Venturers resulted in the actual extension of the cricket field southwards and the creation of a junior football pitch through the use of rubble dug out of Bell Hill to terrace and level. Consequently, it also became possible for the first time to lay out a 440 yard track for athletics to replace the old 220 yard circuit. Frank Taylor, who was at school at the time, later recalled the building of the large retaining wall on Bell Hill and the movement of tons of spoil across the field in tubs pushed by gangs of workmen along a specially-laid tramway.

The Headmaster was quick to reassure governors in December 1926 that he planned to use the new facilities not to increase the capacity of the school, but 'to increase the comfort of the boys at present within its walls'. His consistently-held view was that, under circumstances then prevailing, the maximum size of the school should remain at 180 boys. As events were to prove, there was indeed little fluctuation throughout the years of his headship. He had inherited a total of 167 in 1923, although this quickly rose to 176 by 1927. Thereafter, numbers hovered around the 180 mark (with a short-lived peak of 186 in 1933), including up to 110 fee paying pupils.

There was certainly no shortage of applications for the free foundationer places. In his termly report to governors, he frequently referred to 'the unprecedented number of candidates' for the 7 to 9 places on offer each year - rising to a record 438 candidates in 1931. The problem, however, was that of quality. The best boys in Bristol were being creamed off either by the other direct grant schools in the city or, increasingly, by the new secondary schools opened by the local education authority. In an attempt to improve the quality of his fee paying pupils, Mr Millbourn advertised over a much wider field and therefore successfully recruited boys from such places as Glasgow, Brighton, Nottingham and Chester. The consistency gained in the numerical strength of the school, in the face of a most severe general depression, represents a remarkable achievement.

Forward Planning (2) and Development, 1931-1936

By 1931, the Headmaster's first five-year plan had run its course. He therefore submitted to the governors, in February of that year, a second memorandum outlining his new vision for future policy. This centred on the need to obtain 'Public School' status - although he freely admitted that the time was still somewhat distant before Colston's could feature 'on the pages of the Public Schools' Yearbook'. In particular, they would require better accommodation, more former pupils at the older universities (hence the need for additional leaving exhibitions) and a greater proportion of fee-payers to foundationers. Nevertheless, he claimed, the school already possessed some of the hallmarks of a public school - the high intellectual standard of a number of its boys, its traditional links with a 'great city' and its 'spiritual conception of discipline' rather than 'an imposed repression'. Furthermore, it was a boarding school. The admission of day pupils 'would alter its character and snap its traditions'.

He then went on to make a number of practical proposals to help in achieving his overall aim. Finances should be strengthened, partly through an increase of fees from £60 to perhaps £70 a year and partly through the introduction of a sliding scale of payments for board and lodging by foundationers, according to parental income. While some parents faced great financial difficulties, he argued, some clearly did not - judging by one foundationer who had a car of his own! Secondly, he stressed the need to focus on recruitment. Although 'a quiet revolution' had already seen the proportion of fee-payers in the school increase from 30% in 1901 to 58% in 1931, the school's ultimate aim should be to increase its total strength to 225 boys, thus raising the proportion of fee-payers to 66%. This move would greatly assist in achieving 'public school' status.

At the same time, it was crucial to recruit 'the right type of boy'. Although most of his foundationers did conform wholeheartedly to 'the public school code', the boys recruited from the counties outside Bristol were 'distinctly of the right type' and tended to dominate positions of responsibility. He therefore suggested a redistribution of places in their favour. With regard to fee-payers, he felt that the increase in fees could help to attract 'a better type', because many parents 'were suspicious of cheap products'. Furthermore, he planned to spread his net over a wider area, advertising in the *Overseas Daily Mail*, and the Army, Navy and Air force *Gazettes*. Boys coming from further afield always made their mark on the school and helped to reduce accusations of 'provincialism'. Thirdly, he set out a list of new facilities - two more classrooms for specialist teaching, a fives court, a covered swimming pool, a cricket pavilion and a new school chapel (the present one being too small to accommodate the whole school).

The governors appointed a sub-committee in June 1931 to consider the Headmaster's report. By November, the government inspectors (who had just completed a full school inspection) had lent weight to some of Mr Millbourn's points by recommending the construction of both a swimming pool and a chapel. By the following May, the Medical Officer of Health had tested the water in the old swimming pool by the river and had concluded that, in view of the fact that the river Frome was 'contaminated and consequently unsuitable for bathing purposes', the use of the bath should be discontinued. In the light of this evidence, the governors agreed to build a new swimming bath behind the gymnasium, which was duly opened in 1933. The cost of £1,620 was to be met by a bank overdraft with repayment from annual revenue spread over four years. Three years later, showers were installed and a diving platform erected. The site of the old bathing place was sold (chiefly back to the Society of Merchant Venturers) for £60.

The old bathing pool by the river in 1927 prior to its abandonment in 1932 and the opening of a new swimming bath a year later. (SMV Archive)

Meanwhile, the governors had accepted a generous offer from an Old Colstonian (Mr W.E. Allen) to fund the cost of a new chapel, capable of seating 240 people and estimated at £1,000. This was eventually built on a site next to the gymnasium and opened in 1933 (the old chapel being refurnished as a classroom). Within months a fund, which had spontaneously been opened by parents, had raised £250 towards the cost of an organ for the new chapel (estimated at £350). No sooner had these two major target been achieved, than the Chairman of Governors (Mr Claude B. Fry) launched a personal appeal for funds to build a cricket pavilion (with space for a tuck shop and tea room). The response was so good that, by the end of 1934, the whole cost had been

The new School Chapel, which was opened in 1933 and remained in use until its demolition in 1999. (SMV Archive)

covered, the work completed and the pavilion opened in memory of Mr Mervyn King (the former Chairman, who had just died). Plans put forward in 1936 for the building of a permanent Sick Wing, however, were eventually postponed in the following year because building costs were running 'at such a high level'. All eight estimates submitted were over £6,000.

Nevertheless, the Headmaster was undoubtedly pleased that his proposal for the improvement of facilities had been more than fulfilled. He was equally delighted when the governors submitted an application to the Board of Education in 1934 to amend the 1910 Scheme in line with his plans to attract 'the right type of boy' and to increase the school's revenue. After prolonged negotiation, the Board of Education eventually published a New Scheme for the school on 5th August 1936, which sanctioned most (but not all) of the governors' request. Two major changes were confirmed. In the first place , it was agreed that fees could be raised for fee-paying pupils from £60 a year to £63, inclusive of books and stationery.

Secondly, the allocation of the 75 free places for foundationers from elementary schools would in future be revised so that three-fifths would be taken by Bristol boys (instead of the previous four-fifths), one fifth by boys from the neighbouring counties and one-fifth allocated at the governors' discretion. The important point to Mr Millbourn was that he could in future look for more of 'the right type of boy' in the neighbouring counties rather than in Bristol, where fewer good boys were now available. Bristol LEA had significantly increased its provision of secondary places in the 1930s by building new schools (such as Merrywood and Cotham) and reorganising others as secondary schools (such as St George's and Fairfield). There was far less competition in the countryside! It is also worth noting that the scheme revived the stipulation that the Headmaster should be a communicant member of the Church of England (which had been abolished in 1919 under pressure from the Board of Education), while another clause left open for the future the option of taking in day boys.

Of even greater importance from a financial point of view, however, was an amendment to the clause relating to free places. Although the 1936 Scheme reiterated that the 75 foundationer places should be totally exempt from the payment of tuition and boarding fees, the Board of Education decided later in that year to allow Colston's (as a direct grant school) to exercise such flexibility as their regulations permitted. From 1936/37, therefore, the governors were authorised to convert the free places into 'special places'. The awards, which would give total or partial remission of both tuition and boarding fees, were made subject to a parental means test on a scale laid down by the Board of Education. This clearly eased the strain on the school's limited endowment income. This is exactly what the Headmaster had suggested.

Forward Planning (3) and the Rejection of the Headmaster's Scheme, 1937

By the autumn of 1936, the Headmaster was inwardly feeling pleased with himself. His proposals to date had been welcomed by the governors and had been implemented in such a way as to encourage his dream of gaining public school status. At the Old Colstonians' Annual Dinner in November, he lavished praise on their wisdom. 'The governors', he said, 'had shown a most statesmanlike vision and foresight of the school's position, not five or even ten years ahead, but for generations and generations'. He was perhaps too modest to add that it had all been at his bidding. Certainly his confidence had reached new heights as he submitted, in the strictest confidence, his third forward-looking plan to the Chairman and Treasurer in February 1937. This time, however, he badly misjudged their mood by producing a revolutionary scheme, which was not only misconceived, but also founded on the flimsiest possible arguments.

His proposal was no less than to move the school to a new rural site a dozen or so miles from Bristol. This would help recruitment, he argued, because there was much prejudice against Bristol among parents from further afield and Stapleton had now become 'an undistinguished suburb of Bristol'. Furthermore, although the school needed to expand to around 220-230 pupils, accommodation was 'now taxed to the uttermost'. New facilities were urgently needed; the former Bishop's Palace was 'archaic' and in constant need of repair; the laboratories were outdated; and the playing fields inadequate. The main problem, however, was that the school was now 'engulfed' by housing estates, the roads were dangerously busy and the scope for country walks had been much reduced.

This lack of isolation, he said, brought immense problems. The school was far too close to local Bristol parents, who were 'not conversant with boarding school life' and who therefore brought in 'loads of unnecessary food' - not to mention infections which spread sickness. Worse still, when boys were allowed out on Sunday afternoons, they met 'with other persons', which was 'much to be deprecated'. 'It is a matter of knowledge', he continued, 'that a group of girls, who were causing anxiety in the Sea Mills and Shirehampton district, were recently coming over on a Sunday to keep appointments with some of the boys'. A mother had even asked the school to keep the boys in, because 'she found it impossible to keep her daughter from running after them'.

Another problem centred on the rapid growth in the number of shops (which made it difficult to control boys' purchases of 'forbidden foodstuffs and literature') and 'picture houses'. He despaired at 'the positive craving of a certain type of boy to get to the pictures at all costs' - particularly when they brought back infections with them. Finally he suggested that, once relocation had taken place, the site could be sold to the local education authority as a school for the new housing estates - otherwise, if Colston's remained at Stapleton, there would inevitably be pressure on it to admit day boys from the locality. 'The policy of accepting day boys' he argued, 'is one to be deprecated altogether from this school's point of view' - it would destroy its individual character, alienate its Old Boys and prove difficult to administer.

The Chairman and Treasurer were clearly furious as they read the contents of the memorandum. In a strongly-worded reply, they completely vetoed the Headmaster's scheme. 'The time has come when we should express our views frankly', they stated. His proposal for a change of site was not only out of the question on financial grounds, it also showed great insensitivity, bearing in mind that the past and present chairmen had personally raised funds for major new facilities. They totally rejected his arguments. The present site on top of a hill 'would be envied by more than one public school', while problems raised about the behaviour of boys were not an argument for relocation, but solely a matter of discipline.

The Headmaster's original memorandum is dotted with marginal comments scribbled with feeling by either the Chairman or the Treasurer; - 'this is a *Bristol* school'; 'so do the roads round Clifton College'; 'this applies to Eton and Harrow' (re parental visits); 'more discipline needed' etc. They concluded by instructing him that the proposal, which was 'wholly impractical', be 'indefinitely shelved'. Furthermore, he was forbidden to circulate the plan to other governors, because it 'would do the school incalculable harm'. Future benefactors, for instance, would be discouraged if they picked up any rumour of the school's imminent move. Although they were very conscious of the Headmaster's 'excellent service', their own aim was to concentrate now on 'a gradual process of adaptation of the existing buildings to modern needs'. He was therefore requested to draw up his list of priorities.

The Resignation of Mr Millbourn

There is little doubt that the Headmaster was seriously deflated by this response. His dream of transforming Colston's into a proper 'public school' had been shattered - to be replaced by the nightmare prospect of the arrival of day boys! Nevertheless it has to be said that, however successful his approach had been in the past, he showed himself on this occasion to be out of touch with the traditions of the school and the feelings of the Society of Merchant Venturers. His desire to turn Mr Colston's Hospital into something of an 'isolation hospital'; his increasing rejection of the city of Bristol and the boys it produced; and his contempt for the housing estates in the Stapleton area were indications that he was oblivious to the history of the school and the intentions of its founder. A touch of snobbishness also lurked beneath that modest and self-effacing exterior.

Although, after this rebuttal, the Headmaster retained his dignity and maintained the confidentiality which had been requested, he now saw little future for himself in the school. He continued in his post for just two more years, during which little of any note was recorded in the minute books. Then, on 18th March 1939, he announced his resignation, which enabled him to take up an appointment as Canon Residentiary at Bristol Cathedral where he was installed on 30th June. [He had already been ordained in 1929 to officiate as school chaplain]. At the annual Commemoration in July, Canon Millbourn and his wife were presented with a set of gramophone records and a silver tray, milk jug and sugar bowl by the Old Colstonians, parents and boys - after which he himself preached at a thanksgiving service in the parish church.

The governors recorded in their minute book their 'great sense of loss' and their sincere appreciation for Canon Millbourn 'under whose headship over sixteen years the school has so greatly flourished and has attained its present high position'. He had, they reassured themselves, enjoyed 'the unbroken confidence and regard of the governors on account of his ability and loyal devotion to the school'. There is no doubt that the Headmaster, who took over the school at a time of great difficulty, had not only exercised steady control but had also managed, during a prolonged period of economic stress, to maintain numbers and raise academic standards. His time in office witnessed a remarkable expansion of school facilities - thanks to his own vision and the dynamic support of a vigorous board of governors.

It is true, however, that in everyday life the school lacked the excitement and inventiveness which had been provided by Dr Finn. Canon Millbourn's twice-yearly reports to governors invariably commenced with such uninspiring statements as 'there is little to report'; 'the life of the school has gone on quietly and uneventfully'; or 'a very satisfactory, but uneventful year'. Nevertheless, Roger Newport (1930-37) found him 'a nice chap' and 'quite a good headmaster', in spite of an initial appearance of remoteness. He vividly remembers the Headmaster's habit of stroking the back of his own head while trying to recall a point. John Quayle (1929-1934) also recalls his admiration for the man's real personal qualities: 'I believe he was a very great Headmaster. I had several chats with him at my own request and he never failed to be sympathetic and helpful'.

This view is supported by Stanley Bowell (1924-29), who felt that Mr Millbourn was 'a very good chap' and generally well-liked. He particularly admired the Headmaster's performance on those occasions when, singing as a bass, he joined 'quartet of masters' in a programme of comic songs. Kenneth Hilborne (1934-38), on the other hand, remembers Mr Millbourn, who was nicknamed 'Boas', as a 'somewhat remote figure'. 'He was an urbane and dignified figure, but in retrospect I suspect that he was quite a shy man and it was probably shyness that I mistook for a feeling on my part that he rather disapproved of me. At any rate I had precious little communion with him. His wife, who did not enjoy good health, was *une dame formidable* and a summons to take tea (clearly intended to be seen as an act of grace and favour) was received with fear and trepidation - and sometimes, no doubt, prompted an urgent visit to obtain a sick pass'.

Sources used in Chapter 9

Scheme for the Alteration of the Scheme regulating Colston's Hospital,
       Board of Education, 1936 (printed in Eames, op. cit.,
       Appendix 3)
Society of Merchant Venturers' Archive:
       Colston Hospital Trust:
              Governors' Minute Books, 1875-1934, 1934-1956
              Finance Committee Minutes, 1923-1944
       Headmaster's Reports to Governors, 1926-1987
       (Green file) Colston's School
The Colstonian, vols. 30-47 (Autumn 1923 - Autumn 1939)
Cribsheet (The Old Colstonians' Newsletter), February 1987, October
       1987, October 1988, January 1992, January 1994, January 1995,
       January 1998, January 2001
Sarah Dunn, *Colston's Girls' School: the First Hundred Years* (1991),
       pp 111-112
John Wroughton, *King Edward's School at Bath, 1552-1982* (1982),
       pp 176-7
Personal interviews and written submissions (as acknowledged in the
       text)

TUCK, BOUNDS AND BATHS, 1929-34

J.P. Quayle *(Old Colstonian, 1929-34)*

I arrived at the school in September 1929. That evening I found myself in the South Junior Dormitory over the Chapel. The Chapel in those days was next to the Hall [i.e. just inside the main front door on the right]. On the ground floor, as you entered the Hall from the doors opposite the monkey-puzzle tree (which towered from the round lawn), the statue of Edward Colston was on the left, facing the door of the Chapel. At the end of the Hall was a great chest on which weary boys dumped their 'prep' before climbing up the stairs to the dorm.

Above the brick arches of the shed, which housed our tuck lockers, was a strip of forbidden concrete - the Prefects' Parade. Only Prefects and members of the 1st XV were allowed to parade the length of that sacrosanct strip. Each boy had a school number in those days. It was marked in tacks on your shoes, and all other possessions carried your name and number. Your school number became your identity on roll-calls. More than half a century later, 'Quayle 110' still marks my pride!

The tuck lockers were simply numbered. They were padlocked and in them precious stores of food were hoarded. As in most boarding schools in those days, the food in the dining room was pretty dreadful. How welcome parents were, especially when they came with edible gifts. At the end of the shed were worn stone steps leading down to the 'dugout', a cellar under the old school building. There Sergeant Higgins, at prescribed times, dispensed sweets, jams, marmalade and certain well-defined tins and potted fish and meat products. There were strict rules about what you were allowed to buy and eat and these rules extended to tuck from home or from any other source.

The new swimming pool was great fun [opened in 1933]. In my first year or so we swam in a pool by the Frome. The water was brackish and weedy and there were rumours of carcasses of drowned dogs - though I never saw one. It was thought to be a health hazard so, with the march of progress, the new bath was built. In between exams, we helped by moving soil. When the bath was finished, the Lord Mayor of Bristol, a keen swimmer himself, took the first plunge. Breaking the ice on frosty days was left to those who left water in bowls in the 'washers' [slang for wash room] on wintry nights. There was no hot water and no heating in the dormitories in those days.

Bounds were rigorously enforced. It was strictly forbidden to turn left from the school gates but, when in my later years at school, seniors were permitted to have bicycles in the school it was not difficult to turn right at the gates, thereby maintaining nominal rectitude, but to cycle north and then take one of the roads east and make a foray into forbidden territory. Whether someone was caught I will never know, but an infectious germ reaching the school was made an excuse for a witch hunt.

Obviously the germ had been introduced by one of these clandestine excursions to the 'flicks' [slang for the cinema] and all seniors were assembled, solemnly harangued and asked to own up to their wickednesses. Some did and some didn't; it was noticeable that among the 'didn'ts' were the most inveterate transgressors of the rule - but then life is made that way and we learnt to accept it.

At a solemn meeting with Major Beckett [the Second Master] a selected few of the miscreants were given a choice of punishments, of which one was that they paraded at the school swimming bath in their swimming costumes at 6.30 am to receive eight of the best, and then presumably a swim to reduce the pain. We all agreed to take the medicine, but the execution was commuted to reporting to the master-on-duty at intervals of half an hour in all our time out of school for the rest of that term. We also lost seniority in our various Houses.

(From The Colstonian, *Spring 1982)*

CHAPTER 10

Years of Disruption, 1939-1946

As we reach the end of the first post-war school year, we look back over the last seven years with feelings of thankfulness that we have weathered the storm so well and have suffered so much less than many schools. Though so near a much bombed city, we have not had to leave our buildings, which have suffered very little damage, nor have we been called upon to share them with other schools. (Editorial in The Colstonian, Autumn 1946)

The year has seen the enactment of a Bill which cannot but have a profound and far-reaching effect upon education throughout the country...The Governors have decided that we shall best continue to play our part in the education of the nation by becoming an Independent School. (Headmaster's speech at Prize Giving, 21st July 1945, regarding the Education Act of 1944)

Mr Snaith and Preparations for War

The governors lost no time in advertising for Canon Millbourn's successor. Notices were placed in the *Journal of Education*, *The Spectator*, *The Times* and *The Times Educational Supplement*; and two governors designated to sift through the 111 applications which were eventually received. The names of 18 candidates were then passed on to the selection committee for consideration, of whom six were shortlisted for interview at a special meeting of the governors in June 1939. The man finally to emerge as the new Headmaster was Mr Robert Snaith, MA (Oxon), who was then Housemaster of Pocklington School. He was granted a salary of £600, rising by £5 annual increments to a ceiling of £800. Mrs Snaith was appointed Housekeeper.

The first three Headmasters to be elected during the twentieth century shared one thing in common. They each inherited a school hit by crisis - Dr Finn, a crisis of discipline and staff morale; Mr Millbourn, a financial crisis of major proportions; and Mr Snaith, a crisis brought about by the impact of war, for within weeks of his appointment the country had been plunged into the Second World War. In consequence, much of his time and energy during the early months of his headship were devoted to the task of making the school as safe as possible against air attack. Inevitably, the war was to cause serious disruption to life and work at Colston's during the first two-and-a-half years of the conflict.

A hint of sacrifice to come was given as early as December 1938, when the First Aid Commandant of the local ARP [Air Raid Precautions] casualty service sought permission from the governors to use the gymnasium and changing rooms as a first aid post in the event of emergency. By May 1939, the Board of Education had circularised all direct grant schools emphasising their supreme responsibility for ensuring the safety of the children, especially where large numbers were accommodated in a single building. 'Structural precautions' were therefore to be taken, the cost of which would largely be covered by the local education authority.

The chief danger from air strikes was perceived not so much as that of a direct hit, but rather as one of damage caused by blast and fire - hence the need for secure shelters or 'dug-outs' to be constructed before the boys reassembled for the autumn term in 1939. The governors reacted quickly to the warning and, by working closely with the local authority to ensure that the shelters conformed to Home Office regulations, succeeded in adapting cellars and passages in the basement so swiftly and skilfully that the start of term was only delayed by two weeks. The alterations, which cost £1,001, impressed the City Engineer to such a degree that he was heard to comment that there was 'only one better dug-out in Bristol - the crypt of the Cathedral'. It was reassuring, therefore, that the boys would be much safer there than in their own homes.

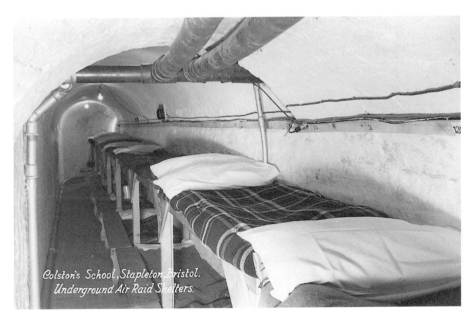

The underground air raid shelter constructed in the cellars and passages beneath the main building in 1939. (SMV Archive)

Meanwhile, other vital preparations were being undertaken during that fortnight by the new Headmaster with teams of staff and older boys. Mrs Snaith recalls that she and her husband actually moved into the school on the day that war broke out, having hurried back from a holiday at their cottage in Devon. Their first task was to black out the windows by covering them with a mash of paper and water to conceal any cracks in the curtains. Blackouts were then put up in the dormitories, dining hall, library, day rooms and changing rooms; sandbags were filled and positioned in vital areas; 3 stirrup pumps, 15 buckets (6 for water and 9 for sand) and 2 shovels were purchased; and a new fire escape erected for the sick wing. Once the boys had returned for the start of term, training was given in fire fighting and evacuation. 'Teams are ready with stirrup pumps, sandbuckets, scoops and rakes, if necessity arises', reported *The Colstonian*. Mrs Snaith vividly remembers a growing anxiety as enemy planes made their regular sorties over the school on raiding missions to Filton airport - openly defying the anti-aircraft gun on Purdown (known affectionately as 'Big Percy').

Staff were also involved as rooftop 'fire watchers' during air raid alerts, working in liaison with local air raid wardens. From 1941, the Board of Education gave permission for senior boys also to be employed in this role, as arrangements for fire watching became more elaborate. Later the school was able to claim a subsistence allowance of four pence an hour for each pupil doing duty during holiday periods. Furthermore, some senior members of the cadet corps joined the LDV [Local Defence Volunteers] and helped to patrol the neighbourhood for one night each week. By 1942, five of the NCOs in the corps had joined the Home Guard, attending their weekly parade and receiving instruction in the use of automatic weapons; while others acted as Home Guard runners during invasion exercises.

The first months of the war (a period known as 'the phony war') saw no enemy action in the locality. However, the spring of 1940 witnessed an increasing number of day-time alerts, which resulted in inevitable disruption to lessons as boys were sent down into the shelters. In actual fact, the strength of the country's defences meant that attacks by enemy bombers were far more likely at night under the cover of darkness. This eventually proved to be the case, when air raids on Bristol commenced in earnest from the end of June 1940. The Headmaster quickly realised that the dug-outs (which up to that point had been used as temporary shelters during day-time alerts) were in need of immediate upgrading, if they were to become the regular sleeping quarters for the whole school. Bunks were therefore quickly fitted during the summer holidays, together with heating and ventilation equipment at a cost of £889. (The governors made a levy of ten shillings a term on each pupil as a contribution towards this extra expense.) During the autumn term, therefore, 'the boys slept in them every night, whether there was a raid or not, and slept soundly'.

The first really frightening moment at the school came on 2nd December 1940, when two high explosive bombs landed on the site. The Headmaster described the incident in a report to governors:

> Our shelters received their first real test on the night of December 2nd. About 7 pm, two high explosive bombs fell in the school grounds and a number of incendiaries in the grounds and on the buildings. The incendiaries, with the exception of one which escaped detection at first, were quickly extinguished by the staff. The undetected bomb caused a fire in small store room attached to the gymnasium and a certain amount of equipment and stores was destroyed. We attacked the fire, as soon as it was observed and, with the assistance of the local wardens, we had it under control before the A.F.S [Auxiliary Fire Service] arrived.
>
> Fortunately for the school, the HE bombs missed the buildings, but one of them fell in the drive and broke our gas and water mains and did considerable damage to windows and roofs in the vicinity. Within a week our water main was mended, and meantime the boys thoroughly enjoyed assisting with water carrying and the general clean-up that was necessary. It was a fortnight before we got gas, however, and the achievement of the kitchen staff in cooking in the open air for the whole school during that time is deserving of the highest praise. As by this time the end of term was near, I decided to relieve the strain on the domestic staff by sending the boys home four days before the appointed day.

Although no personal injuries were sustained, £776 worth of damage to structure and equipment was inflicted (later claimed back in compensation). The memorial window to Dr Finn, for instance, was badly damaged. Mrs Snaith recalls how three of the incendiary bombs landed in a line - one slicing in half the Monkey Puzzle tree (which stood in front of the main door), the second just missing the Chapel and the third narrowly avoiding the swimming bath. The boys, she says, were marvellous, making a camp fire outside the kitchen and helping the cooks to prepare 'stew and milk pudding' over it.

Thereafter the school gradually became accustomed to nightly alerts and disturbed sleep. Nevertheless, by the autumn term of 1941, the majority of boys had abandoned the shelters and returned to sleep in their dormitories, thanks to 'a long spell of quiet nights'. The blitz on Bristol, however, was resumed later that winter and further damage to to the ceiling of a classroom was caused in the spring of 1942 as a result of blast damage. Then, on 16th March, Merchants' Hall in King Street (the headquarters of the Society of Merchant Venturers) was hit for the second time. As the damage was now irreparable, the Society took refuge for the remainder of the war in St Monica's Rest Home at Westbury-on-Trym, an institution for which it was already trustee.

It is interesting to note that, as a result of similar experiences up and down the country, the Ministry of Health issued instructions to Local Education Authorities in 1951 to prepare a comprehensive plan for the complete evacuation of city schools in the event of war. If independent schools chose not to evacuate under these circumstances, they would run the risk of being compulsorily closed or requisitioned. The governors, against the national background of a developing 'Cold War' with Russia, decided to co-operate in preparing a scheme for the evacuation of all Bristol schools into Somerset, Colston's being paired with Monkton Combe School, near Bath. Fortunately, of course, it never proved necessary to implement the plan.

Disruption of Activities

Ordinary daily life at school was to suffer many enforced changes, particularly during the first four years of the war. In July 1941, for instance, the gymnasium was taken over as a store by the Ministry of Food, although the governors did gain a substantial rent for its use (£400 a year). One acre of school land was also taken over for conversion into allotments. More seriously, the lack of blackout in the classrooms not only meant that early evening lessons became impossible, but also that meetings for clubs, societies and lectures were largely suspended for the duration of hostilities. Only the Scientific Society and the Literary and Debating Society managed to escape unscathed.

Boys were therefore forced to seek their own amusements. Pat Mahoney (1940-46) and Doug Winstone (1942-50) recall how time was spent in playing simple games such as 'Jack Across' or 'Strong and Weak Horses', making slides along the Parade during frosty winters and organising shove-halfpenny leagues. Bolder spirits were seen walking on the top of the main block's parapet as a 'dare', while the morale of the boarders was raised by the enterprise of a King's House day boy, Fred Forse (1957-62). He regularly made a drop of contraband goods (cigarettes and certain liquid refreshment), contained in a duffel bag which was placed in his 'contact's' locker. His Housemaster, Mr Cartwright (who had allegedly been in MI5 during the war) never managed to catch him in the act, although - years later at an old Colstonians' dinner - he revealed his suspicion of what had been taking place. Swimming of course was still possible in the pool, though war-time shortages meant that this took place without the usual bathing trunks. According to John Harvey (1940-47), the boys were blissfully unaware of the fact at the time that local girls regularly went up to the top of the church tower with binoculars to view the spectacle!

School matches in rugby and cricket were seriously curtailed, thanks in part to the shortage of petrol (which put a stop to long-distance away matches) and in part to the call-up of young men (which deprived the school of fixtures against the Old Colstonians, Clifton RFC etc.). Large-scale Prize Givings were replaced by much more informal occasions, because it was thought unwise to hold major gatherings of visitors on site; *The Colstonian* was reduced to one publication a year 'in skeleton form', thanks to the shortage of paper; the annual Colston Day parade and service was cancelled; and the July Commemoration weekend was reduced in extent to just one low key service in the parish church.

Nevertheless, boys were still able to enjoy sporting activity, although the departure of several staff for the war meant that the organisation of games was left entirely in the hands of two masters - Mr Rockett (who was aged 55) and Mr Lawrence. At least the house competitions continued as usual in rugby, cricket, tennis, athletics, gymnastics, swimming and music. The school rugby team managed six matches in the autumn of 1939 (but none in the spring of 1940, thanks largely to

Sergeant Higgins, who was the School Sergeant between 1921 and 1942.
(SMV Archive)

snow) and seven throughout the 1940-41 season. The 1st XI cricket team played seven matches and the 2nd XI six in the summer of 1940. Music, too, was affected. *The Colstonian* reported great difficulty in buying new instruments for the orchestra in 1941, appealing to Old Colstonians to donate any which were lying in attics unused.

One group which flourished, of course, during the war was the cadet force with some 90% of those eligible to join by age actually enrolled in its ranks. The corps band was employed in 1940 to lead the procession

which inaugurated Bristol's War Weapons Week - and it was still used
to lead the school's procession for the annual Charter Day service each
November. However, with the evacuation of the Society of Merchant
Venturers from the city centre in March 1942, services were temporarily
held in the chapel of St Monica's instead of the Cathedral. This meant
that the band, corps and most of the school marched the three miles from
school to Westbury-on-Trym (and back again after the service), although
a snack lunch was provided as compensation by the Society. Mr Rod
Pidgeon, who was at school during the war, later recalled those marches:

> By that time [1942] fuel was strictly rationed and the Bristol Omnibus
> Company did not seem anxious to have a large number of boys taking all
> the room on the buses from the Merchants' Arms [in Stapleton] to the city
> centre and then on to the White Tree [in Westbury] - so all of us who were
> old enough had to march from the school to St Monica's and back. The
> youngest boys (and most of the masters) were able to travel by bus.
> The parade, led by the band, consisted of two platoons of cadets in the
> battledress of the Army Cadet Force, a signals sections (later replaced by a
> flight of ATC cadets), a platoon of cadets too young to join the ACF, who
> wore the Colston Cadet Force uniform with breeches and puttees, and a
> group of 'civvies' who brought up the rear.
> We set off in high spirits down Bell Hill, and the first hill to take its toll
> was in Muller Road. By the time we had climbed the long drag through
> Horfield to Kellaway Avenue we were all decidedly jaded - and we
> welcomed the relatively flat stretch through Henleaze to St Monica's. The
> band bugled encouragingly, whenever it was thought necessary by Major
> G.R.A. Beckett, the CO of the ACF Corps and the parade commander. He
> maintained a keen eye on us, but his shouts of 'keep your shoulders back:
> don't slouch' and similar comments were not in the slightest appreciated.

One important development took place in 1941 with the
establishment of the Air Training Corps [ATC] at Colston's, formed as
an off-shoot of the corps by 21 boys who transferred. They formed the
No. 3 Flight of the 1495 Squadron (which also consisted of contingents
from Bristol Grammar School, Queen Elizabeth's Hospital and - later -
both Bristol Cathedral School and Cotham Grammar School). Although
they paraded weekly with the corps at school, they also attended
ceremonial parades in the city, visited RAF stations, studied the theory
of engineering, wireless, navigation and armament, took part in inter-
wing athletic sports and gained opportunities to experience short flights
from Filton. Meanwhile, the War Office had given official recognition to
the Public Secondary Schools' Cadet Association. The school corps
therefore became part of the Army Cadet Force and was duly issued

The School Cadet Corps in the drive of St Monica's at Westbury-on-Trym prior to the Merchants' Charter Day service in 1941. Seen here in service dress (which was replaced by battle dress soon afterwards when the Corps became the Army Cadet Corps), the boys have marched a wet three miles from Stapleton led by Drum Major Beere. (SMV Archive)

with battle-dress uniform - though *The Colstonian* issued this heartfelt lament at this development: 'It must be admitted that we feel we have sacrificed smartness for efficiency'.

New activities also emerged during the war to offset the loss of regular pursuits. As part of the nationwide 'Dig for Victory' campaign, the school was approached by the 'Honorary Organiser of Schoolboy Labour' from the Somerset War Agriculture Executive Committee to help local farmers by joining summer harvest camps. After some initial hesitation, Colston's eventually sent groups to Wickwar in 1943, 1944, 1945 and 1946. The boys also became keen on growing vegetables on the school site. In the spring term of 1940, for instance, they broke up and dug over an acre of ground alongside one of the playing fields, planting it with potatoes. During that first season, the school saved about £50 on the cost of potatoes, thanks in part to relays of boys who went in during the summer holidays to help with the gardening. By the spring of 1941, a further half acre of land had been dug as a result of food shortages which were beginning to bite. Sadly, disaster struck during the course of that summer, for, as the Headmaster reported to the governors, 'after yeoman service in the potato patch, the boys found the greater part of the crop ruined by wireworm'.

Although the war was to drag on to the middle of 1946, everyday life at Colston's gradually returned to more normal levels of activity from 1944, as the threat of air attack receded. Even as early as October 1942, parents and other guests were again invited to attend Prize Giving - and, in 1944, this event was combined with Commemoration in July, together with a School v Parents cricket match, tea on the lawn and the annual Old Colstonians' service. The spring of 1946 brought a relaxation in blackout regulations, enabling the Headmaster to introduce 'Society Time' on Wednesday and Saturday evenings (which also featured a series of lectures). New societies and clubs quickly emerged, including the Junior Science Society and the Bridge and Chess Club; a mock trial was organised; *The Colstonian* reverted to two publications a year; school matches against more distant opponents were revived and fixture cards again printed. The 1st XV celebrated by winning ten and drawing one of its twelve matches in the 1944-45 season.

In November 1946, the school again attended Charter Day, but this time the boys were taken by bus to the new Merchants' Hall on Clifton Down. From there they marched to Emmanuel Church for the service, before returning to Merchants' Hall for their traditional shillings and - for the first time since 1939 - their buns (war-time rationing having previously prevented the distribution of these gifts). Colston's Day was also revived for the first time since the outbreak of war, although the usual ceremony at Colston's statue in the Corn Exchange did not take place owing to the shortage of space caused by the war-time shelters.

On more than one occasion during the war, the Headmaster had remarked on 'the surprising extent to which we have been able to carry on as usual and the very small degree in which we have personally been affected by the war' (1942) or the fact that war had had 'little or no effect on the internal working of the school so far as the boys are concerned' (1940). These reassuring remarks, however, disguised problems behind the scenes which greatly disrupted administration, recruitment, catering and finance.

The Impact of War on Staff and Pupils

Quite apart from the general disruption sustained by normal school activities, the war was to have a more specific impact on the lives of individuals - as members of staff were quick to find out in the autumn term of 1939. In 1929, the governors had very thoughtfully erected 'motor garage accommodation' for the benefit of those masters who owned cars (although they were expected to pay a small rent for the privilege). On the outbreak of war, however, a portion of the garage was immediately requisitioned by the Chief Constable for use by a fire engine.

Even earlier, towards the end of the summer term in 1939, the 6th form had discovered that individuals often lost their freedom of thought and expression in a war situation and that even teenagers could be subject to surveillance. The Headmaster was informed, on instructions of the military, that a police investigation had ascertained that one 6th former (who was shortly due to go to university) was 'a member of a communist organisation'. When he failed to hand over 'all his literature on the subject', he was disciplined by the Headmaster. Furthermore, it was widely known that one of his friends had been 'closely associated' with the culprit and 'was known to share his views'. The governors immediately suspended the leaving exhibitions of these two boys, which had only just been awarded - although these were eventually restored in January 1940, after their universities had confirmed their good behaviour.

Even more regrettable, however, was the inability of two other 6th formers in 1939 (A.G. Harding and R.J. Newport) to continue with their places at university. They therefore surrendered their leaving exhibitions, having received their call-up papers. By 1943, the Headmaster was reporting to governors the fact that call-up regulations made it 'virtually impossible' for any student to make a start at university in an arts course. Students of science were permitted to study, if their work was likely to be of assistance to the war effort. At the same meeting, Mr

Snaith also reported that Lieutenant L.W. Savery, who had been awarded a leaving exhibition for a place at Queen's College, Oxford, had been killed in action.

Meanwhile, several members of staff also waited anxiously to hear whether they would receive their call-up papers. Even the Headmaster, as a keen member of the Territorial Reserve, found himself liable for service in 1940. Mrs Snaith recalls that her husband had fully expected to be called up and was more then willing to go, but - in view of the fact that he was 'as blind as a bat without his spectacles' - he was later granted an indefinite reprieve, following an appeal by the governors. However, by the spring of 1941, three masters had been summoned to join the forces - Mr Whitehead (who was to be an instructor in the RAF Volunteer Reserve), Mr Rich and Mr Addison. Although in theory teaching was a 'reserved occupation', in 1942 the government had ordered the 'de-reservation' of schoolmasters between the ages of 30 and 35.

The Headmaster expressed his grave concern about his ability to find temporary replacements. He warned the governors that 'the field will be unquestionably poor and we may have to appoint a woman teacher'. This would then leave the school with only two resident masters, whereas they had previously thought it vital that six of the ten full-time members of staff should be resident. In order to help the looming crisis at the start of the war, the governors had already persuaded the Society of Merchant Venturers to build a pair of semi-detached houses [numbers 1 and 2 Fry's Close] in 1940 for the use of married staff. In the event, Mr Rich was replaced by Miss K. Harper, an Oxford history graduate - although the Headmaster was frequently forced to appoint non-graduates as temporary replacements (where even these could be found). Nevertheless, the female staff who were appointed (including Mrs Snaith to teach French) turned out to be extremely competent. A similar problem of labour shortage was experienced when Under-Porter Milson was called up in 1942. Eventually, after much searching, Mr Snaith appointed a Mrs Phillips to take his place.

Nor were such problems confined to the academic area of school life. The finance committee faced a serious crisis in December 1943, when it heard that the school had been without the services of a cook or an assistant cook for several weeks, even after 'exhaustive enquiries' had been made. Although the Ministry of Labour had sent a temporary assistant, it was decided to despatch an urgent request to the Board of Education 'to direct suitable staff' to the school - otherwise, the boarding establishment would be forced to close. Eventually, as Mrs Snaith recalls, an Italian cook (Mr Amandini) and a friend 'were supplied to fill the breach from the aliens' camp on the Isle of Man'. The improvement in catering was apparently 'spectacular' - though they soon found a way to secure better jobs in a local restaurant. Exactly the same situation of acute labour shortage also prevailed on the domestic scene, where it proved impossible to find resident domestic staff. Reluctantly, the Headmaster was forced to employ part-time daily workers as much as possible and to turn to the boys for additional help with washing up. The situation was not really stabilised until Miss D. Glastonbury (a former officer in charge of NAFFI catering) was appointed Housekeeper.

Mrs Snaith, who had of course been appointed Housekeeper in 1939, had only continued in that post for the first two years of the war, her husband feeling that the stresses of the job were too often brought home. She recalls: 'I had been sacked as Housekeeper as the Headmaster got sick of being pestered with domestic problems. The official Housekeepers had had fixed times for discussion, but I had to catch him at anytime of the day or night when I could'.

Meanwhile, it was feared that the war would have a damaging effect on the boys' performance in examinations. Indeed, the Headmaster reported to the governors that the 1940 results had been 'distinctly below average'. He attributed this partly to the 'repeated interruption by air raids' of the examinations themselves - 'an inconvenience aggravated by frequent loss of sleep'. The quality of the results, however, was soon to recover. Numbers taking School Certificate averaged 30 throughout the war with an impressive pass-rate, which reached a record 85% in 1942. In HSC, the pre-war numbers were also maintained with an average of five boys passing each year out of the seven or eight candidates.

The best boys continued to win state or county scholarships and governors' leaving exhibitions. Indeed, the school's exhibition fund was further increased by bequests from T.R. Davey (1939) and W.R.C. Parrish (1942) - just as the prize fund was enhanced by Morris Harse (1941), in memory of a son killed in the war, and by the Dr H.J. Wilkins Trust (1942), which endowed a prize for the best sportsman. One other bequest worthy of mention was that of a fund established by Mr Harry Messenger (OC, 1884-87) to provide a leaving award for Pupil Number 152 (his own original number).

The Old Colstonians in Abeyance

By the summer of 1944, it was estimated that about 350 Old Colstonians were serving in the armed forces. Fifty-three of these lost their lives. *The Colstonian* recorded that, by 1941, some Old Boys were serving as far afield as India, Egypt, Palestine, Iceland and Canada, while others were seeing action at sea on the Mediterranean, the Atlantic and the North Sea. Inevitably, some of these fell into enemy hands. By the summer of 1943, therefore, the Old Colstonians' Society was sending regular monthly parcels of tobacco and cigarettes to its prisoners-of-war in Germany and Italy.

As a result of the call-up of many of its members, the society suspended its annual dinner until the end of the war, although the committee continued to hold its annual general meeting in November, followed by an informal get-together at Horts. The Old Colstonian Society in London held its last meeting on 21st September 1939, until a gathering was held of just seven members at the Old Cock Tavern in Fleet Street on 23rd November 1945. This was chiefly devoted to discussing the revival of their bursary scheme for the school, which had been in abeyance during the war. Their first post-war dinner was not held until 1948.

The Welsh Old Colstonians' Society, on the other hand, was much more active once the war had ended. After an annual general meeting had been held on 16th February 1946 in Cardiff, the committee met in April to organise a cricket team to play against the school and a dinner/dance to be held in the winter. The Old Colstonians' Rugby Club also began to show signs of revival in 1946, playing its first post-war matches in the spring. A full fixture list was prepared for two teams for the following season, although kit and equipment remained scarce and was subject to 'clothing coupons'. One element within the ranks of the Old Colstonians, however, continued to grow in strength in spite of (or, perhaps, because of) the war. By the summer of 1946, the Old Colstonian Guild numbered over 500 members.

Impact of the War on Recruitment and Finance

By July 1940, the governors had become seriously alarmed about the effect of the war on the school's financial stability. Their forecast of a substantial loss of revenue by the September as a result of the air raids proved to be accurate - no fewer than 21 fee-payers left as fear set in, some of them without giving proper notice or paying a term's fees in lieu (as under the terms of their agreement). Furthermore, a total of 32 fee-payers had applied for 'dominion evacuation' under a proposed government scheme and a number of older foundationers on 'special places' had suddenly left to secure sound positions with local firms prior to call-up at the age of twenty.

At the same time that numbers were falling, the cost of food was rising with the main ingredients of the school diet showing a 25%

increase. In addition, the laundry contract was suddenly increased by £46 per annum, while the cost of coal also escalated. In the light of all this information, the finance committee resolved on a major cost-cutting exercise, which included decisions not to replace Mr Addison (who had been called up), to reduce the library grant, to suspend the cadet force subsidy, to buy only such books as were vital to examination candidates and to introduce strict economy measures in the use of electricity, gas and water.

In spite of these moves, however, the situation had deteriorated even further by the summer of the following year. Numbers, which had stood at 175 boys in September 1939, had plummeted to 149 by September 1941 - while the school's bank account, which had been consistently in credit since 1934, showed a deficit of £57 in July 1941. Faced with this grave situation, the finance committee took further corrective measures - the masters' 'extra duty' allowances were reduced by a global sum of £100; margarine was substituted for butter in the dining room; and the Board of Education was requested to authorise an increase in fees from £63 to £75 from September 1941 (with a revised income scale for parents of boys holding 'special places').

To their undying credit, the decisive action taken by the governors in the early months of the war eventually proved successful in stemming the drain on finances. By the summer of 1942, a much more stable situation had been established and the bank account was again showing an impressive balance of £2,122. This position was maintained thereafter until the end of the war with the balance fluctuating between £2,571 and £6,393. This more comfortable situation had been helped not only by the increase in fees, but also by the steady rise in numbers - 156 by May 1942, 166 by December 1942 and 180 by December 1943.

The number of applications for special places had continued to increase (from 152 in 1942 to 221 in 1943) as the threat of bombing on Bristol receded, although - understandably - they never matched the pre-war figures. The Headmaster observed, however, that the quality of these applications had noticeably fallen, thanks to the evacuation of many likely candidates from the city. Nevertheless, it always helped the cause of Colston's School to be situated on the edge of the city, rather than in the middle of it. By May 1944, the numbers applying for fee-paying places were so healthy that, for the first time ever, they could only be admitted on a competitive basis. Thereafter the school was full to capacity (i.e. 180 boys) with waiting lists in operation.

As finances improved, the governors wisely decided to plan prudently for the end of the war. In December 1942, the finance committee therefore resolved to set up a 'repairs and buildings reserve' and, later in March 1944, an 'equipment and renewals reserve' as a way of preparing for the considerable outlay required for catching up after the war. As money became available from excess revenue, therefore, sums were transferred into these reserves - £500 in both 1942 and 1944, for instance, into the repairs reserve. Further amounts of unexpended income were temporarily invested in defence bonds - £1,000 in 1942, £2,000 in 1945 and £2,000 in 1946.

At the same time, they were able to relax the economies previously enforced - the 'extra duty' allowances were restored in May 1942 and the library grants in July 1944. Furthermore, they readily paid the 'war bonuses' to staff, as recommended by the Burnham Committee in 1942 and 1944 - even though these added £256 to the salary bill; and they immediately implemented the new Burnham award for teachers, payable from 1st April 1945. Then, in an attempt to attract 'a good type of teacher', the governors issued a new scale of extra responsibility allowances for housemasters (£100 a year) and resident staff (£50) - and bonuses for the quality of the degree (1st class Oxbridge degree £50-£75 a year; 2nd class Oxbridge £25; 1st class Provincial £25). The Headmaster's salary was increased to £875 a year in 1945 and to £950 in 1946.

Establishment of a Preparatory Department, 1942

Throughout the twentieth century, the governors had consistently displayed a capacity to continue their policy of development and expansion, even when times were hard. It perhaps came less of a surprise, therefore, when they decided - in the middle of a world war - to establish a preparatory department. In May 1942, they accepted the Headmaster's recommendation to set up such a department from the following September for a maximum of twelve boys, aged between 8 and 10 years. Mr Snaith was authorised to charge fees of £75 a year and to employ both a mistress (Miss K.D. Webb) and a matron (Miss M.M. Pollard) for that new area of school life. The Prep was immediately successful and, by December 1942, there were already 14 boys on the roll. By May 1943, it was still making excellent progress, although Miss V.I Copley had replaced Miss Webb (who had found it 'difficult to adapt to the conditions and responsibilities of boarding school life').

Meanwhile, there had been an important new development. In the spring of 1943, two Old Colstonians (Mr Fred Organ, who was also a governor, and Mr P.G. Davies) had bought at auction for £1,925 Stapleton Court, Seabrook House and Gordon Ground, all of which stood immediately opposite the school. Although they had acted spontaneously and on their own initiative, they immediately offered their new purchases to the governors for the same price. At their meeting in March 1943, the governors accepted the Headmaster's recommendation that these properties, which had considerable scope for expansion, should be used as a base for the Prep department. Permission was therefore sought from the Board of Education (which was quickly granted) to empower the estates governors to acquire the property as part of the Colston Trust and then to lease it back to the school governors. At this point, Mr Organ generously offered £500 towards new equipment for the school.

Although this was most exciting news, serious problems still lay ahead. The Board of Education made it clear that, in view of the grave shortages in building materials, work on the property was to be restricted to the minimum. A licence would therefore be needed from the Regulations Licensing Office before any 'controlled materials' could be released for work on the school. The governors quickly made up a list of essential repairs and modifications (including plumbing and heating) at an estimated cost of £2,830 - and agreed to an official opening in December 1943.

By that date, however, work had still not commenced and the governors were experiencing 'serious difficulties' with the Board of Education. Then at long last, in March 1944, a licence from the Ministry of Works was granted for expenditure of a mere £700 on sanitation and drainage - with permission to apply for another licence in June, when more materials would have become available. This second licence gave authority to spend £265 on the floors and £130 on decoration and roof repairs. In the end, the governors were permitted to spend a total of £1,408 out of the £2,830 they really needed. They agreed to raise this amount by a loan at 4% interest with repayments spread over 30 years.

These delays caused serious problems with accommodation, because the Headmaster had been recruiting on the basis of a December 1943 opening. By that date, therefore, 30 boys had been enrolled for the Prep - the exact maximum which had been planned from the outset - making a school total roll of 210. There was therefore a good deal of overcrowding in the dormitories and classrooms until Stapleton Court was eventually ready for occupation early in 1945. Thereafter, the Prep School remained full. By December 1945, the Headmaster was able to report to the governors that he had applications for entry 'as far ahead as 1948'. These were 'far in excess of those for the main school'. With future prospects looking so promising, he pleaded with the governors to invest more resources in the Prep, as soon as this became possible, to make it 'the excellent thing I am convinced it could be'

The Reform of Catering, 1943

It was very much to the governors' credit that they were also willing to improve the standard of meals, in spite of war-time restrictions and costs. The problem was brought to their attention by the Headmaster in a memorandum, dated March 1943 and based on his research in twenty-one similar schools. Although he fully realised the financial restraints then prevailing, he felt that it was essential to improve the quality of catering so that the school could compete for recruits on an equal footing, in what would prove to be a highly competitive boarding school market after the war. There were three aspects to the problem - the kitchens needed extensive reconstruction and modern labour-saving equipment; the accommodation for domestic staff was abysmal (seven of the nine domestic staff were forced to sleep in just two rooms, sharing one bath); and the food was totally inadequate in quantity.

He enclosed a sample menu (see below) to illustrate the fact that boys received just one reasonable meal a day (lunch - although this, too, was lacking in size) and were therefore forced to supplement their rations with tuck. He recommended that, at breakfast, the marmalade/honey mornings should be eliminated and that each week there should be one bacon morning, three porridge mornings and three sausage mornings; at lunch, the bulk of the meal should be increased; and at tea, there should be added each day one cold item to the bread and butter already on offer (fresh fruit, cooked meat or cake).

	Breakfast	Dinner	Tea	Supper
Mon.	Bread & honey	Sausages; blancmange	Bread & butter	Buns
Tues.	Sausage	Roast beef; stewed apples	Bread & butter	Buns
Wed.	Porridge	Liver; steamed pudding	Bread & butter; cakes	Buns
Thurs.	Sausage rolls	Beef stew; milk pudding	Bread & butter	Buns
Fri.	Porridge	Baked fish; jam tart	Bread & butter	Buns
Sat.	Bread & marmalade	Mince; bread pudding	Bread & butter	Buns
Sun.	Baked beans	Ham roll; blancmange	Bread & butter	Biscuits

The finance committee accepted the Headmaster's recommendations at its meeting in March 1943. The changes to the menu, which would raise the cost per head from 6s 8d to 7s 6d a week, were to be implemented immediately. They also agreed to modernise the kitchen equipment by installing electricity and purchasing a boiler, tea urn, canteen trolley, steamer, hotplate cupboard and electric potato peeler - followed by a refrigerator, meat-slicing machine and mixing machine as soon as possible. Major reconstruction of the kitchens and provision of better accommodation for the domestic staff, however, would have to wait until the end of the war - once building restrictions had been lifted.

The 1944 Education Act - an Independent School

The governors' decision to improve the standard of catering in the middle of a war did not entirely stem from a feeling of benevolence towards the boys. The year in question (1943) was also the year in which the government's white paper on the future of education was published - a document which heralded their intention to make substantial alterations to the provision of education once the war had ended. There is little doubt that the governors at Colston's, in line with governors at other direct grant schools, felt uneasy about the future and the hidden threats to their position which lay ahead. It is therefore significant that the sub-committee, which investigated the problems of catering in the school, added this preamble to its report:

> The sub-committee, having in mind the fact that the whole question of education is receiving close attention by the government, and that ensuing legislation will inevitably relate, inter alia, to minimum standards both of equipment and accommodation, fully appreciate that, if Colston's is to continue as a non-provided school [i.e. a school not maintained by the local education authority], considerable outlay on these heads will be involved.

Catering reform, therefore, was just one element in the governors' attempt to prove the school's worthiness to retain its status as a direct grant school.

Their own concern was mirrored elsewhere in the Bristol area - hence the meeting called in the spring of 1943 for the chairmen of governors and heads of all local direct grant schools in connection with the new Education Bill, which might contain provisions that would 'adversely affect' their position. Those present, who were also aware of Bristol Education Committee's declaration that it was opposed to any further use of the direct grant schools, unanimously resolved that the system should be maintained. A Bristol Direct Grant Secondary

Schools' Committee was duly formed to fight their case. The Chairman of Colston's governors (Mr V. Fuller Eberle, who had succeeded to the position on the death of Mr C.B. Fry in 1942) and the Treasurer (Commander A.P. Bush) agreed to represent the school on that committee.

By December, 1944 their worst fears had been confirmed with the passing of the Education Act and the publication of the Fleming Committee's Report, *The Public Schools and the General Education System*, which outlined a plan for opening the doors of the English public schools' system to children from all local authority schools. [The committee under Lord Fleming had been appointed by the Board of Education in 1942 to examine the way in which such schools, including direct grant schools, could contribute to the proposed new system of education]. The Education Act, based on an all-party desire to make educational facilities more adequate and more widely available, made sweeping changes - the Board of Education was replaced by a Ministry of Education; 'elementary' schools were abolished in an expectation that all pupils in future would advance beyond basic learning; education was to be organised in three progressive stages - primary (from 5 to 11 years), secondary (from 11 to 16 or 18 years) and further (from the age of 18); the school-leaving age was raised to 15; fees in maintained secondary schools were abolished; and both direct grant and independent schools were to be allowed to exist outside the system. However, the bad news came in the detail of the Fleming Report, which needed to be read alongside the Act. Under its terms, a school such as Colston's would be given a straight (and unpleasant) choice, once the 1944 Education Act had been implemented.

On the one hand, it could apply to join Scheme A of the plan and thus retain its direct grant status. The conditions, however, were to be substantially modified - 25% of places were to be offered as totally free places for children from local primary schools and paid for either by the local education authority [LEA] or (as in the case of Colston's) by the governors from their endowments; a further 25% of places were to be offered to the LEAs as 'reserved places' for boys from any educational background, who reached a minimum standard in the entrance examination; and the remaining 'residuary places' would be filled by the governors on full fees (although the government was to introduce a 'remission of fees scheme' based on a sliding income scale, thus enabling poorer families to claim back from the government a proportion of the full fees). Furthermore, these proposals stipulated that a *minimum* of one-third of the governing body was to be appointed by those LEAs which sent pupils to the school (compared with a *maximum* of 35% in the arrangement which had been operating since 1920). It later transpired that, if these conditions were accepted, the annual direct grant would be increased from £8 13s 0d per boy to £16 - a tempting bait, at first sight.

The alternative was to apply to join Scheme B, which was restricted to existing direct grant schools taking 'a substantial number of boarders'. This offered the possibility of surrendering the direct grant and becoming independent. During the transitional period, the school would offer a minimum of 25% of its places each year to local primary school pupils for a period of five years (with fees paid for by the LEAs); and, in return, would receive a 'tapering grant' for the first three years.

At a special meeting on 12th June 1945, the governors debated in full the agonisingly difficult choice which lay before them. They eventually set out the principles on which a decision would be based - that Colston's should contribute to the national system of education; that the best education should be offered to able children, irrespective of parental income; that they were opposed to 'drab uniformity' in education, believing that schools like Colston's could best contribute 'by preserving their distinctive character and traditions'; that parents should have 'a right by the payment of fees' to choice in education; that education should not just be based on local areas, believing that inter-contact with pupils from further afield was valuable; and that there were real dangers of control by the LEAs, whose policies would be governed by the interests of political parties or rate-payers. They also stressed the vital importance of the independence of the governing body in choosing the Headmaster, the independence of the Headmaster in selecting the staff and the independence of the school in deciding its policy on religious teaching.

The governors then examined the financial and practical aspects of the problem. In addition to periodic gifts from the Society of Merchant Venturers, the school's revenue consisted of interest generated by the Colston's Hospital Trust on its investments, payments contributed by the government under the direct grant scheme and fees paid by the parents of fee-paying pupils. However, whereas the income from the Trust had only risen slightly over the course of years and the direct grant was only contributing 10% of the total budget, the income from fees had grown so rapidly with the expansion in numbers that it was now fundamental to the school's survival and its support of the 'special places' on offer.

After much consideration, they concluded that the increased grant on offer under Fleming's Scheme A, which would amount to just 13% of any future annual expenditure, would make little difference to the overall situation. This calculation took into account their estimate that income would need to grow by £5,500 a year, if they were to finance increases in both local rates and staff salaries under the new Burnham award;

repairs and refurbishments, which had been delayed by the war; and urgently-required new buildings. They feared that the scope of modernising and enlarging the school would 'be lessened' under Scheme A, because the new Ministry of Education and the LEAs would inevitably seek to keep fees as low as possible (i.e. if they were helping to fund the fees of a large proportion of the pupils).

There were other concerns. The governors already knew from past experience that free or special place pupils tended to stay at school longer than fee-payers. They therefore feared that, if 50% of the places were awarded to free place boys under the Scheme A proposals, this would mean in reality as much as 70% of the school being populated by them at any one time. This in turn would seriously alter the existing balance between fee-payers and special or free place boys and would therefore change the atmosphere of the school. Furthermore, from a financial point of view, if they themselves were committed (under Scheme A) to supporting 25% of the entry on 'free' rather than 'special places' (where the parents contributed to the fees, according to their means), the fact that they would stay longer would mean that they would be totally funding some 35% of the school population. The school's finances would therefore be placed under further strain.

Two further worries surfaced. First, the governors sensed that the proposals would result in a far greater number of boys being recruited from Bristol and other urban areas, whereas up to this point some 45% had been drawn from outside the city. This change, they believed, 'would alter and localise the character of the school very considerably'. Secondly, the prospect of changing the composition of the governing board, so that a *minimum* of one-third would be drawn from the LEAs, raised the fear that eventually this figure would be increased and the school would be managed by a majority of local politicians.

After a great deal of careful consideration of all these issues, the governors unanimously decided that Colston's should become an independent school. Three crucial factors were taken into account - the need to carry out the Founder's intention, the question of future finance and their estimate of how, in the long term, they could best preserve the type of education outlined in their statement of principle (see above). In particular, the Chairman expressed their heart-felt concern that the new legislation would tend 'to mould all schools into a drab conformity'. He said: 'I hold that the word education must be considered in its widest terms to include the strengthening of character, the practical expression of the Christian way of life, with the development of a sense of personal responsibility in life to one's neighbours'.

The governors, therefore, forwarded the following proposals to the Ministry on 14th June 1945 - that they accepted the principle of offering places at Colston's to able pupils, 'irrespective of parental income'; that, according to the stipulations in Scheme B, they would offer 25% of the places at Colston's for the next five years to the Ministry (fees being paid by either the Ministry or the LEAs); that they would work closely with the LEAs about filling those places; that they hoped for a continuation of the representation of the LEAs on the governing board as at present; and that the school should now relinquish its direct grant and become independent.

The Ministry of Education eventually confirmed its recognition of Colston's as an 'efficient' independent school (a fact reported to the governors on 22nd May 1946). There is little doubt that the new Labour government, which had replaced the all-party war-time coalition after the July 1945 election, shed few tears over the governors' decision. The Minister of Education (Ellen Wilkinson), who had replaced R.A. Butler (the architect of the 1944 Act), had already announced its intention to reduce the number of direct grant schools. Colston's Girls' School, for instance, had its request to retain its direct grant status firmly refused; and King Edward's School, Bath only managed to reverse the Minister's initial rejection after a prolonged fight, spearheaded by the local MP.

The 'tapering grant' from the Ministry continued, as promised, for the next three years with amounts received totalling £2,336 (1945-46), £1,562 (1946-47) and £778 (1947-48) - after which all contributions ceased. By then, however, the governors had already raised their fees from £75 to £100 a year from 1st September 1945 (but from 1st January 1946 for boys already in the school). This, they believed, would enable them to cover the loss of the direct grant and the extra expenditure now required - assuming, of course, that pupil numbers could be maintained. All the signs, however, suggested that Colston's was now perceived by parents to be a successful school and that it was therefore a popular choice throughout the region.

This optimism was quickly justified. In December 1945, the Headmaster reported that numbers were still running at their very maximum with a waiting list in place for the following September. This was in spite of the fact that the Ministry, the Bristol LEA and the Gloucestershire LEA had all expressed unwillingness to accept and pay for the places offered them under the agreed arrangements (although Somerset had accepted four places). The situation changed slightly however in 1947, when Bristol and Somerset each accepted two; and in 1948, when Bristol took three and Somerset four. Thereafter, Bristol continued to take one or two places annually until 1959. Nevertheless, in spite of an apparently successful outcome, Mrs Snaith later confessed that 'going independent had been a very worrying time'.

Sources used in Chapter 10

Society of Merchant Venturers' Archive:
> *Colston's Hospital Hospital Trust:*
>> *Governors' Minute Book, 1934-1956*
>> *Finance Committee Minute Book, 1945-1956*
>> *Headmaster's Reports to Governors and other papers, 1926-1965*

The Colstonian, vols. 47-165 (Autumn 1939 - Autumn 1946)

Cribsheet (The Old Colstonians' Newsletter), February 1986, October 1987, January 1994, January 1995, January 2000

Personal interviews and written submissions (as acknowledged in the text)

D.J. Eames, *The Contribution of the Society of Merchant Venturers to the Development of Education in Bristol* (unpublished MA thesis for the University of Bristol, 1966), pp 187-99

Sarah Dunn, *Colston's Girls' School: the First Hundred Years* (1991), pp 137-47

John Wroughton, *King Edward's School at Bath, 1552-1981* (1982), pp 176-7, 215-7

'PRISON LIFE' IN THE 1930s

Kenneth Hilborne *(Old Colstonian, 1934-38)*

We endured a secluded life - it would have been a good training for a monastic existence - and from day one of the term, when we arrived with our trunks and boxes, to the last day of term we were up there at the top of Bell Hill, for the most part cut off from the outside world. Coming up that hill with its massive forbidding wall it had every appearance of a prison - and there was no such thing as parole in the shape of weekend passes or easy exeats; once the gates had closed behind you, one had a two-hour Sunday walk as one's allotment of freedom - and I cannot recall finding a deserted and closed Stapleton on a wet Sunday afternoon a venue of excitement, enlightenment or even the slightest passing interest.

Fortunately, and because most youngsters are fairly adaptable and generate their own community spirit, we were not aware of any great loss or deprivation - although some missed home more than others and there were a few (I think about three in the four years I was there) who made a run for it. No sniffer dogs were employed to get them back - they were usually hauled back by the treacherous parent or the maiden aunt who had them in *loco parentis.* These escapes always created a buzz with overt sympathy for the convict on the run, no doubt in heavy disguise and wearing the Housemaster's overcoat.

This kind of incarceration had one reciprocal effect, the flavour of which is still with me over 60 years later. No day boy or even that modern invention, the weekly boarder, can have the slightest idea of the suppressed excitement that the approach of the last day of term engendered. Many boys lived in or near Bristol and some were collected by car - but the best morning departures were by train. On the night before, lists were posted of taxis - Stapleton Road for South Wales (there was at that time a significant Welsh contingent) and Temple Meads for the rest. As soon as the taxi cleared the school gates, the fags came out; with

five of us dragging all the way to the station, there was enough smoke to outdo that on the platform.

Of smoking there was also a certain amount either 'down the Bean Field' or in the 'Booters' (the latter was an underground cellar used by the school janitors, who were good fellows). The discovery rate was low, but one or two masters made a point of making sudden forays into likely places and nabbing a couple of miscreants.

Another crime was going to the 'flics'. This entailed walking through the gates with cap on (5th form and above were allowed into Stapleton) and jumping on a bus when then cap would be stuffed in the pocket. On the one occasion I ventured out, I found to my horror that I had left my cap in the cinema - rather like leaving one's fingerprints on the safe. Fortunately for me it was retrieved in a day or two by the next sortie. The risks were imagined rather than real - a view perhaps not shared by the boy who was watching a film when the person behind tapped him on the shoulder -'Don't bother to get a bus back, I'll give you a lift back to my study'.

We had a weekly or possibly fortnightly bath in a dark, subterranean bathhouse presided over by the School Sergeant. It was certainly a case of getting into hot water and we came out looking like boiled lobsters - after which we dressed and were sent out into a cold winter evening to go to our respective Houses. How we did not catch colds or chills is a mystery. If one was sick or had some reason to pass off as sick, one joined the Sick Parade after breakfast where the Matron, a worldly wise but kind lady, dispensed cures. There were in fact only two that appeared to be available. If the complaint concerned the inside, quinine was administered; and if the outside, Condy's fluid. I cannot recall ever seeing the latter after leaving school, but anything associated with quinine (e.g. Campari) I have since avoided like the plague.

CHAPTER 11

Years of Confidence...and Uncertainty, 1946-1975

Taken in their entirety, the works to which we are already committed, coupled with those which we hope to carry out in the next two or three years, probably constitute the greatest move forward the school has made at one time since the move to Stapleton in 1861.
(Mr Snaith at Prize Giving, 1960)

Under the present Headmaster [Mr Gibbs] some rules have been tightened while several have been relaxed, creating more freedom for the individual than has ever been known at Colston's before...Recent events have indicated that this actively discontented minority is on the increase.
(Editorial in The Colstonian, Spring 1968)

Expansion - Phase 1 (1946-1958): The Admission of Day Boys

In November 1946, the Chairman of Governors (Mr Eberle) outlined his ambitions for the school at the annual dinner of the Old Colstonians' Society. He envisaged an increase in numbers of the combined Upper School and Prep to around 300 boys (from the existing figure of 226), the enlargement of the sixth form and the employment of specialist teachers. There is little doubt that, over the next thirty years, the governors were to provide dynamic and decisive leadership in what proved to be a period of unparalleled growth in the history of the school. In doing so, they showed considerable courage and impressive vision by taking a series of major decisions in a financial and political climate which was far from helpful. On only two occasions, as we shall see, was their judgment later proved to be slightly flawed. For much of the time, of course, they were fortunate to have the guiding influence and long experience of a Headmaster (Mr Snaith), whose commitment and sense of purpose were invaluable.

The first priority, following the loss of the direct grant, was to boost the number of fee-paying pupils. One immediate problem in this connection was to reduce the number of free place foundationers within the school from the existing total of 75, as stipulated by the 1936 Scheme (see Chapter 9). The Colston Trust's meagre resources (with a fairly static income of around £4,500 a year) were no longer able to

The Headmaster, Mr Snaith (on the right), chatting to the Duke of Beaufort (left)
after Prize Giving in 1962. (SMV Archive)

sustain such numbers in the face of rapidly rising costs. After prolonged negotiations (which began in 1946), the Ministry of Education finally agreed to amend the Scheme in 1953, although it was not sealed until 1957.

In short, it was agreed that totally free places should be replaced by 'special places', which would be free of tuition fees, but with boarding fees determined by family income on an approved sliding scale; that awards should no longer be confined to boys from state primary schools (thus opening up opportunities for boys from private preparatory schools - including Colston's); and that the candidate's 'need for boarding' should be paramount. It was also agreed that the total number of special places should be reduced to 32 - and that 'fatherless boys' or those with 'incapacitated fathers' could still be given preference for up to half of the places.

The new arrangements meant, of course, that fewer boys could be admitted on heavily subsidised places, though the demand remained great (307 candidates, for instance, had taken the examination in 1947). Although the governors had originally felt that the Trust's funds could only sustain an entry of three special place boys a year, under the new agreement with the Ministry they actually admitted an average of six boys in each of the years between 1954 and 1959.

Furthermore, the governors did their best to ensure that additional bursary funds were made available whenever possible to encourage bright pupils from poorer homes. In 1956, therefore, Sir Charles Colston (who was a member of the governing board) provided an endowment of £20,000 to help in the support of one or two scholars each year, while in 1958 the Society of Old Colstonians in London offered a bursary of £100 a year towards the cost of a boarding place for one pupil. At the same time, the governors, realising that boys going up to university were now eligible for local authority grants, diverted income from the Proctor Baker Leaving Scholarships and the C.B. Fry Leaving Exhibitions to benefit boys instead who were *entering* the school.

Although the amendment of the 1936 Scheme was of crucial importance, a decision by the governors in 1949 proved to be of far greater long-term significance to the expansion of the school. In the July of the previous year, Mr Snaith had submitted a paper to the finance committee arguing strongly in favour of admitting day boys. After careful consideration of the school's general needs, the governors eventually agreed to admit 20 day boys from September 1949 (with fees of £70 per annum); to increase the number as soon as practicable to 30 or even 60; and to investigate the possibility of admitting day boys into the Prep. The full implementation of this plan, however, was immediately threatened early in 1950, when the Ministry of Education refused to sanction the building of a day boys' common room in view of the acute shortage of building materials.

Fortunately, while these negotiations had been going on, the governors had seized the opportunity to purchase the Old Rectory at Stapleton (which stood next to Stapleton Court) for a sum of £3,500 - the cost being covered by an interest-free loan of £4,000 from the Society of Merchant Venturers (which was actually converted into a gift one year later). Under the circumstances, they now decided to move the Headmaster and his family out of their rooms in the former Bishop's Palace and into the Old Rectory - a move welcomed by Mrs Snaith, who felt that it was more like a proper home with greater freedom from constant interruptions. This enabled them to convert the ground floor of the Palace into a day boys' common room area and the first floor into bedrooms for the assistant Housemasters. The Housemaster of this new 'Dolphin' House (Mr D. Cartwright, who took up his position in

September 1950 when the new facilities were ready) was provided with accommodation in Rose Cottage, which the Society of Merchant Venturers made available to the governors at an 'economic' rent.

The Headmaster was quick to reassure parents at Prize Giving in 1949 that the school would not change its character as a result of this major decision. 'It will remain predominantly a boarding school', he said. 'Our day boys will be required to submit to a discipline comparative to that of our boarders'. There would be no invidious distinction between them, for all would be regarded 'as members of the same family'. It soon became apparent that the newly-arrived part of this family was rapidly growing. By September 1951, there were already 39 day boys in the school with a projected figure of 60 by 1953. Realising the success of this policy, the Headmaster had already begun prompting the governors (as early as 1950) to consider the possibility of a second Day Boys' House.

Encouraged by the offer of an interest-free loan of £12,000 from the Society of Merchant Venturers towards the eventual cost of £17,399, they finally agreed to proceed in December 1955 with the erection of a Day Boys' Block. The building, which was situated behind the gymnasium, was opened in July 1957 and named 'Mervyn King's House' in memory of the former Chairman of Governors. It was designed to accommodate two Houses, each of sixty boys - Dolphin House and the newly-created King's House. This additional facility in turn freed the Bishop's Palace once more for further development. By 1958, the first floor had been converted into a Sick Wing and the ground floor into eight studies for sixth formers. The cost of the latter was covered by a bequest by Mr Fred Organ, who had died in 1950 after serving thirty years as the first Old Colstonian member of the governing board.

Meanwhile, the governors had turned their attention to the development of the Prep School. The Headmaster, realising its growing importance, had suggested as early as 1948 that a Housemaster should be appointed to run that sector on a day-to-day basis. Seabrook, which had previously been occupied by the gardener, was duly adapted as a suitable residence and Mr J.F.C. Brown appointed to that position (to be succeeded in 1956 by Mr L.J.R. Whitby James). Then, in 1951, Mr Snaith, faced by mounting pressure from parents and new local competition, alerted the governors to the urgent need to introduce a day boy entry at that level.

Agreement was quickly reached to provide a new block of four classrooms and a staff room at Stapleton Court; to recruit 20 boys a year, spread over the 8, 9 and 10 year-old age groups (possibly increasing to thirty); and to commence the new arrangements in

September 1952. However, although the Ministry of Education supported the plan, they were unable to grant a licence until the following year owing to a shortage of bricks. It was therefore decided to proceed with the entry anyway, squeezing the boys into existing accommodation while the governors negotiated a £10,000 loan with repayment spread over 20 years. The new block was eventually opened by the Sheriff of Bristol (the Duke of Beaufort) in October 1954. A few months earlier, the governors had agreed to another change which would further the creation of a more self-contained unit - namely, the provision of meals brought from the main kitchens by heated containers and trolleys for consumption at Stapleton Court in a specially-adapted dining room. This, the Headmaster believed, would be of great benefit, freeing the small boys 'from the undesirable trek across the main road'.

In 1949, Mr Snaith had stated at the annual dinner of the Old Colstonians' Society, that 'in these days, it was insufficient for a school to be good - it was necessary for it also to be of a certain size'. The pursuit of numbers had therefore become of paramount importance in an attempt to achieve financial stability, a well-balanced curriculum and facilities which would be attractive in a highly competitive market. Numbers indeed rose rapidly. The combined total for the Prep and the Upper School increased from 210 in 1950, to 295 in 1954 and to 340 in 1957. By then there were 114 day boys in the school, including 88 in the Upper School - although the number of boarders had also increased in the Upper School from 151 in 1950 to 194 in 1957. Facilities, in line with the governors' policy, also continued to grow. In June 1956, a block of three fives courts was opened by Sir Stanley Reed (O.C., 1883-87), who had provided £6,500 out of his own pocket to fund the scheme; in 1955, the kitchens were extended and refurbished with modern equipment in order to cater for the additional numbers; and, in the same year, a new armoury was provided in a Nissen hut by the War Office, the old one being converted into a classroom.

Nevertheless, one of the most important new facilities, in terms of the expansion of the school, had already been provided by the Old Colstonians. In 1947 they had decided, as a War Memorial to those former pupils who had died in the Second World War, to carry out 'a comprehensive levelling and remodelling' of the playing fields. The school's location on a hillside had meant that most of the pitches were not level and a great deal of the ground could not be used. Launching an appeal for £11,000, the Old Boys began work on the project by 1948. For almost two years, the boys were 'gradually driven from one field to another' as the bulldozers took over. Teams were forced to play on borrowed pitches, while the majority resorted to games of handball on the Parade. Once seeded, the new fields were hit by hail storms, drought, weeds and (later) floods.

Eventually, however, they settled down to provide some ten acres of properly laid out pitches, causing *The Colstonian* to report with glee that 'the old [running] track, of a shape to which no name can be attached, has now disappeared to be replaced by a correctly shaped 440 yards track'. The fields had been completed by the autumn of 1949, although the finishing touches were provided in 1955 with the erection of a balustrade and plaque to commemorate the gift. It had also been decided to include, as part of the memorial, a new window in the Dining Hall with the names of the fallen inscribed on oak boards on each side. This was unveiled by the Duke of Beaufort at a dedication service, led by the Bishop, in June 1950. Mike Jones (1945-55), who was present at that ceremony as a small boy, remembers sing Mozart's *Requiem* and witnessing grief for the first time in his life, as the widows of those who had been killed in the war sat sobbing throughout the ceremony. The on-going generosity and loyalty of the Old Colstonians towards the school was noted with gratitude by the Headmaster three years later: 'Few schools', he said, 'can have been more fortunate in their Old Boys'.

Generosity of this level was all the more welcome to governors in the late-1940s and 1950s in view of the school's increasingly alarming financial situation. By 1948, the regular surpluses, which had characterised the annual budgets in the latter stages of the war, had been replaced by repeated deficits. In the April of that year, the finance committee announced a loss on the previous year of over £3,000. Two years later, they reported a deficit of £3,600, which was likely to reach £6,200 for the year ending March 1951. There were many reasons for this slump in fortune - post-war inflation; salary increases made at regular intervals by the Burnham Committee; government legislation on pensions, health contributions and personal injuries; and recent capital expenditure (amounting to over £12,000), which was being 'upheld in the accounts'.

In December 1950 the governors, after considering a special report on the school's finances, decided on a policy of realistic fee increases to rectify the balance. After all, the government inspectors had commented in 1948 that the fees were 'remarkably low'. Boarding fees in the Upper School therefore rose steadily and steeply from £130 in 1948 to £160 in 1951, £185 in 1953, £220 in 1956 and £250 in 1959. Additional measures eased the situation further - the sale of £4,000 worth of defence bonds (which had been purchased with war-time surpluses) and the conversion of the £4,000 loan by the Society of Merchant Venturers into an outright gift. Nevertheless, for two years, the deficit continued to run at between £5,000 and £7,000, causing the finance committee to stress in 1952 that the position was still 'grave'. A policy of strict economy on repairs and provisions was therefore ordered and gradually the deficit was brought under control. By March 1960, the annual accounts were showing a surplus of £2,300, enabling the governors to place £1,500 on reserve.

Expansion - Phase 2 (1958-1965): Restructuring the School

Over the course of two years from June 1958, the Headmaster and governors hammered out a detailed policy for the school's future development. By October 1960, this had been finalised. They decided, bearing in mind the increased profitability of the Prep School and day boy markets, to maintain the Upper School at a level of 200 boarders and 100 day boys (but with an entry at 13 plus) and to enlarge the Prep School to a maximum of 60 boarders and 60 day boys (with an age range of 7 to 13). This would produce an optimum school size of 420, while still retaining a majority of boarders. Increased numbers would necessitate increased classroom, laboratory and (in the case of the Prep) dormitory space - not to mention enlarged playing fields; increased competition would mean the modernisation and refurbishment of existing facilities and the appointment of first-rate staff with 'personality and teaching ability' (particularly at sixth form level).

The governors, who were only too aware of the implications of this new policy, then drew up a financial plan. This was partly based on the launch of an appeal in March 1960, in conjunction with the Old Colstonians' Society, to raise £75,000 in commemoration of the school's 250th anniversary; and partly on a determination to budget each year for a substantial surplus, whilst always keeping fees 'within the reach of parents in the medium and lower income groups' in line with the founder's intention. Underlying the scheme was the desire to gain prestige through future membership of the Headmasters' Conference (the HMC) and the need to cultivate other prep schools as 'feeder schools' at 13 plus.

Meanwhile, attention was being given to recruitment and the problem of restructuring the entry. As an interim measure, it was decided to create an extra fourth form in September 1960, which could receive outside entries at 13 plus - a situation strengthened when the Ministry of Education agreed that two of the six special places each year could be allocated to boarders at that level. Unfortunately, recruitment through the offer of scholarships proved to be extremely disappointing - in 1960, the 13 plus examination was 'a complete failure' with only three poor candidates emerging, while that at 11 plus attracted just 58 entries (of whom only 8 mediocre boys were interested in boarding).

By 1964, concern was still being expressed not only at the shortage of entries, but especially at the poor standard of the applicants - in spite of the fact that the Headmaster was now offering totally free places (which was costly) instead of the partly subsidised ones as previously agreed. In view of the situation, the governors gained the ministry's approval in 1961 to abolish the territorial restriction, which had limited special places to boys from Bristol and the neighbouring counties; and, in 1962, to reduce the number of special place holders from 32 to 24. Such was their anxiety that, in 1965, the governors also decided to extend the catchment area for day boys to include Frampton Cotterell, Yate, Coalpit Heath and Iron Acton.

The new structure became fully operational from September 1961, when the Reverend P. Harper (the Housemaster of Dolphin House) took over as Master-in-Charge of the Prep with 124 boys aged between 7 and 13 (including those transferred from the Upper School). This sudden increase in numbers (up from just 54 in the previous year) was housed in three new classrooms, which had just been completed as additions to the existing block, and extra dormitory accommodation for 18 boys, which had been created out of an existing building. A year later, Mr Harper was re-styled 'Headmaster' of the Prep, only to be succeeded in the post in 1963 by Mr G.S. Jameson, who was Headmaster of the Junior School at King's School, Rochester.

The newly-fashioned Prep School became an immediate success with numbers rising to 142 by 1965. It is interesting to notice, however, that although the overall total for the school (417) had by then almost reached its target figure of 420, the Prep School was 22 over target and the Upper School 25 below. The first signs of a decline in boarding interest were also beginning to appear. Nevertheless, the sixth form had grown to 74 boys by 1963 (including 21 in the General Sixth, who were not aiming at A level); and, in an attempt to attract top quality teachers, a new Colston Scale had been introduced in 1960 to provide salaries above the basic Burnham pay.

For their part, the governors also did their best to raise the school's image in the outside world. They were therefore delighted in 1961 when Colston's became one of the twelve founder members of the Society of Headmasters of Independent Schools (SHMIS) and again in 1962 when the Prep School was admitted to the Incorporated Association of Preparatory Schools (IAPS). This meant that both schools were now at last featured in the Public and Preparatory Schools Year Book, even though membership of HMC still remained elusive.

The years 1958-1965 witnessed a truly remarkable expansion of the school's facilities - an operation masterminded by the Headmaster (Mr Snaith) and the indefatigable Chairman of Governors (Mr Eberle). The first stage of the development was agreed in detail after much discussion in 1959 and early 1960 - and was completed during 1960 and 1961. It consisted of a two-storey block with eight classrooms (including an art room); the creation of two biology laboratories out of the former art room and an adjoining classroom on the top floor of the library block; the conversion of two classrooms on the lower floor of that block into new laboratories for advanced work in physics and chemistry; the creation of a music room and sound-proofed practice rooms out of an old stable block next to the gymnasium; and the modernisation of the Main Block to include improved common rooms, changing rooms with lockers, a hot water system and new shower rooms and ablutions. The total cost of all this work was £71,869, most of which was covered by the highly successful appeal which, by September 1961, had raised £70,500.

Three extra items were subsequently added to this list. It was agreed in 1961 to seize an opportunity, which had presented itself, to extend the playing fields; and in 1962 to modernise the lavatories at the end of the colonnade. The Stapleton Allotment Committee had decided to surrender back to the Society of Merchant Venturers their 11 acres of allotments, which were adjacent to Colston's playing fields. The Society immediately made these available to the school, although it cost £8,000 to level and develop four new football pitches and a cricket square. At

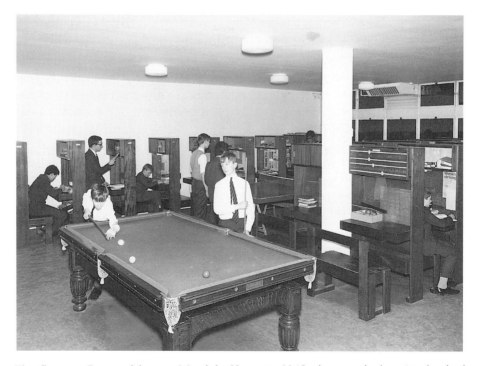

The Common Room of the new Mortlake House in 1965, showing the boys' individual working desks (or 'toyes'). Senior pupils had their own studies. (SMV Archive)

the same time, the governors decided to convert a small field occupied by Mr Flowers off Fry's Close into a playing field for the Prep. All these facilities were ready for use by the summer of 1964.

Meanwhile, throughout 1963, the governors debated with the Headmaster and a planning consultant the details of the second stage of the masterplan. In the end it was agreed that the key elements should consist of a new Headmaster's house, thus releasing the Old Rectory as urgently-needed extra space for the rapidly-growing Prep; a new boarding house to relieve pressure on the existing dormitories; a complete re-vamp of the main dormitory block, creating enlarged accommodation for three Houses (instead of the previous four) and making space for a prefects' room and a library on the ground floor; and six new tennis courts to the east of the classroom block. After some negotiation, Mr Flowers agreed to give up the tenancy of his market garden in the area of Fry's close (with suitable compensation), thus enabling work on both the new boarding house and the Headmaster's house to proceed. As building materials were still in short supply, the governors grasped an unexpected opportunity to buy 20,000 Cattybrook bricks for the latter and have them delivered on site long before work commenced.

All these projects were completed between 1965 and 1966 - although, in order to have the boarding accommodation ready for the start of term in September 1965, some boys spent the latter part of the summer term sleeping in a marquee. Mortlake House was given the privilege of using the new block, while Roundway House had its own new staircase (the Roundway Staircase) next to the main entrance as part of the refurbishment. The two rooms of the new library, which were ready for use in June 1966, were named the Snaith Room and the Harvey Room (the latter in recognition of the generosity of a governor, Mr R.S.S. Harvey, who had funded the panelling). It was subsequently agreed to convert the former library into a sixth form common room complete with television and 'teaching machines'.

Two later decisions in 1965 added to this second stage of the development - the conversion of the colonnaded walkway into a hobbies room area; and the building of a pavilion on the new playing fields (eventually opened in 1967 with the cost covered by individual members of the Society of Merchant Venturers). The governors had also commenced a policy of buying up property in the vicinity of the school, as it came on to the market, with the aim of converting it into staff accommodation - hence the purchase of 2 Church View in 1963 (£2,750), 96 Park Road in 1965 (£3,750) and 25 The Chine in 1965 (£4,250).

***

Boys studying in the old Library in the early 1960s. (SMV Archive)

Boys in their new Sixth Form Common Room, which had been created out of the old Library in 1966. (SMV Archive)

Just before the completion of this phase of the development, its two leading architects departed the scene. In May 1963, Mr V. Fuller Eberle retired as Chairman of Governors after 36 years as a member of the board and 21 years as its chairman. He had during those twenty-one years been a tower of strength to the school through a period in its history which was both difficult and exciting. A man of considerable vision, he was decisive in action and determined in his pursuit of policies which had been agreed. The speed with which the development of the school had been achieved was largely due to his own enthusiasm and drive. Nor could his business acumen conceal his very real human attributes - Mrs Snaith later referring to him as 'a wonderful person'. At Prize Giving in 1947, he had set out his own view of their aim in education: 'What mattered', he said, 'was the building and strengthening of character, the development of the power of leadership, willingness to accept responsibility and the power to stand firm against popular feeling, joined to a Christian outlook on relationships with fellow men'.

In December 1964, the governors were shocked to hear the sad news of the sudden death of Mr Snaith, almost two years before his planned retirement. Mrs Snaith recalls how he had attended the annual carol service, but was taken ill during the night and died two days later of heart failure. She believes that 'the pressure built up over all those years hastened his death'. Headmaster for more than 26 years, he had run the school with quiet dignity and firm control. Both boys and staff showed him great respect mingled perhaps with fear rather than love. In paying tribute to his enormous contribution, *The Colstonian* recalled how he had faced the war situation 'calmly and with no fuss, but complete efficiency', each emergency being dealt with 'quickly and quietly'. After the war, he had gained a reputation for his 'long distance planning', which was always thoroughly researched. No plan was brought forward to the governors 'until it had been discussed, so that any unforeseen difficulty might be met' - but once discussion had ended, he 'proceeded resolutely' with its implementation. His idea to introduce day boys and then to re-structure the school through the development of the Prep proved to be a courageous master stroke, which was crucial to survival.

Although his relationship with the governors throughout had been good, Mrs Snaith recalls that he had from the outset been forced to battle away unceasingly in an attempt to improve the 'Dickensian' conditions which he had inherited. He had been horrified in 1939, for instance, that the boys were still forced to wash in cold water. His request for change, however, was rejected out of hand - 'this isn't Eton', came the reply. Although that particular battle was not won until 1960, the governors had by then grown not only to respect him ('your husband is a gallant fighter', commented one of them to Mrs Snaith), but also to admire the fact that his judgment was usually correct. His one disappointment was his failure to gain membership of the Headmasters' Conference; his one unfulfilled (and unattainable) dream was his wish to transform the parish church into a school chapel. Whenever the history of these times is viewed dispassionately, there is no doubt that Mr Robert Snaith will stand alongside Dr Anthony Finn as the two giant figures of the twentieth century. As *The Colstonian* concluded: 'He is gone, but his work lives on'.

The governors quickly appointed the Second Master, Mr J.A. Campbell, as Acting-Headmaster and immediately set about advertising the vacancy. By March 1965, out of the 61 applicants, seven had been shortlisted (including two existing Headmasters and four Housemasters). The man eventually appointed Headmaster from September 1965 was an Oxford graduate, Mr Nigel Gibbs, who was the Headmaster of Crewkerne School in Somerset and an England Rugby international.

A Period of Great Uncertainty, 1965-1975

There is no doubt that the masterplan for the expansion of the school had been both ingenious and bold. In many ways, it had displayed commendable vision and shrewd forward planning - so much so, that Mr Snaith was rightly proud when he had declared to parents at Prize Giving in 1960: 'Taken in their entirety, the works to which we are already committed, coupled with those which we hope to carry out over the next two or three years, probably constitute the greatest move forward the school has made at one time since the move to Stapleton in 1861'. Later history was to show that the admission of day boys, the expansion of the Prep and the restructuring of the school were vital elements in Colston's future growth and development. Unfortunately, the governors seriously overstretched themselves financially in stage two of the plan; and the reasoning behind its central ingredient - the new boarding House - was quickly shown to be badly flawed.

In 1963, the cost of the stage two developments had originally been estimated at £100,000 - to be under-pinned by an interest-free loan of £80,000 from the Society of Merchant Venturers with annual repayments set at £2,700 over twenty years. One Merchant, however, issued a timely warning that the governors 'should realise that the Society must not be regarded as an ever-ready and easy way of financing the school in future and that the school must aim to be self-supporting'. By 1965, the projected cost had risen to £150,000, forcing the governors to take out a loan for £50,000 from the Bristol and West Building Society at 6.75% over 25 years.

The result of this miscalculation was that the governors were faced with the prospect of suddenly finding £29,268 in the 1966-67 financial year to meet the cost of interest and repayments on the loans, mortgage interest on the three properties recently acquired and the balance of capital outstanding on new projects not covered by loans. This was the prelude to a decade of financial turmoil - greatly exacerbated, it has to be said, by outside pressures, heavy annual deficits and sharply-rising fees.

As early as 1959, the governors had been alerted to the probable consequences of a dramatic fall in the birthrate at the end of the post-war 'bulge' - consequences which were likely to impact on schools from 1964. Furthermore, as early as 1963, it was becoming apparent that the Upper School was not meeting its target of 200 boarders, thanks to a worrying lack of applications even for the heavily-subsidised places on offer. Boys brought up in the emerging 'permissive society' of the 1960s were finding the restrictions of boarding school life increasingly unattractive, especially in view of the greater freedoms on offer as day boys or as members of the newly-established sixth form colleges. Under these circumstances, the decision to invest heavily in a new boarding House was extremely questionable.

The new Mortlake House opened in 1965, when the number of boarders in the Upper School was 182 (18 below the target); by 1970 that number had slumped to 132, before reaching its lowest point of 122 two years later. Thereafter the figure increased again slightly to 137 by 1974. During the same period, however, day boy numbers rose steadily from 93 in 1965 to 144 in 1974 - by which time the combined number of boarders in the Upper and Prep Schools totalled 208 (compared with a target figure of 260), while the number of day boys had increased to 282 (against the target of just 160). Mr Snaith's promise to parents in 1949 that the school would 'remain predominantly a boarding school' had already been shattered. Faced by this situation, therefore, the governors in 1970 considered the possibility of converting one of the boarding Houses into a day boy House, while preserving Mortlake as 'a showplace for parents'. They finally decided, however, that Roundway House in the main dormitory block should be 'infiltrated' by day boys, thus creating a mixed membership of day and boarding.

Quite apart from this growing imbalance between day boys and boarders (with all its implications for annual income), there were other worrying factors for the governors to consider. In the first place, there was a growing crisis over foundation scholarships or special places. Faced by rising costs, income from the Colston Hospital Trust could only support a total of 12 such places, whereas the amended Scheme required 24 - yet recruitment of bright, intelligent boys through this method was crucial to the school's academic performance. The governors did their best to maintain numbers, partly by reducing the value of the awards - but even this was still costly. By 1972, they were spending £4,000 a year on these scholarships over and above the receipts from the Colston Hospital Trust.

Secondly, there were disturbing noises coming from government quarters following the publication of the Report of the Public Schools' Commission (the Newsome Report) in 1967. This contained veiled threats not only to the charitable status of independent schools (estimated to cost Colston's in the region of £8,000 a year), but also the character of the schools that were members of SHMIS. It suggested that these should either become co-educational or accept a lower range of academic ability or become sixth form colleges. The governors, finding these options unappealing, set up a committee in October 1967 to examine the future of the school. One of its members, Professor Rich, urged a fundamental re-appraisal of the sixth form, excellence in which would be vital to future success.

It was therefore decided to attempt full integration with the sixth form at Colston's Girls' School. They recognised that this would require 'a great deal of determination and goodwill' and an 'organised transport system' between the two schools (provided by two minibuses and drivers). The boys and girls would, at the same time, remain 'fully integrated members' of their own schools. The Chairman of Governors (Mr Jack Clarke) was deputed to make contact with his opposite number at the Girls' School (Mr Roger Clarke). The response, however, was disappointing. Reporting back to the board some months later, Mr Jack Clarke said that integration 'might be difficult, because of the very high standard of the Girls' School, where twenty-five subjects at A level were being studied in the sixth form of 170 with considerable success'. By

Mr J.E.C. Clarke, Chairman of Governors, 1963-83 (By courtesy of the Society)

1970, a further meeting with the Girls' School showed 'that almost no integration would be attractive to them'. The scheme was therefore dropped.

Further disappointment came in the regular rejection of the school for membership of the Headmasters' Conference. In 1973, the Chairman was advised unofficially that Colston's academic results were not good enough for the school to be considered. The criteria for election demanded that at least 25% of the Upper School should be in the sixth form and should gain an impressive rate of A level success. The

Chairman bemoaned the fact not only that 'the intellectual quality of the intake from the Prep School was in a temporary trough', but also that the school's lack of resources rendered them incapable of attracting more intelligent boys through bursaries (better candidates invariably being creamed off by the local direct grant schools). This meant that examination results were always 'diluted by fee payers'.

It is true that certain individuals continued to distinguish themselves, picking up well-deserved State or City Scholarships before proceeding to university. Over the 23 years between 1952 and 1974, for instance, no fewer than 16 boys gained awards or places at Oxford or Cambridge (including four in 1969 alone) - while 13 boys won places to other universities in 1966 and 15 did so in 1970.

Nevertheless, in the 23 years between 1952 (when the General Certificate of Education at O level and A level replaced the old School Certificate and HSC examinations) and 1974, the average subject pass-rate at Colston's was just 65% at O level. Although boys in the 'A' stream regularly reached a rate of 75%, those in the 'B' stream struggled to reach 50% - and, when the enlarged entry produced a 'C' stream for the first time in 1965, the results were 'disastrous'. Mr Snaith, who was often tempted to exclude from the examination those who were likely to fail, admitted that he was often too kind when pressurised by individuals. ' Some boys', he said in 1962, 'seem to have the illusion that taking exams is something like shooting at a target, an illusion no doubt fostered by such familiar phrases as 'having a shot at French' or 'aiming at five passes'. In 1963, therefore, boys in the A stream were limited to 7 or 8 subjects (instead of the previous 10) and those in the B stream to 5 or 6. Two years later, it was decided that those in the C stream should take (in the fifth form) the new Certificate of Secondary Education (CSE), which was pitched at a lower level, before staying on for an extra year in the fifth upper remove to take their O levels.

In the sixth form, during the period 1955 to 1963, boys were much more carefully screened before being permitted to take their A level examinations. Therefore, although on average just 13 candidates took A levels each year, they managed to secure an average subject pass-rate of 84%. When, however, the increased numbers in the school reached the sixth form during the late 1960s (many of them with mediocre O level results), the average pass-rate quickly dropped as entry for examinations became less selective. Between 1970 and 1974, for example, an average of 32 candidates gained a 71% subject pass-rate - leading Mr Cartwright (the Acting Headmaster) to remind staff in 1971 that sixth formers 'needed as much pressure to make them work as they had when they were lower down the school'. Some believed that they actually needed more, given the abuse of private study periods in the more liberal regime which prevailed at the time (see below). But however poor their results, the school desperately needed to keep all those boys on board in view of the mounting financial crisis.

After the positive steps taken by the governors during the 1950s, the annual accounts continued for a while in a healthy state - chiefly due to the fact that the expenditure on stage one of the expansion (1946-58) had largely been covered by interest-free loans from the Society of Merchant Venturers. The budget was therefore able to show a surplus of £9,162 for 1960-61 and of £8,448 for 1962-63. By 1970, however, the hard-core overdraft at the bank was being calculated at £20-25,000 (the actual deficit rising at times during the year to as much as £60,000); four years later, 'the operating adverse balance' had grown to £39,000.

The reasons for this decline in fortune are complex. Quite apart from the unexpected overspend on stage two of the expansion (1958-65), teachers' salaries were rising rapidly (by 13% in 1965 alone); inflation was running unbridled (causing the cost of food supplies at school to increase by 13.5% in 1972); and fees were frequently being paid in arrears (with £2,700 owed in 1967, rising to £4,000 in 1973). The governors began to budget £1,000 per year to cover for bad debts, threatened to employ a firm of debt collectors and refused to allow boys to return to school if the previous term's fees remained unpaid.

Particular problems were encountered with the fees of foreign children (by 1966, there were 26 of these in school, although a limit of 30 had been imposed in view of the language difficulty encountered by some). Currency restrictions sometimes made it difficult to transfer funds from Africa, but occasionally boys left without warning - causing Mr Gibbs on one occasion to write for help to the Ambassador in Algiers. Although the governors hesitated to take drastic action for fear of causing 'an international incident', they decided that foreign students in future should pay a term in advance and arrive clutching a return airline ticket!

The slump in the number of boarders in the Upper School was, of course, a major factor in the financial crisis. Although the total number of boys in the two schools combined always exceeded the target figure of 420 from 1967 (rising from 423 in that year to 480 by 1974), this healthy situation was entirely dependent on the huge success of the Prep, which boasted 216 boys in 1973 (96 more than its target), and the day boy entry in general. In the Upper School the situation was distinctly gloomy by the summer of 1970 with only 242 being predicted by the Headmaster (Mr Gibbs) for the September of that year (down by 21 from the previous year) - including just 136 boarders (a drop of 64 from the original target). This was critical to the budget, which had already been set, because the school was still being run as a boarding school with all the implied overheads. In an emergency session, the governors faced up to a probable shortfall in fee income of over £11,000. The budget was quickly revised with major economies and staff redundancies imposed.

Under all these circumstances, the governors had no option but to pursue a policy of major fee increases - not, as in the 1950s, to budget for a surplus in the cause of future development, but rather to budget for survival in a worrying game of 'catch-up'. The Chairman of Governors (Mr Clarke) made it clear in 1967 that 'no future capital expenditure could be contemplated in the immediate future'. By 1973, he was bemoaning the fact that although 'the school was regarded as being the leading hockey school in the region, yet shortly it would be the only school without a hard surface hockey pitch'.

Fees therefore rose steeply and at a rapid pace (almost annually) between 1964 and 1974 - by 10%, 13%, 20% or whatever was needed to cover the immediate crisis. During that decade, the Upper School boarding fee more than trebled from £370 to £1,194 a year, while that of day boys more than quadrupled from £180 to £756. Although this just about enabled the school to weather the storm, unusual circumstances twice plunged the accounts heavily into deficit. In 1972, for instance, the Government's Counter Inflation (Temporary Provisions) Act, which introduced 'the Freeze', forced the governors to postpone the proposed fee increase for the spring term in 1973 - helping to create a budget deficit for the year of £12,971. Worse was to follow.

In January 1974, as the finance committee was wrestling with the muddled state of the accounts, 'at approximately 4.15 pm, the meeting tended to break up in disorder owing to a tornado which was alleged to have hit the school'. Although this news proved to be somewhat exaggerated, a financial tornado did in fact hit the school in August that year, when details of the Houghton Commission's Pay Award for teachers were revealed. Backdated to May 1974, the massive award resulted in an increase of £30,000 to the school's salary bill. The finance committee quickly revised its budget for 1974-75 to reveal an estimated deficit for the year of £49,050 (which also took into account 'a steep inflationary rise'). It hurriedly notified parents of a 20% fee increase from January 1975, reluctantly deciding that the 30% rise which was really needed 'would frighten parents into withdrawing their boys from the school'. In the event, only two parents protested - though Edward Colston must have turned uneasily in his grave.

In the middle of this turmoil, the governors wisely decided to reorganise the accounting system, which had previously been undertaken at Merchants' Hall. From 1969 an 'assistant bursar', based at school, would deal with cheque preparation, answer parental enquiries and maintain financial records, while the Hall would still deal with staff salaries and the signing of cheques. Furthermore, from September 1970, the accounting year would coincide with the school year. By 1972, however, the new Headmaster (Mr King) had persuaded the governors to go even further by appointing 'a strong and well-qualified Bursar', who would be based at school and answerable to him - a man capable 'of exercising effective control of all departments'. Although the first man appointed (who was also made the minuting secretary of all governors' meetings) failed to sort out 'the mess' in the accounts, his successor (Lieutenant Colonel R.F. Alston) undertook an effective reorganisation with the help of a bookkeeper - including the task of getting to grips with unpaid fees (over 80 of which were outstanding when he was appointed in February 1974).

Discipline and the Policy of Liberalisation, 1965-1975

There is no doubt that Mr Snaith had continued to run the school in a fairly traditional and authoritarian manner throughout the post-war years. In 1949, for instance, he had warned parents that uniform regulations would be strictly enforced 'now that rationing was a thing of the past'. The toleration shown during the period of wartime shortages was not to be regarded as a precedent for future laxity. His aim, he told Old Colstonians in 1953, was 'to make the boys into God-fearing men who would be good Christians and good citizens'. A glimpse at the school rules in the mid-1950s confirms the impression of a firm hand at the helm:

> Chewing gum is not allowed...No boy may have his hands in his pockets on meeting a master or other senior person...Boys are expected to raise their caps on meeting any masters, masters' wives or ladies of the staff...There must be no communication of any kind between boys in the Sick Wing and other boys - e.g. dropping notes onto the Parade, lending books etc...Private wireless sets and gramophones are forbidden...Association football is forbidden...No boy may keep in his possession a sum of money larger than two shillings...Only English comics are permitted. All American publications of this kind are banned. In addition, cheap novelettes and such like reading matter are forbidden, but it is understood that this prohibition does not extend to Penguins and reputable publications of the same kind.

These rules were strictly enforced. Michael Wood (1950-56), however, recalls that although boys were in fact caned if they were caught 'kicking a football', some dispensations to the rules were occasionally granted. According to Bill Welland (1959-66), for instance, the occasional game of football was in fact sanctioned 'as long as it took place on Pitch 5, below the horizon of any parent being shown round at the time' - for Mr Snaith lived in fear of the hostile reaction of prospective parents greeted with 'the sight of Colston's boys playing soccer, rather than rugby'. The Headmaster, in another concession to the rules, instructed boys *not* to raise their caps to him, if they passed him as he was driving his car up or down Bell Hill, because it was distracting. Nevertheless, his very presence inspired a certain fear in the hearts of younger boys. David Faulkner (1962-69) remembers the deathly quiet which always descended on the playground whenever Mr Snaith moved from the main building to his home across the road (i.e. the Old Rectory). It was, he said, 'like Moses parting the Red Sea' as boys, who had been milling around noisily on the drive, suddenly opened up to permit this stately and austere figure (who looked neither to left nor right) to pass through their midst.

There was only one occasion on which his authority was challenged (a sign perhaps of the changing attitudes in society, which were shortly to make their impact on the school). Fred Forse (1957-62), Peter Mitchell (1960-65) and other Old Colstonians vividly recall the sense of outrage and injustice among the boys caused at the end of the summer term in 1961 by the suspension of the Head Prefect - especially in view of the fact that it was almost the end of his final term. An extremely popular boy and all-round sportsman, he had been reported for a visit to The Beehive after a cricket match against Clifton College, where shandies had allegedly been bought for other members of the team. According to Adrian Williams (1956-64), several of the other team members pleaded with Mr Snaith indirectly on his behalf - but to no avail. 'The school', he recalls, 'was livid and a demonstration was planned for lunch. It was Snaith's tradition to enter the dining hall last and to walk its length as the school quietened before the Head Boy said grace. As he entered there was the continuation of jeering and foot stamping. He hesitated and then did his usual walk down the hall. The noise subsided and the revolution petered out'.

Mr Gibbs, on the other hand, who joined Colston's in 1965 as the new Headmaster, was a man of much more liberal outlook. Sympathetic and compassionate by nature, he was determined to make the school into a more civilised and enlightened place. His arrival coincided with great changes which were taking place in society at large and which challenged established attitudes in a reaction to the restrictiveness of the 1940s and 1950s and the threat of nuclear war. This was the age of the permissive society, student protest, university riots, 'flower power', drugs, the Beatles, rock-and-roll and Harold Wilson's Labour government which attempted to redress the inequalities of life. Schools were not immune from these pressures.

Mr Gibbs quickly demonstrated his belief in consultation and free expression. The format, content and style of *The Colstonian* magazine were immediately changed to provide a platform not only for original articles and poems, but also for personal opinions and grievances. The editorial committee, consisting chiefly of sixth formers, encouraged 'letters to the editor'. These inevitably voiced grumbles about such matters as school caps and the new 'multi-coloured House ties', which had replaced a plethora of older designs. 'It does seem rather strange', commented one boy in 1967, 'that the House ties were introduced without asking the opinion of the boys'. Another correspondent seethed with anger in 1966 about the use of non-CCF members for community service. 'The school appears to be making use of cheap labour, in sending boys to cut down long grass...This is not part of our education'.

The editorial committee also voiced its own opinions in a series of forthright editorials - deploring the attitude of some boys and staff 'who

Boys in the entrance hall, overlooked by the statue of Colston on the left and his portrait in the rear. (SMV Archive)

strongly object to having to live with the increasing number of foreign students in the school'; condemning the lack of any kind of aesthetic education within the school'; and criticising the proliferation of societies - 'Are we suffering from too much activity?', they pondered. On a more positive note, however, one sixth former was delighted to point out 'the breakdown of the strict public school uniformity, where no sixth former would be caught dead talking to a year below him'. This barrier, he believed, had now been broken down 'to reveal a society and community where all boys are equal, where all are friends in 'a liberal and free society'.

Sadly, the evidence does not support this optimistic view. In the very year when that letter was penned (1969), a group of sixth formers had combined to produce a new magazine for internal consumption - *The Libertine*. [One of its editors later admitted that 'the name *Libertine* was mistakenly chosen - 'we thought it had something to do with freedom', he explained.] This publication, which they claimed was not merely designed as 'a vehicle of public protest', actually contained a fair proportion of news, sport, correspondence, reviews and original poetry. Indeed, the first issue was so well received that the Headmaster, wishing to encourage enterprise, offered 'to pay the cost of future issues'. That first issue, however, also contained a proposal that the sixth form should become a separate entity within the school with the same privileges as those enjoyed by prefects. This set the tone for later editions, which became so hard-hitting that Mr Gibbs quickly felt obliged to impose censorship. He would therefore in future forbid publication of 'any material in bad taste', any 'misstatements about school policy' or any articles which 'in seeking to point out faults or weaknesses (whether real or imagined) in the school's organisation or ethos, are likely, by the very fact of publication, to hinder the correction of those faults'. *The Libertine* quickly fell into abeyance.

In the same year, a School Council was established, raising hopes in *The Colstonian* that it would bring changes in policy over school uniform, smoking 'and other points of such gravity'. Disillusionment very soon set in. Although the body discussed a whole range of topics - including punishments, haircuts, the use of sixth form studies and the running of the library - boys quickly realised that it was 'purely an advisory body' with no real power (although hopes were harboured in some quarters that this situation could be changed). Secondly, it was criticised by some sixth formers for 'the evident lack of democracy in the election of its members'. At first consisting chiefly of school prefects, it was later composed (under Mr King) of the captain and one representative from each House. *The Colstonian* editorial claimed to be perplexed at the lack of reaction to this injustice: 'The surprising and somewhat disturbing thing is that there have been no cries for democracy from the rest of the school. Why?'

Nevertheless, in spite of the apparent impotence of the School Council, Mr Gibbs pressed ahead steadily with a policy of reform. He outlined to governors in 1969 some of the concessions he had made (which were already common practice in other schools) - sixth formers would be allowed their own cars for transport; there would be 'a controlled freedom' in the choice of games; clothing regulations would be relaxed, including the abolition of caps; boarders would be permitted to use 'leisure wear' after tea; rules on the number of exeats would be eased; and a joint committee of boys and masters would be established to consider chapel services, food and dining arrangements. As early as 1965, he had modified the rules on the use of sixth form studies, permitting boys to play radios, record players and tape recorders at specified times during the day; to brew tea at the same times and to make social visits to other studies. Mr King (Headmaster, 1972-74) continued this policy of liberalisation by agreeing in 1973 to reduce by half the number of Sundays when compulsory chapel services would be held. Voluntary services would in future be held at 9.00 am on the other

A daily service in the School Chapel. Opened in 1933, it was eventually demolished in 1999 to make way for the Chatterton Hall. (SMV Archive)

Sundays, followed by coffee in the library. This did not, of course, herald the collapse of religion within the school - mid-week services and confirmation classes continued unscathed and the Christian Union was established as one of the new societies.

History shows that the introduction of limited reform, after a period of restriction or repression, often serves to whet the appetite of those involved rather than to satisfy their complaints; and that newly-acquired freedom is sometimes abused. *The Colstonian* was, therefore, most perceptive in its comments on the malaise which was sweeping the school in 1968. 'Under the present Headmaster', it pointed out, 'some rules have been tightened whilst several have been relaxed, creating more freedom for the individual than has ever been known at Colston's before'. However, it deplored the fact that 'passes out' were seen by some as 'an opportunity to break school rules'. This created bad feeling among the staff that rules were being disobeyed; and 'among the majority of the boys that disobedience brings greater restriction'. Although the troublemakers were comparatively few in number, it concluded, 'recent events have indicated that this actively discontented minority is on the increase'.

By 1971, this active minority was causing concern through its associations outside school. Five sixth formers had (with the Headmaster's permission) attended a meeting of the Bristol Union of Secondary Schools - although Mr Gibbs had warned them that any suggestions they might have for the improvement of school life were to be put forward 'through constitutional channels'. The governors debated this matter at length and were most concerned about the influence of 'this extreme left-wing' organisation with its 'alarming literature' However, although they regarded 'the long term canker of such a group with great suspicion', they felt it would be 'improper for the Headmaster to forbid boarders to attend meetings, when it would be difficult to prevent the attendance of day boys'.

Faced by all these new pressures, which were totally outside all previous experience, both Headmaster and governors understandably displayed an uncertainty of touch on occasions as they veered between freedom and restriction. Nor had the situation been helped by government policy. In 1968, the Secretary of State had sent a letter strongly recommending that all schools should abolish corporal punishment. The governors decided to leave the matter to the Headmaster's discretion. Then, in 1971, they were alerted to the possible implication of the Family Reform Act, which had lowered the age of majority to eighteen. This would therefore give the oldest boys in the school rights of their own, making them no longer bound by the school rules which their parents had contracted for them to observe. The governors felt on balance that, until the question had been fully investigated, it would be 'unwise to alert the boys to the implications of this new legislation'.

The truth of the matter, however, was that discipline of young people nationally was already under severe strain. In 1970, the school experienced its first case of illegal drugs. A boy had been apprehended on his return from Ghana with three ounces of cannabis in his possession, together with a diary revealing the names of other boys involved. After a three-day police investigation in school, two other boys were found to be in possession of the drug and twelve confessed to smoking it outside school. As a result, Mr Gibbs expelled four boys and severely disciplined several others. It has to be said, however, that this sort of situation was being repeated in schools all over the country. Indeed, the police said at the time that, in comparison with other similar investigations, 'the amount of smoking and the number of boys involved was not large'.

Nevertheless, this was no isolated example of serious indiscipline. Three years later, Mr King expelled three more boys for 'truancy and discreditable public behaviour'. In 1971, the finance committee criticised 'the permissiveness of wall decorations in the studies, which it appeared were now used more for social than industrial purposes'. In the same year, an A level student had left the school half way through his course 'as a protest at a rebuke from the Headmaster' and had gone off to a technical college. In 1974, the Bursar, in explaining to governors the rising costs of maintenance, repeatedly referred to the 'increased vandalism' within the school.

By 1975, therefore, many of the traditional elements of school life had been eroded, including school uniform, compulsory chapel and the rigid control of leisure time. A further blow to tradition had been struck by the Society of Merchant Venturers in 1969, when it was decided that, on Charter Day in future, there would no longer be a procession to church or a parade by the CCF and its band. [This decision was taken partly on the advice of the police, who felt that they could no longer hold up traffic as they had previously done.] *The Colstonian*, in its editorial for the summer edition of 1975, bemoaned the fact that freedom had brought with it a terrible apathy. The support for societies was 'lamentable', *The Colstonian* itself had failed to appear over the previous two years, the 1975 school play had been cancelled... 'Does anyone care?', it wondered. The school had not yet adapted to the less structured environment which was now in place and individuals had not yet learnt (or been taught) the art of self-discipline. Nevertheless, some comfort could be drawn from the fact that the 'revolution' of the 1960s and 1970s had been far less dramatic and violent than that of the 1780s!

(see Chapter 4)

Changes in Headmastership, 1971-1974

A number of long-established members of the Colston's community passed from the scene during the years 1946 to 1975. These included four retirements - Mr F.A. Rockett in 1955, after 36 years service as Latin master, Housemaster and Second Master; Miss Lewis, the senior Assistant Matron, in 1956, after over 40 years at the school; Mr Frank Noddle, in 1958, after 39 years as physics master; and Mr J. Milsom in 1972, after 48 years service (latterly as Head Porter). In addition, the School Doctor (Dr E.C. Bernard) died in 1968 after holding the position for 32 years, and was succeeded by his son, Dr Richard Bernard. The Bernard family (which was related to the family of the famous cricketer, W.G. Grace) actually celebrated its 100th year of association with the school in 1971 - a dynasty which had consisted of Dr D.E. Bernard (1871-1905), Dr Claude Bernard (1905-1936), Dr E.C. Bernard (1936-1968) and Dr J.R. Bernard (1968-97).

This tradition of long service had of course also applied to the school's twelve Headmasters, who had been appointed in the 254 years of its existence to 1964, each averaging 21 years in office. This tradition came to a sudden end, however, during the decade which followed Mr Snaith's death, when no fewer than three new Headmasters were appointed.

When Mr Nigel Gibbs arrived in September 1965, the school was already in a precarious state - numbers were falling, examination results were mediocre and finances were distinctly brittle (see above). He arrived, too, just at the time when, in the nation at large, the 'permissive society' of the 1960s had taken root and the whiff of student protest was in the air. He was, however, an existing Headmaster and a charming person, who was already well known to a number of members of the governing board. His six years at Colston's (1965-1971) witnessed the blossoming of extra-curricular activities, the rise of the school to excellence in sport (see Chapter 12) and the introduction of a policy of liberalisation, which brought many fundamental reforms to the life of the community (see above). Unfortunately the period also witnessed a further (and dramatic) fall in numbers and a series of disciplinary problems, which were in part the product of changing attitudes in society.

By the autumn term of 1970, the governors (many of whom had been doubtful about the need for change) were deeply anxious about the state of the school. Although they had the highest regard for the

'Christian and gentlemanly qualities' of Mr Gibbs and 'the civilised culture which he had introduced into the school', they were increasingly concerned about his ability to revive its fortunes in the face of mounting difficulties. They were also disturbed about morale in the Common Room. Many of the staff, including the Second Master, had experienced serious misgivings about the introduction of a School Council and the relaxation of sixth form rules, fearing that such reforms would create problems by loosening the structure of discipline. They found it hard to accept that, even in the new climate, boys should be accorded some minimum 'rights'. Mr Gibbs, on the other hand, felt that 'a lot of things needed turning round' to bring attitudes at Colston's in line with other schools - including methods of teaching and basic relationships between staff and pupils. He later reflected that his aim had not been to rule by fear, but 'to speak to boys in a much more flexible fashion' and to deal with them as individuals. The staff, many of whom had experienced the authoritarian regime of Mr Snaith, were wary of this new approach and concerned that, with a more democratic approach to policy-making, the previous decisiveness had been lost.

Mr Nigel Gibbs, Headmaster 1965-71, in retirement (2001)

The good relationship, which the Chairman of Governors enjoyed with the Headmaster, enabled him to discuss these anxieties openly with him. Eventually, after much thought, Mr Gibbs decided to resign in order to pursue some new interests in education - a fact which was communicated to parents in May 1971. He therefore joined a post-graduate course at Bristol University on the care and nurture of disturbed children, before taking up a post as Housemaster at the Cotswold Community for disturbed children. He was subsequently appointed Senior Master of North Foreland Lodge, near Basingstoke.

The Colstonian paid a warm tribute to a man, who had undoubtedly found himself caught up in difficult circumstances: 'He was an extremely kindly man, whose immediate desire was always to make others happy, but never at the cost of any sacrifice of his strongly held moral principles. He was, indeed, a truly Christian gentleman. He loved the Chapel, where he was a faithful communicant...In his time with us, he made many friends and no enemies'. He had got to know the boys well through his coaching of the younger teams, while - outside school - he was held in great respect by his fellow Headmasters, who had elected him onto the Council of the Headmasters' Association for 1971. In his final Prize Giving speech that year, he said 'that his decision to leave had not been easy as he had been happy here and had regarded being at Colston's as a privilege'. He left the school 'with sadness and affection'.

The governors hurriedly advertised the post and eventually interviewed a shortlist of five, composed of four existing Headmasters and one Housemaster. They were most anxious to make an immediate appointment of a man with dynamic leadership qualities, who would raise the school out of its malaise and on to new heights. They were therefore dismayed when their first choice turned down the offer. They then agonised over whether to re-advertise (which would 'look bad'), offer the job to Mr G.S. Jameson, the highly successful Headmaster of the Prep (which would be most unusual) or appoint the next in line, Mr A.E. King.

They eventually decided on the latter. Mr King was a Cambridge graduate, who had at one time taught French at Bristol Grammar School, but who had just returned from a spell as Headmaster of the General Wingate School, Addis Ababa in Ethiopia. They believed that he would bring clarity to policy-making and 'would impose proper discipline upon the boys, which many of them seek as much as we do'. Perhaps, with hindsight, they were too eager to make a quick appointment - for, if they were anxious to recruit a man who would provide continuity over many years in the Colston tradition, then they had failed to note the warning signals. Mr King had taken up teaching in 1950 - and Colston's was his eighth school in 22 years!

Nevertheless, there is no doubt that Mr King did a highly competent job, following his arrival in January 1972. He immediately set out his short-term targets for the school to both the governors and the editorial committee of *The Colstonian* - namely, to establish a better administrative structure with a strong Bursar at its head (see above); to make the school compound more attractive; to increase the range of extra-curricular activities; to forge closer relationships with the Old Colstonians in the hope of gaining careers advice for the boys; to establish a 'Colston's School Society', thereby forging closer links with the parents; to establish a covered swimming pool and a well equipped careers room; and, above all, to create 'an aura of purpose' and a 'broader outlook', which would produce well-balanced citizens.

Many of these objectives were achieved - a Bursar was appointed for the first time in May 1972; the Colston School Society was established at the same time; a careers library and parents' waiting room were created in November 1972 out of the former Aldington common room; new societies and activities suddenly abounded (see Chapter 12); and the site, which Mr King had called 'generally scruffy and unattractive', was given a major facelift - thanks to a sum of £5,000 authorised for this purpose by the governors. His greatest delight, however, lay in the organisation of a series of weekly sixth form lectures - engagements which gave him the opportunity to lavish lunchtime hospitality not only on the visiting speakers, but also on members of staff and selected sixth formers (often making them, in the process, late for their afternoon lessons!). The Headmaster also did his best to promote the school - partly through a new prospectus in 1972 and partly through membership of ISIS (the Independent Schools' Information Service), which had been formed that year. Numbers in the Upper School certainly staged something of a revival, rising from 250 in 1970 to 281 in 1974 (though boarding figures had only slightly improved). However, although many aspects of school life had been tightened, there had been no major initiatives or far-reaching reforms.

In October 1974, just under three years after taking up his appointment, Mr King tendered his resignation at a meeting of the governors. 'I leave with much regret', he said, 'but a particularly attractive post [teaching French] was available in Tasmania and it was a case of now or never'. The Chairman spoke warmly of his 'stewardship and success' during his period in office (January 1972 - December 1974). By November, the governors had appointed Mr King's successor - Mr Graham Searle, an Oxford graduate (aged 37 years), who was then Head of History and senior Housemaster at Stamford School. In a letter to parents, they praised both 'his enthusiasm and his thoughtful, balanced outlook'. For the second time in four years, Mr D.W. Cartwright (the Second Master) was appointed Acting Headmaster during a short interregnum before the arrival of Mr Searle for the summer term in 1975.

Sources used in Chapter 11

D.J. Eames, *The Contribution of the Society of Merchant Venturers to the Development of Education in Bristol* (unpublished MA thesis for the University of Bristol, 1966), pp 309-326
Society of Merchant Venturers' Archive:
    Colston Hospital Trust:
        Governors' Minutes, 1934-1956, 1956-
        Finance Committee Minutes, 1934-1956, 1956-
        Headmasters' Reports to Governors, 1926-1965
        Treasurer's Paper for Governors, 'Colston's Boys' School - Foundationers', December 1952

Mr Eberle's paper for Governors, 'The Future of the Public Boarding School', August 1959

The Colstonian, 1946-1975 issues

Cribsheet (The Old Colstonians' Newsletter), February 1986, October 1987, October 1988, January 1999, January 2000

Personal interviews and written submissions (as acknowledged in the text)

LIFE AS A BOARDER, 1957-64

Murray Wilson *(Old Colstonian, 1957-64)*

Dormitories had absolutely no heating, and we could take an extra blanket or overcoat. The beds were so old that the springs had sagged so that we slept 'within' rather than on the beds, but at least it was warmer.

'Boots and shoes' was called each week, and the shoe-mender came in a three-wheeled vehicle with a motor cycle front wheel suspension. Shoes were to be worn during the day, but not upstairs when you had to change into Cambridge-style slippers. Before prep you had to put on these slippers.

We prided ourselves on how fast we could descend the main stairs, two at a time. Some slid down lying across the banisters. I was walking through the hall one day when a body landed beside me. He had been sliding down and someone ascending had spun him round and over the edge. He only broke an arm. The studs in the banister rail were replaced next day.

We had house rooms to which to retire, but before us they only had the 'Arches' [i.e. the space under the colonnaded walk to the toilets] for all activities apart from games and class work. Nevertheless, we managed to read a lot and educate ourselves. The main activity was ping-pong, unless you were in North House where there was a billiard table. Each house purchased a newspaper, paid for from compulsory 'house subscription'. Normal pocket money was 10 shillings [50p] per term, and no one was allowed 'more than one shilling in his pocket'. Walls ice cream and a packet of Smith's crisps each cost 3d [a quarter of one shilling].

When I started, there were no mirrors in the school! We did our hair by the reflection of the glass of the door outside the headmaster's study. When mirrors were introduced, it was a great day. The only clock was in the doorway of the science block, so there was a steady stream of boys finding the time. Watches were expensive.

What was so different then from now is that everyone did the same thing at the same time. Everyone was in class together, everyone went to chapel together, everyone played games at the same time. In winter we had 'late clar', when we had games in the afternoon first and then classes until tea time. We marched everywhere - breakfast, chapel, tea and church. Not lunch; this had been stopped to the disgust of older people in about 1945. Very untidy, having people hanging around the dining room doors. The parades gave the opportunity of an inspection of hands, shoes, ties etc.

Roll call was a regular feature of games afternoons, presumably to make sure that no-one had wandered off, or was engaged in nefarious activities. We filed past 3A (junior library) steps calling out our number to a prefect. No chance of signing in for a friend! Then on Sunday were the walks. Second and third form boys were sent on a walk on Sunday afternoons as far as Hambrook or Winterbourne.

Those whose parents came to see them for the only possible visit of the week were accompanied on the walk. The parents must have been fit. The destination, and whether the fourth form would undertake the walk, relied on how malevolent the duty master felt. Whitehead always sent the fourth form on the longest walk. At the destination you gave you name to the prefect who had cycled there. It was only later that boys were allowed home on Sundays - first after lunch, and then before lunch.

(From *Cribsheet* January 2000)

CHAPTER 12

Years of Enrichment, 1946-2002

Schoolteachers provide pupils with opportunities...The greater the opportunities, the greater the likelihood a pupil has of becoming a knowledgeable, well-rounded, cultured individual. At Colston's we are very fortunate to have teachers who want to provide a wider education than that which is just based on national curriculum subjects. (Mr Crawford, Headmaster, at Prize Giving in 2001)

A quality education will blend academic prowess with personal development, and we are proud that so many of our pupils are so successful in sport, music and drama and are able to take their places in adult life as well-adjusted and informed men and women. (Mr Michael Graham, Director of Studies, in *School Ties*, 1992)

The Expansion of Extra-curricular life, 1946-2002

(i) Dormitories, Meal Times and Playground, 1946-1965

The arrival of day boys in 1949 created an immediate problem for the running of the House system. In view of the fact that there were only four main points on the compass, Mr Snaith drew up a completely new set of House names, each with a Colston connection - Mortlake (formerly North House), Roundway (South), Beaufort (East), Aldington (West) and Dolphin (Day Boys). Roundway House was named after a governor, Mr C.E.H.A. Colston, who had been elevated to the peerage in 1916 as Lord Roundway. To strengthen a sense of loyalty to the new Houses, the school cap was modified so that 'the band as well as the badge' carried the House colours.

The boys continued to sit in House groups for meals with House staff moving around the tables in rotation. The school rules made it clear that all boys were to have 'something of everything provided', although masters were empowered to use their discretion in giving small helpings on request. Alan Hale (1958-64) recalls that Major Creek (who was assistant Housemaster of Aldington House, commander of the corps and the 'hardest beater' of recalcitrant boys) used these meal times also to pick up incriminating detail from the boys' idle chatter for use in his amusing songs at the House Christmas party. Boys were expected to take turns on a rota system with waiting at table, serving on high table and assisting with the stacking of empty dishes. Grace in Latin was said by a prefect at the start of each meal (*Benedic nobis domine deus at donis quae ex liberaletate tua sumpturi sumus. Per Iesum Christum Dominum Nostrum. Amen*) and at the end (*Benedicto benedicator. Per Iesum Christum Dominum Nostrum. Amen*).

The governors did their best to ensure that the boys were adequately nourished, in spite of post-war shortages. From 1946, therefore, they joined the 'Milk in Schools Scheme', by which the government provided each boy with a third of a pint of milk a day free of charge; and in 1959 they replaced the 'cereal or porridge' breakfasts with a cooked meal. However, amid growing concern about the acute shortage of cooks and domestic staff, they eventually decided in 1962 to place the school's catering in the hands of outside contractors under the Bursar's general oversight. This system lasted for just eight years, before the governors (having experimented with large-scale use of convenience foods in an attempt to cut labour costs) finally agreed to resume total control of the catering operation under the school's own catering officer. Shortly after the introduction of the new system, they noted with satisfaction in their minutes that 'the standard of catering had improved; and the cleanliness and the hygiene were so much better that parents no longer had to be shielded from visiting the kitchens'.

Mrs Snaith recalls one other consequence of the post-war labour shortages:

> In the very early days, it was impossible to get staff, so we were glad to employ 'girls' and later 'boys' (aged about 30) from what we called 'the Colony' - an institution for girls and boys in need of care and control. This Stoke Park Colony was housed opposite the school in the old Dower House of the Dukes of Beaufort. I remember one day my husband was driving home up Bell Hill when a figure emerged from the school gates and ran down Bell Hill brandishing a dustpan and brush. My husband recognised him as one of 'our boys' and led him gently home (i.e. back to school).

Ten 'colony boys' were still being employed in 1954, their wages having been increased from 10 shillings to 15 shillings a week, and they continued to be part of the scene until the early 1970s. The boys and girls were employed primarily to work in the kitchen, to wait at table, to assist with domestic chores and to assist in the grounds.

Life in the dormitories was occasionally enlivened by a fire practice. Bill Welland (1959-66) has advanced a theory that it was always held on Thursday nights between 10.00 and 10.30 pm to interrupt Jimmy Saville's radio programme, *Teens and Twenties' Disco Club*, which some of the older boys listed to (illegally) in bed. Each dormitory had its own canvas chute with a steel frame at the top which clipped onto a bar across one of the windows. The boys were instructed to avoid possible burns by holding their arms in tightly as they slid down inside the tube. It was, however, a 'scary' experience, as Murray Wilson (1947-54) later recalled:

> Fire practice was held in the summer term - that is after we had been there for over two terms! The machine was rolled forward and the chute fell out. Two older boys then descended by rope inside the tube and three more gingerly slid down. Four then held the chute out and the fifth threw you aside when you arrived. It was very like a low technology form of the escape chutes from the 747s. It was great fun, especially the ritual of throwing shoes out of the window before descending. I was in the eighth dorm [in the attic], so we went to the South dorm for the practice! How we were meant to escape from a fire in the eighth dorm no-one ever explained - but it was near the end of term so it did not matter.

The dormitories themselves, according to Murray Wilson, 'were enormous' to the eye of a small boy. In the late 1940s and early 1950s, 'younger boys went to bed at 8.30 pm and the older ones after second prep at 9.30 pm.' They simply had to learn 'to stay asleep, while others came in and got undressed'. Sergeant Hannaford sounded the wake-up

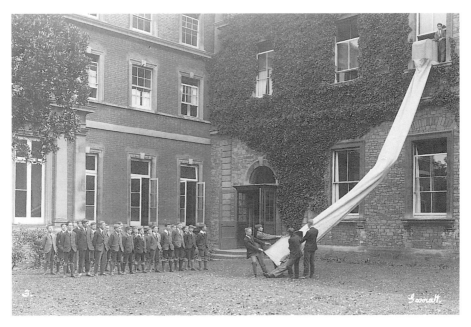

Fire drill in operation in the 1920s. The canvass chute is being used to 'rescue' boys from the old Mortlake House dormitory. (SMV Archive)

bell at 7.00 am, followed by a second bell fifteen minutes later. Boys then ventured out 'to the freezing water of the washroom'. Hot water was not introduced into the main block until 1960-61, when a new shower room was installed in the basement (below the present library). Until then the only hot showers were situated in the changing rooms just inside the main gate - reached in all weathers by boys from their dormitories clad in dressing gowns. According to Bill Welland (1959-66), boys in his time were allocated two showers a week, the rota for which was posted by the Sergeant on a board under 'the Arches'. This was the colonnaded walkway which led to the toilet block. Until the mid-1960s, it was open-sided and paved with flagstones. Notice boards hung from several of the pillars and tuck boxes lined the back wall. A more regular chore, of course, was that of making of beds after breakfast. According to Alan Hale (1958-1964), 'hospital corners were the order of the day' - and the prefect on duty ensured that they were done correctly.

Life in the playground continued much as normal during the 1940s and 1950s. School slang, unsurprisingly, enlarged its repertoire to keep up with the times. Familiar words and expressions included 'the Crib' (the School), 'toke' (bread), 'dunny' (lavatory - the sit down variety), 'bunje' (rubber), 'pavy' (pavilion), 'sickers' (sick room), 'caddy' (cadet corps). 'cosh' (the cane), 'Crib rookie' (a thief), 'Crib tick' (school jam), 'oats' (bread), 'grease' (butter), 'grit' (sugar), 'knobshave' (school haircut), 'stow' (watching out for those in authority), 'squipps' (the hard red soap provided by the school), 'tuckers' (tuck shop), 'wads' (buns distributed during prep), 'Weston mud' (chocolate semolina) and 'Tom Shaw' (the two-wheeled cart used in gardening and apparently named after the boy who built it).

Other terms applied to punishments imposed by the prefects - 'pres coshing' (one stroke of the cane from each of the six prefects applied in turn), 'drill' (the punishment session after school) and 'getting the dap' (being beaten in one's pyjamas for misdemeanour by a prefect or monitor using a plimsoll). Mike Newman (1947-55) and Mike Jones (1945-55) remember only too well the severity of punishments awarded by the prefects in their time. Corporal punishment was inflicted by means of the dap (six of the best) in the washrooms after lights out. With the culprit forced to bend over the washbasin immediately opposite the door, the prefect would often gain momentum (and dramatic effect) by starting his run from the corridor outside. Punishments for misdemeanours in the Dining Hall included two particular methods of 'torture'. The offender would be forced to spread out a hand on the table with fingers splayed and the prefect then would either press down on top of it with the large brown teapot (which of course was very hot) or would stab a fork rapidly between the fingers in turn, increasing in speed until a finger was 'accidentally' struck. Nevertheless, Alan Hale (1958-64) makes the point that prefects sometimes resorted to milder punishments - such as the favourite imposition of writing two or four sides of foolscap on 'How to grow hair on a billiard ball'.

For their part, members of staff were empowered either to use the cane or to sentence a boy to the punishment of 'drill'. This was administered by Sergeant 'Herbert' Hannaford (later by Sergeant Warburton) for an hour on Tuesday afternoons. It consisted essentially of running round the Parade with the Sergeant yelling at boys to lift up their feet - or moving coal from the store to the boiler house. The Sergeant was also responsible for the regular inspection of hands and shoes before meal times. Summoned either by bugle or bell, the boys would assemble on the Parade, line up by House tables and march into the Dining Hall. If a boy was found to breach the rules of cleanliness, he would be sent away to rectify the matter while the rest of the table was kept waiting outside.

The Sergeant also carried out a weekly inspection each Wednesday lunchtime of the length of each boy's hair - although, according to Nigel Hurley (1959-65), Mr Snaith was also seen on occasions holding out a boy's hair to see if it covered his ears. Boys who failed the inspection were detailed to attend the weekly session of the travelling barber, who set up base inside the pavilion. Old Colstonians agree that in those days the Sergeant was 'the central figure in your life' - a man who was 'ever present' throughout each day from the morning rising bell onwards. Sergeant Hannaford himself was always extremely smart in appearance with shining boots ('as if he had come straight off the parade ground'). Behind his crimson face and loud voice lurked a man who was 'incredibly fair', bore no malice and commanded the highest respect.

Not all boys, however, were deterred by the fear of punishment. Smoking in particular had its attraction for some (often using 'liquorice-flavoured Rizla paper' to roll out their own cigarettes) - especially if they could remain undetected in the toilets ('senior bogs') at the end of the 'Arches', in the 'pipe room' just inside the entrance to the changing rooms or at 'the overhang' outside the school on the way down to Stapleton village. One boy, however, was uncovered in a most dramatic manner. David Faulkner (1962-69) recalls that the Motor Club, which met in a section of the Arches set aside for the use of societies, had on one occasion spilt a quantity of petrol in its inspection pit. Later that evening, a boy went into that area for a smoke, climbing down into the pit and pulling the boards back over his head to remain concealed. Suddenly, there was a loud explosion! The boy allegedly spent the next three months in hospital.

Very few parts of the school remained secure from enterprising boys. Mike Newman (1947-55) admits that he was quite skilful at copying keys in the workshop for use in most locks. Masters, of course, were not always able to solve petty crimes with the speed they would have preferred - hence their frequent resort to bluff. Bill Welland (1959-66) recalls a spate of thefts involving geometry boxes taken from boys' lockers in the common rooms (many of the keys apparently fitted many of the locks!). On hearing this, Mr Baxter, the art and woodwork master who was the Master-on-Duty, stood up at the end of a meal and demanded information coupled with their immediate return. 'I want to know - and I want to know by Thursday', he said. No culprit was identified, but the boxes were subsequently found in a neat pile on the playing field.

(ii) The Combined Cadet Force, 1949-2002

The cadets continued to play an important part in school life. In 1949, with the winding up of the Army Cadet Force, the school corps was transferred to the Combined Cadet Force (the CCF) - although, even by December 1951, the revised uniform, which consisted of a new-style battledress with collar and tie, had only been provided for 12 out of the contingent's 119 cadets. Realising that the shortfall was entirely due to the prohibitive cost of equipping the entire force (c. £200), the Society of Merchant Venturers again came to the rescue, as it had done on so many previous occasions, by providing a complete set of shirts worth £94. The War Office, too, responded to the call for improved accommodation for this rapidly-growing unit, which was finding the restricted space of the armoury insufficient for all its activities. By 1954, an additional hut had been erected within the grounds.

The CCF more than justified all this investment by offering boys a variety of experiences and challenges. For instance, it enabled them to take part in a number of memorable activities such as providing a guard-of-honour for General Sir John Harding at Prize Giving in 1949 and for Princess Margaret in Bristol in the same year; or participating in a ceremonial parade in 1953 during Coronation Week and again in 1965 to celebrate the 50th anniversary of its own foundation. According to *The Colstonian*, it also provided valuable training in leadership, especially after the formation of the cadre in 1963 as 'a hatchery for NCOs'. One President of the Examination Board, after witnessing a 100% pass-rate in the Certificate A examination, commented that in five years 'he had never met such an efficient unit with such excellent instructors'. It is therefore hardly surprising that three of the Under-Officers went on to Sandhurst during the mid-1960s. Many boys seized the chance to

The CCF wearing its new-style battledress uniform with the cap badge of the Gloucesters' Regiment. The inspection is being carried out in the early 1960s by Mr Snaith (left), Sergeant Warburton (centre) and the visiting inspecting officer. (SMV Archive)

become expert shots on the Pilning Open Range or the school's miniature range, three of them being classed as Colston's first-ever 'marksmen' in 1954. Many also attended the annual camps at such places as Warminster (1949), Aldershot (1956), Windmill Hill (1959), Dartmouth (1961) and Germany (1973); or took part in arduous training from 1957 in the Lake District, North Wales and Argyllshire.

Murray Wilson (1947-54) later recalled - without any great enthusiasm - his own experience of the corps:

> The cadet corps, first ACF, later CCF, was like many things - minimalist. Whereas other schools had naval and air sections, we had the army. Every Tuesday afternoon and every Saturday in the fifth period we paraded. Some were more enthusiastic than others. One day I was in charge of a section sent to the Bean Field. Major Creek came along. 'What are you teaching, Corporal Wilson?' 'Camouflage and concealment, sir'. 'Where are they?' 'Don't know, sir, they are so well camouflaged'. You can see why I never got to be a full corporal...

Inspection Day was a great occasion. We had endless rehearsals. Non-caddy blokes were under no circumstances to be seen by the inspecting general. I always wondered why not. Would it have been thought letting the side down to acknowledge that were in fact other boys, most of them too young, in the school? Snaith put on his ceremonials and appeared with the general. We marched up and down, were inspected, and marched up and down again. The day was always the same. Marching in the morning, a demonstration of field craft during which people crawled about firing blanks in the afternoon - and then the general said that we were just as good as real soldiers. That always made me wonder about the efficacy of the real Army.

Those old enough to join the corps, but who did not wish to do so, were considered a lesser breed and referred to as 'non-caddy blokes'. They undertook good works, mainly involving maintenance of the fields and heavy rollers, every Tuesday and Saturday afternoon.

Nevertheless, the popularity of the CCF among most boys never wavered throughout the period 1946-1975, its numbers ranging between 115 in 1948, 150 in 1961 and 130 in 1974. Unfortunately, its very existence was threatened in 1970, when Major C.N. Creek announced his intention to resign as commanding officer owing to ill health. Furthermore, the acute shortage of teachers, who were willing to assist in the corps, meant that it had only two additional officers at its disposal

Cadets shooting on the school's miniature (or tube) range in the late 1970s or early 1980s. (SMV Archive)

instead of the five who were needed. The Headmaster (Mr Gibbs) therefore gave notice to both the War Office and the parents that the unit would be closing down in the autumn. It was, however, reprieved at the eleventh hour 'in a modified form', when Major Creek agreed to continue on a temporary basis. Unfortunately, the CCF band was one immediate casualty of the crisis - although that, too, was briefly revived in 1974.

It was with some relief, therefore, that the arrival of a new member of staff boosted morale with an injection of fresh enthusiasm. By January 1972, he had persuaded the new Headmaster (Mr King) to agree to the establishment of an RAF section within the CCF with an initial membership of 16 boys. By 1974, this total had grown to 35 cadets, who very much enjoyed the opportunity to fly from Filton and to be trained in gliding. Meanwhile, in 1964, those boys who were not members of the CCF were required to choose between two other activities - 'social service' (which saw them helping the elderly with jobs about the house and garden or visiting the disabled in Purdown Hospital) or 'pioneers' (which involved them in building paths, chopping wood or weeding around the grounds at school). In 1979, for instance, no fewer than 120 boys were involved in social service in the Stapleton area with 50 homes visited each Monday to offer help with shopping, repairing, cleaning or dog-walking. This operation was closely monitored by the Second Master, Mr Cartwright, who took a genuine interest by visiting each disabled person himself in rotation. The options for social service were slightly modified in 1980, when all fourth formers were required to enter the cadet force for at least one year. Five years later, however, membership of the CCF became a totally voluntary activity.

In spite of the growing difficulty in attracting officers to help with its organisation, the CCF continued to flourish throughout the 1970s. Two members of staff - Major Robin Lee and Flight Lieutenant Martin Tayler were subsequently awarded the Lord Lieutenant of Avon's Certificate for their sterling work in keeping the CCF going during this period. Termly field days were revived in 1977 (normally based at Yoxeter); annual camps were held much further afield (with the army section in Berlin in 1978 and the RAF section at Laarbruck in Germany in 1979) and gliding courses were well attended. Although still suffering badly from an absence of officers from within the teaching staff, the CCF was given a further lease of life in 1983 when Major Frank Brace was employed for two days a week to run the unit. Finding it in a 'very run down condition', thanks partly to the fact that membership was no longer compulsory, he set about introducing more professional standards and built up a store of good, serviceable equipment to replace the poor quality kit he had inherited. Facilities were also improved with the provision by the Ministry of Defence in 1985 of a new CCF complex,

*Major Roger Clements leading a CCF mountain walking expedition in the early
1990s.*

consisting of offices and two classrooms on the site of the old nissen hut
and a new store next to the fives courts. Enthusiasm returned and in
1987 victory was secured in the Avon Jubilee assault course
competition. Sadly, Major Brace died suddenly at the summer camp in
1988 and was replaced as commander by another outsider, Major Roger
Clements.

By 1990, numbers had again fallen - a decline blamed on the fact that
non-members were being given the opportunity to go home on the CCF
afternoon. Therefore, in spite of the fact that boys in the RAF section
began to train on an RAF flight pilot simulator, that the school's unit of
just 16 cadets at the 1991 summer camp actually emerged as overall
winners of the competitions, that girls began to join the ranks from 1992
and that individuals were beginning to win RAF sixth form scholarships
and flying scholarships, the corps found itself on the brink of extinction
early in 1993. Although it was given a temporary reprieve in the autumn
(on condition that its numbers increased to a minimum of 60), the RAF
section was closed down.

Three years later (in October 1996), a reviewing officer from the 43
(Wessex) Brigade, having inspected the CCF, reported that in spite of
good facilities, the contingent had 'a very poor record of attendance and

activity' and the training was 'lifeless and unimaginative'. There were just 17 cadets on parade - almost the entire contingent - who were well turned out, cheerful and keen to learn. Nevertheless, he concluded, 'on most counts, the CCF should close down'. His mind was changed, however, by the supportive attitude and interest shown by the new Headmaster (Mr Crawford), who had already reverted to the old policy of making membership of the CCF compulsory. The school was therefore given to the end of 1997 to reorganise the leadership within the corps and to build up its strength.

From that moment, a remarkable transformation took place. An army report on the contingent in August 2000 proclaimed that 'Phoenix has well and truly risen from the ashes. Now sporting three sections, all with commissioned officers and a regular parade strength of 140, this is one of the most successful CCF contingents within the 43 (Wessex) Brigade area'. The transformation, it concluded, 'was entirely due to the unstinting support of Mr Crawford, the Headmaster, and the almost unbelievable commitment of Major Steve Waters, the contingent commander'. Mr Waters, who was also the School Chaplain, had been appointed commanding officer in January 1997. He was given massive support in achieving this revival by two Staff Sergeant Instructors (Harry Wiltshire and Tim Scarll), who provided the necessary equipment and specialist back-up. By September 1998, a Royal Naval

Petty Officer Matthew Jelf receiving instruction in a Royal Navy helicopter when it visited the school in 2001. It was part of the 702 squadron from RNAS Yeovilton, which had adopted the school's naval section. (Photograph by Clive Warren)

section had been formed, followed a year later by a re-formed RAF section.

Between 1997 and 2002, groups of cadets regularly participated in the Ten Tors Expedition, the Three Peaks Challenge, Easter and summer camps, weekends on Salisbury Plain, Dartmoor and the Brecons, arduous training courses and leadership/survival exercises. Year 9 [i.e. 3rd form] pupils were taken on the Colston Challenge during Activities Week (a 4-day trek on Dartmoor); sailing, shooting and flying options appeared on the games programme; and visits were made to the Royal Artillery and HMS Raleigh. The rapid growth in interest and enthusiasm was further illustrated by the fact that, in 1999-2000, no fewer than five cadets gained entry to Sandhurst - Alex Brighton, Rebecca Wegener, Sam Poulson, Simon Griffiths and James Bratby (the first two of whom were also awarded army sixth form scholarships) - while one other pupil (Brett Jones) won an RAF flying scholarship.

Cadets on a visit to the Bristol T.A. Royal Artillery Battery in 2000. Richard Coussins is holding the 105mm shell with Rebecca Wegener (who had gained entry to Sandhurst) on his immediate left. (Photograph by SSI Timothy Scarll)

In October 2001, Under Officer Samantha Poulson was appointed a Lord Lieutenant's Cadet and both Major Waters and SSI Wiltshire were awarded Lord Lieutenant's Commendations. By 2002, the CCF had not only been revived to something like its former strength, it had emerged as an essential and vibrant part of the school's programme of character development - illustrated by the fact that, in the autumn of 2001, the contingent organised and led a two-day-and-night leadership and induction course for the school's 80 new lower sixth formers at Caerwent. Equally ambitious was a planned expedition in 2002 from Land's End to John O'Groats by ten cadets in aid of charity.

(iii) Expeditions

Nor was the opportunity to take part in expeditions limited to members of the CCF. The post-war period witnessed a rapid growth in foreign travel and exploration as the school became much more outward-looking. French exchange visits were resumed as early as 1947, for instance, while Colston's itself hosted parties of twelve Swedish students in 1967 and fourteen boys from the East End of London in 1972. Groups of sixth formers took part in camping expeditions to the Lake District in 1955 and 1956; a fourth form party cycled round the youth hostels of Snowdonia in 1959; and the first-ever ski trip was organised to Austria in 1959 for eight fifth formers - followed by annual trips thereafter to various continental resorts. As time progressed, more ambitious expeditions of a general or cultural nature were sent out to destinations which included Paris (1960), Russia (1967), America (1968), Liechtenstein (1970) and Tunisia (1974). In addition, there were regular language courses in France and family to family exchanges with French pupils. Individuals, too, were sponsored by the governors from 1959 to take part in 'outward bound' courses, while groups of A level geographers regularly went out on fieldwork trips. This idea was taken further in 1992 by the School Chaplain, who took a group to the Holy Land for GCSE field work in religious studies. Five years later, another party crossed to Belgium for an exploration of 1st World War battlefield sites.

Local visits were increasingly organised by the school from the late 1950s for lectures at the university, concerts and plays at the theatre, conferences on such topics as world citizenship and educational tours of both nature reserves and industrial factories. Practical arrangements for this broadening work in education were made much easier for staff after the purchase of a second-hand 36-seater bus in 1968 (later renovated in 1973), together with two minibuses - the first in 1967 and the second, purchased by the Colston's School Society, in 1974. A new 45-seater bus was bought in 1976, making travel even more comfortable. By then the concept of 'outdoor pursuits' was becoming much more firmly established with mountaineering expeditions to Snowdonia, the Lakes, the Brecons and the West of Scotland on numerous occasions (many of them organised by Mr Keith Brook) - and to the Pyrenees in 1978, Iceland in 1985 and the Ardeche river in 1988 for canoeing. This was particularly pleasing to the Headmaster (Mr Searle) who firmly believed

Presentation of a minibus by the Colston's School Society in 1974. The Headmaster, Mr Alan King, is seen at the front on the left receiving the keys, while the bus is being driven by Mr Martin Tayler (the-master-in-charge of both rugby and cricket). Mr Donald Cartwright (the Second Master) and Mr Alan Brown (the Head of Science) are seen in the group on the left. (SMV Archive)

that some boys 'found themselves for the first time' through the challenges offered in this way.

(iv) Clubs and Societies

Both Mr Snaith and Mr Gibbs were very keen on the expansion of school societies as a way of enriching the personality and experience of each boy. Although very few such societies existed in 1948 (restricted chiefly to the Literary and Debating Society, the Science Societies and the Chess Club), the list rapidly grew thereafter with the addition of the Photographic Society and the Harmonia Society in 1950 (the latter expanding members' knowledge of music through records and organ recitals), the Phoenix Society in 1956 (for play readings, discussions and debates); the Philatelic Society, the Caving Club (which offered expeditions to the Mendips) and the Archaeological Society (with both excursions and excavations) in 1960. During Mr Snaith's time, in the 1950s, societies (which were largely for the fourth forms and above) met on Saturday evenings, when two separate sessions were organised between 7.00 and 8.00 pm and between 8.15 and 9.15 pm.

Many boys, of course, were quite content to make their own amusements, as Murray Wilson (1947-54) later recalled:

> The old fields, prior to their remodelling [in 1950], were very rough in places. It was possible to dig tunnels and generally act like young boys. Some built model aeroplanes and flew them from the banks. They used long lengths of rubber band for the engines. These were, on occasions, used to catapult bent bed springs at those hiding in the bushes. The school gardens were quite extensive, but seemed to be put exclusively to cabbage and rhubarb - explaining their frequent appearance on the menu.

There was a second period of growth under Mr Gibbs and Mr King between 1965 and 1972, which saw the establishment of the Shooting Club, the Bridge Club, the Modern Languages Society, the Sixth Form Historians, the Christian Union, the Model Railway Society, the Motor Club, the Woodwork and Modelling Club, the Art Club, the Basketball Club, the Badminton Club, the Table Tennis Club, the Cycling Club and the Railway Society (which featured trips to the Severn Valley and Dart Valley Railways). Further interest was created on Saturday evenings by both Mr Snaith and Mr Gibbs (particularly after the purchase of a 16 mm projector in 1947) through a programme of classic films (including *Great Expectations, Hamlet, The Cruel Sea* and *The Wooden Horse*) and visiting lecturers. Mr King, too, was particularly keen on the idea of bringing in outsiders to share their experiences with the sixth form through a series of Friday morning lectures - an initiative which was later expanded further by Mr Searle (1975-88).

Clubs and societies, of course, were constantly changing in both number and character, according to the boys' latest fads and interests. Some fell into abeyance, only to make a reappearance a few years later (such as the Photographic Club and the Badminton Club, which were revived in 1980, or the Chess Club re-formed in 1981). A number of totally new societies, however, emerged to reflect teenage taste and ambition - the Motor Cycle Maintenance Club (1978), the Computer Club (1981), the Kit Car Club (1986) and the Mountain Bike Club (1988) - while, in 1992, the Chatterton Society was formed to give older pupils the opportunity to express themselves through debates, discussions and quizzes. Interest in public speaking and current affairs was also stimulated by the school's participation in the Model United Nations Assembly from 1992. By 2002, in addition to the CCF, the Duke of Edinburgh's Award Scheme and various musical groups, there were some 26 clubs and societies operating weekly - including fantasy football, first aid, internet, jigsaw, scrabble, war games and web page design.

(v) Drama

Two other activities enjoyed considerable development during the post-war years - namely, drama and music. The annual school play was revived in December 1947 with a performance of *The King's Jewry*, although the most ambitious enterprise came in 1973 with the production of *Anthony and Cleopatra*. This involved 31 actors (including girls from La Retraite School) and 40 people backstage. Furthermore, a lecture and discussion session was arranged in the afternoon prior to each performance with invited audiences totalling 121 sixth formers from eleven local schools. Another memorable event in 1970 was the world premiere of *Aella* by Thomas Chatterton, O.C. to commemorate the bi-centenary of his death. The script had been specially modified by Dr Basil Cottle of Bristol University with incidental music composed by Mr Christopher Walker, a former member of staff. By 1968 a Junior Dramatic Society had also been established and was beginning to stage such plays as *The Devil's Disciple* and *Under Milk Wood.*

The cause of public speaking, which was dear to Mr Snaith's heart, was undoubtedly helped in 1956 by the gift of 'a tape recording

A scene from The Rivals, *which was the annual school play in 1954. (SMV Archive)*

machine' from a governor. The Headmaster stressed at Prize Giving its undeniable benefit in 'improving the English accent of those of our number, and they are not a few, who leave something to be desired in that direction'. This process was assisted further by the establishment in 1975 of the Allen Elocution Prize for sixth formers and the introduction of a fifth form elocution competition in 1977. These were both later styled 'Public Speaking Competitions'.

There is no doubt that the arrival of Mr Searle as Headmaster in 1975 gave a great boost to drama within the school. Although some individual productions had unquestionably been good, they were infrequent and catered for comparatively few pupils. Mr Searle, who was determined to raise the profile of cultural activities within the school, was anxious to offer the chance of involvement to as many boys as possible. This aim was achieved in two ways - by establishing an annual inter-House Drama Festival in 1976, which featured sixth formers as producers and directors with middle school boys as actors; and by launching of a series of sixth form plays in 1977.

These experiments proved a great success in stirring up enthusiasm and building confidence. The sixth formers staged a wide variety of productions, including *Waiting for Godot* (1977), *The Caretaker* (1978) and *Androcles and the Lion* (1982). With such valuable experiences available, it is hardly surprising that the standard reached by the main school play each autumn became increasingly impressive. Memorable productions included *All My Sons* (1981), *When we are Married* (1982), *The Boy Friend* (1983) and *Outside Edge* (1985). Female parts were now increasingly played by girls from Red Maids School and Redland High School - and, from 1985, from the school's own sixth form.

The arrival of Mr Stephen Pritchard on the staff in 1987 heralded a major advance in both ambition and quality - an advance greatly encouraged by the new Headmaster, Mr Howarth. Mr Pritchard's first production, *The Winter's Tale*, involved no fewer than 70 pupils in the company and was hailed by *The Colstonian* as 'a spectacular piece of entertainment, including live music, dance, songs, thunder lightening, fog and snow'. This set a future pattern in which modern technology played an important role in a series of highly professional productions - including *Dr Faustus* in 1990 ('a triumph of ambitious technological wizardry'), *Caucasian Chalk Circle* in 1992, *Peer Gynt* in 1993 ('a pyrotechnic kaleidoscope of dazzling images') and *Yerma* (1998). The opening of the Harry Crook Theatre in 1992 provided both the setting and the facilities which these plays deserved - 'the artistic completeness of which rivals anything seen in Bristol'.

The experience gained by those who took part was invaluable and the confidence given immeasurable. Furthermore, an awakened interest in

A scene from Stephen Pritchard's production of The Insect Play *in 2001 with (from the left) Joseph Cook, Claire Timbrell and Matthew Crawford.*
(Photograph by Mr & Mrs George Phillips)

drama motivated increasing numbers to opt for GCSE and A level courses in drama and theatre studies. Indeed, the whole nature of drama had been transformed under Mr Pritchard from that of a mere extra-curricular activity into a mainstream academic subject. This quickly proved to be one of the most successful and most popular subjects in the curriculum - a fact illustrated by the fact that, in 2000, 48% of the school's candidates gained A* at GCSE (compared with just 4% nationally).

(vi) Music

Music, which had languished during the 1930s, mounted a revival during the mid-1950s under the direction of Mr D.C. Johnstone. By 1954, 'a staunch band' of instrumentalists were working enthusiastically on Saturday evenings to re-establish the orchestra 'undeterred by their sometimes unlovely harmonies'. The Christmas Concert by choir and orchestra soon became once more a regular feature; visits to hear the D'Oyle Carte and Sadler's Wells Companies were arranged to stimulate interest - as were the two programmes of gramophone recitals each weekend; and much more ambitious productions were staged by the choir with professional soloists - including *Merrie England* (1956), an Elgar Centenary Concert (1957) and *The Bartered Bride* (1958). By then there were 60 boys in the choir. Four years later, school music was restructured with the establishment of a Chapel Choir of 32 selected voices and a Choral Society of 100 members, including four masters.

The Society frequently combined with a rejuvenated orchestra to perform such works as *Trial by Jury* (1962), *The Messiah* (1963), *HMS Pinafore* (1966) and Borodin's *Petite Masse Solennelle* (1967), which also featured the Colston's Girls' School Choir and two sixth form soloists (Anthony Wright and Gerald Hawkins). By 1968, the music programme included monthly invitation concerts, organ recitals, summer concerts and recitals by the Choral Society in Bristol churches. In 1969, the Society's ambitions were taken a stage further with the production of a '12-inch LP record' - although, in doing so, they were merely copying their predecessors in 1955, who had made 'a gramophone record' containing various songs. They had proudly confessed in *The Colstonian* that 'several members of the school *outside* the choir' had been tempted to buy copies - though they could not 'report a similar trend in the sale of the choir photographs'.

Thereafter music at Colston's went into a period of temporary decline and, by the time of Mr Searle's appointment as Headmaster in 1975, it was 'at a very low ebb'. Determined to raise the profile of cultural activities within the school, Mr Searle soon found himself in a position to appoint a new Head of Music - Mr Christopher Swain - who rapidly transformed the situation. By 1979, he had established two choirs (including a four-part chapel choir), an orchestra (with 34 members), an 18-strong brass band, a jazz group and a new Choral Society (including parents, staff and pupils), which performed such works as Haydn's *Nelson Mass* and Mozart's *Requiem*. He also ensured maximum involvement in musical activity by revamping the House music competition in 1979 into an Eisteddfod-type festival; and by commencing a series of concerts for soloists. Furthermore, in 1978, he formed a Music Society to stage regular concerts - often in conjunction with the Bristol Chamber Orchestra, which was conducted by Swain himself and included six boys. It was at one of these concerts in 1981 that Wei Kiat Ong, a most talented young pianist, was the soloist in Rachmaninov's 2nd Piano Concerto. Before he left in 1982, Mr Swain produced a record entitled *Music at Colston's*, which was recorded over a special 'Music Weekend'.

From 1982, musical activity in the school became much more low key, although the inter-house competition continued (re-styled the Colston School Music Festival in 1989) and the Choral Society successfully performed a number of works. The choirs, too, played a full part on major occasions. In 1989, for instance, the Chapel Choir sang at the Charter Day service in the Cathedral, while the combined choirs of the Upper School and the Prep participated in the Colston Day service in St Stephen's Church - followed by a chamber group playing baroque music in All Saints' Church during the wreath-laying ceremony at Colston's tomb. In 1990, a new instrumental teacher inspired the formation of both wind and brass ensembles, while the arrival of co-education in 1991 boosted the choir and heralded the start of recorder groups. Individuals continued to excel. Rachael Kear, for instance, performed Shostakovich's 2nd Piano Concerto in 1993, although the orchestra had, of necessity, been 'augmented by staff and friends'. Indeed, the growing shortage of instrumentalists had become all too evident, making it impossible to revive - at least for the time being - the excellent concerts and lively musical activities which had been such a feature of the late 1970s and early 1980s. [It is worth noting that Rachael Kear distinguished herself not only by becoming the first Head Girl of Colston's in 1992 but also the first girl from the school to enter Oxford University, where she subsequently gained a 1st class degree in music].

The appointment of Mr Ian Holmes as Director of Music in 1997 marked the emergence of the school's music from a lengthy period in the doldrums. The department quickly enlarged its ambition. Initial activity was based on the Chapel Choir, which gave performances in Bristol Cathedral and sang each year at the Guild of Guardians' Christmas Service in the Lord Mayor's Chapel; and the Choral Society, which was re-formed in 1997 after a gap of ten years. The two groups frequently combined - in 1999 to perform Faure's *Requiem*; in 2000 (in combination with singers from nine other independent schools in the Colston Hall) to sing *MM*, a new work for massed choir and orchestra; and, in the same year, to undertake a short concert tour around Lake Garda in Italy - followed in 2002 by a similar tour to Barcelona in the company of Colston's Swing Band.

Meanwhile, instrumental music had been stimulated by the creation of music scholarships in 1998; the appointment of an Assistant Director of Music and a School Organist in 1999; and the opening of the Chatterton Hall in 2000 as a base for the department with six practice rooms - as well as a fine area for concerts. The new Viscount organ, purchased by the Parents' Society, was immediately put to good effect by Martyn Rawles, who won an Organ Scholarship to St Catharine's College, Cambridge in 2001. Interest in music was also created through the visits of accomplished performers - the Central Band of the Royal Air Force in 1999 and the children of the Mathieson Music School in Calcutta in 2000. By 2001, there were 250 pupils learning musical

The School Choir performing with the Colston's Choral Society at the Christmas Concert in 20001. (Photograph by Graham Ricketts)

instruments; the Lower School was providing a choir, orchestra, wind band and two string ensembles; while the Upper School boasted an orchestra, chapel choir, choral society, swing band, wind band, string orchestra, 'clarinet clique', a music scholars' group and a middle school choir. A striking transformation was therefore already under way.

(vii) Sport

(a) 1946-1975

Perhaps the greatest transformation during these years, however, came about in the realm of sport. Far more choice was on offer, especially for those boys who were not so good at rugby and cricket, with the introduction of new competitive games. Regular fixtures were therefore arranged in fives (1957), judo (for sixth formers, 1961), volleyball (as an alternative to cricket, 1969), basketball (1969), handball (1975) - and, more importantly, hockey (1954) with the first match in 1955 against a Bristol Grammar School 'B' XI. By 1959, 40 boys from the fifth and sixth forms were playing the sport on a regular basis. Badminton and table tennis had also become popular as leisure activities by the mid-1960s. Much of this diversification, of course, could not have taken place without the provision of the new facilities, including the gymnasium, the fives courts and the re-modelled games pitches.

Meanwhile, the school's major sports - rugby and cricket - continued to struggle in the pursuit of real success. Although Colston's had produced a number of skilful games players over the years, including several rugby internationals, consistency had always been lacking at first team level. The same pattern repeated itself to a large extent throughout the 1940s and 1950s. It is true that, in swimming, the school beat 40 other schools to win the Royal Life Saving Society's Shield in 1946, 1949, 1954 and 1957 - but such elation was never experienced by the rugby players and cricketers. 'A disappointing season' or 'a team capable of both brilliance and mediocrity' were typical comments in their magazine reports. For instance, the 1st and 2nd XV's somewhat dismal record of losing 19 out of the 20 matches played in 1958-59 was more than matched by the 1st XI's performance in failing to win a single game in 1960.

This increasingly despondent situation, however, was suddenly transformed in the mid-1960s, thanks to a number of factors. In the first place, boys were beginning to gain far greater continuity of coaching and much more experience of competitive play at an earlier age, both in the Prep School and in the lower part of the Upper School. From 1959, for instance, fixtures were being arranged for the first time at under 13, under

A gymnastics lesson in progress in the old gymnasium in the mid-1960s. (SMV Archive)

14, under 15 and under 16 levels - instead of simply for the 'junior' team. Furthermore, the number of boys within the two parts of the school (an important factor when competing against other institutions) had risen from 295 in 1954 to 480 in 1974.

The quality of coaching had also improved. In cricket, from 1960, the school had adopted with the junior teams methods advocated by the MCC Youth Coaching Scheme; by 1965, under the enthusiastic direction of the master-in-charge of cricket (Mr Morgan Johnson), coaches from the Gloucestershire County Cricket Club were also being employed on a regular basis. In hockey, no fewer than seven members of staff were Hockey Association coaches by 1974; and, to provide example of the highest quality, the school hosted not only the England Men's Trial in 1965, but also two full internationals against Pakistan and Australia in 1970 and 1971.

In rugby, the purchase of a scrummaging machine in 1965 and the arrival of Mr David Rollitt in 1964 gave the sport a new momentum. Mr Rollitt, who represented England in the Five Nations' Championships in 1967 while on the staff, joined Mr Dennis Price (the master-in-charge of rugby) to spearhead the coaching in what *The Colstonian* described as 'their new and successful tactics'. They introduced not only a rigorous fitness schedule, but also 'a coaching scheme' which taught 'the same techniques to all the school teams'. The presence on site of top-class sportsmen undoubtedly provided both inspiration and example. There is no doubt, too, that the appearance of Mr Gibbs as the new Headmaster in 1965 gave an enormous boost to sport within the school. An international rugby player himself, he offered a personal lead by taking responsibility for the coaching of junior teams. After Mr Price left in 1969 to become Headmaster of Rendcomb School, Mr Martin Tayler brought long-term continuity to the sport by remaining as master-in charge of rugby for the next twenty years.

Whatever the reasons, however, the change from mediocrity to excellence was most dramatic. In **cricket**, for instance, while the junior teams were 'seldom beaten' between 1961 and 1964, the four most senior sides together won 21 out of the 27 matches played in 1965 with the 1st XI itself unbeaten for two seasons - a performance almost matched in 1973 and 1974, when they recorded a total of just two defeats. In 1966, Bruce Thompson captained the Somerset Youth XI and also played for Somerset 2nd XI while still at school; and in 1973, Ian Crawford, who scored the school's first century since the war, became one of two boys to represent England Schoolboys (the other being Andrew Bromley) - the first Colston's cricketers to gain international caps. Crawford went on to play county cricket for Gloucestershire.

In **hockey**, the 1st XI made rapid progress, losing only two matches in 1969, winning the Bath Hockey Festival in 1968 and the Bristol six-a-side tournament in both 1970 and 1971, being invited to the Oxford Public Schools' Hockey Festival for the first time in 1973 and producing a regular stream of county representatives. By 1971, Colston's was being praised by the famous Occidentals Club 'as one of the two schools in the west country who were outstanding for the type of hockey played and good sportsmanship'. Two years later, the Headmaster reported that 1973 had been the school's 'most successful year ever in hockey' with the 1st XI 'rated among the best in England'. The next year saw 12 boys taking part in the county hockey festival and no fewer than seven representing the West at either under 19 or under 16 level. Boyan Wells eventually went on to captain Oxford and gain his hockey blue.

In **rugby**, the school was also enjoying considerable success in spite of a much-strengthened fixture list, which in 1969-70 included such schools as Bradford Grammar, Sevenoaks, Belmont Abbey, Millfield and King's (Worcester) - not to mention Balliol College, Oxford. This extension was organised largely by Mr Wally Feiner (who had taken over the fixture lists in all sports) with the prompting and encouragement of the Headmaster (Mr Gibbs). In 1969, the latter also accompanied the 1st XV with Mr Martin Tayler on a tour of Yorkshire, playing such schools as Silcoates, St Peter's (York) and Giggleswick. The same year saw the 1st XV win 12 out of its 14 matches; Austin Sheppard playing for both Somerset Schools and Harlequin Wanderers; and Paul Atterbury and Alan Morley playing for Bristol RFC at the age of seventeen. Three years later, after leaving school, Morley was to win his first cap for England, scoring a try against South Africa - while, back at Colston's, Gareth Denley and Ian Crawford were playing in the English Schools' Trials. It is however true to say that the success of the glorious 1968-69 season was difficult to match over the next decade.

Nor was sporting glory limited to the major games. The **fives** team was consistently successful, the first pair winning the finals of the Schools' National Tournament in 1971 and John Uwins going on to gain a half blue in the sport at Cambridge; and the **tennis** team (benefiting from the six new courts provided in 1965), not only reached the finals of the South-West Schools' Tournament in 1970, but were unbeaten during the 1973-74 seasons. It is perhaps hardly surprising, therefore, that *The Evening Post* should offer the opinion in 1972 that Colston's 'must rank as one of the country's best sporting schools for its size'. Nevertheless, the greatest delight was expressed by the Headmaster (Mr King) in 1974, when he reported to the governors that the school had that year beaten Clifton College in *every* sport - chess, fives, tennis, hockey, cricket and rugby.

Swimming, of course, remained a popular leisure activity for many boys - but this meant that the bath had first to be cleaned at the start of the season. Murray Wilson (1947-54) explains how it was done:

> Summer started properly when the bath was emptied by Mr Rockett, and parties were detailed off to spend an hour or so cleaning it with razor blade scrapers, pumice stones and - for big boys - enormous grinding stones dragged across the floor on ropes. When judged sufficiently clean, it was filled with mains water - and eventually the first swimmers were allowed in. It was bitterly cold, having come straight from the underground pipes. No costumes were allowed. However, if you intended to dive from the top board, then a slip (now described as a bikini bottom) was worn.
>
> The pool was disinfected by 'the Voxan boys'. Voxan was a chlorine-containing liquid added each evening. Voxan boys were not the brightest, always selected from Rockett's House and always in the B stream, but having achieved high swimming standards. They completed their prep quickly and went to the pool to measure and add the voxan and then swim round to stir it in. Maybe they were not bright to start with, but swimming in concentrated bleach every evening cannot have improved anything. They were, probably unjustifiably, the main suspects when the Sergeant's beans in a garden next to the pool were cut at ground level. We all stood for hours on the parade ground in an effort to make the guilty party own up. This didn't work.
>
> A swimming gala was held and dining room benches were carried round to line the sides of the pool. Curiously no one thought it strange that all the participants were naked except for the high divers, of course.

(b) 1975-2002

The arrival of Mr Searle as Headmaster in 1975 gave a further boost to sport - but not to the exclusion of other activities. A keen sportsman himself, he made a point of watching not only the matches on Saturdays, but also (whenever possible) the mid-week practices. Furthermore, he was anxious to broaden the scope of the games programme so that all boys could find at least one choice they could enjoy. After the opening of the squash courts in 1978, a 'racquets option' was therefore introduced for non-rugby players enabling the boys to play squash, tennis and fives in rotation. In the following year, shooting was also added to the list following the opening of the new covered range. **Squash** quickly established itself as a favourite sport. A junior House competition was organised, a team entered for the local under-17 league - and, in 1985, Peter Ward was selected to represent England at under-16 level. **Cross country** running was another sport to grow in popularity with regular fixtures arranged against other schools from 1984 - and Simon Mugglestone emerged as the United Kingdom under-19 cross country champion (before going up to Oxford to win blues for both cross country and athletics). The sport continued to thrive in the early 1990s with Colston's emerging as Bristol Schools' champions in 1993.

Nevertheless, in spite of much greater interest and involvement, success at first team level in the three major sports was distinctly patchy during the years 1975-1987. In **hockey**, over a twelve-year period, the 1st XI won just 26% of its matches. However, three boys had appeared in an under-19 West of England team in 1976 - the year in which England played Wales in a full international at the school - and a girls' hockey team had made its first appearance in 1985 (in spite of the fact that there were only 13 girls in the school). Thereafter regular fixtures were arranged for the girls (as well as in tennis, rounders, squash and netball) and by 1996 two girls were representing Avon at under-16 level. The year 1988 - rated by *The Colstonian* as 'the best for many years' - heralded something of a revival for hockey, when the school won both the under-18 and under-16 county championships. These successes were followed up in 1990 by an unbeaten under-15 team and in 1993 by a 1st XI which won 11 out of its 13 matches. Furthermore, Roly Ward gained an England cap at under-16 level in 1994 - to be followed by an under-18 cap in 1995 and a full England cap in 2001; while Dan Moore won Welsh caps at under-16 and under -18 level in 1998 and 2000. One particular highlight of this decade came in 1998, when the hockey club organised a tour to Barbados in conjunction with the cricket team.

In **cricket**, the 1st XI (over the twelve-year period, 1975-1987) won 29% of its matches with a further 42% of them drawn. However, this slightly disappointing record disguises a number of real successes. In 1976, for instance - the year in which the 1st XI lost only one of its games - Andrew Bromley broke the school bowling record with 76 wickets (having taken 75 wickets in the previous season); and in 1978, the under-15 team remained unbeaten. Furthermore, a number of highly talented individuals made their mark. The school batting record was broken on three occasions - by Antony Lawrence in 1978 with 705 runs (including three centuries); Lawson Roll in 1982 with 757 runs; and Jeremy Stutt in 1984 with 904 runs (including four centuries). In 1983, Lawson Roll gained wider recognition by being selected to play for the National Association of Young Cricketers XI, while Warren Smith was chosen for the MCC Schools' XI. They both went on eventually to play for Gloucestershire - the county which Chris Broad (who had been a member of the school's 1st XI between 1973 and 1975) had originally represented. Having moved to Nottinghamshire, he won his first of 25

England caps in 1984, scoring six centuries in the process throughout his England career (see page 345).

The years 1989 to 2001 also provided a number of striking successes in cricket. The under-15s won the Avon Schools' Cup for three successive seasons (1989-91); the under-16s won a similar cup (1992); the 2nd XI was unbeaten for two years running (1991-92); the 1st XI lost only two of its 17 matches in 1992 and enjoyed two outstandingly successful seasons in 1994-95; Joe Ewens scored three centuries at under-14 level (1992); David Carter took all ten wickets against Christ's College, Brecon (1994); and, in a match against The Downs School (1997), Colston's scored the highest total ever made by an under-12 team, totalling 224-1 (including two centuries). Two other individual feats should also be recorded - Andrew Holloway scored a record 628 runs during the 1994 season at under-14 level; and James Franklin (1990) not only achieved the highest individual score in a match of 186, but also the highest aggregate for the season of 906 (just beating Jeremy Stutt's previous record). Even more spectacular, he hit six sixes in one over in the match against Queen Elizabeth's Hospital School in 1989.

Andrew Holloway in 1994, having scored a century for the under-14 cricket team - part of the 628 runs he scored in the season. (By courtesy of R & P Photographic Services)

The most outstanding of all batsmen, however, was Chris Taylor (who went on to become a regular for Gloucestershire, having scored a century at Lords on his debut). In four seasons in the 1st XI (1993-96), he scored no fewer than 16 centuries and a total of 3,824 runs, breaking in the process Franklin's record aggregate for the season with 1597 runs in 1995. He can also claim to have recorded the highest score ever made in a school 1st XI match in England with his total of 278 not out against Hutton Grammar School. Unsurprisingly, he gained schoolboy international honours for England in 1995 - as did Joe Tucker and Jonathan Pick in 1999. Tucker went on to play county cricket, making his debut for Somerset against the West Indies in 2000. Mr Martin Tayler, who was master-in-charge of cricket between 1973 and 1996, feels that the school's remarkable success in producing outstanding batsmen is partly due to the benign nature of the wicket which, from the 1970s, benefited in its preparation from the addition of Surrey loam. So prolific were the run-makers during this period that the school was forced to abandon its policy of awarding a bat for each century scored, limiting itself instead to a bat for the *first* century achieved by an individual.

Hannah Wright-Davies with the Loveband Trophy in 1996. (School Archive)

Meanwhile, **tennis** had also gained quite considerably in popularity and, by the early 1990s, the school was fast becoming one of the top tennis schools in the country. In 1992, Paul Martin, the boys' under-16 national doubles champion, represented Great Britain in the under-16 World Championships; while in 1993, Simon Pender won the bronze medal in the Youth Olympics in Holland. By 1994, Martin was ranked number 2 in the United Kingdom at under-18 level; Pender number 5 at under-16 level; and Rebecca Dunbar number 6 at under-18 level. Others quickly followed on the trail they had blazed. Charlotte Wallace and Hannah Wright-Davies jointly won the Loveband Trophy in a national schools' competition (1996), the latter going on the represent Great Britain at junior level; the under-18s reached the national final of the Glanville Cup (1997); Hannah Wright-Davies and Caragh White reached the final of the national schools' doubles championships (1997); and Paul March and Mark Willis became south-west schools' doubles champions (1999).

Colston's pupils also distinguished themselves in a range of other sporting activities - Oliver Bright, the Avon under-11 chess champion, played for England juniors against Czechoslovakia (1995); Hannah Wright-Davies became Avon under-18 squash champion at the age of 14

(1995); Matthew German represented England in the United Kingdom schools' swimming championships (1996), while James Mason won five gold medals in the Gloucestershire championships (1997); and the under-14 netball team (who were unbeaten as under-13s) won all but one of their matches in 1999.

In **rugby**, the school enjoyed two glorious seasons in 1979 and 1980, winning 23 out of the 29 matches played and organising two memorable tours to France. According to *The Colstonian*, the 1980 season (in which only one game was lost) was 'the most successful in the school's history'. This level of performance, however, could not be sustained and, over the ten other years of the period 1975-87, the 1st XV won only 36% of its matches. Nevertheless, interest remained high. Andrew Thomas and Andrew Joyce went on to gain rugby blues at Oxford; the first-ever junior rugby tour (for the under-14 and under-15 teams) was organised to Worcester in 1982 - and, by 1985, far more boys were representing the school than ever before with no fewer than eight teams regularly playing on Saturdays. 'B' team fixtures had become a regular feature of the programme.

There is no doubt that, over the course of the century, Colston's had produced a number of boys with outstanding rugby talent. Henry Shrewring had played for England ten times between 1905 and 1907; William Johnston sixteen times from 1910; Tom Brown nine times from 1928; Alan Morley seven times between 1972 and 1975, plus a British Lions' tour in 1974 (also gaining the world record for the number of tries scored in first-class rugby - 479); and Austin Sheppard twice in 1981. Nevertheless, for a variety of reasons, the school 1st XV had never managed to become a major and lasting force in school rugby. This situation, however, was to change in a most dramatic manner during the 1990s.

In 1991, Mr Alan Martinovic became 1st XV coach (assisting the master-in-charge of rugby, Mr Peter Johnson) and immediately introduced new ideas on training and tactics, coupled with a much more ambitious vision for the development of rugby at school. Colston's became the first Bristol school to undertake a major overseas tour when, in 1991, seven matches were played in Australia, Fiji and Thailand. This was later followed by tours of South Africa in 1995 and Australia and New Zealand in 1997. The 1992 season proved to be important in the emergence of Colston's as a top rugby-playing school - the 1st XV remaining unbeaten in all its matches against local opposition and Richard Bryan becoming the first pupil to gain an England Under-16 cap. Another England schoolboy international, Duncan Bell, joined the school from outside in the same year - the first of many boys to do so, who were attracted by the quality of rugby on offer. By 2000, no fewer than

30 boys had been capped at Under-18 level for England, Wales and Scotland with several going on to play for their countries at a more senior level (Joe Ewens, for example, captained the England Under-18 side in 1996). In 2001, three Old Colstonians, Oliver Barkley, Alex Brown and Joe Ewens, were selected for the England tour of North America and one, Andrew Lloyd, for the Wales tour of Japan - two of them (Barkley and Lloyd) subsequently winning their full international caps.

Meanwhile, the 1st XV had gained enormous country-wide prestige through its performances in winning two major national competitions - the St Joseph's College National Schools' Festival in 1994, 1996, 1998 and 2001; and, of far greater significance, the *Daily Mail* Cup with its final at Twickenham. Colston's in fact, won the cup for a remarkable six years in succession (1995-2000), before they eventually withdrew from the competition having defeated some of the best sides in the country in the process. Largely as a result of this notable success, the England Schools' Rugby Union awarded Mr Martinovic a special trophy in

Richard Hunt bursting through with the ball in the semi-final of the Daily Mail Cup
against Hutton Grammar School in 1998.

recognition of his immense services to the game. Gradually the school had also been extending its fixture list to include some of the best schools in Wales and Ireland - and, in 2001, it took part in international schoolboy tournaments in Dubai and Bordeaux playing against teams from New Zealand, South Africa, France, Italy, Ireland and Zimbabwe. By 1996, a girls' rugby team had also been formed - a team, which two years later, had not only won an international tournament in the Oxford Sevens but had also provided four girls as members of the south-west and northern regional squad at under-16 level.

During this period, great benefit had been gained from the close relationship which had developed between Colston's and Bath Rugby Club, which had generously funded a number of sixth form rugby scholarships and equipped the new fitness rooms in 1999. A further boost had been given to the image of the sport by the arrival on the staff in 1994 of Mr Andy Robinson, an England international and British Lion, who remained at Colston's for two years. Subsequently coach to Bath Rugby Club, England and the British Lions, he helped to create 'a winning mentality'. There is no doubt that, over the course of a decade, Colston's had emerged in a most striking manner as the most successful rugby-playing school in the country. According to *The Times*, their fourth victory in the St Joseph's National Schools' Festival in 2001 'reiterated their pre-eminence in British schoolboy rugby'. This was of enormous importance to the general reputation of the school on a national level and its ability to recruit pupils from a wide area.

(viii) The Chapel

In 1971, an anonymous correspondent had written in *The Colstonian*: 'At the moment, chapel is a painful experience for many people, both the religious and the non-religious. The ideal would be a voluntary chapel with good attendance and real Christian worship'. As we have already seen, Mr King began the process of ending compulsory chapel in 1973 by reducing by half the number of Sundays when compulsory chapel would be held (see Chapter 11) and substituting voluntary services at 9.00 am on the other Sundays. Thereafter, between 1973 and 1987, successive chaplains did their best to maintain interest and involvement in the religious life of the school by inviting lively and well-known preachers (including Cliff Richard, General Sir Arthur Smith, the Bishop of Oxford and the future Bishop of Liverpool), establishing Christian Fellowship groups, using a Retreat House for meditation, organising 'House' chapel services (often led by Prefects) and raising considerable amounts of money for charities through sponsored activities. By 1987, mid-week chapel services were still being held on a daily basis, although

Fund raising for charity in 1985. The presentation of a cheque for £2045.95 by the Head Boy (Julian Daven-Thomas) to Mr Bob Woodward, Chairman of CLIC. (By courtesy of The Picture Company Ltd.)

the Chapel itself - in view of increased numbers - could only house the whole school with difficulty. At the same time, there were four or five compulsory services each term on Sundays, which parents were actively encouraged to attend (the Remembrance Day and Harvest Festival services proving particularly popular).

Outside the Chapel, the school was still involved in the two traditional November services - the Merchants' Charter Day Service (10th November) and the Colston Day Service (13th November). Although the traditional school procession behind the CCF and its band had been abandoned for both these services in 1969 (see Chapter 11), the school still attended the Charter Day Service *en masse*, having travelled there by coach. By the mid-1970s, however, the school was celebrating Colston's Day at Stapleton with a short service in the Chapel, a wreath-laying ceremony on Colston's statue in the Entrance Hall, a reading by the Head Prefect on the founding of the school and a prayer by the Chaplain. Nevertheless, the school continued to be represented at the official Colston Day Service in Bristol by the Headmaster with a group of Prefects and younger boys, who placed a wreath on Colston's statue in the city centre.

In 1988, important discussions took place over future policy concerning chapel and Sunday services. In view of the shortage of accommodation in the school's own chapel for mid-week services, the Headmaster opened negotiations with the Rector of Stapleton Church to explore the possibility of using the church for daily services. Agreement on this, however, proved impossible. Then, in September of that year, the governors endorsed the recommendation of the Headmaster (Mr Howarth) that compulsory attendance at Sunday church services should be abandoned. Taking into account the school's more recent status as a predominantly day school and the long distances travelled by pupils, it was felt that compulsion was no longer reasonable. By 1989, therefore, a new pattern of worship had developed. Daily chapel services continued as normal; each term began and ended with a church service; three mid-week services with sermons were also held each term in church; and a voluntary communion service was held on Sundays. The Prep School, however, decided to continue with its existing arrangements - namely a

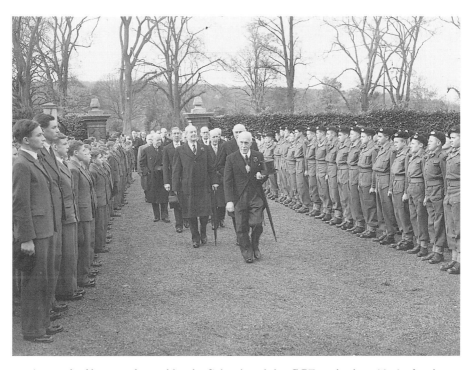

A guard of honour formed by the School and the CCF in the late 1940s for the Merchants arriving back at their new Hall after the Charter Day Service at Emmanuel Church, Clifton. (SMV Archive)

church service on the first Sunday of term and further compulsory services on two Sundays each term in church.

Two major steps forward were taken between 1999 and 2001 to benefit the religious life of the school. In 1999, the governors decided to pull down the old Chapel (which was now much too small for daily services) and to build a new hall, which would be used both as a concert hall and as a chapel. The Chatterton Hall (as it was named) was opened in the summer term in 2000. A year later, when the Rector of Stapleton moved to another parish, the governors reached an agreement with the Bishop that the new Rector should be employed partly by the parish (for two-thirds of his time) and partly as Assistant School Chaplain. It was hoped that this arrangement would also make possible the additional use of the church for chapel services several times each term.

The Revival of the Old Colstonians, 1946-2002

Having fallen into abeyance throughout the war period, the various branches of the Old Colstonians' Society gradually staged a revival in the years that followed. The year 1946 saw the resumption of both the annual dinner in Bristol and the dinner/dance of the Welsh Society in Cardiff; while 1948 heralded both the restart of the bi-monthly gatherings of the London Society at the Old Cock Tavern and the first stirrings of the Sports Club after nine years of inactivity. The next decade was to feature some memorable events, including the Centenary Dinner at the Royal Hotel in Bristol in 1953, which was attended by the Lord Mayor, the Duke of Beaufort and 161 guests; the Silver Jubilee Dinner of the London Society held at the De Vere Hotel in 1958; and the Diamond Jubilee Dinner of the same society in 1968. The Old Colstonian Guild also celebrated its 50th anniversary during the Commemoration Weekend in 1957, when it was calculated that over its history no fewer than 1213 Colstonians had been members, including 390 OCs who were still active and 80 boys who were then at the school. The Commemoration itself was well supported with 100 members sitting down to supper after the Old Colstonian service on the Saturday and 60 Old Boys attending the Guild's corporate communion on the Sunday morning.

Much has already been stated in the sections above about the generosity of the Old Colstonians towards the school through the provision of newly-levelled fields as a War Memorial in 1950, the organisation of a 250th Anniversary Appeal in 1960 (which made possible the new classroom block and the refurbishment of the main dormitory block), the renovation of the Chapel in 1967 as a memorial to Mr Snaith (according to Peter Mitchell, 1960-65, he had made it clear before his death that he 'did not want a window') and the establishment of a bursary fund by the London Society. This fund not only offered in 1958 a bursary of £100 a year for five years to a boarder (preferably the son or grandson of an Old Colstonian resident in the London area), but also in 1967 a scholarship of £100 (known as the London Scholarship) to a non-foundationer of Oxbridge potential to enable him to stay an extra year to take the examination; and in 1968 a grant of £120 per annum for the son of an Old Colstonian at 13 plus. In the same year, the Old Colstonian Society itself announced a bursary of £120 a year for the top candidate in the 13 plus examination.

By 1987, when the London Bursary Fund celebrated its 50th anniversary, almost £7,000 had been paid in bursaries to support a total of eleven pupils and a further £2,530 expended on the London Scholarships (shared between some forty pupils in all). The capital value of the fund had risen to £9,000, producing an annual income of over £1,300. Together these bursaries had represented an enormous boost to the school's meagre scholarship resources and their ability to attract intelligent boys from less affluent homes. It is hardly surprising, therefore, that Mr Snaith expressed his heartfelt gratitude to the Society at Prize Giving in 1960 by saying: 'If Edward Colston is the parent of the school, the Society may justly be called its foster parents'.

The school's success over many years in nurturing the potential of its brightest pupils was most vividly illustrated throughout this period by the achievements of a number of distinguished Old Colstonians - Sir Charles Colston, who was appointed President of Hoover in 1954; P. Matthias, who was elected Fellow and Director of Studies at Queen's College, Cambridge in 1955; F.A. Bishop, who became Principal Private Secretary to Mr Anthony Eden in 1959 and subsequently to Mr Harold Macmillan; H. Pitman, who was elected Fellow of St John's College, Cambridge in 1959; Ian MacDonald, who was appointed Queen's Counsel in Scotland in

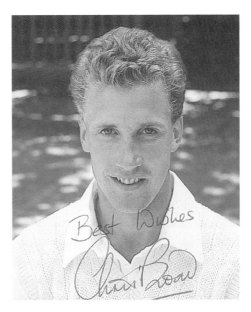

Chris Broad, Old Colstonian, who won 25 England caps for cricket from 1984, scoring six centuries in the process.

1964 and, as Lord Mayfield, Senator of the College of Justice in Scotland in 1981; and E.E. Rich, who was elected both Professor of Imperial History at Cambridge and Fellow of St Catharine's College in 1953 and who subsequently became a governor of the school in 1961. It is also worth recalling that, in 1967, when Professor Rich was President of the Senior Common Room at St Catharine's, Adrian Williams (who was at school between 1956 and 1964) was President of the Junior Common Room there.

Perhaps the most exciting development of the post-war years was the resurgence of the Sports Club. In 1948, a plot of nine acres at Mile Straight in Filton was offered by the Bishop Monk's Trust at a rent of £50 a year as a base for the club. After some hard work in 1950 to prevent flooding and to keep out the neighbouring cows, the ground was eventually ready for use. In fact a full fixture list for two teams (30 matches in all) had been drawn up for the 1950-51 season - the first games in fact to be played since the war. Facilities, however, remained somewhat spartan - as George Moore (1941-47) later recalled:

> I remember this time clearly. I was then a newcomer to the Club and not involved on the committee. Baths after the match on Saturdays were fun! The changing room was an old nissen hut. The ends had fallen out. Bathing was in four old bath tubs. Water was heated on two old army field stoves. This gave six inches of tepid water per tub shared by 7 or 8 husky young men. If anyone moved, the tub tipped over upsetting the water and the other contents on to the rough concrete floor. When bathing was over, the water was no disgrace to Weston-super-Mare. Normally nobody cleaned the tubs out until the following Saturday - by which time the contents had solidified and could be tipped out. The whole thing was more fun in the middle of winter with a north-east wind blowing and no lights.

Unsurprisingly, therefore, a decision was taken in 1952 to lay a concrete base and build a proper hut of concrete blocks and to install hot water fed from a new boiler. The most exciting moment, however, came in 1956 when the ground at Mile Straight was bought by the Old Colstonians for £2,122 - thus fulfilling their long-held ambition to possess a ground of their own. By 1958, the club was not only putting out three rugby teams, but had also revived the cricket section and the annual ball (held at the Grand Spa Hotel, Clifton). In addition, a social club had been formed with its main focus of interest (a bar) centred on the pavilion. Four years later, plans were made to raise at least £300 a year through bar profits, a weekly football pool and an annual fete to fund a new clubroom with a bar, tea room, ladies' room and refurbished changing rooms for 60 people. This was eventually opened in October

1977 by Bruce Hockin, the HTV News presenter, who had a boy at the school.

Blazer badges were awarded for playing a hundred games for the club - and tankards for two hundred! The club further illustrated its successful revival by organising an Easter tour of Devon and Cornwall in 1964, followed by a series of tours to France from 1975. In 1977, the Sports Club celebrated its 75th anniversary with a rugby match against Alan Morley's Invitation XV - and the news that it was raising no fewer than four rugby teams and three cricket teams (the 1st XI winning Division 4 of the Bristol and District League). Nor were these the only sporting interests catered for by the Club. 1971 had seen the launch of a thriving Golf Society, which went on to celebrate its silver jubilee in 1996.

Meanwhile, the Welsh Society had celebrated its 50th anniversary in 1975 by presenting the school with a clock for the teaching block, followed by two display cases in the next year. Although the Welsh Society itself had ceased to function by 1985, the generosity of the Old Colstonians towards the school continued unabated with the gift of an honours board for the Dining Hall (1979), a sophisticated music centre together with the school's first-ever computer (1980) and a number of musical instruments (1984). All this was in addition to the inauguration of a careers' counselling service in 1985, which later became a fully fledged Old Colstonians' Careers' Fair in 1993; and grants awarded to individual pupils for adventurous pursuits and other worthwhile projects. The latter, known as the Personal Initiative Enterprise (P.I.E.) Awards, were financed out of the Society's old bursary fund from 1979. Furthermore, in 1993, it arranged for a legacy of £20,000 from the widow of an Old Colstonian to be ear-marked for the refurbishment of an old physics laboratory (the M. Jenkins Memorial Laboratory).

Major changes to the annual programme of events were announced in 1984. In view of the fact that numbers attending the Commemoration Weekend in July had noticeably declined, it was decided to abandon the dinner, the chapel service and the Sunday communion of the Old Colstonians' Guild and to restrict activities to the traditional cricket and tennis matches against the school. The dinner itself was then amalgamated with the Society's annual dinner on 10th November, although - significantly - the venue was switched to the school. This proved to be an immediate success with no fewer than 180 attending the event in 1984.

The late 1980s and 1990s were to witness not only the continued growth of social activities (the annual Bristol versus London Clay Pigeon Challenge, treasure hunts and rounders tournaments), but also further reforms to the Society itself. The Old Colstonians' Charitable Trust was established in 1993; work was started by Mike Dymond on the Colston Collegiate Register in 1995; the Old Colstonians' Office was opened at the school in 1998, a year which also saw the first OC's Open Day; the first Lady President of the Society (Mrs Ann Miller, who was married to an OC and whose father, Dr C.L. Thresher, had served on the school staff) was elected in 1998; the Pupil Purchase Scheme was commenced in 1998, enabling parents to purchase future life membership for pupils on a termly basis; and the Society moved firmly into the age of modern technology by acquiring its own e-mail address in 1999 and website in 2000.

However, perhaps the most important development during these years concerned the Sports Club. After the Society had sold half an acre of its sports ground at Mile Straight in 1992 to the adjoining builders' merchants for £175,000, it began to consider the possibility of selling off the remainder for a large profit and moving to a new location. Although provisional planning permission for housing development on the site was refused in 1993, the idea remained firmly on the agenda until 1999 when an ambitious plan was agreed in conjunction with the school. In what was later styled The Pavilion Project, the Society agreed to develop the area known as The Arches into two changing rooms for use by the school and the old latrines at the end of The Arches into two more changing rooms for the OCs.

In return, the school sanctioned the conversion of the pavilion into a clubroom for the OCs with a social/bar area, committee room and office. This enabled not only the Old Colstonians' Society to have a base within the school, but also the Old Colstonians' Rugby Club to move to the school in 2001 (just in time for the celebration of its centenary in the following year) and thus to make the school's extensive sporting facilities available to members of both sexes. The plan was then to sell off about one-third of the Mile Straight ground for housing development and invest some of the proceeds into improving the remainder as a first-rate sports field. This could then be rented out to various sports clubs including the Bohemians' Cricket Club, which had amalgamated with the Old Colstonians' Cricket Club in 1987.

Sources used in Chapter 12

Society of Merchant Venturers' Archive:
    Colston Hospital Trust:
        Governors' Minutes, 1945-1992
        Minutes of Colston Collegiate Governors Ltd, 1993-2001
        Finance Committee Minutes, 1945-2001
        Education Committee Minutes. 1982-2001

Headmasters' Reports, 1946-2001
The Colstonian, 1946-1994
School Ties (the termly newsletter), 1988-2001
Cribsheet (The Old Colstonians' Newsletter), 1986-2001
Personal interviews and written submissions (as acknowledged in the
    text)

MISCHIEF AND LEISURE, 1959-66

Bill Welland *(Old Colstonian, 1959-66)*

Challenge Bowl points in cross-country running were influenced by the number of House members reaching the 'standard' time of, I believe, 35 minutes for 'The Five'. Once it became clear that you were going to miss that time, the run became still harder to bear so, as a House Prefect and Third Year Sixth Former, I decided to miss out part of my run when the opportunity arose. Unfortunately, my lead was followed by perhaps a dozen younger boys and, still more unfortunately, I was as a result twice overtaken by the same School Prefect (who, in fairness to him, had already told me what would happen to anyone he caught taking a short cut). The result was that we were summoned by the Headmaster (Mr Gibbs) and sentenced to an afternoon's gardening in the ploughed field that was to become his garden. My Housemaster (Mr Brown) was appalled that such a breach of trust by a House Prefect could be treated so lightly!

When the Headmaster's study overlooked the Parade, the school's front door bell rang in his secretary's office. One of our number, whom we shall call by Mr Campbell's name for him (Fisher-Woosher) noticed that the bell-wire ran through Q room (then the Roundway common room), and was apparently sufficiently knowledgeable about electrical things to realise that this was low-voltage cable. He was able to demonstrate that, if an optical pin was inserted into each of the wires, and the two pins were then touched together, the Headmaster's secretary could be seen (through the open door of Q room) walking briskly to the front door and, shortly afterwards, returning with an annoyed expression on her face!

The early days of rock'n'roll coincided with the arrival of the transistor radio and, though radios were forbidden (except, I believe, in Prefects' studies), these were small enough to be easily hidden, for example, in hollowed-out books. Consequently there was general familiarity with the pop music of the moment (especially that played on Radio Luxembourg between 10.00 and 10.30 pm). The appearance of the new Music Room in the autumn of 1960 - which had its own, if ancient, radiogram - led to the appearance of a lunchtime pop music club, where members could listen to *Runaway* (and whatever else had been purchased with their membership fees) in the half-hour or so between lunch and resumption of classes. Eventually this came to Mr Snaith's ears and he drew the not unreasonable conclusion that the need for ever more new records might easily lead to membership fees being extracted under duress. That was the end of that.

After the morning celebrations of November 10th and 13th, school was given a half holiday and passes were available. However, these were to permit travel to the only two authorised destinations: the Zoo and the Museum. A number of masters, meanwhile, were rumoured to be spending the afternoon on watch outside the cinemas in case any boy should dare to flout the rules.

The timetable meant that almost everyone was in a class almost all of school hours, but occasionally 'private study' had been allocated where no suitable teacher was available. I found that the most effective way of walking round the school unimpeded during these times was to carry a single sheet of paper. Anyone carrying nothing was clearly up to no good; a pile of books meant that you were late for a lesson; but a single sheet of paper could only be a message being carried from one staff member to another - so you could pass unchallenged!

Despite the reputation which single sex public schools seem to hold with the general public, sexual malpractice seemed a rarity in the '60s - and I am only aware of two boys who were accused of, and expelled for, taking an unnatural interest in their fellows. The small bedroom in sick bay (overlooking the Parade) was used as their 'condemned cell', where they awaited collection for the last time.

CHAPTER 13

Years of Rising Optimism, 1975-2002

We are entering a period of intense competition amongst independent schools and it must be our aim to continue to raise our standards - in the facilities offered by the school, in the academic performance of the boys, in their general bearing, in societies and on the games field. (Mr Searle, Headmaster, to the Governors in January 1976)

Anticipating change and managing change is something that this school has had to do, and I believe it has done so successfully. (Mr Crawford, Headmaster, Prize Giving in 2001)

Growth of the Prep and the Lower School, 1966-2002

Although the Prep School had been given a separate identity in September 1961, it continued to enjoy a close relationship with the Upper School - sharing teachers in art, music, woodwork and physical training; and combining for major concerts and services. Nevertheless, it quickly developed a life of its own. The cub pack (the 68th Bristol, Colston's School), which had been established in 1958, flourished; soccer, cricket and rugby teams were formed; Sports Days and Prize Givings arranged; a choir organised and a nativity play produced as an annual event.

However, it was with the arrival of Mr Geoffrey Jameson as Headmaster in September 1963 that the Prep really developed into a vibrant and dynamic community. A man of infectious enthusiasm and drive, he quickly set about the task of involving all the boys in extra curricular life. He immediately established a House system for sports competitions, dividing the school into Stapleton and Court Houses for boarders and Merchants and Venturers Houses for day boys. Anxious also to see as many boys as possible taking part in musical activities, he introduced compulsory violin lessons for all first formers, set up informal instrumental groups, organised lunchtime concerts and and established both the Carol Service and the Christmas Concert as regular events. The Prep choir gave a recital in the Lord Mayor's Chapel in Bristol in 1965, while in July of that year a major open air concert was

Prep School boys working on painting and pottery in the Upper School's Art Room in the late 1960s. (SMV Archive)

staged for parents. It was, however, so windy that 'the music racks not only needed clothes pegs to hold their precious sheets, but even boulders to which they could be tethered'. By 1967, dramatic productions, as well as plays performed by glove puppets, were regular items in the calendar - including the staging of *Joseph and the Amazing Technicolour Dreamcoat* in 1974.

Sport, too, was immensely popular and increasingly successful, especially after the introduction of a more organised coaching policy in conjunction with the Upper School (see Chapter 12). The years 1969 and 1970 were something of golden years for the first teams, with the cricketers enjoying their 'most successful season ever', the footballers winning 7 out of their 8 matches played and the hockey players being unbeaten in all 1st and 2nd XI games. Indeed, the school had a reputation as 'the best Prep side in the West' for hockey. Mr Jameson, however, believed that sport should be played for enjoyment and was highly critical in 1973 'of the present-day attitude of winning games at all costs and the animosity thus created between schools by such an approach of mind'. He equally deplored, in the following year, 'the influence of the first-class game [in rugby], where roughness and toughness had infiltrated down to Prep school level'. He therefore introduced plenty of other options - fives, judo, swimming and tennis.

He also placed a great deal of stress on outdoor activities and adventurous pursuits. A scout troop, which was formed in 1964 to supplement the cubs complete with tents and equipment, was given its own headquarters at school in 1971 when two second-hand huts were erected on site. In the same year, 28 scouts camped on Mr Densham's farm in Publow and were surprised not only by his frequent visits, but also by the fact 'that any governor could be so human'. [Mr Jameson was later awarded the Chief Scout's Medal of Merit for his outstanding contribution to Scouting.] For other boys, caving became a particularly popular activity with instruction by an Old Colstonian - as did water sports on Chew Valley Lake, thanks to four dinghies and six canoes purchased by the Prep School Parents' Society, which Mr Jameson had established in 1969. Holiday expeditions of various kinds were also organised on bicycles, on canal barges (in both Oxfordshire and Holland) and by bus (to see Concorde or to inspect IBM computers). Practical arrangements for all these activities were made easier from 1967, when an old 18-seater minibus was bought from the Upper School.

The Parents' Society at work on renovating the cottage at Cryn Fryn in the early 1970s. (Photograph by John Wilson-Smith)

One of the most important advances, however, came in 1970 with the purchase of a disused farmhouse with adjoining land at Cryn Fryn in the Wye Valley. After complex negotiations lasting three years, the governors paid £1,100 out of capital drawn from the F.A. Clark Trust - although the parents of a special place boy were 'so pleased with the education and progress of their son' that they gave the equivalent of one term's fees (£100) towards the purchase. Thereafter the house was constantly improved by further gifts and voluntary work. With the farmer's permission, it had in fact already been in frequent use since 1967 as an adventure centre with small groups of staff and boys making regular visits. It was to prove both popular and invaluable as a base, thanks in no small measure to the commitment and energetic lead provided by Mr Keith Watts, who regularly took trips to the cottage over many years after his arrival on the staff in 1974.

As numbers grew in the Prep (see page 296), so it became necessary to add to the facilities which had already been provided in the years to 1965. In spite of their self-imposed 'freeze' on all new development, therefore, the governors eventually agreed to erect (in 1969) a temporary building as a dining area for 140 boys (paid for again out of the F.A. Clark bequest); and, in 1972, to install three second-hand terrapins on the roof of the classroom block out of the Charles Colston gift. Mr Jameson was equally keen to promote the school's academic progress, the Nuffield Science Course being introduced in 1966 and a 'scholarship class' being established in the same year for boys aiming at the Common Entrance Examination. All these successes and activities of the Prep were faithfully recorded each year - at first (from 1966) in a coloured pull-out section of *The Colstonian* magazine and later (from 1972) in its own publication, *The Young Colstonian*.

After eleven years of distinguished service, Mr Jameson left Colston's in 1974 to become Headmaster of Swanbourne House, Bletchley. He was succeeded in September of that year by Mr Michael Kefford, who was Housemaster at the Royal Russell School, Croydon. The new Headmaster continued the development of the Prep on much the same lines. Sport was encouraged (the 1975 rugby team emerging as 'one of the best ever' with 8 wins out of 11 matches played - and both squash and fives gaining popularity on the new courts); a wide range of activities put into operation (including model aeroplanes, fencing, judo, scouts, cubs, sailing and canoeing); skiing trips to the Dolomites started; drama developed (including a performance of *The Thwarting of Baron Boligrew* in 1976, which was attended by 1,200 people over the course of a week); music expanded (with an enlarged choir, an orchestra and a brass band) and special events organised (such as the school's involvement in a Christmas broadcast to the antipodes in 1977).

The unbeaten 1978 cricket team. Warren Smith (2nd from the left on the back row) and Lawson Roll (seated on the far right) both went on to play for Gloucestershire at senior level. (Lower School collection)

According to Mr Kefford's notes in *The Colstonian*, that year was the year 'of white rabbits and yo-yos, marbles and conkers'. Everything, however, was now on a much grander scale. 'Whereas before boys were content to hold a few marbles in a sweaty hand or ink-stained pocket, now modernity demands that you should own 200 or more to achieve respectability'. The following year (1978) in fact saw everything in the school performed on a much grander scale. The Prep celebrated its Silver Jubilee by arranging a Jubilee Exhibition at school, building a float for the annual Bristol procession, arranging a Jubilee Eisteddfod (featuring twenty events from public speaking to cake baking) and staging a production of *Tom Sawyer*.

Meanwhile, the popularity of the Prep was reflected in its continued numerical growth. Whereas in 1961 there had been 124 boys in the school, by 1973 this total had grown to 216. Although numbers declined slightly to 195 in 1977 (reflecting a national trend), they recovered dramatically thereafter to reach 244 by 1980. It is worth noting, however, that boarders only accounted for 27% of this total, dropping to

16% by 1987. The Headmaster and governors considered various methods of maintaining recruitment and, in 1976, even considered admitting girls for the four years between 7+ and 11+. Two new policies, however, were successfully adopted - the introduction in 1978 of a 'dyslexia facility' (the first in a Bristol school), which by 1983 was assisting 16 pupils; and the establishment of a Pre-Prep for the 4-7 age group in 1986 under its own Head, Mrs Elizabeth Coatsworth.

This rise in numbers and extension of age groups inevitably put pressure on existing facilities - a problem which the governors readily tackled. In 1977, a new science building was opened, generously equipped from funds raised by the Parents' Society and a pedestrian crossing was installed on the busy main road to cater for increased movements to the sports facilities; in 1980, an additional classroom was authorised to adjoin the main block and, in 1986, an assembly hall with five adjacent classrooms was built as part of the appeal (see below). 1988 saw the opening of a new unit with toilets, changing rooms and showers below and classroom above to house the Pre-Prep; the establishment of a computer room with 12 Amstrad computers; and the

The opening of the new classroom block in 1986 by Sir John Wills, Master of the Society of Merchant Venturers, seen here with (from the left) *Alastair Harwood (Head Boy), Mr John Cross (Headmaster of the Prep) and Mrs John Spielman (wife of the former Chairman of Governors). (SMV Archive)*

creation of a newly-furnished art department.

The 1980s witnessed two changes in Headmastership. Mr Kefford left in 1983, after serving nine years. His successor, Mr John Cross, remained at Colston's for just four years until 1987, when he returned to the Brecon School, Amersham as Headmaster. He was followed by Mr John Aveyard, a Cambridge graduate, talented sportsman and accomplished organist, who had been Director of Music and Housemaster at Rossall School, Fleetwood. It is perhaps not surprising, therefore, that music was given some prominence in the years that followed, the Prep School choir singing in the cathedrals at Llandaff, Brecon, Bristol and Wells and a home-grown musical, *Change of Opinion*, being produced in 1990.

Sport remained a popular activity, the rugby team scoring over 400 points in twelve victories in 1988 and winning the Cranleigh Schools' Sevens Tournament in 1990. Individual successes abounded - Paul Martin in 1989 and James Frost in 1990 each won the singles title at the IAPS national tennis tournament at Chiswick; numerous boys represented either Avon or Gloucestershire at cricket, rugby and hockey; six boys won their athletic events at the south-west area Prep Schools Championships in 1991, progressing to the national in consequence; and Roland Ward represented the West of England in under-14 hockey in 1990. Extra-curricular life was by no means limited to music and sport. By 1991, no fewer than 22 activities were on offer to boys (and, by then, to girls), including cookery, ballet, riding and calligraphy. Inside the classroom, Mr Aveyard welcomed the new National Curriculum, advising parents in 1989 that pupils at Colston's would eventually take part in official assessments at the ages of 7, 11 and 14.

Nevertheless, in spite of these encouraging signs of life and vigour within the school, recruitment of pupils into the 7-11 age group was giving cause for concern, while the number of boarders had slumped from 68 in 1982 to just 14 ten years later. The reasons for this (which included a national decline in boarding, a country-wide recession and fierce competition within the Bristol area) are examined later in this chapter. The merger with The Collegiate School (a girls' school) in September 1991, however, gave the school a welcome, though temporary boost, increasing its total population to 346. As a result, the new nursery of three-year olds, which was housed in a conversion of the old dining room, was completely full with 35 children; the Pre-Prep (4-7 years) contained 71 pupils (55 boys and 16 girls), the Lower School (7-11 years) 112 (97 boys and 15 girls) and the Middle School (11-13 years) 128 (110 boys and 18 girls). The merger coincided with the conversion of three classrooms into a science and technology unit. It also witnessed the removal of the Middle School onto the Upper School

Colston's Prep School competing in the Avon Schools' Regatta on Chew Valley Lake in 1992. (Photograph by John Wilson-Smith)

campus, whilst remaining under the control of the Prep School Headmaster (see below).

Mr Aveyard left in the summer of 1993 to pursue his musical interests. A believer in firm discipline, the Christian basis for education, the boarding school ethic and high standards in every aspect of school life, he had seen the school through a difficult period of change. His successor inherited one further fundamental reform, which became effective from September 1993. The Middle School now became part of an 11-18 secondary unit (with its main entry at 11+) under the Upper School's Headmaster, leaving the newly-styled 'Head of Lower School' to be responsible for pupils in the 3-11 age range. The Prep School as such had therefore ceased to exist - a recognition of the fact that Colston's had in reality become a day school with a small boarding house attached. The man appointed to this post from January 1994 was Mr Graham Phillips, a graduate of Southampton University, former Headmaster of Lawrence House School in St Anne's and an England

Trialist at rugby.

The task facing Mr Phillips was not an easy one. Morale among both staff and parents had been affected by the rapidity of change brought about by the merger, the restructuring and the change of Head. A period of stability was therefore a priority. Alongside this was an urgent need to halt the decline in numbers which, by 1993, had become serious. Whereas in 1991, the combined total of pupils in the 3-11 age groups had been 218, two years later it had dropped to 164. The story of the next eight years, however, was the story of a most remarkable recovery. This was brought about partly through a dynamic whole-school recruitment campaign centred on a newly-styled Open Day (see below) and partly by specific policies adopted in the Lower School to raise its profile in the locality and to forge closer links with parents. In consequence, total numbers rose steadily each year (193, 220, 228, 240, 251, 263) to reach a new peak of 281 in 2001.

High among the objectives of Mr Phillips was to raise academic standards and to restructure the curriculum. Subject based teaching was therefore introduced for all pupils from the age of seven; children were setted according to ability in mathematics and English in the top two years of the school; staff were appointed to be responsible for particular areas of the curriculum and to familiarise parents with what was involved at specially-arranged meetings; the profile of the scholarships on offer at 7+ and 9+ was raised; and an 11+ transfer examination was introduced for the first time. The modernisation of the curriculum was greatly assisted through the establishment of a design and technology classroom in what had been the old scout hut (1998); the equipment of a new computer room (2000); and the provision of 12 electronic keyboards for the music room (a gift from the Parents' Society in 2001).

The performing arts again became an important ingredient of the all-round education which the Lower School sought to offer. The choir and wind band grew in strength from 1998, the choir participating in the IAPS Millennium Concert in Exeter Cathedral in 2000; the school regularly took part in the Kingswood Arts Festival; and enthusiastic, large casts were involved in the annual school play, which ranged from *Voyage of the Dawn Treader* (1996) to *Voyage of the Jumblies* (1998) and *Captain Blackboot and the Wallamgrumba* (2001). Horizons were extended by regular ski trips to the continent and visits to Normandy - not to mention frequent camps and adventurous activities. However, pupils were also given the opportunity to show their concern for others through a large-scale expansion of fund-raising activities to raise money for the needy in Kosovo and The Gambia as well as for a variety of charities, including Mencap, NSPCC and CLIC (which had been founded in memory of Robert Woodward, who had died while still a pupil at

Robert Channon in action on the slopes during the school's ski trip to Notre Dame, France, in 2000. (Lower School collection)

Colston's Prep). The 'Walk to Wells' in aid of the *Save the Children* fund also became a regular feature in the annual programme.

The school, which continued to excel in a whole range of sports, encouraged maximum involvement in physical activity (witnessed by the occasion in 1994, when the entire school took part in a hockey match against King Edward's School, Bath). There were regular sports tours to Jersey for soccer and rugby; and inter-schools tournaments in netball, rugby and cricket (sometimes hosted by Colston's). The year 1999 proved to be a particularly outstanding one for the school with the girls' netball team winning a tournament held at Colston's; the boys' hockey team winning all but one of its matches; the soccer team reaching the semi-final of the Coronation Cup; four boys representing their respective counties at cricket or swimming; one pupil becoming Avon under-9 tennis champion - and, most praiseworthy of all, the under-11 rugby team winning in the *Daily Telegraph* National Prep Schools' Championship competition at Harrow School. This feat was almost matched in 1999 by the under-9 team, who ended as runners-up in a similar competition.

By 2002, the Lower School had been revived in numerical strength, morale, community life and academic achievement - a fact emphasised by the highly favourable reports received after the ISJC (the Independent Schools' Joint Council) inspection of the Lower School in 1995 and the OFSTED inspection report of the Nursery in 1999. Its growth in reputation locally and nationally owed much to the clear and calm leadership provided by Mr Phillips, whose high standards and good-humoured approach had produced such a positive response from

Mr Graham Phillips, Head of the Lower School, taking part in a Scottish theme day in aid of 'Children in Need' on St Andrew's Day, 2001.
(Photograph by George Phillips)

parents, pupils and staff. The level of activity and enthusiasm within the school was reflected annually in the publication of *The Young Colstonian* and the Headmaster's lively and informative Prize Giving speech.

The Searle Years, 1975-1988

When Mr Graham Searle took up the post of Headmaster of the Upper School in the summer term of 1975, he was faced with a number of problems - some of which were acute. There was, for instance, a general unease and lack of confidence within the community, brought about partly by frequent changes in headship over the previous decade and partly by strained relationships between the Upper School and the Prep. Overall numbers within the school were not in a healthy state and recruitment was proving difficult - in 1976, for instance, only 18 boys applied for the Foundation Scholarship examination (including 8 from Colston's Prep). The fact was that Bristol was a highly competitive area for independent schools, particularly after the withdrawal of the direct grant by the government in 1976. This immediately resulted in a lowering of entry standards by some of those schools, which were now forced to rely more heavily on a fee-paying entry - thus competing for the sort of boys who would previously have gained entry to Colston's. Furthermore, although the school's finances were now on a much stronger footing (the 1975/76 accounts showed an operating surplus of £38,697 and a further £80,000 on deposit), they were under constant pressure from major salary awards for teachers (particularly the Houghton Award of 1974 and the Clegg Comparability Award of 1980) and roaring inflation (which stood at 25% in 1975). This situation resulted in massive increases in fees (20% in 1975, 15% in 1976 etc), which was a further deterrent to recruitment.

There were other worrying aspects which confronted the new headmaster. Although the Governors had invested heavily in new buildings during the period 1950-1965, maintenance of the fabric (which was always costly) had been so neglected that the site appeared somewhat scruffy and uninviting. Conditions within the boarding houses were far from ideal with a distinct lack of study bedrooms and an abundance of old-fashioned furniture, including beds. There was also an urgent need to expand sports facilities, which (apart from the school's fine games fields) seriously lagged behind those provided locally by comparable establishments.

Of even greater concern, however, was the continuing mediocrity of the school's academic performance - a fact which repeatedly undermined its ambition to become part of the Headmasters' Conference (HMC). Although the results at O level and A level were quite good for boys at

The staff in the mid-1970s - a drawing by John Paice (Head of Art), who is seen on the right sitting on the window ledge. Mr Graham Searle (Headmaster) is just inside the door talking to Mr John Campbell (former Second Master) with Mr Donald Cartwright (Second Master) in the check jacket behind. (By courtesy of John Paice)

the top of each year group, they were noticeably weak for the remainder. This was partly due to the shortage of really able pupils, which a more competitive entry would have produced, and partly due to the curriculum, which was much too rigid and failed to offer appropriate options for the less able. The sixth form in consequence was always far too small in size (with usually no more than 50 or 60 in total), because many fifth formers failed to qualify for entry with a minimum of five O level passes, while others joined the exodus to further education colleges. 'The increase in numbers in the sixth form', stated the Headmaster to the Governors in 1976, 'is of crucial importance to the future of the school'.

Mr Searle was also concerned about the lack of quality in the range of extra-curricular activities and, especially, about the apparent divisions between sporting and cultural pursuits. In October 1976, he outlined to Governors his policy on this - even though he was a keen games player himself. 'I have attempted to promote the development of a wide range of activities in the cultural field to provide outlet and interest for all types of boy. It has been my aim to bridge the gap between sporting and cultural activities and to make boys realise that the two are not incompatible. Only when we have managed to do this shall I feel that we are producing boys of a properly balanced outlook'. (See Chapter 12 for his success in developing this policy)

Faced by all these problems, the Headmaster quickly drew up a detailed plan of action with the energetic assistance of the Bursar, Lieutenant Colonel R.F. Alston (until his retirement in 1977), and wholehearted support of the Chairman of Governors, Mr Jack Clarke. Described later by Mr Searle as 'a wonderful man, who loved the school dearly', Mr Clarke (by the time of his death in 1983) had been a governor for thirty years and Chairman for twenty. Within two years of Mr Searle's arrival, the school had been given a major face-lift with a comprehensive programme of redecoration and repair, the refurbishment of common rooms and dormitories, the re-wiring of large areas of the site, the fitting of new pipes in the science block and the purchase of new equipment for the maintenance of the grounds.

By February 1977, therefore, a delighted Headmaster was able to inform the governors that 'there are now no areas to which I will not happily take a parent'. Determined that this progress should be maintained, the governors thereafter adopted a policy of progressive improvement and upgrading - including a regular programme of redecoration, the renovation of the fives courts, the installation of a new fire precaution scheme (1978), the heating of the swimming pool (1979) and the creation of three new all-weather cricket nets. To assist in this on-going programme of development on all fronts, they established in December 1981 two sub-committees - one responsible to them for building developments and the other for educational policy.

Meanwhile in January 1976, the Headmaster had produced a list for the governors of seven projects to be tabled for future consideration as a way of extending and improving the school's resources. These consisted of the refurbishment of the kitchens, the improvement of stage equipment, the extension of the Day Block and the building of four new facilities - squash courts, an all-weather hockey pitch, an assembly hall for drama and concerts and a sports hall. An immediate start was made in 1976 to the improvement of the stage and kitchen areas (the latter benefiting from redecoration and better ventilation prior to a major refurbishment in 1982 costing £92,000). The two Day Houses (King's and Dolphin) were then provided with additional accommodation in 1979 when an extension was made to the original building at a cost of £24,000. Four squash courts with their own changing rooms were completed in September 1978 for a sum of £72,000 in the area between the five courts and the tennis courts - and a squash club for outside members formed as a way of financing their maintenance. By March 1980, the club, which had already reached its maximum membership of 372, was producing an annual turnover of £10,000 (although it has to be said, that membership had slumped to 124 by 1988). The next major project, an all-weather shale hockey pitch, was constructed for use in 1985 at a cost of £38,500.

At this stage in the development programme, the governors readily acknowledged the fact that the remaining targets could not possibly be financed without additional resources raised through an appeal. It was therefore decided to launch such an appeal, directed by a professional organiser, in January 1985 to coincide with the 275th anniversary of the school's foundation. It was planned that the target figure of £275,000, supplemented by money from budget surpluses, would achieve six main developments - an assembly hall and five adjoining classrooms for the Prep; a sports hall; the conversion of the gymnasium into a concert hall/theatre; the conversion of a classroom into an electronics laboratory; four new classrooms for the Upper School; and the establishment of a bursary fund.

The appeal was an immediate success. By March 1985, £200,000 had already been raised; by September, the figure totalled £273,000 and the overall target had been increased to £325,000; by March 1986, the revised figure had also been passed. This fine achievement was due in

A cheque for £50,000 is presented by the Society of Merchant Venturers as the lead donation for the 1985 Appeal. Seen here, from the left, are Mr Graham Searle (Headmaster), Mr David T. Quilter (Master of the Society), Mr John Spielman (Chairman of Governors), Mr John Cross (Headmaster of the Prep School) and Mr Bernard Ashford (Appeal Director). (SMV Archive)

part to the generosity of the Society of Merchant Venturers (which gave £50,000 as the lead donation), the Old Colstonians (£5,000) and a number of individuals - including one anonymous Old Colstonian, who expressed a wish to repay the school for the seven years' free education he had received during the 1930s. Scaled up to the modern value of a boarding place, he calculated that his debt amounted to more than £21,000.

It was at this moment, too, that Colston's benefited from the extraordinary generosity of a Bristol millionaire businessman, Mr John James. At the outset of the appeal, he had already pledged to donate an annual sum of £1,000 to fund a research prize for sixth formers. He subsequently invited the Headmaster to his office to discuss the progress of the appeal (then standing at £225,000) and immediately offered to give £100,000 in ten yearly instalments to the bursary fund. This wonderful gesture enabled the school to establish in 1986 four new scholarships for 9+ pupils either already in or entering the Prep. It also meant that the sixth target of the appeal - the establishment of a bursary fund - had now been achieved, thus making it possible for all other money raised to be donated to the outstanding building projects. The Chairman of Governors, Mr John Spielman (who had succeeded Mr Jack Clarke in 1983), told the governors that Mr James's gift 'had been solely due to the efforts of Headmaster Searle'. In 1988, Mr James increased his annual bursary donation from £10,000 to £20,000.

The first appeal building project - a two-story block containing an assembly hall and five classrooms for the Prep and costing £235,000 - was opened in January 1986 by the Lord Lieutenant of Avon, Sir John Wills (who was also Master of the Society). This was followed in September of that year by a new sports hall for the Upper School (£215,000), which was opened by Mr John James. Having spent heavily on these two items, the governors understandably paused for a while before pressing on to achieve the two major appeal targets which remained - the building of two full-size classrooms and four smaller sixth form rooms (£300,000), which were opened in January 1990 (Mr Searle, who had by then resigned as Headmaster, having returned in the previous October to cut the first sod on site); and the conversion of the old gymnasium into a concert hall/theatre (£300,000), which was opened in February 1992. It should also be noted that, amid all these large-scale developments, the Parents' Societies in the two schools had continued to raise money in a most energetic manner through a wide range of social activities and sales - money which was dedicated to ambitious projects such as the heating of the swimming pool in 1979 and the provision of a multi-gym in 1987.

While dramatic progress was being made with all these new facilities

Boys at work in the workshop in the 1970s. (SMV Archive)

(vitally important in themselves for the marketing of the school and the recruitment of pupils), the Headmaster was also giving his attention to the need to improve academic performance. During his very first term in 1975, he had been asked by the governors to consider 'the Cartwright Plan', which had been drawn up by Mr Donald Cartwright, the Second Master. The idea was to establish a Sixth Form House by taking all sixth formers (day boys and boarders) out of their original Houses and placing them in a more adult and congenial atmosphere with their own studies or study bedrooms. It was hoped that this would tempt more fifth formers to stay on at Colston's as well as attracting new pupils to join the school from outside. In spite of a great deal of internal opposition to the scheme, Mr Searle successfully steered the plan through to adoption. Based on the old Roundway House, the new Sixth Form House opened in September 1975.

Another urgent reform witnessed the complete revision of the curriculum for the 13 to 16 age group in 1976. The Headmaster's aim was to improve the quality of examination performance of the weaker boys by increasing the choice of subjects and introducing setting instead of the more rigid streaming. Music, art and divinity therefore became new O level options (with technical drawing added in 1978); these subjects, together with woodwork, were also made available to A form boys, so that the ablest and the less able worked together - thus improving the morale of the latter; and all subjects were setted across the B and C forms, so that a boy would not be confined to working in one form only. 'I hope', said Mr Searle, 'that this will give opportunities to weak boys who have strength in one or two subjects only and will decrease the C form mentality which I have seen in the past'.

There is no doubt that these changes, together with increased expectation and dedicated teaching, succeeded in bringing about a substantial improvement in O level performance. In 1975, the O level pass rate had been a disappointing 66%; while in the following year, although boys in the A form had averaged seven passes each, those in the B form had only managed four (and had thus failed to qualify for sixth form entry). In 1978, however, A form pupils had improved on average to eight passes each and B formers to six. In this connection, it was perhaps significant that one of the new subjects - art - had secured an 88% pass rate. 'These results must rank amongst the best achieved at the school', claimed the Headmaster. Two years later, he again praised 'the best set of O level results in the school's history', while at the same time delighting in the knowledge that the sixth form had increased in size to eighty.

Meanwhile, attention had also been given to the development of the sixth form itself, against the background of the new Sixth Form House. In 1976, in an attempt to attract boys of a high academic standard into the sixth form from outside, two day boy scholarships had been established. A boost of this kind was certainly needed, because in 1975 the A level pass rate had been a dismal 69%. However, with improved O level results and the consequent increase in sixth form numbers, the situation quickly improved. By 1980, the A level pass rate had increased to 81% with 25 boys going to university and 8 to polytechnic; by 1983, it had improved further to 85% with 34 out of the 37 candidates passing in at least two subjects; and by 1987, the figure stood at 87%. During these twelve years, a total of 22 pupils had also succeeded in gaining places at Oxford or Cambridge. Sixth form numbers had been further bolstered by a decision in 1983 to admit girls. The Headmaster, who had first mooted the idea in 1978, recommended the admission of 12 girls for each of the two A level years. Recruitment, however, proved to be disappointingly slow with just six girls (3 boarders and 3 day girls) recruited into the lower sixth in September 1984. Two years later, the total number of girls in the sixth form had risen to sixteen.

The process of recruitment into the sixth form and the motivation of pupils to proceed to university, had been partly aided by the great attention paid to individuals in helping them to examine various options for higher education and careers. A structured careers programme was set in place for fifth formers and above, which included visits to universities and major employers, films, lectures and personal interviews conducted by the Independent Schools' Careers Organisation (ISCO), which by 1983 included computer-based testing. The sixth form lectures on Fridays, which had been started by Mr King, were continued and extended, introducing boys to the experiences of a wide range of eminent speakers. In 1985, an Understanding Industry Course was organised for the lower sixth and an advanced reading programme for the middle school to help them to become more efficient in academic work. One further service was offered to sixth formers immediately following the publication of A level results. This proved to be of enormous value. Those who had not quite achieved their grades for university entry were

Prize Giving in 1984. Seated behind the table from the left are Mr Christopher Thomas (Master of the Society), Mr Duke Hussey (Chairman of the BBC) and Mr John Spielman (Chairman of Governors) - with Mr Graham Searle presenting the Headmaster's Report. (SMV Archive)

given individual help and advice in applying for other universities and courses in the 'clearing house' operation - many of them gaining places in consequence.

As a result of the increasing and visible success of the school on so many fronts, numbers in the Upper School increased in a most dramatic manner. When Mr Searle arrived in 1975, he inherited a total of 277 pupils (including 139 boarders and 138 day boys; by February 1977, this figure had slumped to 270. Then suddenly the tide turned. By 1978, the total had reached 298, including a large increase in day boys to 171; by 1987, it had grown to 341 with a sixth form of one hundred. There were a number of additional factors at work to explain this increase, quite apart from the introduction of girls and a growing dissatisfaction with education in the state sector. The Headmaster had worked hard on publicity, inviting Prep school heads to look round the school, improving the school's advertising programme, introducing a new prospectus and, from 1978, taking part in the annual exhibition organised in Bristol by the Independent Schools' Information Service. Of greater importance, however, was the cordial relationship which developed between Mr Searle and Mr Kefford, the Headmaster of Colston's Prep. Parents of boys at the top of the Prep were carefully cultivated through invitations to tour round the Upper School. However, it was the success of the Prep School in boosting its own numbers during this period which contributed in great measure to the success of the Upper School. Against the national trend, the roll (which had slumped to 195 by 1977) had risen to 233 by 1979.

This encouraging situation helped to ensure a substantial basis for Upper School recruitment over the coming years - just as the Conservative government's invitation to the school to join the new Assisted Places Scheme in 1981 provided a welcome opportunity to enlist able pupils from lower-income families. Colston's was offered a total of 20 such places each year (eight at 11+, seven at 13+ and five at sixth form level), which were funded by the government with parents making contributions on a sliding scale based on income. The invitation was itself the fruit of the school's increasingly successful examination results - as was the Headmaster's election in 1984 to the Headmasters' Conference (a group of some 220 Headmasters from the country's leading independent schools). Only six years earlier, the school had been in no position to apply for membership, bearing in mind that its performance at A level was consistently below the standard required. The election was a great personal triumph for Mr Searle in finally achieving what had been the ardent ambition of successive governing boards since 1931. The benefit to the reputation and prestige of the school was immeasurable.

Diana, Princess of Wales, being greeted by the Headmaster in November 1983, when she landed at the school in her helicopter on her way to visit the Maytrees Home for the Blind. Lady Wills, wife of the Lord Lieutenant of Avon, is on the left of Mr Searle. (SMV Archive)

Colston's lost three of its most experienced members of staff within the space of a year. In 1987, Mr John Campbell, who had been Housemaster, Second Master and Acting Headmaster on the death of Mr Snaith, retired after 37 years at the school; and Mr Donald Cartwright, who had served as both Housemaster and Acting Headmaster on two occasions, retired after 29 years service. He was later described by Mr Searle as 'a wonderful teacher' and 'the solid rock', who had provided vital continuity during a period of rapidly-changing headships. Then, at the end of the spring term in 1988, Mr Searle himself resigned to take up a position as National Director of the Independent Schools' Careers Organisation in Camberley. In his thirteen years of Headship, he had presided over a remarkable and exciting period of progress and growth. 'Change and improvement will, indeed, always be associated in everyone's mind with his Headmastership', commented *The Colstonian*. 'His self-effacing manner belied his determination to see ideas through and to pay attention to the finest detail'. Contemporaries praised not only his 'total and selfless personal commitment', his hard work and the great thought he gave to each issue, but also his approachability and the time he spent with prospective parents. They were impressed, too, with his determination to ensure that each boy achieved his potential and developed into a balanced personality - for he believed that 'no pupil was beyond redemption'. One former colleague summed it all up by describing these as 'the golden years' which really established the school as a major force. Certainly the first stage in laying down solid foundations for future success had now been achieved.

The Howarth Years, 1988-1995

Mr Searle's successor as Headmaster in April 1988 was Mr Stephen Howarth, an Oxford graduate, who was previously Head of History at Whitgift School. His Chairman of Governors, Mr Andrew Reid (formally elected to the office in March 1987 following the sudden death of Mr John Spielman and a brief spell as Acting Chairman by Mr Tony Hooper), was a distinguished industrialist. Deputy Chairman of the Imperial Group and former Chairman of Imperial Tobacco Ltd., he was later to become Master of the Society of Merchant Venturers and the Queen's High Sheriff of Avon. His experience of problem solving in major companies was to prove vital during these years - for, in spite of the visible success of the school in 1988 on so many fronts, serious difficulties lay ahead.

First, it was crucial to maintain numbers in the face of stiff local competition, bearing in mind that the 'bulge' in figures (caused partly by disenchantment with the state sector following the teachers' strike in 1986) was gradually passing through. Furthermore the difference - at least in academic performance - between Colston's and the comprehensive sector was too narrow to convince parents of the advantages of sending their children there. Areas of distinction, therefore, needed to be created. Mr Reid also felt that 'the atmosphere in the school was immediate post-war and was a time warp of that period'. In addition, the culture was 'strongly masculine'. According to Mr Howarth, parental perception locally was that the school 'was a bit too robust and philistine' (in spite of Mr Searle's valiant efforts to change the situation). Such was the strength of competition within the Bristol area that it was crucial for Colston's to find its own niche or selling point in the market.

Secondly, there was the whole future of boarding to be considered against a background of national decline (independent schools had reported a 17% fall in demand for boys' boarding between 1980 and 1988). At Colston's, with boarders then accounting for just 19% of the Upper School's population and 18% of the Prep School's, a decision was long overdue on the question of whether the day or boarding ethos should prevail. Saturday school (until 4.00 pm) and compulsory Sunday chapel still existed, presenting a further deterrent to day boy recruitment. The old boarding school ethos, which had imposed a particular structure on the school with a transfer at the age of thirteen, was also undermining recruitment. In a city where most other secondary schools recruited at 11+, the Prep School was experiencing serious problems in recruiting day boys for just two years into its senior classes and Mr Howarth found it 'monumentally difficult' to recruit day boys at 13+, because most of them had already found places elsewhere. Furthermore, the Prep School still regarded itself as an independent institution (rather than a 'feeder' for the Upper School) and prided itself on sending its able boys on scholarships elsewhere.

Thirdly, there was a need to scrutinise the school's policy on sixth form girls for, although their introduction in 1984 had been reasonably successful, numbers remained modest. Fourthly, there were major problems with the fabric. Mr Reid later commented that, in spite of the efforts made in the late 1970s, 'there was no sinking fund available to finance capital projects and, in particular, to renovate the school buildings which were very run down and shabby'. The visual impact of the school was of course vital to the perception of prospective parents - and this applied to an even greater extent with regard to boarding facilities, which were visibly inadequate.

The Headmaster and governors tackled these problems with vigour, trying at the same time to open up the minds of long-serving staff to the idea of change. In September 1988, the governors accepted the Headmaster's recommendation to end compulsory chapel on Sundays in the Upper School (though, at its own request, not in the Prep) in recognition of the fact that the school had largely become a day school; a few months later, Dr Stephen Fenton from Bristol University was commissioned to undertake an 'Attitude Survey' of parents, while a survey of staff attitudes was carried out in parallel; and, throughout 1990, the governors held various meetings to discuss future strategy - including co-education, boarding, school structure and possible mergers. At the same time, a decision was taken to introduce the option of weekly boarding from September 1990.

There was by then a strong tide of opinion running in favour of co-education. When, therefore, informal discussions revealed that a merger might be of interest to The Collegiate School in Winterbourne, the governors decided to give urgent consideration to the idea. The Collegiate School, an independent and interdenominational establishment founded in Redland in 1903 by the three Adam sisters, had moved to Winterbourne in 1945 after a brief wartime evacuation to Langford Court in Somerset. By the 1950s, it had developed a strong boarding tradition with a distinct international flavour. Mrs Susie Hopes (the youngest of the Adams sisters, who did not finally retire until 1970 after 67 years as Headmistress) had firmly established the school's own ethos and family atmosphere - a fact recalled by Mrs Carole Jenkins, a former pupil and governor: 'She was an educator in the widest sense possible. Morals, social skills and Christian belief were high on her list of teachings, as well as elocution lessons!' The school's motto, *Ye are...that ye may*, was chosen to inspire girls with the notion of responsibility and service - sentiments which were not alien to the traditions of Colston's School.

By 1990, with 230 girls aged between 3 and 16 (plus a small preparatory department for boys), The Collegiate was struggling in a fiercely competitive market - a situation which had been exacerbated by the withdrawal of government allowances for the children of service personnel. The Chairman of the Collegiate School Council, Mrs Gillian Woolley, later said: 'The answer for The Collegiate School has been to find a stronger partner whose aims and traditions we share'.

The governors at Colston's immediately appointed educational and financial consultants, who reported back favourably on the proposed merger in January 1991. It was therefore agreed to establish on the Stapleton site from September 1991 a fully co-educational school for pupils aged between 3 and 18 years; to offer secondary education from 11+ with a curriculum designed for the 11-18 age group; and to establish a new nursery for three-year olds. The two schools were therefore to combine, with the Colston Hospital Trust taking over responsibility for both the assets of The Collegiate (the site was eventually sold for £600,000) and the substantial merger-related costs. Under a new management structure, Mr Howarth was to become Headmaster of the whole operation and Mr Aveyard Deputy Headmaster with autonomous responsibility for both the Lower School (7-11 years) and the Middle School (11-13 years). However, in what proved to be a transitional arrangement, the Middle School was to be sited on the Upper School campus as 'a separate, self-contained unit'. Mrs Lesley Sharland, who had been Headmistress of The Collegiate since 1981, was to be the Senior Mistress in the combined institution which was renamed 'Colston's Collegiate School'.

The merger brought with it immediate benefits, which went some way to providing a solution to the problems outlined above. In order to fit in to the structure of The Collegiate (with admissions into the senior school at eleven, not thirteen), Colston's was finally transformed into a secondary school drawing on recruitment at 11+, with a Lower School dealing with children from the ages of three to eleven. At the same time, the introduction of girls not only settled the matter of co-education and gave a boost to overall numbers, it helped to introduce a more relaxed and civilised climate to counter that somewhat 'robust and philistine' atmosphere. For their part, the girls from The Collegiate were offered the chance to continue their education (at a specially subsidised rate) with their own friends and some of their teachers - and to progress into a sixth form, which had not been available at their own school. Furthermore, the benefits of the Susie Hopes Scholarship Fund (which had been established in 1977 as a permanent memorial to the former Headmistress) were now made available in their new school. Since 1991, therefore, an annual scholarship has been awarded to a sixth form girl wishing to study a course in the creative arts.

The merger was organised with smooth efficiency and was broadly accepted by parents at both Colston's and The Collegiate (although a handful removed their children in protest after expressing their views very forcibly at a series of parents' meetings) and by staff (although this was not entirely the case in the former Prep). Nor did the media help in calming passions - an article appeared in the local press (based on leaked information) on the Friday before the official press release was issued on the following Monday (8th February 1991). Nevertheless, the controversy quickly subsided.

The curriculum was expanded, partly to cater for girls, through the introduction of home economics, textiles and fashion, drama and German as an option alongside Latin; and a new boarding House (Winterbourne) was established for girls aged 13 to 18. When the re-named school assembled in September 1991, eight members of The Collegiate staff had transferred and just under 50% of the girls (the parents of some preferring their daughters to continue with single-sex education). This gave a total school roll of 639 (against the consultants' predicted total of 684), plus 35 in the fully-booked nursery. There were in all 119 girls in the school or 18.6% of the total. By September 1992, in the face of a recession and strong local competition, the school population had slumped to 608 (against the consultants' prediction of 703) with the Middle and Lower Schools most affected. Furthermore, boarding numbers had dropped from a total of 96 in 1991 to 73 in 1992. 'To say that HMC, SHMIS and ISIS are worried about boarding is an understatement', reported the Headmaster. 'Schools are now under fierce pressure'.

Faced with these stark statistics and a considerable bank deficit brought about by declining numbers, the governors called for an urgent review of future prospects. Nevertheless, the outlook was not totally clouded in pessimism. The survey they had conducted in 1989 had revealed that the *potential* for enlarged recruitment was considerable. ISIS surveys had revealed that the impact of the fall in the school-aged population was now over and that therefore the size of the potential market would steadily increase; that sixth forms provided schools with real opportunity for growth; and that, although boys' boarding had declined nationally by 17% between 1980 and 1988, there had been an increase in *girls'* boarding of 18% during the same period. The governors, who were already employing a public relations officer, set up a strategy committee, a public relations committee and a marketing committee to grapple with the task of recruitment, the future of boarding and the high cost structure of the school, which had resulted in the fact that day fees were not competitive alongside those of other local schools.

Throughout the autumn of 1992 and the spring of 1993, these groups worked hard to tackle some highly complex problems. After the Headmaster had presented a paper on *A Vision for the Future*, the governors decided that Saturday school (which had existed for 283 years, but was now seen as a serious barrier to the recruitment of girls) should cease from September 1993; that boarding below the age of eleven should end, as it was no longer viable; and that salaries should be restructured in an attempt to limit costs. Then, in February 1993, the Headmaster submitted a second paper on restructuring and reform. In consequence, it was agreed that a new senior management structure should operate from the following September, consisting of a Headmaster, Deputy Headmaster, Director of Studies and Head of Lower School. The Middle School would become part of the Upper School under the Headmaster's direction, although it would continue to be administered as a separate pastoral unit for 11-13 year olds. At the same time, it was agreed to bring day fees more into line with those of local schools through the use of concessions to pupils of high quality; and to introduce a wide range of examination subjects at A level to cater for weaker candidates (including business studies, theatre studies and - from 1994 - sports studies). Boarding itself was considered likely to end in 1996.

By September 1993, Mrs Sharland had retired; and Mr Aveyard had left to pursue his musical interests 'after six very happy years with Colston's' to be replaced as Head of Lower School by Mr Graham Phillips (see above) and as Deputy Headmaster by Mr Alan Martinovic. Mr Michael Graham had already been appointed Director of Studies in 1989. The news greeting this team, however, was not promising. Numbers in the Middle and Lower Schools had fallen from 240 in 1991 to 176 in 1993, posing a real threat to the future health of the upper part of the school. They were therefore instructed by the governors to undertake 'a pro-active recruitment programme'.

Backed by the efforts of the marketing committee and a new scholarships and bursaries committee to co-ordinate the award of assisted places and bursaries, the Headmaster and his senior colleagues launched a highly effective campaign based on the transformation of the Open Day in October. Whereas previously such occasions had consisted of tours round the school followed by a short talk by the Headmaster - a pattern repeated almost exactly in all other local schools - the Colston's Open Day was now totally re-shaped following an idea put forward by Mr Martinovic. At the heart of it was a highly professional presentation in the new Harry Crook Theatre (see below) by the Headmaster and a cast of over 30 pupils. This carefully-rehearsed production, staged and masterminded by Mr Stephen Pritchard (the Head of Drama) gave an audio-visual overview of the school, using slides, music, dance and drama. At the same time, as visitors were shown round the school by a host of pupil-guides, the modern languages department welcomed them into their Parisian cafe, serving hot croissants and freshly-brewed coffee; the classics department, having donned togas, offered them grapes; and the science team invited them to participate in experiments.

This first-ever Open Day for the entire school attracted some 550 visitors (thanks to a well-planned advertising campaign) and resulted in 102 external candidates sitting the 11+ entrance examination. This initial success was followed up vigorously in February, when the Headmaster and two senior colleagues spent half term week in making personal contact with all those parents whose children had been offered places. As a result, 52 outside candidates made acceptances for entry in September 1994 (compared with 21 in 1992 and just 14 in 1993). The total school roll (including the nursery) rose in consequence from 557 in 1993 to 623 in 1994, enabling the finance committee to report a substantial surplus for the year. This new, successful approach was continued in 1995, witnessing an increase to 663, including an additional 30 pupils recruited into the Lower School (thanks partly to a 'leaflet drop' in the Bradley Stoke district).

There were, of course, other contributory factors in this rapid revival. The outstanding success of the school's rugby teams (see Chapter 12) was beginning to have a beneficial effect on recruitment into the sixth form and also on sixth form boarding. This process became even more marked from 1995 (see below). In addition, although performances in GCSE remained somewhat patchy (averaging a 70.5% pass-rate between 1988 and 1994), the results at A level were beginning to show a marked improvement in quality from the 76.1% pass rate experienced in 1989 to the 91.7% gained in 1994 (with the percentage of those candidates going on to university or higher education rising in consequence from 65% to 90%).

The curriculum too had been thoroughly modernised to make the school more appealing. Craft, design and technology had been introduced from 1989 as part of a creative arts 'circus' for the fourth forms; a Head of Design and Technology had been appointed for the first time in 1990, followed by a Head of Information Technology and Business Studies and a new Director of Sport in 1994; a programme of personal and social education (PSE) had been drawn up in 1992 with sixth form lectures arranged on drugs, health and hygiene; and, from 1990, an activities programme arranged on Monday afternoons, with options including the CCF, the Duke of Edinburgh Award Scheme, social service, cooking and many other creative pursuits.

At the same time, considerable advances had been made to the facilities on offer. In January 1990, the new classroom block was opened (see above); and in September of that year the old workshop was converted into a technology centre at a cost of £34,500. Then in February 1991, the cause of scholarship and private study was given a major boost through the total refurbishment of the library. This was made possible through the generosity of Mrs John Spielman, wife of the former Chairman of Governors, who donated £30,000 - including a sum of £8,000 towards the purchase of new books (a sum which was doubled by the governors, enabling the establishment of a library of 7,000 books - twice the previous number). The Harvey Room was converted into a reading/recreational area, the stock including fiction, newspapers, magazines, videos and audio-tapes, while the Snaith Room housed non-fiction and was designated for private study. Re-named The Spielman Library, the complex was opened in February 1991 by Mrs Spielman. A part-time librarian was appointed soon afterwards for the first time and, by 1994, the first computers with CD Rom facilities had been installed. There is no doubt that the new library not only helped to create a more scholarly atmosphere, which the Headmaster had long been anxious to establish, but also raised the status of academic work in the eyes of pupils.

Exactly a year after the opening of the library, the long-awaited conversion of the old gymnasium into a theatre/concert hall was finally achieved. The refurbishment, which included the installation of a lighting gantry, retractable seating, dressing rooms, drapes, roof insulation, projection equipment and a cloak room area, eventually cost over £300,000. This was only made feasible through a generous donation of £200,000 from the Harry Crook Trust [Harry Crook, founder of the Kleen-e-ze Brush Company, was a former Lord Mayor and Sheriff of

Mr Graham Searle (former Headmaster) cutting the first sod on the site of the new classroom block, which was opened in 1990. Seen here with him are Mr Stephen Howarth (Headmaster - left) and Mr Andrew Reid (Chairman of Governors - right). (SMV Archive)

Bristol], supplemented later by further sums from the Old Colstonians, Parents' Society and the governors. The Harry Crook Theatre was opened in February 1992 by Mr John Bickle (who was the brother-in-law of Harry Crook and an Old Colstonian) on behalf of the trustees. It was to become the setting for a remarkable rise in the standard of drama, a cause which was dear to the Headmaster's heart (see Chapter 12).

The outdated elementary laboratories were also refurbished - the physics laboratory in 1992 as a result of a £20,000 legacy from the wife of an Old Colstonian (Mrs M. Jenkins); and the biology and chemistry laboratories in 1995, following funding from the John James and F.A. Clark Trusts. Meanwhile, in 1993, the appeal of boarding had been made more attractive by improvements to Mortlake House, which included carpets and curtains (for the first time) and individual units for sixth formers; and in 1993, a vital step had been taken by establishing a new information technology centre equipped with a network of thirteen IBM compatible 386 computers, file server and laser printer.

While all these exciting developments were taking place, two important changes had been made to the school's constitution. First, in 1988, the Charity Commissioners approved a new scheme of government for the school to consolidate and update in one document the six previous schemes issued between 1936 and 1986. As a result, the governing body was reduced in size to 18 members, including 10 nominated by the Society of Merchant Venturers, 6 who were co-opted and 2 who were ex-officio (i.e. the Bishop of Bristol and the Rector of Stapleton); and the governors and Headmaster were given both flexibility in awarding fee exemptions and power to run a school for pupils aged between 4 and 19 years. The latter two clauses were of course important in terms of the reforms introduced in subsequent years. Secondly, in December 1992, the governing board was re-established as 'Colston Collegiate Governors Ltd.' to set a limit on the financial liability of its members.

At the very time when detailed plans were being formulated for the merger with The Collegiate School in 1991, an incident occurred which was both frightening and distressing - an incident which threatened to rock the very foundations of the new proposals. A pupil at the school burst into a classroom and shot the master who was teaching in the arm. This action was totally out of character with the atmosphere which existed within the community at the time. The rebelliousness of the 1960s was by then a distant memory and a caring, trusting environment had been established between pupils and staff. This was immediately demonstrated by the 4th form boys who witnessed the shooting and who reacted quickly to the urgency of the situation by applying a tourniquet to stem the flow of blood. Tom Roberts, in particular, was later to receive three awards for 'his calm influence and brave actions'. The master concerned, who later recovered from his injuries, was greatly touched by the upsurge of sympathy and support from the pupils, which resulted in 600 get-well cards being sent to hospital and enough flowers 'to stock a small florist's shop'. At the same time, the Headmaster's skilful handling of the episode helped to avoid any collateral damage which might have resulted from bad publicity.

In July 1994, Mr Andrew Reid retired as Chairman of Governors after a period of momentous change. He had successfully steered the school through eight years in which outside factors (affecting independent schools throughout the country) had threatened to undermine its position. Undeterred by mounting pressure, he and the governing board had transformed the school into a co-educational establishment, restructured it to take account of its growing day school status and modernised it to face up to the challenge of increased parental expectation. In doing so, they had helped to create a particular niche in the local market, offering a school which provided a rich educational experience for pupils of wide-ranging abilities. Colston's could now boast several particular selling points - strong sport (based on its outstanding rugby), excellent drama, impressive art and a clutch of new subjects, which few other local schools could match at the time. The merger with The Collegiate had proved to be the catalyst for a number of crucial reforms - just as it had protected the school from the worst effects of the recession (during which three independent schools in the area had been forced to close). Although some staff later confessed that they had found the rapidity of change somewhat confusing, the second stage of establishing foundations for future success had now been completed.

Mr Reid was succeeded by Brigadier Hugh Pye, who was Treasurer of the Society of Merchant Venturers. A governor since 1992, he had enjoyed a distinguished military career, serving in Northern Ireland, Germany, Cyprus and the Middle East and working as Chief of Staff at the Staff College in Camberley. He brought with him a fund of experience, enthusiasm and decisive leadership. A year later, Mr Howarth also left the school to become Headmaster of the King's School, Grantham, feeling that - after seven years at the helm - he had 'done everything he could to meet the challenges facing the school'. Although his relationship with the governing board had not always been easy and that with the Prep had suffered from fundamental differences in outlook, he had nevertheless brought his acute mind to bear on the problems and had implemented the changes with efficiency. A modest and likeable character, he had worked hard to create a friendly, relaxed and purposeful atmosphere within the school and had developed a more democratic approach to management, introducing a sixth form council, a parents/staff consultative committee and a senior management team. More symbolic changes, in the view of *School Ties*, included 'his burning of the canes which stood in the corner of his office on his arrival in 1988, and allowing pupils to use the main front door'.

The Crawford Years, 1995-2002 (continuing)

The new Headmaster appointed in September 1995 was Mr David Crawford, who had previously been Headmaster of Cokethorpe School in Oxford. A county rugby player and a keen sportsman, he brought with him considerable experience of managing both the educational and financial aspects of school life. His task was to build on the progress which had been made over the previous two decades (particularly with regard to the recruitment of pupils and improved facilities) and to tackle a number of remaining problems. These were quickly identified by Mr Crawford in a strategic plan outlined to governors during his first term - the need to invest in the infrastructure and its maintenance, which - as previous Headmasters had also pointed out - had been badly neglected over many years; the need to develop an even more caring ethos in the school with equal value being given to all activities and all pupils; the need to raise the expectations of both staff and pupils, thereby increasing the level of academic performance; and the need to improve the financial management of the school in order to generate surpluses, while at the same time to improve recruitment by restructuring school fees to bring Colston's into line with other Bristol schools.

Fundamental to a range of other problems was the importance of improving the school's financial base. When, therefore, the Bursar left in 1996, a new structure was established under the Headmaster with a Facilities Manager to supervise both non-teaching staff and maintenance and a Finance Officer to handle the accounts. Then, over the course of the next few years, two crucial changes were made to the policy on fees with the aim of cutting the high operating costs, while at the same time generating larger surpluses through the recruitment of additional pupils. Therefore, although the level of concessions on basic fees was eventually reduced by half, the steep rise in fees, which had previously operated when a pupil transferred from the Middle School to the Upper School, was abolished. This removed at one stroke a powerful deterrent to recruitment and made Colston's much more competitive within the local market. The Headmaster also persuaded the governors to establish a sizeable contingency fund within the annual budget, which - if not spent during the year on emergencies - could be released for projects to improve the infrastructure. As a result, considerable headway was made at last with regular programmes of maintenance, redecoration, landscaping, refurbishment and renewal. The visual impact of the whole site, therefore, was greatly improved - an important factor in improving morale within the community and attracting new members to join it from without.

There is no doubt that these new initiatives - linked with the continued success of the school in so many ways and the dynamic operation of its Open Day policy - helped to generate a most dramatic rise in numbers at all levels in the school. In September 1995, Mr Crawford had inherited a total of 443 pupils (aged 11-18) in the Upper School and 220 pupils (aged 3-11) in the Lower School. By September 2001, these figures had risen to 568 and 281 respectively. During the same period, sixth form numbers had increased from 114 to 152 and the percentage of girls in the whole school to one-third. By 1999, no fewer than 86 pupils (the highest number ever) had been admitted into the first form (now re-styled nationally 'Year 7') with some 200 children taking the entrance examination in the following year. Numbers in the boarding house, which had seemed threatened with extinction by 1996, had risen to 56 by 2001 - thanks in no small measure to the remarkable success of Colston's rugby (see Chapter 12). During the six years, 1996-2001, out of 109 boys who were recruited into the sixth form from outside, no fewer than 89 of them were keen rugby players, who had been attracted by the quality of coaching at Colston's. In view of the fact that many of these were drawn from all over the United Kingdom, the availability of boarding facilities was clearly important.

The increased size of the school inevitably led to the need for a more extended management structure in both parts of the establishment. By 2001 this consisted of the Headmaster (Mr Crawford), the Deputy Headmaster (Mr Martinovic), the Director of Studies (Mr Graham), the Senior Tutor (Mr Tayler) and the Senior Mistress (Mrs Brighton) in the Upper School; and the Head (Mr Phillips), the Deputy Head (Mrs Coatsworth) and the Director of Studies (Miss Tailby) in the Lower School.

The record numbers also meant that, by 1997, budget surpluses were again being generated, which could be reinvested in school facilities. The increasingly healthy state of the school's finances was boosted further by the generosity of a number of benefactors - Bath Rugby Football Club (under Mr Andrew Brownsword) granted £30,000 a year to the school in 2000 for the development of rugby (initially used for the setting up of new fitness rooms - see below); Mr Andrew Reid (the former Chairman of Governors) who, with the Old Colstonians' Society, funded a much-needed sixth form private study room in 1995; the Parents' Society, which paid £15,000 to equip the Chatterton Hall with a new organ in 2000; and the Educational Trust of Hebron and Medlock Ltd, which not only sponsored a new minibus and a range of computers, but also part-funded the salary of a new Head of Design and Technology for three years from 2002. Furthermore, the professional guidance of Mr David Medlock, a governor, was crucial in developing this new subject area.

Mr David Medlock presenting a new minibus to Mr David Crawford (Headmaster) on behalf of the Educational Trust of Hebron & Medlock Ltd. Mr Alan Martinovic (Deputy Head and 1st XV rugby coach) is on the right with members of Bath Rugby Club immediately behind. (SMV Archive)

Of even greater long-term significance, however, was the outstanding munificence of an Old Colstonian (who wished to remain anonymous) in establishing a major fund for the award of bursaries. His intention was to offer a partial replacement for the government's Assisted Places Scheme, which was abolished in 1997 when the school was educating no fewer than 101 assisted place holders. The objective of this most generous gesture was to ensure that Colston's tradition of providing places for able pupils from less affluent homes would continue and that the social mix, which had characterised the school over the last century, should not be lost.

The launch of a development appeal in October 1997 was also important in terms of the overall strategic plan to develop the school.

Organised by a full-time Appeal Director, who drew heavily on a newly-compiled register of Old Colstonians, the appeal was given an immediate boost by a lead donation of £200,000 by the Society of Merchant Venturers - followed by one of £100,000 from the Harry Crook Trust (which was earmarked for the bursary fund). Within two years, a total of £850,000 had been raised to fund a number of important projects. Foremost among these was The Chatterton Hall (costing £410,000) to provide, on the one hand, a replacement for the old chapel, which was by then totally inadequate in size; and, on the other, to establish a first class centre for instrumental tuition and the performance of music. By the time of its opening in the summer of 2000, several other appeal projects had already been completed (the first two of which were in immediate response to recommendations made in the HMC Inspection Report of 1999) - a new computer room with 30 computers and internet access (making a total of 90 in all on the school's network); a new

The opening of The Chatterton Hall in 2000. From the left: Sam Haire, Hollie Grant, Mr David Crawford (Headmaster), Mr Bob Musson (Managing Director of the contractors), Mr Ian Holmes (Director of Music), Mr Hugh Morris (School Organist) and Dana Drake.

science laboratory; the conversion of the old fives courts into state-of-the-art fitness rooms; the creation of new girls' changing rooms; and the establishment of new bases for members of the senior management. The final target of a covered swimming pool was, by the autumn of 2001, awaiting the outcome of a bid for lottery funding.

Meanwhile, progress in recruitment and the development of modern facilities had been more than matched by advances in academic work. When the government had introduced the national curriculum in the late 1980s, the school had decided to follow its provisions - even though, as an independent school, there was no obligation to do so. Indeed, there was a determination to go beyond what was offered in state schools. As Mr Michael Graham, the Director of Studies, put it, '*National curriculum plus*' had become the school's motto - in other words, 'to offer a curriculum which is at least as extensive as that found in the maintained sector, yet enriched by a wealth of provision in the aesthetic, creative and sporting realms'. In reality this meant offering a range of 15 subjects at the Key Stage 3 (11-14 years) level, including drama, design technology, information and communication technology and social education (incorporating careers); and at Key Stage 4 (15-16 years) GCSE level, a core of 7 subjects plus a further two or three chosen from a list of nine options. At sixth form level, a new system came into operation nationally in 2000 aimed at introducing more breadth into the curriculum. This meant that pupils in the lower sixth took 4 AS (advanced supplementary) level subjects from a total of 17 on offer, before proceeding to take 3 (or even 4) of them at A2 level (or full advanced standard) in the following year.

What was particularly striking over the period 1995-2002 was the major impact of developments in information and communications technology on the way in which pupils learn. As Mr Graham explained: 'Pupils are taught to use ICT as a tool not only for researching information, but in communicating it in a clear and relevant manner. Staff use computers in their teaching and for administration; the school has its own administration network; and the school timetable - once produced by hand - has been computerised since the late 1980s'.

There is little doubt that, at the time when all these changes were increasing the breadth of education at Colston's, the quality of academic performance was also being improved in a most striking manner. At A level, for instance, there had been a pass rate of 84.5% in 1995 with 28% of those passes recorded at A or B grade and an average points score per candidate of 13.4. [Points are calculated as follows: A=10, B=8, C=6, D=4, E=2]. From 1996, the pass rate was always over 92% (reaching 98% in 1998) - and in 2001, it stood at 95% with a new record of 51% of the passes at A or B grade and an average points score of 20.09 per candidate. The quality of these performances was such that a large proportion of the pupils gained places at first-grade universities. Five of these secured places at Oxford or Cambridge, the highest-ever Oxbridge total in the school's history - Martin Rawles, who also won an organ scholarship at St Catharine's College, Cambridge; Alex Brighton, who was also awarded an army scholarship; Richard Cousins, Peter Ibraihim and Rachel O'Neill. As a result in this surge in excellence, Colston's moved up no fewer than 56 places in the 2001 *Daily Telegraph* league table of independent schools (based on A/B grades) from its position in 1996 - and 82 places in the *Financial Times* table (based on points per pupil) from its average position over the previous five years.

At GCSE (which had replaced the former O level examination in 1988), the school had made similar progress. Whereas in 1995 the overall pass rate (grades A*-C) had been 82.7% with 25.4% of the grades at A* or A, in 2001 the pass rate had risen to 92.1% with 38% of the grades at A* or A. Similarly, the percentage of pupils passing in at least 5 subjects had risen from an average of 77.3 in the years 1992-96 to 95.8 in 2001. Earlier in that year, *The Daily Telegraph*, in an analysis of results, had placed Colston's as the 9th most improved school in the country at GCSE, while a 'value-added' table produced in 2000 had highlighted the pupils' success in achieving considerable improvement in performance between GCSE and A level - thanks to good teaching.

There were, of course, many factors involved in this transformation of the academic standards in the school. A much more able intake of pupils had been recruited from 1994, which had helped to create a more positive attitude to work; staff of high quality had been newly-appointed in a number of key areas to join a highly professional and committed Common Room; a programme of in-service training had become effective from 1996, coupled with that of staff appraisal from 1992; improved private study facilities had been established to encourage scholarly learning; and the library had been upgraded with the appointment of a full time librarian in 1997 and an increased stock of 11,000 volumes by 2001. Above all, expectations had been raised and a more conducive atmosphere created by the Headmaster's *It's smart to work* campaign. The introduction of the Gold Academic Awards, which gave recognition to the individual who performed above the normal expected standard, sent out signals that achievement in the classroom was valued just as highly as achievement on the games field. Furthermore, the HMC Inspection Report of 1999 praised both the overall quality of teaching and the excellent relationships which existed between staff and pupils - factors which were at the very heart of success.

Mr Crawford had inherited from his two immediate successors not only some solid foundations for future success, but also a number of intractable problems. The strong and energetic leadership he brought to the scene, coupled with a clear vision and a real sense of purpose, enabled him to overcome many of the latter, while building steadily on the former. His period in office to 2002 brought increased richness and success to extra-curricular activities, firm management to the finances, noticeable improvement to the visual impact of the site, a dramatic rise in numbers and a significant growth in the quality of academic performance. His election in 1997 as Chairman of SHMIS (the Society of Headmasters and Headmistresses of Independent Schools) - along with the school's remarkable achievements on the rugby field - helped to increase its national reputation. Equally important to the school's development was the strong backing he received from the governors in general and the Chairman of Governors in particular. Brigadier Pye's boundless enthusiasm for the school, his optimistic and decisive handling of difficulties and his active involvement in both social events and fund-raising gave enormous impetus to the emergence of Colston's as one of the west country's leading schools.

*****

POSTSCRIPT

The pupils are guaranteed a happiness and security that enables them to be notably tolerant, courteous, friendly and caring. Their pride in their school, their concern for each other's welfare, their clear recognition that the school rules are sensible and applied fairly, and their confidence that all boys and girls are treated equally regardless of creed, race or academic ability all guarantee that the pupils grow up in an atmosphere of trust, purposeful behaviour and mutual respect. The pastoral side of the school is well organised: the quality of care is good.

The pupils are in every way a credit to their school: they are open and friendly, polite and welcoming, self-assured without arrogance. They are proud to be members of the school and determined to take every opportunity to enhance its reputation. They are splendid.
(HMC Inspection Report, 1999)

The school has visibly adapted, therefore, to the needs of the modern world and in 2002 is enjoying one of the most successful periods in its long history. Its impressive facilities, buoyant numbers, vibrant community and academic achievement testify to a school with first-rate leadership and a highly-motivated staff. It has also become a much more compassionate and caring place, which continues to cater for a broad level of ability. The spartan conditions and brutal punishments, which were still evident in the 1950s and 1960s (see Chapter 12), have given way to more civilised surroundings and a less harsh regime. Nevertheless, discipline remains firm with clear regulations on uniform and behaviour, including great emphasis on courtesy and the total prohibition of bullying. The eighteen or so prefects, who now exercise leadership in a much more positive and constructive manner, work closely with staff to implement a number of sanctions based on detentions rather than beatings.

Each pupil is attached to a tutor group, where individuals can find personal encouragement and advice; and close contact is maintained with parents through regular reports, newsletters, parents' meetings and termly issues of *School Ties* (an illustrated news sheet, which had first been published in 1985 and which, by 1995, had superseded *The Colstonian*). Another indication of a more sensitive approach to parental needs is the introduction, from 2000, of a system of 'flexi-boarding', which enables pupils to board for short periods. Jonathan Mills, who joined the school as a sixth former, commented on the supportive atmosphere which was evident to newcomers in 2001: 'When I started boarding at Colston's I was very nervous, but I was helped by the more established members of the House to feel at home. As I began to settle in, I quickly realised how close the boarding community was. Everyone started to feel like your brother and you felt part of a family'. The years 1975-2002 have, therefore, witnessed a remarkable transformation in the school's ethos, atmosphere, structure, facilities and ambition - but how far is all this in line with the intentions of its founder, who continues to look down on the scene from his portrait and who is still remembered each year on Colston's Day?

In setting up his Hospital in 1710, Edward Colston aimed to pluck a hundred boys from their squalid background, to instruct them in the Christian faith, to provide them with a rudimentary education and then eventually to place them out as apprentices - all to be provided free of charge, thanks to his generous endowment. Stewardship of the Hospital was entrusted to the Society of Merchant Venturers, which was duly charged with management, control and close involvement.

Although, in 2002, the school has moved from its original site, the traditional dress has long since disappeared, the majority of pupils no longer board, girls have now entered the scene and family backgrounds are much more affluent, four important elements in the life and work of the school can still be traced back to its foundation. Of prime importance is the continuing concept of the School Chapel with its daily act of worship and its close connection with the neighbouring parish church of Stapleton. Although the Catechist of Mr Colston's day has for many years been replaced by the School Chaplain, his task remains much as before - to instruct the pupils in the Christian faith (to which has now been added an understanding of other world religions). The annual presentation of bibles to sixth form leavers is another indication of a legacy which was so close to the founder's heart.

Secondly, in spite of the fact that the school is now entirely fee paying, there remains a strong commitment to cater for children from less affluent homes. Colston's original endowment, which in 1710, covered the entire cost of running the school, has steadily been eroded over the years by inflation and the need to purchase two new school sites (the one at Stapleton for boys in 1858 and the one at Cheltenham road for girls in 1890). Free education for all pupils out of endowment funds is therefore no longer practicable. Indeed, with the annual cost of a boarding place standing at £12,603 in 2002, it would require funding of around £1,260,000 a year to maintain the education of 100 boarders, as envisaged by Colston. Instead, the school offers a number of scholarships (provided by the Merchants' Scholarship Fund, the Harry Crook Trust and the Susie Hopes Scholarship Fund) and bursaries (made possible through trust funds established over the years by former governors, staff and pupils) - all of which offer assistance to promising pupils in need of support. Furthermore, the Colston Hospital Foundation injects a sum each year into the school for educational purposes, representing current income from the founder's remaining endowment.

Thirdly, although Mr Colston's stipulation that all boys should be found apprenticeships lapsed some 125 years ago, the principle that pupils are properly 'placed' on leaving school remains. The comments made by the visiting inspectors in 1999 (see above) are a tribute to the quality of the school's pastoral care, which ensures that boys and girls find appropriate destinations either at university or in employment. Sixth form tutors and careers staff today are the rightful heirs of the 18th century Masters, who used personal contacts and eloquent testimonials to ensure that their charges were entrusted to the best local employers and craftsmen.

Fourthly, the Society of Merchant Venturers remains today - after nearly 300 years - as the guardian of Colston's vision. It has been passionately loyal to the trust placed in it by the founder, stoutly defending its independence from local authority control and vigorously fighting for its survival when threatened by outside forces. For almost two centuries, it has masterminded a remarkable transformation of the old Hospital, in the face of constant difficulties, with ambitious policies courageously implemented. The school, which over the years has seemingly lurched from one financial crisis to another, has repeatedly drawn strength and renewal from the boundless generosity of the Society - generosity expressed through a succession of gifts, interest-free loans,

The Society of Merchant Venturers' Master's XI, which played in the annual match against the School in 1977. Seen on the front row (from the left) are Moger Woolley (who in later years captained the side), Graham Searle (Headmaster), John Camm (captain) and Martin Tayler (master-in-charge of school cricket, 1973-96). On the back row (3rd from the left) is Andrew Bromley, the school's prolific wicket-taker between 1975-77, who also played for England Schoolboys. (SMV Archive)

cancelled debts, appeal donations, bursaries, scholarships and prizes. Nor does this list take any account of the many acres of its own land, which the Society released for use as playing fields - or the remarkable contributions made over the years by individual members on their own initiative. With a majority still on the Governing Board, the Society continues its policy (commenced in 1836) of close involvement with the school by entertaining groups of governors, staff and senior pupils at Merchants' Hall, actively supporting school functions and challenging the 1st XI to the annual cricket match against the Master's XI.

There is no doubt that Lieut. Col. R.F. Alston was right in 1977, when he paid tribute to the wisdom and foresight of Edward Colston 'in placing the care of the school in the safekeeping of the Society'. Colston would, he said, be rightly proud of all those Merchants who, over the years, have 'dedicated themselves unstintingly' to the task.

Sources used in Chapter 13

Society of Merchant Venturers' Archive:
  Colston Hospital Trust: Governors' Minutes, 1975-1992
        Minutes of Colston's Collegiate Governors Ltd.,
        1993-2001
        Finance Committee Minutes, 1975-2001
        Education Committee Minutes. 1982-2001
        Headmasters' Reports, 1975-2001
The Colstonian, 1975-1994
School Ties (the termly newsletter), 1988-2001
Cribsheet (The Old Colstonians' Newsletter), 1986-2001
HMC Inspection Report, 1999
Personal interviews and written submissions (acknowledged in the text).

A drawing by R.W. Keen, which was presented to Mrs Winifred Snaith (wife of the former Headmaster) by Old Colstonian, H.B. Thompson. It depicts the school at Stapleton sometime before 1928. (By courtesy of Mrs Winifred Snaith)

A VIEW FROM THE COMMON ROOM

Michael Graham *(Director of Studies & former Housemaster)*

Beef curry was on the menu when I came for interview in May 1977. Sitting in a dignified elevation with the Headmaster and Prefects on High Table, I pondered a scene before me quite clearly reminiscent of Tom Brown's schooldays: a master at the end of each long oak table, and six boys either side. Colston's - with its Latin graces, roll calls, prep, chapel, remove, school sergeant, beatings, boarders and gowns - was a mile away from the comprehensive school I was teaching in, and even further from the world of industry I had previously known. Yet it seemed a welcoming place with a sense of purpose and achievement, and I was pleased to accept the position of mathematics teacher and boarding tutor of Roundway House.

On my first day I went dutifully to the stationery cupboard to collect my box of chalk, board rubber and cane. The latter might occasionally be needed, I was told by an old hand - even though the Headmaster, whose philosophy was that 'boys, like ships, are best steered through the rear', had left some years since.

All boys and staff were referred to by their surnames - and were disciplined with almost equal severity by the Second Master of the day. Whilst staff were spared the embarrassment of queuing up at morning break for the ritual caning, it was not uncommon for their wives to be phoned at home with a curt message that '[surname] has failed to enter his Upper Fifth grades and is instructed to do so without delay'. Needless to say, not many of us were bold enough to step out of line.

The Masters' Common Room when I arrived seemed full of colourful and rather eccentric characters. There was, for instance, the bachelor housemaster who taught trigonometry by mnemonics ('Silly Old Harry Caught a Hot Tomato Over Algeria') and whose dog 'Sas' was named after one of the conditions of proof (Side, Angle, Side) for congruent triangles. Then there was the classics master who wrote of a particular boy:

'Whilst we do not scale the heights in this class, he is the vanguard of our assault on the lower slopes', and the biologist (well known for using a femur rather than a cane for discipline) whose stock phrase on reports was 'he is the typical curate's egg'. I eventually discovered that a curate's egg is good in parts. The poor woodwork master had so many reports to write that he resorted to something akin to a John Bull printing kit: for all the boys his simple stamped comment was 'making good progress with his joints'.

With the decline in boarding, schoolboy pranks have not loomed as large as I remember them in the 70s and 80s. I can well recall the occasion when a member of staff's bubble car appeared on High Table at breakfast. Then there was the time when some ingenious pupil broke into the organ loft and rigged up the keys to the wrong pipes - with amusing results at Chapel the following day. However, perhaps most memorable of all was the mysterious appearance of some toe nail clippings alongside the lock of Edward Colston's hair in the entrance hall display cabinet, accompanied by a label affirming that they, too, belonged to our founder.

Over twenty years on, Colston's is a very different place. The dining hall now sports modern formica-topped tables and a cafeteria system. We have fewer boarders but the school has almost doubled in size, there is a growing number of girls and rugby has rocketed. New buildings have sprouted; most recently the Chatterton Hall, which provides a far brighter venue for morning worship than the old chapel. Common Room hair (where present) is far less grey than formerly, though its wearers are every bit as dedicated to their task. Much has been gained, and the school is in good shape. But perhaps something of the fun and eccentricity of the old order has sadly been lost in today's high-pressured educational climate. But I imagine it is the same in all schools. For all that, Colston's is still a rewarding place in which to live and work.

APPENDIX

Chairmen of the Governors

(from the start of the New Scheme in 1875)

1875 - 1906:	Mr W. Proctor Baker
1907 - 1916:	Mr W.W. Jose
1916 - 1929:	Mr M.K. King
1929 - 1941:	Mr C.B. Fry
1942 - 1963:	Mr V.F. Eberle
1963 - 1983:	Mr J.E.C. Clarke
1983 - 1985:	Mr J. Spielman
1985 - 1987:	Mr A.S. Hooper (Acting Chairman)
1987 - 1994:	Mr A.S. Reid
1994 -	Brigadier H.W.K. Pye

Headmasters

1710 - 1717:	Mr Sylvester	(dismissed)
1718 - 1740:	Mr Samuel Gardner, senior	(died in office)
1740 - 1762:	Mr Samuel Gardner, junior	(resigned)
1762 - 1784:	Mr William Haynes, senior	(died in office)
1784 - 1787:	Mr John Watkins	(resigned)
1787 - 1836:	Mr William Haynes, junior	(resigned - terminally ill)
1836 - 1848:	Mr John Lewis	(dismissed)
1848 - 1870:	Mr Richard Rowlatt	(forced resignation)
1871 - 1901:	Mr John Hancock	(retired)
1901 - 1922:	Dr Anthony Finn, MA, DLL	(died in office)
1923 - 1938:	Canon Anthony Millbourn, MA	(resigned)
1939 - 1964:	Mr Robert Snaith, MA	(died in office)
1965 - 1971:	Mr Nigel Gibbs, MA	(resigned)
1972 - 1974:	Mr Alan King, OBE, MA	(resigned)
1975 - 1988:	Mr Graham Searle, MA	(resigned)
1988 - 1995	Mr Stephen Howarth, MA	(resigned)
1995 -	Mr David Crawford, BA, DLC	

Heads of the Prep/Lower School

1962 - 1963:   Rev. P. Harper. BA
1963 - 1974:   Mr Geoffrey Jameson, MA
1974 - 1983:   Mr Michael Kefford, MA
1983 - 1987:   Mr John Cross, BA
1987 - 1993:   Mr John Aveyard, MA, BMus
1993 -   Mr Graham Phillips, BEd

The School Song

(This was composed in 1902 and sung on various public occasions. The words printed here are taken from the programme of a school concert in December 1907)

O stand we together, together let us call
On God on high who loves us, who loves and cares for all.

This world is for all men to learn to do His will,
And school it is the world to us, our world for good or ill.

Let's live from henceforth truthful, from strife and discord free,
Let sin be seen how hateful, let goodness cherished be.

But slow are we to goodness, and prone are we to sin,
We cannot fight our foes without, nor quell our foes within.

Yet if God be our bulwark, we'll stand tho' foes surround,
Our unity made stronger by hands of love fast bound.

But soon shall all be scattered and tossed the wide world o'er,
Where then shall be our unity, when hand joins hand no more?

O! one we shall in heart be, God's spirit ever nigh
Will guide us all, where'er we are, to God our Tower on high.

Select Bibliography

1. Unpublished Manuscripts:
The Society of Merchant Venturers' Archive

Hall Book of Proceedings, vols 3-25, 1694-1875
Hall Book of Charity Proceedings, vols 1-2, 1852-81
Book of Orders and Minutes for Electing Nominees, 1708-1874
Minutes of the Meetings of Mr Colston's Nominees, 4 vols, 1748-1875
Proceedings of the Colston's Hospital Visiting Committee, 3 vols,
        1836-75
Annual Reports of the Colston's Hospital Visiting Committee, 1842-58
Colston's Hospital Trust:
        Governors' Minute Book, 3 vols, 1875-1992
        Management Committee Minutes, 1887-1923
        Finance Committee Minutes, 1923-2001
        Education Committee Minutes, 1982-2001
Minutes of Colston's Collegiate Governors Ltd., 1993-2001
Headmasters' Letters and Reports, 1870-1921
Headmasters' Reports to Governors, 1926-2001
Copies of Mr Colston's Settlements, 1708-20 (printed volume)
Box of Appendices (bundles of papers relating to period 1780-1912)
List of Boys taken in and bound out by Mr Samuel Gardner, 1718-62
Diary of Mr William Claxton, 2 vols, 1841-73
Pupils' Records, 1861-62
Admission Registers - Paying Scholars, 1875-1926
Admission Registers - Nominated Scholars, 1875-1926
Newspaper Cuttings, 1901-22 (scrapbook)

2. Official Publications:

Scheme for the Management of Colston's Hospital in Bristol, 1873
Scheme for Public and Secondary Schools for Boys and Girls, 1910
Scheme for the Alteration of the Scheme regulating Colston's Hospital,
        1936
Schools' Inquiry Commission - Southern Counties Report, vol. 7, 1868
Charity Commission - Charities under the Management of the Society of
        Merchant Venturers of the City of Bristol, pt. 3, 1871
Regulations for Secondary Schools, 1907
Educational Reconstruction (White Paper), 1943
Fleming Report: Public Schools and the National System, 1944
Education Acts 1902, 1918, 1944

3. Printed Material

Barnard, H.C: *The History of English Education, 1760-1944* (1947)

Bristol Times & Farley's Bristol Journal (November & December 1856)

Cribsheet (the Old Colstonians' Newsletter, 1986-2001)

Dix, John: *The life of Thomas Chatterton* (1836)

Dictionary of National Biography (1900 - article on Thomas Chatterton)

Dunn, Sarah: *Colston's Girls' School: the First Hundred Years* (1991)

Eames, D.J: *The Contribution made by the Society of Merchant Venturers to the Development of Education in Bristol* (unpublished MA thesis for the University of Bristol, 1966)

Garrard, Thomas: *Edward Colston, the Philanthropist, His Life and Times* (edited by S.G. Tovey, 1852)

Gregory, G: *The Life of Thomas Chatterton* (1789)

Latimer, John: *The Annals of Bristol in the Eighteenth Century* (1893)

Latimer, John: *The Annals of Bristol in the Nineteenth Century* (1887)

Latimer, John: *The History of the Society of Merchant Venturers of the City of Bristol* (1903)

McGrath, Patrick: *The Merchant Venturers of Bristol* (1975)

Morgan, Kenneth: *Edward Colston and Bristol* (1999)

Powell, Cecil: *A Great West Countryman* (Somerset Year Book, vol. 35, 1936)

School Ties (Colston's School termly newsletter, 1988-2001)

The Colstonian (School Magazine, 1894-1994)

Wilkins, H.J: *Edward Colston* (1920)

Wroughton, John: *King Edward's School at Bath, 1552-1982* (1982)

INDEX

(Page references in bold type indicate illustrations)